The Chinese State at the Borders

Contemporary Chinese Studies Series

This series, a joint initiative of UBC Press and the UBC Institute of Asian Research, Centre for Chinese Research, seeks to make available the best scholarly work on contemporary China. Volumes cover a wide range of subjects related to China, Taiwan, and the overseas Chinese world.

Glen Peterson, *The Power of Words: Literacy and Revolution in South China, 1949-95*

Wing Chung Ng, *The Chinese in Vancouver: The Pursuit of Power and Identity, 1945-80*

Yijiang Ding, *Chinese Democracy after Tiananmen*

Diana Lary and Stephen MacKinnon, eds., *Scars of War: The Impact of Warfare on Modern China*

Eliza W.Y. Lee, ed., *Gender and Change in Hong Kong: Globalization, Postcolonialism, and Chinese Patriarchy*

Christopher A. Reed, *Gutenberg in Shanghai: Chinese Print Capitalism, 1876-1937*

James A. Flath, *The Cult of Happiness: Nianhua, Art, and History in Rural North China*

Erika E.S. Evasdottir, *Obedient Autonomy: Chinese Intellectuals and the Achievement of Orderly Life*

Hsiao-ting Lin, *Tibet and Nationalist China's Frontier: Intrigues and Ethnopolitics, 1928-49*

Xiaoping Cong, *Teachers' Schools in the Making of the Modern Chinese Nation-State, 1897-1937*

Norman Smith, *Resisting Manchukuo: Chinese Women Writers and the Japanese Occupation*

Edited by Diana Lary

The Chinese State at the Borders

UBCPress · Vancouver · Toronto

15 14 13 12 11 10 09 08 07   5 4 3 2 1

Printed in Canada on ancient-forest-free paper (100% post-consumer recycled) that is processed chlorine- and acid-free, with vegetable-based inks.

Library and Archives Canada Cataloguing in Publication

The Chinese state at the borders / edited by Diana Lary

(Contemporary Chinese studies, ISSN 1206-9523)
Includes bibliographical references and index.
ISBN 978-0-7748-1333-4 (bound); ISBN 978-0-7748-1334-1 (pbk.)

1. China – Territorial expansion – History. 2. China – Boundaries – History. 3. Minorities – Government policy – China – History. 4. China – Ethnic relations – History. 5. Regionalism – China – History. I. Lary, Diana II. Series

DS736.C54 2007   9517   C2007-902086-0

Canadä

UBC Press gratefully acknowledges the financial support for our publishing program of the Government of Canada through the Book Publishing Industry Development Program (BPIDP), and of the Canada Council for the Arts, and the British Columbia Arts Council.

This book has been published with the help of a grant from the Canadian Federation for the Humanities and Social Sciences, through the Aid to Scholarly Publications Programme, using funds provided by the Social Sciences and Humanities Research Council of Canada, and with the help of the K.D. Srivastava Fund.

Financial support from the Chiang Ching-kuo Foundation is also greatly appreciated.

UBC Press
The University of British Columbia
2029 West Mall
Vancouver, BC V6T 1Z2
604-822-5959 / Fax: 604-822-6083
www.ubcpress.ca

Contents

Maps

Preface

The reach of the Chinese state has expanded and contracted over the two millennia since its foundation. From the Qin campaigns in the eighth century BCE to the present-day campaign to develop the West (*Xibu kaifa*), successive central governments have never been free of pressure regarding the borderlands, either through their own expansionist visions or from fear of external encroachment. The state, its bureaucracy, and its financial system were all deeply concerned with the borderlands, and all were involved in a process whereby the borders often had as much influence on the centre as the centre did on the periphery.

Alexander Woodside has devoted part of his distinguished academic career to looking at the form and the functions of the Chinese state as well as those of its neighbour to the south, Vietnam. The original versions of the chapters in this volume were presented at a conference held at the University of British Columbia in February 2004 to mark his retirement. Most of the people who came to the conference were either his colleagues or his former students – in many cases both.

Alex was born into the intellectual world. He grew up in Wychwood Park in Toronto, part of a discreet but brilliant community of academics that included Marshall McLuhan and Northrop Frye. He followed his father Moffatt Woodside into the university world, first to the University of Toronto as an undergraduate and then to Harvard as a graduate student and faculty member. For the last three decades, he has been back in his native land at the University of British Columbia.

Alex's career has taken him to the heights of academic achievement. He is Canada's leading Sinologist and the West's leading expert on Vietnam. Japan and Korea have a title for their citizens who reach Alex's level of distinction: "national living treasures." The title is given for pure accomplishment, not for time-serving or for political contributions. It goes to artists, craftspeople, and performers. If Canada were to follow Japan's example, and to include academics among its national treasures, Alex would be one of the first nominees for the title.

Alex has an encyclopedic knowledge of Chinese and Vietnamese history, stretching from the distant past to the present and even into the future. He can talk with authority about the latest trends in Chinese popular ideas as well as about what Qianlong thought about border defence. He knows as much about Western history as does any specialist, and more about Canadian history than almost anyone else. One of the sad outcomes of regional specialization is that he has never taught Canadian history.

Alex is known in the field of Asian history not only for the great range of his knowledge and his writings but also for his generosity with ideas and advice, manifested in his thoughtful critiques of manuscripts, his support of younger scholars and, above all, in his clear-eyed, humane evaluations of the work of his colleagues. Alex is never mean, but he is insightful. Presented in his inimitable wry and witty style, his considered opinions count for more than do the paeans of praise or the broadsides and vindictive carping of other scholars.

Alex's career has been influenced by his devotion to his country as much as it has been by his devotion to scholarship. He is a dedicated nationalist and a devout believer in the values of fairness, understatement, and generosity, which he associates with Canada. He comes from a long line of Canadians of Scottish and Irish ancestors, from whom he has learned sobriety and carefulness. But somewhere along the line a great sense of humour has crept in, and this has served to give him a sense of proportion and a deft ability to make fun of the pompous. Alex is an enemy of pomposity and of self-importance. In the politest possible way, he gently deflates people who have pretensions beyond their abilities.

Alex has never restricted himself to academic history. He has an encyclopedic knowledge of several quite disparate topics – early movies, hockey greats, and, above all, birds. No visit to Vancouver by an Asianist is complete without a Woodside-led visit to the Reifel Bird Sanctuary. The culmination of our conference was a trip to Reifel to see the great flocks of snow geese that stop for long periods at the mouth of the Fraser River on their migrations between Russia and Mexico, with absolutely no recognition of borders or frontiers.

Our conference was funded by a grant from the Social Science and Humanities Council of Canada. The Institute of Asian Research and its Centre of Chinese Research provided further financial and logistical support, and the Department of History at UBC provided funds for a reception. Many people made valuable contributions to the conference: Alison Bailey (UBC), Timothy Cheek (UBC), Arif Dirlik (Oregon), Caroline Ford (UBC), Samuel Ho (UBC), Steven Lee (UBC), Stephen MacKinnon (Arizona State), Daniel

Overmyer (UBC), Glen Peterson (UBC), Allen Smith (UBC), and Michael Szonyi (University of Western Ontario). Colin Green (UBC) planned the conference with immaculate skill, with help from Allan Cho, Jakc Hayes, Kenneth Ho, and Judy Maxwell. Eleanor Gill did a wonderful job of putting all the papers in order, Judy Maxwell organized the last stages of production work, and Desmond Cheung collated the complex bibliography. We thank all these people for their contributions.

At UBC Press, our thanks go to Emily Andrew, Jean Wilson, and Holly Keller. We also thank Eric Leinberger for producing the maps in this volume.

The Chinese State at the Borders

Introduction

Diana Lary

The Peoples Republic of China claims 22,000 kilometres of land borders, with eight other states, and 18,000 kilometres of coastal borders. How did this vast country come into being? The credo of the Chinese state describes an ancient process of cultural expansion, as less cultivated peoples accepted high culture from China and became inalienable parts of China. Successive governments (imperial, Guomindang, Communist) have held devoutly to the view that the Chinese state reached close to its current extent in the early stages of the Empire (3rd Century BCE). There have followed more than two millennia of unity, broken only by the aberration of periods of disunity. The centre (wherever the Chinese capital was located at any given time) rightfully controls the borderlands, in a paternalist, one-way relationship in which benevolence comes from the centre and is gratefully received by the benighted border peoples, once referred to as barbarians, now known as national minorities.[1]

This credo is not as straightforward or as linear as it seems: it contains fundamental contradictions and is quite obscure. One contradiction concerns the physical extent of the state. There *were* periodic Chinese incursions out from the centre from the foundation of the Empire on, but most of the current borderlands were not fully incorporated into the Chinese state until the eighteenth century, in a process that stretched the centre to its limits – a process usefully described as "imperial overreach." Even then the process was incomplete. Many of the regions that have been claimed by successive centres as part of China remained outside direct control until quite recently.

A major area of obscurity is the actual location of many of the borders. Some of them follow natural features – the crest of a mountain chain or the coastline – but others are less clear. In the deserts to the north and northwest, tracks through the sand are soon blown away. Even river borders are less fixed than they seem. The line of the Heilongjiang/Amur border in the northeast shifts as the course of the river shifts; in winter, when it freezes, it becomes a highway rather than a border. This confusion led to an armed conflict with the Soviet Union in 1969. The Great Wall gives the impression of being the most permanent boundary marker on earth, but for much of its history it has lain well within China, not on the state's borders.

Few of China's borders were marked until quite recently. In Chinese historical accounts, China's southern border was marked in the Han Dynasty with a bronze pillar, but the pillar has not survived (or has not been found); the formal borderline with Vietnam/Indo-China was only established in 1894. The Sino-Russian border is even more recent: the final demarcation was made in 2004.

The communiqué issued at the signing ceremony for this border agreement points up another contradiction: the way in which control of the borders has normally been established. The communiqué sets a high moral tone: "the correct and effective way in settling complicated and sensitive issues like border issues lies in peaceful dialogue, fairness, equal consultation, mutual understanding and concession, and balance in each other's interests."[2] These bland, confident assertions obscure the actual nature of much of China's physical expansion – a heavy dependence on the force of arms. This forcible expansion has often been regarded as permanent only on the incoming (i.e. Chinese) side; on the other side, that of the indigenous peoples of the borderlands, the Chinese presence either remains contested or is seen as an occupation.

Another area of contradiction is the assumption that, since time immemorial, China has existed in a state of unity. Unity is not a natural state of affairs but, rather, a condition that the centre goes to great lengths to ensure. The present centre is assiduous in putting down threats to national unity. The most obvious form that this takes is the putting down of any manifestations of discontent in the border regions.

The centre has another, underlying reason for its stern attitudes towards the border peoples: it is concerned not only with maintaining control over the border regions themselves but also in preventing a loss of power at the borders of the state, which might trigger a general process of regional devolution in the Han Chinese provinces. The threat of devolution is always real. At the moment, some of the citizens (including members of the government) of the putative Chinese province of Taiwan express their belief that Taiwan does not belong in China, and this is a direct threat to the ideal of a united nation. Quieter but equally threatening are the unspoken attitudes and behaviour of some of the most developed regions in China: Guangdong, Fujian, Zhejiang, and Shanghai have evolved strong regional identities, and they use them (and the regional dialects that are part of them) as mechanisms of inclusion and exclusion. These regions show levels of autonomy that strong centrists can only find to be disturbing.

These contradictions and obscurities take away from the elegance and simplicity of the official credo of an ancient, united state. They imply that the relationship between the centre and the borderlands was and is a conceit, an imperial conceit that disdains the problems inherent to controlling a vast state.

The chapters in this book look at the relationship between the state and the borderlands over a long period of time, and they cover most of the borderlands. Alexander Woodside's overview, "The Centre and the Borderlands in Chinese Political Theory," looks at the continuities between the distant past and the present as well as at how the centre's ambition to control a vast country have influenced capital politics and state administration.

Control of the borderlands demands a large and creative repertoire of tactical devices. Map-making is a key element of border demarcation and is the basis of claims to sovereignty. Benjamin Elman's chapter, "Ming-Qing Border Defence, the Inward Turn of Chinese Cartography, and Qing Expansion in the Eighteenth Century" looks at Chinese cartography. Nicola Di Cosmo, in his chapter, "Marital Politics on the Manchu-Mongol Frontier in the Early Seventeenth Century," looks at how border stability was peacefully maintained. The borders were always major topics of policy debate and factional fighting at court. Timothy Brook's chapter on the great philosopher official Wang Yangming – "What Happens When Wang Yangming Crosses the Border?" – looks at how border issues were manipulated at the centre. Leo Shin's chapter, "Ming China and Its Border with Annam," discusses the creative and multiple solutions the Ming court found to deal with the southern border regions.

The most ambitious expansionists were the Manchu emperors of the mid-Qing dynasty. Their dynasty was a conquest dynasty, and military might continued to be its raison d'etre under the first four emperors. Their campaigns into the western borderlands were successful and consolidated China's expansion; others, to the southwest, were less successful. In his chapter, "Embracing Victory, Effacing Defeat: Rewriting the Qing Frontier Campaigns," Peter Perdue shows how the impression of successful expansion was constructed and promoted.

Nothing was ever quite settled in the borderlands. The Qing had to deal with borders that were never permanently stabilized (e.g., the border with Korea). Andre Schmid's chapter, "Tributary Relations and the Qing-Chosŏn Frontier on Mount Paektu," looks at a border where tributary relations governed interstate relations, yet the border had a life of its own. Other border regions were beyond anyone's control. One of the wildest was the northeastern border. In the late Qing it became a focus of Russian interest, a place where Chinese and Russian worlds met. Victor Zatsepine's chapter, "The Amur: As River, as Border," looks at the vast, remote, cold border region of the

Amur River Basin. Another kind of interaction, a *metissage,* where Chinese values were transformed through acculturation to accommodate local systems, is described in Van Nguyen-Marshall's chapter, "The Ethics of Benevolence in French Colonial Vietnam: A Sino-Franco-Vietnamese Cultural Borderland."

After the fall of the Qing, and the loss of central power for several decades during the Republic, China's control over the borderlands was drastically reduced. Border relations became the preserve of regional governments rather than of the state. Diana Lary's chapter, "A Zone of Nebulous Menace: The Guangxi/Indochina Border in the Republican Period," shows the relationship between a single province and its neighbour. In the period after its conquest of China in 1949, the Chinese Communist Party (CCP) government restored Chinese control over many of the border regions and started a campaign (that continues today) to settle Han Chinese in the borderlands. One method of doing this involved forced migration and the use of the borderlands as places of punishment. Wang Ning's chapter, "Border Banishment: Political Exile in the Army Farms of Beidahuang," looks at banishment and exile. Banishment was a traditional practice, as was using borderland leaders as proxies for the centre. Stevan Harrell looks at this issue within a contemporary context in his chapter "L'état, c'est nous, or We Have Met the Oppressor and He Is Us: The Predicament of Minority Cadres in the PRC." Finally, in his chapter, "Theoretical and Conceptual Perspectives on the Periphery in Contemporary China," Pitman Potter looks at how the periphery and the centre continue to have great importance for each other.

The chapters in this book cover a millennium. Though the parallels from one period to another are often striking, the chapters show how, over time, the richness and diversity of the interactions between the central state and the borderlands evolved. This is a field of research that offers great possibilities to better understand not only China but also the borderlands of other large states.[3]

Terminology

Any work that covers a long time span and uses more than one language is bound to present terminological difficulties. In our case this is exacerbated by the fact that many of the terms commonly used to discuss China are anachronistic, starting with the word "China" itself. The term "Zhongguo," the current translation of "China," has only been in common use since the nineteenth century; the term "China" has been used in Western languages dating from the same period.[4] We acknowledge the anachronism but, for the sake of convenience, continue to refer to "China."

Another terminological confusion concerns place-names (toponyms). Place-names have changed frequently over the millennia. A whole subset of historical writings in Chinese is devoted to the study of place-names (*diming*). This variability occurs just as much with the names of provinces as it does with the names of individual places. We are quite aware of these variations, but in most cases, again for the sake of convenience, we employ the names in use at the moment.

Equally confusing is the naming of peoples. The dominant people, the Han, have only been known as such since quite late in the imperial period, while the names of the various non-Han peoples have changed repeatedly over time. Over seven hundred different ethnonyms are found in Chinese sources for different periods; there must be high levels of overlap within this group of names, but these are confusions that are almost impossible to resolve, in spite of the valiant efforts of Chinese scholars to do so.[5]

English terms give us problems that Chinese terms do not. In English there are various ways of referring to the edges of a state, the ends of a state's claim to territorial sovereignty. The term "marches" was once a useful one, suggesting regions where states and cultures connected to each other in ways that were sometimes hostile (often a stand-off) and occasionally amicable. But this term is so out of date that using it might give the impression that we ourselves are stuck in the past. The term "frontier" has much greater currency. It has more than one meaning, yet these meanings are not contradictory. "Frontier" may refer to a zone without clear boundaries, where cultures meet, overlap, and compete, as in Frederick Jackson Turner's "frontier thesis" or in Owen Lattimore's notion of the "inner Asian frontiers of China." "Frontier" may also mean a fixed, clearly demarcated line on the map or even an actual, physical barrier between two states. The same dual meaning applies to the word "border." A border may be an actual line, as in the line guarded by the Canada Border Service or the US Border Patrol (or the line crossed by cross-border shoppers). It may also be a zone of transition, a zone in which two or more states meet – and where a distinct society emerges. "Border" also refers to non-physical entities, as in the term "border-crossing," which is now popular in the study of cultural and social issues, with the idea of transcending previously fixed and restrictive limits.

The distinction between "frontier" and "border" is not a hard and fast one. In fact the two are often used interchangeably. In French the international medical aid agency is *medecins sans frontieres*, in English "Doctors without Borders." In Chinese there is less of an issue with terminology. The common terms are *bianjiang* and *bianjie*, the first translated fairly indiscriminately as frontier or border, the second as frontier zone or border zone. The neologism *guojing/guojie* is used in formal contexts, such as immigration and emigration procedures.

We have chosen to use the term "border," without giving it the implication of a fixed line but, rather, a gradual break, a transition between two entities, the end of one and the beginning of another. It is implicitly permeable, flexible, and interpenetrable. Our usage includes the conception of border zones, places inhabited by people who do not recognize border divisions, moving across them as though they did not exist.

Discourses on the Borderlands

The Centre of Civilization

In China, all history is official, constructed to provide proof of the state's right to rule. The state has often been successful in getting non-Chinese to follow its interpretations, and this success is reflected in many academic and popular writings on China. *The Chinese State at the Borders* breaks with the dominant view in political and academic discourses on the Chinese state, in which centre/borderlands relations have been seen as *de haut en bas*, with the borderlands being inferior, benighted places, their darkness lit by the distant rays of the brilliant centre. Versions of this view have been prominent in several fields of study: ethnicity, state economic development, China's relations with neighbouring states, and cultural absorption. All have put the centre on a higher level than the borderlands. These views have also been widely accepted by national governments, international organizations, and non-governmental organizations (NGOs). In academic circles this acceptance is becoming less standard as lessons have been learned from the transformation in our views of indigenous peoples in North America, once referred to as "Indians" but now known to themselves and others as First Nations peoples.

In China, this change has not occurred. Though the term "barbarian" has quite disappeared, and the use of disparaging written characters with the dog radical is gone,[6] the centre describes China's border peoples as ethnic minorities (*shaoshu minzu*). They are made up of fifty-five officially designated peoples who live mainly in the border regions and who account for about 8 percent of the population. The rest of the Chinese population is Han. This description stresses the word "minority." The border peoples are numerical minorities, and they are also minorities in the sense of being different, strange, exotic, at a lower level of cultural evolution than the Han. They have picturesque cultures, well suited to attracting tourists and to providing colour (unlike the rather dour Han). The exotic depiction of minorities finds its ultimate statement in the "minority theme parks" now found in many parts of China, the largest one being the Chinese Ethnic Culture Park in Beijing, where all the minorities are lumped together in a saccharine display of unthreatening cuteness.[7]

The "Under-Developed" Peoples

The assumption that the border peoples are backward is underlined by the recognition that many of them are poor. The borderlands are seen as less developed, either because the terrain they inhabit is hard (deserts and mountains) and the climate harsh or because the peoples themselves lack interest in material culture, being steeped in "backward religions" that value faith above material accumulation. The efforts of international aid agencies and NGOs are now concentrated in the border regions, while the centre implements the "Develop the West" policy that aims to integrate the western border regions into the rest of China, an effort blurred by the fact that the "West" now includes provinces normally considered to be Han, such as Sichuan and Shaanxi. What is not mentioned is the fact that the border regions may be poor because of long-term economic changes, such as the decline of traditional trading patterns (e.g., the ancient decline of the very prosperous Silk Road economy, the impact of China's international rivalries, and the damage caused to the Xinjiang-Central Asia trade by the Sino-Soviet split in the early 1960s).

Threats from the Borders and at the Borders

The view from the centre gives the impression that the ethnic minorities belong only in China and that they live at the ends of the world. Many of the border peoples in fact have long historical connections across the borders and are parts of ethnic groups separated from each other by a fairly artificial state border. The Korean, Kazak, Mongol, and Russian minorities in China are all tied to states dominated by their own ethnicity. Other peoples are parts of ethnic groups represented in several countries; the Uigurs have close connections right across Central Asia to Turkey, their languages mutually intelligible. These ancient connections are treated with some nervousness at the centre. A good knowledge of history brings with it a knowledge of the might of the Mongol Empire and of other great centres of power in Central Asia. China's nightmare would be the revival of these conglomerations of power.

The borderlands may be seen as *potential* threats to the centre. They were quite clearly the places where China has confronted imperial expansionism, from well before the Mongol Empire to the modern era. From the mid-nineteenth century on, China confronted France across the borders of Indochina in Yunnan and Guangxi. In the northeast, in the Heilongjiang/Amur region, China had to deal with Russian expansion. In the high mountains in the west, China was drawn into the Great Game between Britain and Russia. In remote Kashgar, the Russian and British consuls kept their lonely vigils, collecting intelligence about the schemes of the other's masters for regional dominance. Most dangerous of all for China was the new imperialist power, Japan; from 1895 on, Japan annexed Korea, detached the island of Taiwan, pushed in on Manchuria, and eventually threatened the heartland of China. The threats of imperialism came not in the heartland of China but on its borders.

Homes for the Han

From the beginning of the empire, the centre has periodically looked for ways to solidify its partial control of the borderlands. Brought in by conquest, they could only be held securely by force of arms or by permanent settlement. The early dynasties achieved control by setting up civilian government in the wake of military conquest, sending out officials, and settling demobilized soldiers. Neither of these tactics was ever very successful in the long run. The officials felt (usually quite rightly) that they were being banished, while the soldiers (who were single men) married local women and were absorbed into the indigenous populations. After each period of conquest, civilian control gradually withered away. Not until the mid-Qing did serious settlement start. The pace has speeded up in more recent times, especially since 1949. But the forms of migration have seldom been positive: the continuing practice of settling unwilling migrants, demobilized soldiers, famine victims, and prisoners means that there is no excitement or enthusiasm for migration at the sending end, and even less at the receiving end. The common observation that vast borderlands are the ideal place to settle China's surplus population, heard now for many decades, will not become a reality until the lack of enthusiasm for Han settlement, on the part of borderland peoples and the Han themselves, changes. Even now, when millions of Han have moved to the borderlands, few regard their settlement as permanent; they are sojourners, making money so that they can eventually go back to their own homes.

Recurrence and Evolution

The issues that confront the state in the borderlands often recur, but these recurrences are offset by continuous evolution. The ebb and flow of Chinese influence that characterized the early dynasties has given way to a much more permanent, concentrated Chinese presence. Changes within the borderlands and beyond them have altered the nature of the relations between the centre and the borderlands. The rise of nationalism has made the peoples of the borderlands more aware of their own identities at the same time that their incorporation into China has become an integral part of Chinese national identity. Other changes have happened far away. The 911 events have had a huge impact on western China in that they have made it possible for the centre to associate those who want greater autonomy for the Uigurs with terrorism. There are undoubtedly more changes – perhaps equally unexpected ones – to come. The centre will never be able to take the borderlands for granted.

Centre-border relations are never static. In many ways, the current relationships between the border regions and the centre are different than they were in the past. The centre is acutely aware of the importance of the borderlands and their inhabitants to its vision of China's future, for traditional but also for new reasons, particularly resource extraction:[8]

1. *Resources:* the borderlands contain large quantities of untapped mineral deposits, most of the forest land, and over 80 percent of the country's animal products. These resources are very important for China's economic development.
2. *Geography:* though small in number, non-Han groups occupy 63.7 percent of the land area of China. The less densely populated minority regions may provide an avenue for relief from China's overpopulation problem.
3. *Strategic:* non-Han inhabit over 90 percent of China's border regions, making minority issues vital to national security.

Modern technology has had major impacts. It is now a five-hour flight from Beijing to Urumqi rather than a four months' trek across the desert. It is possible to travel from Beijing to Lhasa by train. Television programs from Beijing are broadcast in all parts of the nation at the same time: Beijing time. There is no recognition of the east-to-west time lag, no official time zones (as there are in North America). The borders are integrated into the state in other ways and are no longer anything like as isolated as they once were. Border guards are issued with phone cards so that they can keep in touch with their families. The Internet reaches all parts of China – though sites that discuss autonomy or religious freedom for peoples in the border regions are quickly closed down.

These technological innovations make control easier, but they have not managed to destroy the consciousness of many of the people of the borderlands that they are not Chinese.

In this book, we see the border regions as places in their own right, as places that have given the centre great problems and have sometimes dominated state policies because of the centre's self-imposed need to dominate them. Our approaches tend to share the following ideas:

- that the present extent of China, and the consolidation of the state, dates from the eighteenth century rather than from time immemorial;
- that there was an ebb and flow to Chinese control in the border regions rather than a long, continuous process of expansion and absorption;

- that the borderlands were brought into China by military conquest rather than cultural conquest (i.e., by a benevolent "civilizing" mission);
- that permanent Han settlement in the borderlands, so far from bringing high culture often brought people who were convicts, demobilized soldiers, and famine victims;
- that the peoples of the borderlands were and are closely connected – by ethnicity, history, religion, and economic ties – to peoples beyond China rather than constituting the ends of the Chinese world.

The current centre goes to great pains to present China as a stable, multicultural, multiethnic state – a model of harmony, equality, and unity for other states. In tandem with these upbeat views goes an intolerance of those who do not accept Han rule – "religious zealots," "feudal thinkers," "splitists," "terrorists." This toughness appears to contradict the form of government that exists in many of the borderlands. Many of the border regions are administered as "autonomous regions" (Tibet, Xinjiang, Inner Mongolia, Guangxi). Until the present, in practice "autonomous" seems to mean its opposite – that is, a high degree of direct control. This notion of autonomy has no room to accommodate the persistent desire of many of the peoples of the border regions for real autonomy or actual detachment. The challenge for the near future is to see whether there can be some evolution, whether the centre can recognize that there may be means of governing the borderlands that are less painful than force, and less demanding of its time and attention. In meeting this challenge China might look to Canada, which has one of the world's most stable political systems. Canada balances federal and provincial powers, and, although the threat of separation is a constant concern, no one contemplates resolving the problem through force.

Notes

1 Stevan Harrell, *Cultural Encounters on China's Ethnic Frontiers* (Seattle: University of Washington Press, 1995).

2 *Peoples Daily*, 15 October 2004.

3 For new views on the frontier in North America, see Jeremy Adelman and Stephen Aron, "From Borderlands to Borders: Empires, Nation-States and the Peoples in between in North American History," *American Historical Review* 104, 3 (1999): 814-41.

4 Endymion Wilkinson, *Chinese History: A Manual*, rev. ed. (Cambridge: Harvard University Press, 2000), 132, 753.

5 Ibid., 710-12.

6 The word for the Zhuang, the people of the Guangxi Zhuang Autonomous Region, used to be written with a dog radical to the left of the character for a child. It is now written with a homophone meaning "strong."

7 Dru C. Gladney, *Dislocating China; Reflections on Muslims, Minorities, and Other Subaltern Subjects* (Chicago: University of Chicago Press, 2005), 28-29, 32-48.

8 Wang Bing, "Multiculturalism in China," *Canadian Diversity Canadienne* 3, 3 (2004): 36.

1
The Centre and the Borderlands in Chinese Political Theory

Alexander Woodside

The Quixotic Nature of China's Political Centre

During his presidency in Russia in the early 1990s, Boris Yeltsin asked Russian thinkers to engage in a contest to create a new concept of the Russian nation-state. A newspaper close to the Yeltsin government, noting that both communism and Russian Orthodox Christianity were too weak to supply useful ideologies, even offered a US$2,000 reward for the most acceptable new conceptualization of the Russian polity. To the apparent satisfaction of Chinese observers, the prize went unclaimed; and the "spiritual crisis" in Russian politics remained unresolved.[1]

It is hard to imagine a Chinese newspaper offering any such prize in China. Some sort of notion of a Chinese state, as based upon an eternal civilizing political centre, committed to the unification of ever-widening areas and the peoples around it, has survived for several millennia. It continues to influence the People's Republic of China (PRC). The notion of an imperial centre was originally mythic and pre-bureaucratic, preceding the actual centralized emperorship of China created in 221 BCE. In the Chinese classics, the political culture's "Central Domain" (*zhong zhuo*) was one of the nine regions into which legendary rulers like the Yellow Emperor or King Yu of the Xia dynasty had divided the ancient world, with the other eight regions offering tribute to the region at the core.

During the Chinese Empire itself, the centre received its tribute from the provinces and expelled convicts, deserters, and dissidents to its outer regions, as in the First Emperor's use of banished prisoners more than two thousand years ago to colonize what is now the south Chinese province of Guangdong. But if Guangdong as a convict colony anticipated the much later history of Australia under British rule, there was no Australian-type romance about this in later Cantonese writings, no celebration of the liberating frontier through which the convict colony would become freer than the metropolis. The historical heroes in Guangdong, for great Cantonese poets like Qu Dajun (1630-96), were two strongman emperors – the First

Emperor (221-209 BCE) and Han Wudi (140-86 BCE), who, from a northern power base, had forcibly created Chineseness in the south.[2]

Chinese leaders have found great comfort over the centuries in embracing a cluster of fictive historical continuities concerning a unifying political centre. The ideal of the unifying centre was and is self-validating: its very persistence is taken to be proof of its rightness and objectivity. In September 1999 the Chinese State Council in Beijing published a detailed justification of China's ethnic minority policies. This text argued that a unified multiethnic state had existed in China since the unification of the empire in 221 BCE and that such unity had been the "main trend" of Chinese history. What's more, non-Chinese peoples themselves had contributed to this trend. The great Mongol Yuan government of the thirteenth and fourteenth centuries had refined China's system of "provinces" (*sheng*) as centre-dependent secretariats, and the influence of the Mongol province had survived to the present. China's Mongol rulers had also established agencies of military control in Tibet, which from this point on had become an "inalienable" part of Chinese territory and had set up patrols to manage the affairs of the Pescadores islands and of Taiwan. The Manchu Qing Empire (1644-1911) had made Xinjiang into a province; had imposed central bureaucratic control over the selection of the Dalai and Panchen Lamas in Tibet; and had introduced centrally appointed officials into the lives of the minority peoples of the southwest. The "mutual dependence" and "common development" of China's ethnic peoples, furthered by such statemaking, had in turn created "Chinese civilization."[3]

In 1999, the State Council's seductive grand narrative placed its faith in the existence of a time-transcending structure inherent in the past, which non-Chinese as well as Chinese agents served. The benefits of the structure supposedly remain available – without needing any complex strategy of accommodation – to contemporary Chinese politicians. Yet it is the centre that really transcends time in this narrative, not the borderlands or their peoples. Their identities fluctuate. The same 1999 justification of China's ethnic minority policies conceded, without embarrassment, that, after 1948, the Chinese political centre had not been able to make up its mind about the number of ethnic minorities in China. It had decreed 38 official ethnic minorities in 1954; 15 official ethnic minorities in 1964; and 55 official ethnic minorities in 1979. If the centre is eternal and the borderlands and their minorities are far less certain, there is seemingly less need to study the minorities' impact upon Chinese culture itself, apart from their service to the centralizing ideal. Not until well into the twentieth century did Chinese scholars begin comprehensively to examine the obvious subject of Central Asian influence in the Chinese core, as in the pioneering effort of the historian Xiang Da (1900-66) in the 1930s to uncover the connections between the Tang dynasty capital of Changan and the "civilization of the Western region." Significantly, Xiang Da relied heavily upon the research of the British Central Asia specialist Aurel Stein (1862-1943), whose works he translated into Chinese.

The problem with the ideal of the unifying centre is that, even since the first century of the common era, when Han dynasty leaders talked of pacifying the fifty-odd "countries" of pre-Islamic Xinjiang, China's borderlands have been too big and too various for any political centre, even a semi-mythic one, to control. The quixotic nature of the political centre's all-encompassing image of itself, and the discrepancies between the self-image and the almost impossible scope of its ambitions, explains why the political problems of the borderlands, in Chinese theory, have so often been disguised versions of political problems at the centre. And political problems at the centre were frequently pressing: in the two thousand years between the First Emperor and the Opium War in the 1800s, China had no real semblance of unity for almost half that time.

There are parallels in European history to the Chinese disjunction between the teleological approach to political power (attributing to the state an inherent ideal purpose) and the functional approach (concerned with the state's more modest actual behaviour in the exercise of its tasks). The German scholar Ernst Kantorowicz once noted the "double truth" in the Aristotelian formula that, for centuries, European lawyers tirelessly applied to the often ineffectual empires associated with the "eternal city" of Rome. As the formula presumed, the Roman and the Holy Roman Empires remained unchanging in their ideal essence, even if they were mutable and corrupt in their dispositions. Western writing down to the 1800s preserved this theme, as in Nathaniel Hawthorne's double vision of Rome as a timeless model of human civility and a time-bound place of corruption and squalor.[4]

However, the Chinese version of such a "double truth" has survived longer and been more potent than has the European version. Unlike the latter, the Chinese version could celebrate centralization without so much attachment to a specific city; and it did not have to mediate the competing claims of politics and religion. This gave it a flexibility that disguised its weakness: the underdevelopment of any critical intuitions that there could be polities that were united without being centralized. If it survives today, it finds its context in the life of an emerging superpower that has land borders with fifteen countries and maritime frontiers with six more (ranging from Korea to Brunei). Indeed, China now claims a coastline of 18,000 kilometres plus territorial waters – two-thirds of them disputed with other countries – covering 3.6 million square kilometres.[5] And, as the first round-the-world voyage of Chinese warships in 2002 suggests, the whole notion of a limited oceanic "borderlands" for China may rapidly be becoming obsolete.

The Psychological Symbiosis of Centre and Borderlands

Both foreign and Chinese critics of the overweening political centre in Chinese political theory have taken its apparently absolute claims at face value, and they have stressed the malignant effects of the ideal upon China's development. The sociologist S.N. Eisenstadt, in a stimulating 1978 book about "revolution and the transformation of societies," proposed that the Chinese political centre, with its strong "Confucian orientation," was more "monopolistic" and more "rigid" than were equivalent political centres in Western Europe. Its alleged "rigidity" even accounted for the supposedly greater violence of the Chinese revolution compared to the English and French ones. The more extreme Chinese revolutionary violence was a response to the frustration that "major strata" in China suffered from their political centre's coerciveness.[6]

Chinese critics of the centre ideal have been even more severe. At the outset of the People's Republic of China, in 1951, the long-time Qinghua University ethnologist Pan Guangdan (1899-1967) published a newspaper article assessing what he called the historic ethnic chauvinism of the Chinese people. Pan attacked the "chronic disease" of the Chinese people, their boastful view of themselves, expressed in the fantasy that their polity contained everything "under Heaven" and that their rulers could convert the entire world into a family. The strong political centre was a necessary accompaniment of this notion of the legitimate conversion of the world into a household. Such a centre had to be all-encompassing in its view of itself, comprising definitions of its identity that were at once geographical, patriarchal, cultural-ritualistic, and military. But – Pan wrote in 1951 – the geographical element in the centre's definition of itself was a fabricated value that would become increasingly problematic once it was discovered that the earth was round; and as the Chinese political centre's fictive geography, patriarchal emotional foundations, and cultural mobilization ambitions hardened over time, that centre would require more and more military force to repress opposition to it.

In Pan's perspective, the borderlands minorities would be the principal victims. The political centre's language, in talking about these minorities, resembled the language with which parents "humbugged small children." The centre's policy towards its minorities, who were regarded as though they were children, could be described as a policy of "mama-ism" (*mama zhuyi*) (Pan's Chinese rendering of the then fashionable American term "momism," which was popularized by the writer Philip Wylie). The Chinese Communist Republic was as guilty as was the Empire. Pan scathingly observed that all the new PRC had done, in dealing with its minorities, was to change the bottle in which the anti-minority "medicine" came. The "medicine" itself remained unchanged: the PRC's Mongolia-Tibet Commission of 1951 was nothing more than the Qing dynasty's old Court of

Colonial Affairs (*Lifanyuan*), which had administered the peoples of central Asia from the 1600s to the 1800s, in a different guise.[7]

Up to a point there were, indeed, bloody collisions between the "rigid" political centre and the peoples of the borderlands, whose ethnic and cultural and political boundaries (including those of Han Chinese settlers) were shifting and negotiable. When the bureaucratizing centre did try to impose its ideas of administrative integration upon the mutable and pluralistic border world, the result could be something like the Guizhou killing fields of the Ming and Qing dynasties. This was the great slaughter of aboriginal peoples in the Chinese southwest that began roughly about the time of the initial slaughter of aboriginals in the Americas in the aftermath of Christopher Columbus's voyages.

But the sheer ecological variety of the borderlands dictated that there would be variety in the interaction of central designs and local histories. Of all the border wars conducted by China's imperial centre in the 1700s, the campaign that lasted longest, cost the most, and probably involved the mobilization of the greatest number of Qing troops, was Beijing's struggle to subdue about thirty thousand Tibetan Khamba hill people in the mountains of west Sichuan. The terrain here made central Asia's, by contrast, seem ideal for warfare; and the centre's effort to control the relative handful of west Sichuan Tibetans – the Chechens of eighteenth-century Asia with regard to their skill at humbling a bigger opponent – probably cost it more than twice what it had cost Beijing to conquer all of Xinjiang in the same century.[8]

Nor were ecological limits the centre's only problem in managing its borders. The central realm and the borderlands realm were locked into a psychological symbiosis. In this symbiosis, the borderlands might compel institutional change at the centre (as with the creation of the Qing dynasty's secretive "Grand Council") or raise subversive questions about the political centre's own inconsistent bureaucratic culture. In the 1700s and 1800s, for example, the Beijing government's great project to reduce the hereditary power of almost eighteen hundred minority chiefs (*tusi*, "local officers") in the south and southwest inspired academicians in the court to ask why the political centre itself tolerated so many haughty hereditary clerks in its own Six Ministries.[9] The borderlands, in other words, compelled the centre to confront the tensions between its own publicly universalist, but privately counter-universalist, political tendencies.

It was not just the borderlands whose boundaries were shifting and negotiable; it was also the boundaries of what the political centre itself was supposed to be or to mean. To put it in social science language made famous by Pierre Bourdieu, the centre tried to concentrate different types of political capital: military, fiscal, cultural-informational, and moral-symbolic.[10] But it did so in varying degrees, with the needs for the concentration of one type sometimes colliding with those for another. As the paymaster of one of the world's oldest bureaucracies, the imperial centre was often insolvent. (Things are better now; but two experts recently calculated that, at the end of the 1980s, the Chinese central government administered a smaller percentage of China's GNP than did the central governments of India or Indonesia for their countries.)[11] The centre's shifting boundaries of action and meaning ensured that borderlands political theory would be part of a long Chinese debate about bureaucracy as a whole. Such theory was not just a relentless project to impose demeaning ethnic and cultural categories upon non-Chinese peoples.

The centre's obsession with the utopianization of place-names was no doubt part of its effort to reconcile the two parts of the state's "double truth": the teleological and the functional. The names of countless Chinese administrative bailiwicks, ranging from Changan to Nanning, included vocabulary elements (*an, ning, ping*) that evoked peace or tranquillity. (Pan Guangdan thought that, in 1951, about one-quarter of Guizhou's counties had traces of the "pacification" ideology in their names.) In contrast, the naming procedures under European colonialism were far more miscellaneous, being a welter of saints' names (San Francisco), borrowed aboriginal terms (Toronto), transposed European place-names (New York), sailors' names (Vancouver), and a small number of names with utopian implications (Philadelphia). But if the Chinese centre's hope for "tranquilized" borderlands contrasts with the more heterogeneous naming practices of European colonialism, it is clear that its naming game encoded needs at least as much as it did facts. And the primary need was, through subliminal persuasiveness and with little cost, to enable a chronically weak imperial core to achieve an idealized administrative model of space. Significantly, the Chinese state intellectuals who helped make the names were frequently accused of taking an insufficient interest in China's borderlands.

The Borderlands and State Intellectuals' Imperial Amnesia

The criticism that Chinese thinkers were indifferent to their borderlands is current in China today. But it also has a long genealogy. If we sample its genealogical layers by beginning in the present and working backward, the first stop must be the China Borderlands History and Geography Research Centre that was set up by the Chinese Academy of Social Sciences in 1983. Its purpose was to produce a series of encyclopedic anthologies under the heading "China Borderlands History and Geography Library." Something of the energies behind this project is suggested by one of its first works, a 1992 anthology of documents concerning the history of the boundary between China and Vietnam, which runs to over 1,100 pages and translates into Chinese roughly 3 million words' worth of French language materials found in France and dating back to Vietnam's French Indochina period.

The general preface to anthologies like this one charges post-1949 China with suppressing research about China's frontiers, declaring it for a long time a "taboo area." Coming close to substituting a borderlands explanation of Chinese history for the old Maoist class warfare explanation, the preface claims that borderlands crises, and their management, have determined the problem of order and disorder in China as a whole. And the recent suppression of Chinese borderlands research has played into the hands of China's near neighbours, whose own research momentum on this subject is great.[12] The preface stops just short of proclaiming the cognitive equivalent of a missile gap in armaments.

But it is all old stuff. In 1934, the well-known professor and nationalist journalist Lin Tongji (T.C. Lin, 1906-80) told the readers of a celebrated journal that, for several thousand years, Chinese elite education had been an "anti-frontiers education." The orthodox literature that Chinese schools had taught had reviled the frontier-developing feats of the First Emperor and of Han Wudi. As a result, attitudes hostile to the frontiers, which were considered to be "rustic and unlivable," had become second nature for the Chinese people.[13]

Elite indifference to the borderlands was also a staple complaint in the pre-1911 empire. In 1820, the reformer Gong Zizhen (1792-1841) had attacked people whom he called "stupid literati of shallow experience" and "rustic students down in the villages" for questioning *both* the Qianlong emperor's intelligence and his humanity because he expanded China's borders by conquering Xinjiang.[14] Even earlier than that, in the Ming dynasty, the scholar-official and iconoclast Lü Kun (1536-1618) had denounced the Chinese elite strategists who did think about the frontiers for the complacent staleness of their theories of frontier defence, which privileged the building of brick walls and more brick walls. Women and children all "laughed" at the futility of such schemes, Lu said, yet "border ministers" declined to abandon them.[15]

In fact the criticisms were exaggerated. Major Chinese elite thinkers, including Gong Zizhen and Lü Kun, did pay attention to the borderlands. But it is worth looking at Chinese state intellectuals' alleged avoidance of the topic of their expanding empire and its borders from a global history perspective. As a general rule, all imperial powers have intellectuals who tend to avert their gaze from empire.

In the sixteenth century, when Spanish America was taking shape, Europe's imperial new world was hardly mentioned in the European chronicles and memoirs of the time; European schools continued to use classical cosmographies that the new world had rendered outdated.[16] During the heyday of the British Empire, in the 1800s, J.R. Seeley advanced the claim (in his *The Expansion of England, 1883*) that the British had conquered half the world "in a fit of absence of mind." While the British were seizing much of Asia and Africa, "we did not allow it to affect our imaginations or in any degree to change our ways of thinking."[17] More recently, in 2002, the American historian Thomas Bender complained that, "save for what I will call the William Appleton Williams era, empire has been invisible in American history," despite empire's "centrality" in that history.[18]

What David Armitage usefully calls the "imperial amnesia" of intellectual elites is a widespread phenomenon. The reflex has less to do with pacifism than with the ways in which imperial expansion threatens or subverts the principles of the political theory in circulation among the elites at the time the expansion occurs. The French Enlightenment tribune Denis Diderot made this point in the 1700s, when he warned Dutch republican theorists that predatory Dutch trade monopolies in Dutch colonies would eventually undermine the chances for democratic republicanism in the Netherlands itself.[19]

In the sixteenth century, the Spanish Crown feared its borderlands conquistadors (like Hernan Cortes) because their tendency to create their own feudal estates in Mexico and Peru seemed to contradict the Spanish government's own political centralization efforts in Spain itself. Surely one of the reasons that British thinkers of the 1800s "absented their minds" from the British conquest of half the world lay in their commitment to the Whig theory of British history as one of expanding constitutional liberties. What the British were actually doing in Burma and India was hardly compatible with pictures of British history as being about the growth of liberty. And as Bender observed in 2002, the American elite's denial of empire was part of their immersion in a general view of the United States as being politically exceptional rather than as resembling the "old" and decadent European powers.

So if there is any truth in the accusations that Chinese state intellectuals did not celebrate China's expanding borderlands, we have to ask which important political theory traditions in China appeared to be the most imperilled by the Ming Empire's huge frontier armies or by the incorporation into China of Xinjiang in the 1700s. There were at least two, one of which was the welfare-based approach to political obligation. It went back to the reciprocity principle of the classical pre-imperial period of small political jurisdictions in China, when the people, according to legend, obeyed their rulers because "they ate their princes' food and wore their princes' clothes." The numerous thinkers who wrote about poverty in the Ming-Qing period were quick to blame poverty not on the sinfulness or the shortcomings of the poor but, rather, on the excessive administrative scale of the empire and its corresponding decline in feudal political intimacy. It was thought to foster alienation and to frustrate proposals for the effective redistribution of wealth.

The second tradition that was contradicted by China's expanding borders was that of the empire's faith in a salaried bureaucracy that could employ poor but talented officials who lacked private fortunes and that, through its law of "avoidance," proved its principled indifference to local family or geographical loyalties. The law of avoidance, continuously elaborated since the Han dynasty, compelled officials to serve in government positions far from their homes. It was – when it was enforced (which was not always) – one of the most physically and economically exacting public interest principles ever devised, even if it was a bureaucratic rather than a constitutional one. The bigger the empire, the further officials might have to travel, on inadequate salaries, to their appointments.

Lü Kun, the Ming scholar-official already mentioned, significantly linked the two concepts of "border planning and popular distress" in his dissection of the Ming border crisis at the end of the 1500s. Lü insisted upon looking at the administrative space of the Ming Empire from the viewpoint of its postal relay stations' sedan chair bearers and horse coolies. They were the suffering peasants conscripted to leave their families in order to move promoted or transferred bureaucrats hundreds of miles or more in compliance with the law of avoidance. (Lü's writings anticipated George Orwell's later look at the British Empire's frontiers in Burma from the perspective of its clerks and policemen.) To reduce the misery of the empire's conscripted coolies, Lü thought, the distance its promoted officials had to travel must be reduced. His scheme for doing this was to shrink the law of avoidance by subdividing China into three bureaucratic appointment zones (South, North, and Centre) and by stipulating that no civil officials (with his conscripted servants) should have to cross more than one zone to take up an appointment away from home.[20]

Lü Kun – like the other mandarins of the Ming and Qing dynasties who proposed China's conversion into multiple bureaucratic appointments and travel zones – reflected Chinese political theory's quest for subimperial forms of administrative space. In comparative terms, this was looking for a bureaucratic equivalent of the more feudal low-cost "composite monarchies" of Europe, with their patchwork juxtapositions of realms with separate laws, immunities, and even ecclesiastical establishments. The concern with cost-cutting forms of subimperial space creation clearly worked against the emergence of Chinese Horace Greeleys or John Buchans – mandarins with an urge to incorporate distant borderlands. But the high rates of indebtedness of the Chinese civil officials who did have to travel great distances to their posts, without being able to acquire feudal estates (like Spanish officials in the Americas) when they got there, does make their distaste for the borderlands more understandable. And there was another threat to the well-being of mandarins that encouraged them to see the borderlands as a breeding ground of potential catastrophes, whose management – even at the best of times – was a Sisyphean enterprise. This was the threat of imperial overstretch.

The Imperial Overstretch Fear in Views of the Borderlands

The political theory of China's Ming dynasty (1368-1644), much of it still unexplored, is probably one of the greatest repositories we have of preindustrial wisdom about the only too enduring subject of imperial overstretch. Ming China apparently mobilized something like 4 million soldiers (ranging from hereditary army troops to auxiliary mercenaries) with varying degrees of dependency on the centre's budget. Globally, at that time, this was probably a unique situation. Even Europe's dominant ruler, Louis XIV of France, commanding the biggest armies in French history at the end of the 1600s, only had to pay for about 400,000 soldiers.[21]

Frontier armies' endless drain on the centre's resources only reinforced the civil elite's borderlands hypochondria, for reasons both obvious and not so obvious. In 1605 the Ming grand secretary Xu Guangqi (1562-1633), Paul Xu to Chinese Christians, publicly asserted that the two greatest dangers to the stability of China were its monarchy and its frontiers. What they had in common was runaway spending: it was bound to lead to a terminal financial crisis.

To save the empire, Xu told the Ming court in 1605, the tens of thousands of descendents of the polygamous royal house would have to have their stipends cancelled and be returned to self-supporting occupations like farming (a not very reasonable remedy). As for the extended frontiers, they could only be sustained by the resurrection of self-sufficient military colonies whose soldiers also farmed.[22] But military state farms on the frontiers were a Han dynasty practice, making the idea more than seventeen centuries old in 1605. Not surprisingly, frontier-based state farms were unpopular in the 1600s. They had high desertion rates, anticipating the current flight of able personnel from their obvious successor in Xinjiang – the Production-Construction Army Corps (*bingtuan*) created by Mao Zedong in the 1950s. Changing values made Chinese not only less willing to work land they did not own but also to be both farmers and soldiers.

But as with the law of avoidance, the general issue of the performance of China's civil service was also what was at stake in this frontier-hating debate. The borderlands got absorbed into battles over the theorization of consumption standards in the Chinese core itself. To high officials like Xu Guangqi, only "rich frontiers" – by which they meant economically self-sufficient ones – would permit the political centre to pay salaries to its officials (who were spread all over China) that would be decent enough to keep them free of corruption. The elite's borderlands hypochondria therefore stemmed from its view of the borderlands as being part of a fiscal zero-sum game. Increased costs on the frontiers were thought to undermine the material upkeep, and thus the behaviour, of the political centres' administrators. Here there was a sharp contrast between the Ming Empire and more capitalist modern empires like the British Empire of the 1800s, whose London money markets had surplus capital to export and whose elite was dominated not by impecunious salaried mandarins but by the richest hereditary aristocracy in Europe.[23] The greater theoretical contingency of consumption standards, in a Chinese empire ruled at least in part by poorly salaried officials, influenced Chinese elite views of borderlands space. For Chinese political theorists, until recently, the problem was not an imperial centre that created underdevelopment on its borderlands but, rather, imperial borderlands that threatened to create underdevelopment at the centre.

The Qing Empire, in its prime, modified this situation without completely banishing it. In the 1700s, Manchu-ruled China much more resembled a successful empire of the sort that a historian like Immanuel Wallerstein would recognize: that is, an empire with a dominant core and the capacity to transfer wealth efficiently from its peripheries to that core. For one thing, there was more wealth to transfer in the Qing Empire than there was in the Ming, thanks to a more rapidly commercializing economy that China's rulers could exploit. Demographic trends also made Manchu-ruled China look more like a modern empire: remarkable population growth encouraged a migration of perhaps 10 million Han Chinese settlers, between 1644 and 1799, to the southwest borderlands, to Mongolia and Manchuria, to Taiwan, and even to Xinjiang.[24]

Equally remarkable, Chinese elite thinkers began to take a more benign view of the borderlands as a place where wars and popular welfare could be reconciled. In 1820 Gong Zizhen previewed more modern forms of the utopian production of frontier space with his proposal to make Xinjiang the antidote to a decadent China. In his reform plan, all the rootless poor people in north China, beginning in Beijing, would be rounded up and moved to Xinjiang to make a fresh start. Gong's version of a mandarin New Jerusalem in the Chinese northwest included the characteristic hope that Xinjiang could be kept pure for such people by restricting the import of corrupting consumer goods from the Chinese core.[25]

But the Manchu emperors themselves still upheld old negative views of the borderlands, and they converted Xinjiang into a banishment site for the officials, both Manchu and Chinese, whom they punished by sending into exile. Even major Chinese scholarly authorities on Mongolia and Xinjiang in the early 1800s, such as Qi Yunshi (1751-1815) and Xu Song (1781-1848), hardly resembled Aurel Stein: both had backgrounds as involuntary Chinese official exiles in the region. Down to the late 1800s, the emerging welfarist definitions of the frontiers coexisted with the old

Sisyphean view that saw them as spaces that generated cycles of crisis and catastrophe. Zuo Zongtang (1812-85), the general who reconquered Xinjiang in the 1870s from Ottoman Empire-backed Islamic rebels, could still write in his old age that only the Han and the Tang dynasties had had winning policies on their frontiers. Zuo also wrote that the Manchu emperors had seized Xinjiang in order to protect Beijing: if Xinjiang became unstable, the Mongols would be disturbed; and if the Mongols became restless, then, in a chain reaction, the political centre itself would be jeopardized.[26]

Thus the whole story of the triumphant conquest of Xinjiang could be made to serve the purpose of a much older, more pessimistic theme: that of the vulnerability of the imperial centre. Zuo's view – if Xinjiang goes, then Beijing goes – has to be one of the most extravagant domino theories ever conceived, at least up until the American war in Vietnam in the 1950s and 1960s.

The Decline of the Catastrophic View of the Borderlands

At the end of the 1800s, the Chinese elite began to shift its outlook on China's borderlands. The Sisyphean, or cyclical-catastrophic, view of the borders faded in favour of a perspective that might be called linear-providential. This entertained visions of frontier development in which frontiers were seen as part of a willed progress towards some emancipatory goal.

Chinese ethnic nationalism promoted the shift. After the Japanese annexation of Manchuria, for example, in 1932 the young Pan Guangdan warned that what China had lost to the Japanese in its northeast borderlands was not just mineral wealth and an outlet for its surplus population but also a "great garden area" in which the superior, more fit elements of the Chinese people could test themselves and improve the race.[27] (Imported theories of ethnic struggle influenced Pan, most notably those of the Yale University geographer Ellsworth Huntington, who had praised Chinese colonists in Manchuria in a study of "natural selection and Chinese national characteristics.") But Chinese nationalism could combine with another tendency, this one borrowed from Western Enlightenment thought: the tendency to link planned social progress, including the remaking of nature, with ventures in spatial engineering. In this synthesis, frontier space might be imagined more as artificially designed "virtual territory" that could satisfy national needs and less as historically lived space with its own particular identities.

The modern Chinese fascination with Christopher Columbus and his career is surely a symptom of this shift in Chinese views of the borderlands. Reading and writing about Columbus evidently allowed Chinese thinkers to participate vicariously in the celebration of border expansion as positive wealth creation or even as the positive outcome of the maximization and projection of scientific research and knowledge.

About 1902, Liang Qichao began Chinese thinkers' obsession with comparing Christopher Columbus with the fifteenth-century Chinese admiral Zheng He. Liang asserted that Columbus's achievements had created a progressive "new era" in world history and that Zheng He's had not. Between 1900 and 1949, the boom in Chinese Christopher Columbus studies continued, as is seen in Zhang Xiangwen's school geography textbooks of 1901 and 1908, and in books about Columbus written by Lin Wanli in 1915 and by Liu Linsheng in 1921, and by Wu Zhiyi's biography of Columbus written in 1933. After 1949, Chinese studies of Columbus (by, among others, Zhu Huan, Wu Yujin, Yan Zhongping, and Sun Jiakun) began to come closer to resembling the more conflicted interpretations of Columbus that one finds in the Western world itself. Yan Zhongping even called Columbus a "genocidal pirate." But at the end of the twentieth century, the Beida historian and "modernization" specialist Luo Rongqu returned compulsively to the comparison between Columbus and Zheng He, using it to differentiate two types of border expansion: the Columbus type, driven by the search for markets and by constructive government cooperation with private businesspeople, and the more sterile Zheng He type, allegedly driven by the Chinese political centre's desire to flaunt its power.[28]

New models of developmental colonialism accompanied the Chinese elite's abandonment of the old pessimistic "border planning and popular distress" anxieties of the pre-1911 mandarins and its growing interest in prescribing history-accelerating manipulations of borderlands space. Not surprisingly, Xinjiang was especially vulnerable to this trend. In 1910 one of the last Qing dynasty governors of Xinjiang, Yuan Dahua, summarized the disastrous effects, in this newly created province, of trying, in the spirit of the Qing emperors' neo-Confucian universalist creed that "all things are of one body" (*wanwu yiti*), to impose Chinese schooling on a sparsely populated homeland of Turks, Kazakhs, Mongols, and Chinese Muslims. Yuan wrote that the results of forcing the children of Xinjiang's "turbaned peoples" to go to Chinese schools were that their parents hired the children of "beggars" to go to school in their children's place; or sold their property and fled to Russia; or rallied at their mosques and talked of vengeance. Chinese teachers had to put Turkic students in fetters and handcuffs to keep them from fleeing Chinese schools.

Yuan's solution, which was characteristic of the new era, was to borrow a spatial model from abroad. Yuan urged the Beijing court to try to reimagine Xinjiang as a Chinese version of the northern Japanese island of Hokkaido. Treating Xinjiang in a Hokkaido-like way would mean separating it from the main body of the empire; scrapping Qing educational universalism in the region; and concentrating on special programs of industrial development and infrastructure creation. Little came of this in 1910; yet the free-floating attractions of the developmental model of Hokkaido have persisted in modern Chinese thought concerning the ethnic minority borderlands. In 1981, for example, Yu Guangyuan, a state council development expert and Hu Yaobang adviser, proposed that Thai-speaking areas of southern Yunnan be made a pilot project for the transfer of Japan's successful Hokkaido formula to China.[29]

But despite the transition to a more providential view of the borderlands, and the use of foreign developmental models, the Chinese political centre, minus its monarchy, remains intact. China's sufferings in the first half of the twentieth century only strengthened its persuasiveness. Before the 1937-45 Sino-Japanese War, Chinese Communist leaders talked of creating a "Chinese federal republic," or a China that was a "federation of soviets." After the war broke out, they became wary of entertaining the idea of even a nominal federalism – the post-1911 version of subimperial space creation. What Eisenstadt called the political centre's "monopolistic" instincts also remained strong; for example, the PRC's 1995 law for producing and publishing maps gives the Beijing State Council and Foreign Ministry exclusive authority to produce standardized maps of China, going all the way back to 1840.[30] The quixotic nature of the political centre's ambition to impose a single normative managerial framework upon its far-flung borderlands is still apparent. Yet the borderland societies are too complex for such a framework. Their past histories are so diverse as to compel the untidy coexistence of different mentalities, from different periods, even among the centre's own strategists in Beijing (and Shanghai). The contrast between China's northwest and northeast frontiers underscores this point. In the northwest, almost utopian formulations of multi-state cooperation seem plausible to the Chinese centre; in the northeast, at the end of the twentieth century, multi-state cooperation seems very difficult to conceptualize.

To take the northwest borderlands first, in 1996-97 China joined Russia, Kazakhstan, Kyrgizstan, and Tajikistan in founding an association of the "Shanghai Five" countries. The "Shanghai Five" were dedicated to multilateral border cooperation, especially in the exploitation of energy resources. (By 1999, imported oil supplied more than 20 percent of China's needs; nearly half of it had to travel by sea from the Middle East.) But it was surely characteristic that the rise of the Shanghai Five generated quasi-utopian enthusiasms among Chinese thinkers that went far beyond technical debates over the location of oil or natural gas pipelines.

One Chinese Russia specialist wrote that the purpose of the Shanghai Five must be to construct a high-tech Silk Road. This new Silk Road would have to be both spiritual and material; visible and invisible; underground, above ground, and in the air; and capable of weakening all frictions caused by differences in ethnicity, religion, and language. China's mission, as the leader of the new Silk Road commonwealth, would be to "congeal," or "coagulate," Central Asian economic life by transmitting Chinese reform experiences to

Central Asians. China would even have to "fill in the historical blank spaces" of countries like Kazakhstan and Kyrgizstan, whose national identities were weak.[31]

This vision – of a Christopher Columbus-like Chinese political centre heroically constituting a new multicivilizational world on China's borders – transcended economics. And, in so doing, it failed to capture the sheer technical difficulties of coordinating energy, land, tax, and currency policies among the five countries, let alone the difficulty of coordinating even the different prices in China's own natural gas market. But, as in the old days, a "double truth" was at work here, with its teleological and functional concerns far from perfectly aligned. And the transposition of Mao Zedong's old "blankness" metaphor, from the Chinese people themselves to the countries of the Central Asian borderlands, was suggestive on a number of counts: in both instances the metaphor justified the prescriptive activity of a strong central leadership.

After 1978, China's northeast borders stimulated a long list of proposals for multi-state cooperation. Some Chinese writers even referred to an eruption in China of "Northeast Asia fever." The fever's ideas included plans for a Yellow Sea Economic Circle, a Three Seas Economic Circle, and a Northeast Asia Economic Circle (all of which would take in Russian Siberia, north China, Mongolia, the two Koreas, and Japan). Perhaps the most ambitious proposal, made in 2002, was the one to create a Sea of Japan science and technology alliance modelled on the European Union's Eureka Plan, which had required European countries to pool their science and technology in order to boost their competitive position vis-à-vis the Americans and the Japanese. The two Fudan University economists who proposed the alliance warned that China must use Northeast Asia cooperation – among China, Japan, Russia, and South Korea – to construct a "tripolar" world order instead of a Euro-American bipolar one. Otherwise the "natural laws" of the strong-eat-the-weak global economy might "eliminate" China as a serious competitor.[32]

But differences in the borderlands lead to differences in the Chinese centre's self-image. Unlike in Central Asia, in the northeast the Chinese centre must deal with other states with global power and few "blank spaces" in their historical national identities. Forms of bilateral cooperation between China and other Northeast Asian states – such as nuclear energy cooperation agreements with Japan and South Korea or a Harbin economic cooperation zone shared with Russia – are achievable. Forms of multilateral regional cooperation of the European Union kind, or even the Shanghai Five kind, have been slow to develop. (The Tumen River regional plan, which involves China, Russia, and North Korea, was originally organized by a non-Chinese centre – the United Nations development planning office in New York.)

Northeast Asia is special. In no other Chinese borderlands does the long shadow of modern history so complicate the Chinese centre's sense of its own capacity to cooperate with other powers. In much of the northeast, serious state boundary creation, at least of the European post-Westphalian type, did not begin before 1858. This was late and, more important, it was virtually on the eve of Japan's prodigious self-modernization. From this point on, Japanese scholars dominated the study of Northeast Asian societies and their histories; a specialized Chinese understanding of the region remained comparatively shallow, and there were no European scholars of the region who achieved for it what Stein, Chavannes, Pelliot, or Kozlov and Oldernburg had achieved for Central Asia. For China now, the Japanese economy remains that of a rival whose power must be overcome rather than that of a neighbour, like Kazakhstan, whose economic activities must be "coagulated" by Beijing. As one Chinese strategist wrote in 1999, China must use Northeast Asia cooperation schemes to smash Japan's hierarchical "flying geese" model of economic progress for Asia. This could only be done by using European investment capital to upgrade China's industrial technology faster than the Japanese lead goose might like, Europeans having fewer "misgivings" than the Japanese about investing in the improvement of Chinese technology.[33] As a Chinese environmentalist complained in 2002, the main reason for the failure to create a borderlands environmental community in Northeast Asia was China's view of itself – in its relations with Japan and South Korea – as a victimized developing country. Influenced by this view, China's only interest was how much financial aid the Chinese government could extract from Japan, its richer counterpart; the Chinese government showed far too little interest in its own managerial and technical contributions to Sino-Japanese environmental cooperation.[34]

As in the past, therefore, different borderlands created mutable "dispositions" at the political centre, even if the centre's teleological "essence" remained constant. The Chinese political centre today is embodied in a much more complex array of formal institutions than it was two hundred years ago: the CCP Central Committee, the Standing Committee of the Chinese People's Consultative Conference, and the Central Military Commission. This centre also rules over the most extensively militarized state in Chinese history; its resources and ceremonies include the People's Liberation Army, the armed police, the people's militia, eleven military industrial groups, a state border defence commission (charged with everything from improving roads to television broadcasting in border areas), the roughly 60 percent of Chinese college students who receive some form of military training, and (since 2002) an annual September National Defence Education Day. But China remains, as in the past, a huge country with one political centre and multiple types of borderlands. The sheer breadth of the political engineering required to reconcile the two ensures that, in the minds of the Chinese elite, the imagining of borderlands space (and the logic of visualization applied to the process of such imagining) will continue to be affected by efforts to resolve perceived problems of power and knowledge – problems that exist quite independently of the real borderlands. Or, to put it another way, elite pictures of the borderlands are, as often as not, displaced forms of more general concerns in political theory – concerns that have arisen elsewhere.

Of course, to some extent, this is also true in the Western world. Frederick Jackson Turner's famously optimistic picture of the American frontier as a source of freedom was designed to celebrate American ideals of economic autonomy and political participation. Gloria Anzaldua's more recent hymn to the American-Mexican borderlands, as the basis for a new, more flexible and pluralistic Mexican American "consciousness," rewrites this freedom script from the viewpoint of a Chicana feminist.[35]

The difference is that the Chinese teleological sense of life as having a developing purpose uses China's borderlands but remains tied to faith in a commanding political centre. And if the catastrophic view of the borderlands has gone, the centre's borderlands hypochondria has nonetheless enlarged its rhetorical character. As changes in missile development and information technology have increased the spaces the centre must guard (land, sea, air, space, cyberspace), the perceived threats to those spaces have also increased. Now border threats are defined as including "terrorisms, separatisms, and extremisms" (in the words of the State Council's December 2002 paper on national defence). Here is a potential border defence overstretch problem such as the Ming dynasty critics of imperial overstretch could scarcely have imagined.

Notes

1 Zhao Shufang, "Eluosi waijiao wenhua de tedian yu yingxiang" [The characteristics and influence of Russian foreign policy culture], *Dongbei Ya luntan*, Changchun 4 (2004): 50-54.

2 Qu Dajun, *Guangdong xinyu* [New discourses of Guangdong] (Hong Kong: Zhonghua shuju, 1974), 232.

3 For the text see *Renmin ribao* [People's Daily], 28 September 1999, or *Xinhua yuebao* [New China Monthly Report], 1999, 12, 138-47. For a good and different look at the real centre and its borders see, among other sources, Susan Blum and Lionel Jensen eds., *China Off Center: Mapping the Margins of the Middle Kingdom* (Honolulu: University of Hawaii Press, 2003).

4 Frank Kermode, *The Classic* (Cambridge, MA: Harvard University Press, 1983), 32, 106-12.

5 You Ji, *The Armed Forces of China* (London: I.B. Tauris, 1999), 160-63.

6 S.M. Eisenstadt, *Revolution and the Transformation of Societies: A Comparative Study of Civilizations* (New York: The Free Press, 1978), 228-41.

7 Pan Guangdan, *Minzu yanjiu wenji* [A collection of writings on nationalities research] (Beijing: Minzu chubanshe, 1995), 146-59.

8 Alexander Woodside, "The Ch'ien-lung Reign," in *The Cambridge History of China*, edited by Willard J. Peterson, 9a: 230-309 (Cambridge: Cambridge University Press, 2002).

9 Fang Junyi, "Shili shiyi shuo" [Hereditary clerks and hereditary office servants], in *Huangchao jingshi wen xubian* [A continuation of the statecraft essays of the present court], comp. Sheng Kang, 28: 29-30 (Taibei: Wenhai, 1972).

10 Pierre Bourdieu, *Practical Reason: On the Theory of Action* (Stanford: Stanford University Press, 1998), 40-58.
11 Wang Shaoguang and Hu Angang, *Zhongguo guojia nengli baogao* [A report on the Chinese state's capabilities] (Hong Kong: Oxford University Press, 1994), 37-38.
12 Xiao Dehao and Huang Zheng, comp., *Zhong Yue bianjie lishi ziliao xuanbian* [Anthology of documents about the history of the Chinese-Vietnamese frontier boundaries] (Beijing: Shehui kexue wenxian, 1992), vol. 1, general preface.
13 Lin Tongji, "Bianjiang wenti yu lishi jiaoyu" [The border areas question and history education], *Duli pinglun* [The Independent Critic], 18 November 1934, 8-12.
14 Gong Zizhen, *Gong Zizhen quanji* [The complete works of Gong Zizhen] (Shanghai: Renmin Chubanshe, 1975), 105-6.
15 Chen Zilong, ed., *Huang Ming jingshi wenbian* [A collection of statecraft essays of the imperial Ming court] (Taibei: Guofeng chubanshe, 1964), 416: 1-22b.
16 J.H. Elliott, *The Old World and the New, 1492-1650* (Cambridge, UK: Cambridge University Press, 1970), 13-14.
17 Quoted in David Armitage, *The Ideological Origins of the British Empire* (Cambridge: Cambridge University Press, 2000), 16.
18 *Items* (New York Social Science Research Council, 2002), no. 3-4, 17.
19 Armitage, *The Ideological Origins*, 16; Sankar Muthu, *Enlightenment against Empire* (Princeton, NJ: Princeton University Press, 2003), 97-104.
20 Chen Zilong, *Huang Ming jingshi wenbian*, 416: 3b-5.
21 John A. Lynn. "Recalculating French Army Growth during the Grand Siecle, 1650-1715," *French Historical Studies* 18, 4 (1994): 881-906.
22 Ding Shouhe, comp., *Zhongguo lidai zhiguo ce xuancui* [Selected highlights of Chinese state administration policies through the centuries] (Beijing: Gaodeng jiaoyu chubanshe, 1994), 664-67.
23 Dominic Lieven, *Empire: The Russian Empire and Its Rivals from the Sixteenth Century to the Present* (London: Pimlico, 2003), 102-3.
24 Cheng Chongde, "Qingdai xianqi bianjiang tonglun, xia" [A general discussion of the earlier period Qing borderlands, part 2], *Qingshi yanjiu* [Studies in Qing History] 1 (1998): 14-27; Peter C. Perdue, "Military Mobilization in Seventeenth and Eighteenth Century China, Russia and Mongolia," *Modern Asian Studies* 30, 4 (1996): 757-93.
25 Gong Zizhen, *Gong Zizhen quanji*, 110.
26 Zhang Hao et al., *Zhongguo jindai kaifa Xibei wenlun xuan* [Selected official discussions of China's modern development of the northwest] (Lanzhou: Lanzhou daxue chubanshe, 1997), 1: 147-50.
27 Pan Guangdan, *Minzu yanjiu wenji*, 22-27.
28 Shen Minhua, "Zhongguo dui Gelunbu yanjiu de pingxi" [A critical analysis of the Chinese approach to Columbus studies], *Shehui kexue* [Social Sciences] 11 (1992): 67-70.
29 Li Yushu, comp, *Xinjiang tuzhi* [Illustrated gazetteer of Xinjiang] (Taibei: Wenhai, 1965), 106: 5-9; Yu Guangyuan, *Yu Guangyuan duanlun ji* [A collection of the brief writings of Yu Guangyuan] (Shanghai: Huadong shifan daxue, 2001), 1: 389-92.
30 *Renmin ribao*, 20 July 1995; *Xinhua yuebao*, 1995, 9, 110-15.
31 Ding Peihua, "Luelun 'shanghai wuguo' fazhan de jichu" [A brief discussion of the basis of development of the "Shanghai Five" countries], *Shehui kexue* 7 (2001): 45-49.
32 Liu Junmei and Wu Huajia, "Guanyu jianli huan Ribenhai siguo keji lianmeng de kexingxing yanjiu" [On studying the feasibility of building a science and technology alliance of the four countries around the Japan Sea], *Dongbei Ya luntan*, 2002, 1, 65-68.
33 Li Jingyu, *Zhongguo yu Dongbei Ya quyu jingji hezuo zhanlue duice* [China and its strategic measures for Northeast Asian economic cooperation] (Beijing: Renmin chubanshe, 1999), 174-75.
34 Xu Songling, "Zhongguo – Dongbei Ya guojia zhi jian de huanjing hezuo" [Environmental cooperation between China and the countries of Northeast Asia], *Dongbei Ya luntan*, 2002, 1, 49-54.
35 Gloria Anzaldua, *Borderlands/La Frontera: The New Mestiza* (San Francisco: Aunt Lute Books, 1999).

2

Ming-Qing Border Defence, the Inward Turn of Chinese Cartography, and Qing Expansion in Central Asia in the Eighteenth Century

Benjamin A. Elman

Since the Song dynasty, China has sometimes supported a massive navy, which the Mongols expanded to invade Japan in 1274 and again in 1281 and to attack Java. Subsequently, the early Ming navy carried out enormous excursions into Southeast Asia and the Indian Ocean from 1403 to 1434. Ming rulers also declined any political accommodation with the Mongols and their nomadic neighbours, a policy that lasted from 1368 until 1570. They saw in such accommodations, which included possible diplomatic and commercial relations, one of the reasons for the fall of the Song in 1280 to the steppe barbarians. As a result of its more narrow-minded defensive and punitive measures, the Ming dynasty faced continual threats from their Mongol neighbours on the steppe.[1]

During the first century of Ming rule, for example, the "perennial problem of the Mongol menace" became so acute that officials in Beijing feared an imminent reconquest by the Mongols. The infamous Tumu debacle of 1448-49, for instance, began when the Oirats, who had reunified Western Mongol forces on the steppe, had captured the reigning Zhengtong emperor (r. 1436-49) when he led a Ming military campaign against them. In the climactic battle, the Ming army lost half of its 500,000 soldiers. Rather than capitulate to Oirat extortionist demands for ransom or move the capital from Peking back to Nanjing, the Ming court chose to replace the captured emperor with his younger brother, who was then enthroned as the Jingtai emperor (r. 1450-56) and led the successful defence of Beijing. The proposal to retreat to the south reminded Ming officials too much of the disastrous experiences of the Southern Song when it had moved its capital from Kaifeng to Hangzhou.[2]

The crisis continued when the Zhengtong emperor, a worthless hostage by then, was returned by the Oirats in 1450. Several years later, he retook the throne as the Tianshun emperor (r. 1457-64) in the coup d'état of 1457, during which the officials who had sacrificed their emperor in 1449 were accused of treason and executed. After 1457, the Ming pulled its army back from the Inner Mongolian steppe, and the rebuilt Great Wall became, in the sixteenth century, the only immediate barrier separating the capital from the Mongol tribes.[3]

In the 1460s, the Ming court terminated naval expeditions to Southeast Asia and the Indian Ocean, which had been especially prominent from 1403 to 1434, in favour of maintaining a strictly coastal navy. The Tianshun emperor, who had already suppressed the great "Treasure Ships" of the Ming navy before his capture by the Oirats, maintained a military vigil on his northern borders after returning to power. In 1474, only 140 of the 400 warships that had comprised the main fleet remained. Thereafter, all seagoing ships of more than two masts were scrapped and used as lumber, while the court attended to military campaigns against the Mongols and rebellious southeastern tribes. A coastal navy thereafter defended the China coast from Japanese pirates in the sixteenth century, albeit in vain. This northern border focus on steppe defences lasted until the mid-sixteenth century, when the Wokou pirate menace loomed in the Yangzi delta and the southeast.[4]

Chinese naval power revived briefly in the late Ming as a result of Ming efforts to aid Korea and to halt Hideyoshi's (1536-98) invasion of that country. Ming loyalists at first defeated the Manchu Qing dynasty in major naval and land battles along the Fujian coast. This brief naval efflorescence lasted until the 1680s but, thereafter, new types of sailing vessels continued to be developed (such as the Zhejiang junks first built in 1699). They were used in northern waters for the Ningbo-Nagasaki trade between Japan and China, which lasted into the eighteenth century despite Japan's alleged "closed door" policies.[5]

Pre-Jesuit Cartography and Descriptive Geography

During the late Ming, native attempts at serious cartography and descriptive geography provided the Chinese with a foundation that cumulatively helped bridge the gap between the orthodox symbolic geography popular since the Song period and the Jesuit techniques that stimulated the emergence of more precise cartography in the seventeenth century. Chinese achievements in geography climaxed with the production of schematic grid-maps, sailing charts, and relief maps. Although few maps from early dynasties have survived, two other extant maps, which demonstrate the remarkable development of map-making in China, were carved on stone in the twelfth century. Informed by Tang models, the maps were entitled the *Map of China and Foreign Areas* (*Huayi tu*) and *Map of the Tracks of Emperor Yu* (*Yuji tu*). The latter (see Figure 1), carved in 1137 as a grid based on a scale of approximately 1:1.5 million, is described by Needham as "the most remarkable cartographic work of its age in any culture."

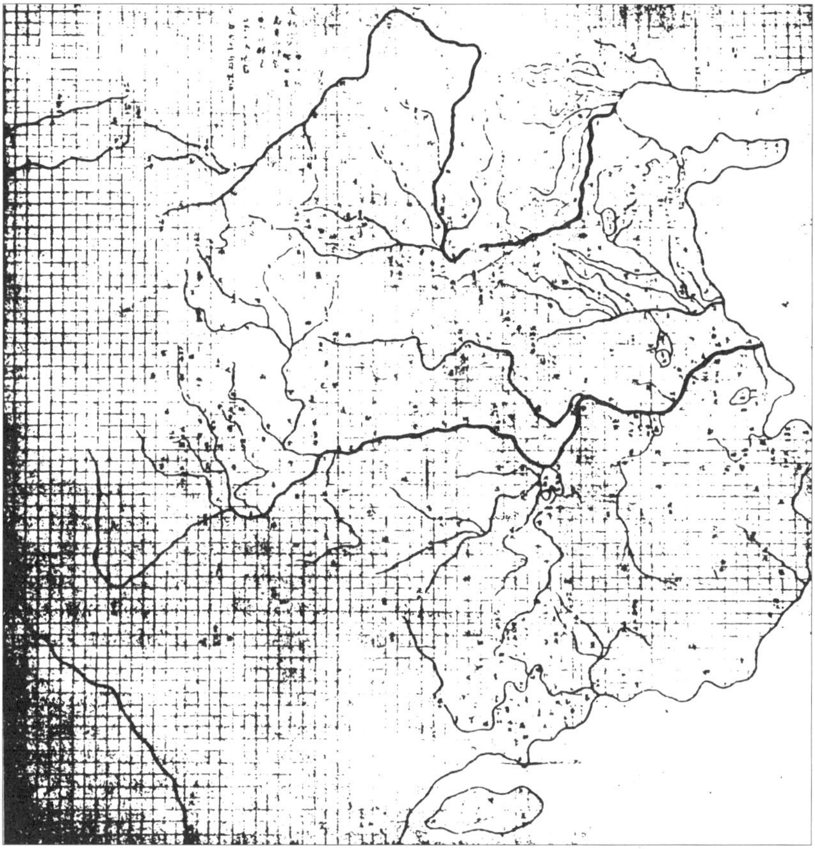

Figure 1 Map of the Tracks of Emperor Yu (*Yuji tu*).
Source: Reprinted from Joseph Needham, *Science and Civilisation in China,* vol. 3, Cambridge University Press, 1959. Copyright © 1959. Reprinted with the permission of Cambridge University Press.

The medieval cartographer Pei Xiu (224-271) first used the method of indicating distances by a rectangular grid system. Since then, cartography in China was often based on the grid tradition, although many important maps still followed the *Map of China and Foreign Areas* model and were not rendered using a grid. Jia Dan (730-805), the greatest Tang cartographer, constructed a map of Chinese and foreign regions for the emperor. The map, now lost, was thirty feet long, thirty-three feet high, and used a grid scale of one inch for one hundred Chinese miles (equal to about thirty-three English miles), the same scale used in the Map of the Tracks of Emperor Yu. Jia Dan's map, given its huge scale, likely depicted all of known Asia.[6]

Zhu Siben (1273-1337) inherited this grid format. Perhaps the best known Chinese cartographer until the twentieth century, Zhu used grid-maps to summarize the large body of new geographical information that the Mongol conquests in Asia had added to the earlier fund possessed by Tang and Song geographers. Zhu's map, circa 1320, was known as the "Mongol Atlas of China" (*Yutu*). An early Ming map, circa 1390, replicated the imperial pretensions of Mongol maps and charted the empire's sway from Central Asia and Japan to the Atlantic via Southeast Asia and the Indian Ocean world.[7]

In the sixteenth century, Luo Hongxian (1504-64) discovered a manuscript copy of Zhu Siben's map of the known world, which Zhu prepared between 1311 and 1320 but never printed. Luo revised and enlarged Zhu's grid format in 1541. He also added new information, some derived from the early Ming naval explorations led by Admiral Zheng He. Luo's map (*Guang yutu*, lit., "Enlargement of a map of the earth"), printed about 1555, included a clear depiction of the Cape of Good Hope and southern Africa, leading some to speculate that Zheng He was the "Vasco da Gama of China" and had traversed from the Indian to the Atlantic Ocean and back some seventy years before da Gama did it in reverse.[8]

Ming Knowledge of Foreign Countries

Geographers and cartographers in Ming China were fairly knowledgeable about the southern regions (*nanyang*, i.e., what Chinese referred to as Southeast Asia) and foreign countries in the Indian Ocean and Arabian Peninsula (*Xiyang fan'guo*, i.e., "Western tributary states"). Information of this type peaked in China as a result of the early fifteenth-century voyages of the Ming fleet. Zheng He, the eunuch commander of seven Ming expeditionary fleets launched between 1405 and 1433, at one time or another reached Sumatra, Java, Ceylon, Hormuz, Aden, and East Africa.

The expeditions overlapped with the Ming maritime tributary system, around which trade and diplomatic relations were organized in Ming China. Moreover, Ma Huan left a descriptive account of Zheng's fleets in 1433, which was based on his service as Muslim translator for three of the seven expeditions (1413-15, 1421-22, and 1431-33). Ma's *Captivating Views of the Ocean's Shores* (*Yingyai shenglan*) described the countries the fleet visited and portrayed the customs, religions, and lifestyle in each place. He also depicted topography, geology, and wildlife.[9]

Subsequently, other members of Zheng He's expeditions described their adventures. For example, Fei Xin's (1388-1436?) *Captivating Views from a Star Guided Vessel* (*Xingcha shenglan*) and Gong Zhen's *Gazetteer of the Western Tributary States* (*Xiyang fan'guo zhi*, 1434) were based on first-hand visits and help fill the gap in Indian Ocean accounts that occur between Marco Polo's *The Travels* and Portuguese reports in the late fifteenth century. References to the expeditions and the exotic gifts brought back to China were added, for instance, to Cao Zhao's (fl. 1387-99) *Key Issues in the Investigation of Antiquities* (*Gegu yaolun*), which was published in the early Ming and was enlarged several times. The work originally appeared circa 1387-88 with important accounts of ceramics and lacquer as well as of traditional subjects such as calligraphy, painting, zithers, stones, bronzes, and ink-slabs.[10]

Excerpts and extracts were subsequently included in the massive early eighteenth-century *Synthesis of Books and Illustrations Past and Present* (*Gujin tushu jicheng*), the largest encyclopaedia in Chinese history. The Qianlong Imperial Library also included a 1520 annotation of Ma Huan's account by Zhang Sheng (1442-1517). In addition, the Imperial Library summarized the content of Gong Zhen's work and mentioned Huang Shengzeng's 1520 *Records of Western Tributaries* (*Xiyang chaogong dianlu*), although neither was copied into the collection. Huang's work drew on and cited earlier sources.[11]

Within China, Ming dynasty explorers such as Wang Shixing (1547-98), Xie Zhaozhi (1567-1624), and Xu Hongzu (also known as Xu Xiake, 1586-1641) travelled to the most remote borders of the empire. In their travels they collected notebooks outlining in descriptive terms the river systems, topography, and cultural aspects of the places they visited. Xu Hongzu, for example, discovered the main source of the West River in his travels through much of Southwest China and was able to determine that the Mekong River and the Salween River were different river systems.[12]

Cartography and Ming Military Defence

Interest in cartography and geography in China was tied to problems of border or maritime defence. Luo Hongxian became interested in geography because of Japanese pirate raids on the maritime provinces in the Yangzi delta and along the Southeast Coast in the sixteenth century, which were aided by Chinese accomplices. The Ming government urgently needed maps and geographical advisors to cope with the situation. Luo spent three years collecting geographical materials for military defence and, in the process, discovered the manuscript of Zhu Siben's grid-map.

Zheng Ruozeng (1505-80), a native of Suzhou prefecture, was also involved in coastal defence because of the Japanese pirate threat. In the 1540s, Zheng compiled a strategic atlas of China's coastal region, extending north from the Liaodong Peninsula to southern Guangdong, which included maps and strategic information. More important, however, was a work on coastal geography compiled under then Zhejiang governor Hu Zongxian's (1511-65) auspices by Zheng Ruozeng.

First published in 1562, the resulting *A Maritime Survey: Collected Plans* (*Chouhai tubian*) was modelled after Luo Hongxian's work. The *Maritime Survey* was an ambitious survey of geographical minutiae about the China coast, and it contained accurate accounts of China's neighbours, Japan and Korea. Hence, it was not simply an atlas. A major contribution to Chinese historical geography, the *Maritime Survey* marked a major turning point in Chinese geographic studies. Arguably, its completion provided the impetus for later literati to incorporate Jesuit information into the Chinese tradition of geography and cartography.[13]

Prior to the sixteenth century, threats to China's security had mainly come from the north and northwest (e.g., the Jurchen, the Mongols, and the Manchus). Hence, earlier geographers such as Zhu Siben focused attention on the northern frontier areas. In the sixteenth century, however, the primary military menace came from Japanese pirates and their Chinese collaborators along the South China Sea coastline. Zheng Ruozeng's research on the maritime provinces in the southeast thus stimulated a shift in geographical research. A number of sixteenth-century geographical treatises on maritime defence were either inspired by or followed the pattern of the *Maritime Survey*.[14]

Because of their travels, European Jesuits could claim expertise in world geography when they arrived in Ming China in the late sixteenth century. Their charts of the globe were based on the New World discoveries of the Portuguese and Spanish explorers they often accompanied. The mappa mundi that Matteo Ricci (1552-1610), his collaborators, and others produced for literati in the late sixteenth century caused an uproar because the Ming imperial system was based on a cosmological view of its geographical centrality in the world, which the Jesuit maps seemed at first to challenge. It was difficult, for example, for literati to accept the Jesuit claim that the earth was round because this suggested that the "vaulted heavens" (*gaitian*) were circular as well. Many literati considered the earth to be flat and the sky to be a finite vault overhead.[15]

Matteo Ricci's Mappa Mundi

Jesuits added to the geographical knowledge that Ming literati already had in the late sixteenth century. Produced with the help of Chinese converts, the first edition of Matteo Ricci's mappa mundi, entitled *Complete Map of the Earth's Mountains and Seas* (*Yudi shanhai quantu*), for instance, was printed in 1584. A flattened sphere projection with parallel latitudes and curving longitudes, Ricci's world map went through eight editions between 1584 and 1608. The third edition was entitled *Complete Map of the Myriad Countries on the Earth* (*Kunyu wan'guo quantu*) and was printed in 1602 with the help of Li Zhizao (1565-1630; see Figure 2). Li studied European mathematics and astronomy, in addition to geography, after meeting Ricci in Peking in 1601.[16]

Ricci's description of the form and size of the earth obliged many seventeenth-century Chinese literati to revise their views of the world. For the first time, Chinese became aware of the exact location of Europe in relation to their own country. In addition, Ricci's maps contained technical geo-

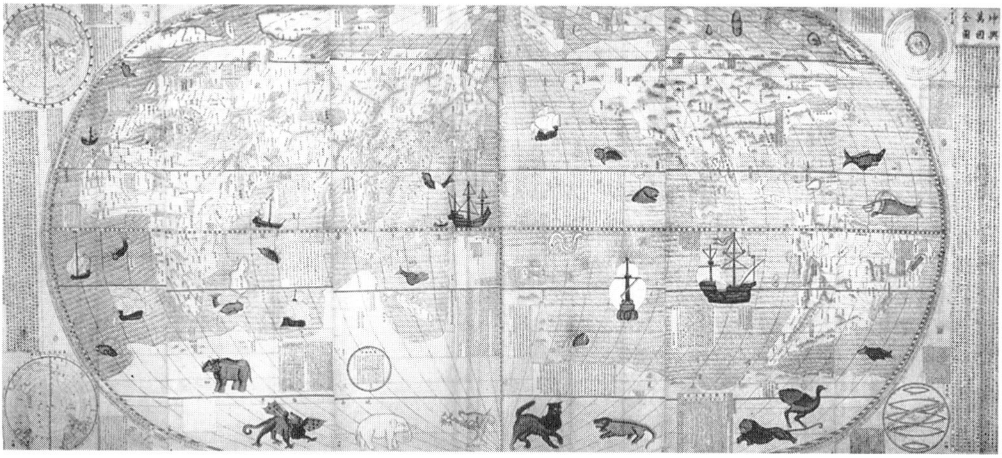

Figure 2 Complete Map of the Myriad Countries on the Earth (*Kunyu wan'guo quantu*).
Source: http://geog.hkbu.edu.hk/GEOG1150/Chinese/Catalog_main_11.htm.

graphical lessons for Chinese geographers: (1) Ricci taught Chinese cartographers to localize places by means of circles of latitude and longitude; (2) he invented many geographical terms and names, including Chinese terms for Europe, Asia, America, and Africa; (3) his maps transmitted to China the most recent discoveries made by European explorers; (4) he described the existence of five terrestrial continents surrounded by large oceans; (5) his maps introduced the sphericity of the earth; and (6) he spoke of five geographical zones and their location on the earth (i.e., the Arctic Circle, the Antarctic Circle, the zone between the Arctic Circle and the Tropic of Cancer, etc.).[17]

An indication of the initial impact of Ricci's maps, especially the 1608 edition printed in Beijing, was its inclusion in geographical works produced by literati scholars in the closing years of the Ming dynasty. For example, Zhang Huang (1527-1608), who had met Ricci in Jiangxi in 1595, added Ricci's Complete Map to his own illustrated collection, which Zhang called *The Compendium of Maps and Materials* (*Tushu bian*, 1613). In addition to Ricci's 1584 map of the world, in his massive collection Zhang also printed European depictions of the northern and southern hemispheres, along with traditional maps of the four seas.[18]

The only known copy of the first Chinese map of the world produced in 1593 was entitled *The Comprehensive Map of Heaven and Earth and the Myriad Countries and Ancient and Modern Persons and Artifacts* (*Qiankun wan'guo quantu gujin renwu shiji*) and included geographical information brought by the Jesuits. It was based on Ricci's first world map of 1584, which is now lost. The map offered a traditional representation of China, with foreign lands arranged around the periphery. It served chiefly as an administrative map for officials and thus included statistical information such as population (based on families) and locally produced commodities.

Topological rather than topographical, the 1593 Chinese version fit European lands in along its edges without affecting traditional cartography. The New World was shown as a series of small islands surrounding the "Central Kingdom." Methodologically, however, the compiler stressed the "achievements of investigating things and extending knowledge," which by now served as a native trope for the accumulation of knowledge. The linkage of the world map of 1593 to classical studies based on investigating things and extending knowledge heralded the application of such native terminology to European scientia.[19]

The 1602 *Complete Map of the Myriad Countries on the Earth* corresponded to one of the first issues of Ricci's third world map and is the earliest version that survives. This 1602 edition followed the *Typus Orbis Terrarum*, which was produced by the Flemish scholar and geographer Abraham Ortelius (1527-98) and was first published in a 1570 European atlas called the *Theatrum Orbis Terrarum*, itself based on Gerardus Mercator's (1512-94) prominent 1569 world map. The chief alteration for the Chinese version was that Ming China was placed at the centre of the map to appeal to Chinese dynastic sensibilities. The New World was located on the eastern borders. A fourth edition of the map was prepared in 1604.[20]

Ricci's map-making was continued by later Jesuits who, in 1623, produced a lacquered wooden globe, which updated Ricci's map and also stressed the sphericity of the earth. Giulio Aleni (1582-1649) and Yang Tingyun (1562-1627) quickly followed with their *Account of Countries Not Listed in the Records Office* (*Zhifang waiji*), a treatise on world geography that was later included in the 1628 *First Collection of Celestial Studies* compiled by Li Zhizao. Aleni's *Account* grew out of notes on Ricci's 1601 mappa mundi that Pantoja and Ursis had prepared for the Ming court.[21]

Aleni's translation represented the first detailed exposition in Chinese of a world geography that drew on Renaissance traditions of local lore and Ptolemaic cosmography to describe Asia, Europe, Africa, and the Americas. Another section focused on the oceans. In addition to the *First Collection of Celestial Studies*, other Chinese collections reproduced Aleni's treatise in the eighteenth century, thus making it more influential during the Qing dynasty than Ricci's maps, which were quickly forgotten by literati. In the nineteenth century, Aleni's work was reprinted three times in sixty years after Euro-American geography became de rigueur for literati trying to understand the military consequences of the Opium War (1839-42).[22]

A world map composed by the Naples Jesuit Father Francesco Sanbiasi in 1648 was designed as a simplified version of the large maps produced by Ricci. It was drawn as an oval projection, with China at the centre. Later,

Michael Piotyr Boym, a Polish Jesuit who had served the embattled Southern Ming in the 1650s, produced the *Map of the Middle Kingdom* (*Zhongguo tu*), circa 1652, which he brought back to Rome in 1656. The original manuscript was compiled to convey Jesuit knowledge of China to Europe. This version was superseded by Martinus Martini's (1614-61) *Novus Atlas Sinensis*, which was published in an Amsterdam atlas series in 1655.[23]

Although Matteo Ricci introduced the system of longitude and latitude to Ming China, the grid system employed by Luo Hongxian and his predecessors continued to exercise a dominant influence on Chinese cartography throughout the late Ming and Qing periods. For example, an admired genre known as "Complete Maps of All under Heaven" (*tianxia quantu*) was initiated by the Ming loyalist Huang Zongxi (1610-95) in 1673 and was continued by a number of talented literati scholars who were interested in map-making. Cao Junyi's ambitious *Complete Map* of 1644, for instance, mixed inaccurate classical geographical lore with a precise recognition of Europe, Africa, India, and Central Asia (which was provided through the use of longitudes and degrees for estimating their distances from Nanjing, the Southern Ming capital).[24]

In the early Qing, Ferdinand Verbiest (1623-88), with the help of others, produced two works that dealt with world geography. His 1674 world atlas included a comprehensive map in two hemispheres, with gazetteer information about each part of the globe. Later abridged, it was based largely on Aleni's *Account of Countries Not Listed in the Records Office*. Similarly, Verbiest's *Main Records about the West* (*Xifang yaoji*) drew on the topical organization in Aleni's 1637 *Answers about the West* (*Xifang dawen*), which compared China to Europe in light of geographical lore. During the Qianlong reign (1736-95), the compilers of the Imperial Library considered these works important enough to be copied into the collection in the 1780s.[25]

The final stage in the development of traditional Chinese map-making came in the eighteenth century when French Jesuits, on behalf of the Kangxi emperor (r. 1662-1722), conducted systematic surveys of the entire Manchu realm between 1708 and 1718. They drew up a series of maps of the Qing Empire and its border areas, which became known as the 1718 *Kangxi Atlas* (*Huangyu quanlan tu*). Along with succeeding maps in the Yongzheng (r. 1723-1735) and Qianlong periods, the *Kangxi Atlas* surpassed earlier Jesuit surveys completed in the seventeenth century. Although the Manchu court restricted access to and reproduction of these surveys and maps, they remained the chief sources of foreign geographical information concerning China until the twentieth century.[26]

Rather than switching to Jesuit cartography, late eighteenth-century literati such as Ma Junliang sometimes presented both a traditional picture of a China-centred world and global maps that loosely duplicated Ricci's mappa mundi. Ma's *Capital Edition of a Complete Map Based on Astronomy*

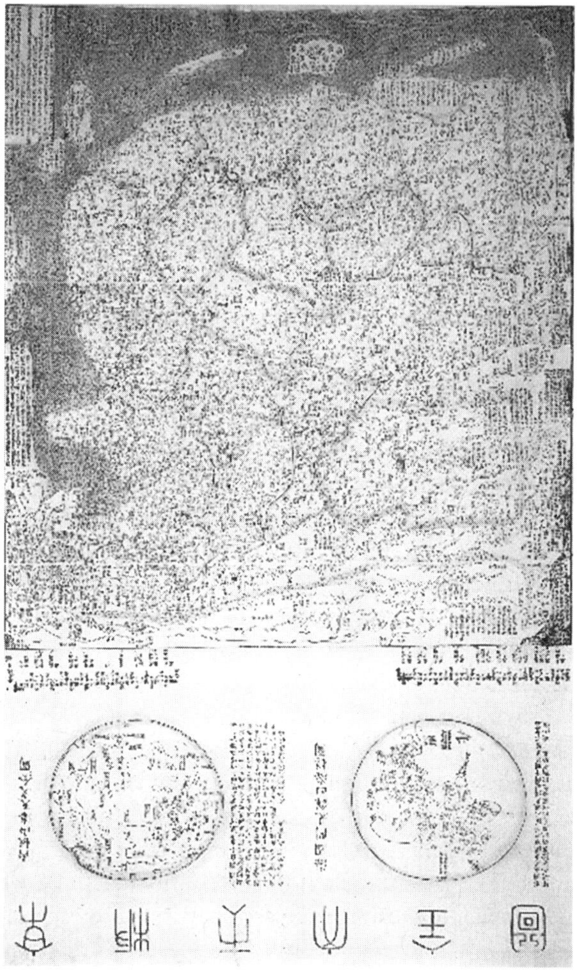

Figure 3 Capital Edition of a Complete Map Based on Astronomy (*Jingban tianwen quantu*).
Source: The Woodson Research Center of the Fondren Library, Rice University.

(*Jingban tianwen quantu*; see Figure 3) circulated widely in the 1790s and included two smaller global maps of the Euro-Asian-African and Pacific hemispheres above his detailed map of the Qing Empire, which roughly corresponded to Ricci's *Map of the Myriad Countries on the Earth* rendered in a late Ming encyclopaedia.[27]

Despite displaying substantial variations, the "Complete Maps" shared as a prominent feature the mingling of traditional and newer techniques, such as the hybrid overlap between the grid and latitude-longitudinal approach for large-scale land maps. Indeed, Li Zhaoluo's (1769-1841) famous 1832 atlas of the Qing Empire showed both grid and latitude and longitude lines on the same map, indicating, long after the Jesuit mappa mundi were introduced, the reluctance of native geographers to give up the traditional system. This nativist pattern for domesticating European learning was repeated in other new fields of learning, such as mathematical astronomy, during the late eighteenth century.[28]

Mensuration and Cartography in the Eighteenth Century

The late Kangxi and Yongzheng bans on propagating European natural studies did not suffocate literati learning, where a decisive sea change in classical learning was occurring. Eighteenth-century "evidential research" (*kaozheng*) scholars stressed painstaking research, rigorous analysis, and impartial evidence drawn from ancient artifacts and historical documents and texts. They made verification a central concern for the emerging empirical theory of knowledge – namely, "to search truth from facts" (*shishi qiushi*), a Han dynasty expression used, in the eighteenth century, as a slogan for impartial scholarship.[29]

In geography, moreover, evidential scholars during the late seventeenth and eighteenth centuries reacted to the Jesuit contributions in world geography by domesticating such new knowledge in the midst of Qing empire building and the court's use of Jesuit surveying techniques to measure its domains. At the same time that the Manchu dynasty took advantage of international changes in Central Asia, Chinese literati took an internalist turn by focusing on native topics in their new geographic works.[30]

The Seventeenth-Century Turn Inward

Ming naval power revived when the Ming joined forces with the Korean navy to resist the Japanese invasions of the Korean peninsula in 1592 and again in 1597. In particular, hundreds of Ming coastal ships joined the Korean "turtleboats" (i.e., sailing vessels also propelled by oars and reinforced with iron plates, ringed with spikes, and equipped with cannon) to gain control of the sea war. Their combined forces of some five hundred ships and fifteen thousand men were decisively superior in technology and continually threatened Japan's land-based supply lines. Despite mobilizing a Japanese fleet of twelve thousand men on five hundred ships for the climactic battle at the Noryang Straits in December 1598, Hideyoshi failed in his grandiose plans to use Korea as a stepping stone to conquer China. Some three hundred Japanese ships with ten thousand sailors were lost.[31]

Despite the increased awareness of foreign nations as a result of the Korean wars, contact with Jesuits, and/or the border treaties between the Qing and Russian imperial governments in 1689 and 1727, Han Chinese scholarly interest in such global knowledge waned. Due in part to wide travel in North and South China by many eminent scholars in the seventeenth century, particularly as a response to the Manchu military conquest in the 1660s, research on geography in the early Qing returned to traditional questions of regional military strategy and local, coastal defence. Meanwhile, the Dutch increasingly colonized Taiwan beginning in 1623, when the Dutch East India Company contracted Chinese traders and farmers from Southeast China to settle the island.[32]

Subsequently, southern Ming loyalists led by Zheng Chenggong (Koxinga, 1624-62) resisted the Manchus in major naval and land battles along the Fujian coast in the 1640s and 1650s. Zheng's land and sea forces took heavy losses, however, when they moved up the Yangzi River to Nanjing in 1659, and they were forced to retreat to Xiamen (Amoy). Southern Ming naval forces then challenged the Dutch garrison in northern Taiwan (called "Formosa" by Europeans) at Castle Zeelandia in April 1661 with a force of six hundred ships and twenty-five thousand sailors. The Dutch capitulated after a bitter nine-month siege.[33]

In 1662, for its part, the Qing government ordered coastal inhabitants from Shandong in the north to Guangdong in the south to move inland to cut Zheng's supply lines and to negate the value of the coast as a battleground. In addition, the Manchus developed a naval fleet to defend the coastline. When Shi Lang (1621-96), one of the Southern Ming's most capable admirals, joined the Manchus in 1646 because of a dispute with Zheng, he took command of Qing naval forces along the Fujian coast (during the 1650s and 1660s. In July 1683, Shi Lang commanded the Qing fleet of some three hundred warships and twenty thousand sailors, which first subdued the Pescadores. Taiwan fell to the Qing navy in October, and for the first time the island became part of the "Chinese" Empire.[34]

The Qing navy no longer remained on a war footing after Taiwan was annexed, and the Manchu emperors became increasingly preoccupied with the land-based expansion of the Russians from Siberia into the Manchu homelands and the renewed dangers posed by the Zunghars in Central Asia. In addition, the Qing sought to expand its empire into Tibet and Turkestan. By the end of the eighteenth century, the Qing had doubled its size. When the Opium War broke out in 1839, therefore, the Qing fleet was again mainly a coastal navy used principally for defence against outside pirates and local marauders. For the land-based Qing, the maritime world remained a "center of subversion."[35]

Furthermore, even before the conquest of Taiwan, maritime considerations evoked less interest among Chinese literati. Because the Manchu conquest emanated from the northern steppe, Gu Yanwu (1613-82), a leading voice of the early Qing turn towards precise studies, emphasized China's strategic positions vis-à-vis its traditional foreign neighbours to the north and northwest in his influential geographical treatise entitled *The Strategic Advantages and Weaknesses of Each Province in the Empire* (*Tianxia junguo libing shu*), compiled between 1639 and 1662. Ironically, such "foreigners," particularly the Manchus, Mongols, Tibetans, and Uighurs, would in ensuing years become part of the political-cultural unit that nineteenth-century Europeans referred to as "China."

Gu Yanwu did not even mention Ricci's mappa mundi. He was concerned with the effects of topography on political and economic development within China. His findings, however, were based on his wide travels, careful first-hand observations, and the study of written materials. Likewise, Gu Zuyu's (1631-92) *Essentials of Geography for Reading History* (*Dushi fangyu jiyao*), written between 1630 and 1660, was a study of native historical, administrative, and natural geography, with an emphasis on the importance of topography for military strategy. Ricci's world map was disregarded, and late Ming interest in the maritime nations waned.[36]

Zuo Zongtang (1812-85) read Gu Yanwu's and Gu Zuyu's geographical treatises in 1829, and they inspired in him a life-long interest in Chinese topography and military strategy. His interest in Chinese Turkestan grew out of his early reading and underscored his later insistence that troops be sent to Northwest China in the 1870s to prevent that area from falling permanently into Russian hands. Zuo's campaigns provoked the opposition of Li Hongzhang (1823-1901) and other Beijing officials who regarded naval power for coastal defence and protection of Korea from Japan as more pressing needs than the recovery of territory in the distant interior.

The compilers of both the official Ming dynastic history and *The Comprehensive Geography of the Great Qing Realm* (*Da-Qing yitong zhi*) had access to Ricci's and other Jesuit geographical works, but they dismissed as fictitious many of the Jesuits' claims and the information on their mappa mundi. Nevertheless, Xu Qianxue (1631-94), who chose scholars to work on the Comprehensive Geography project when he was appointed director in 1687, had a high regard for the emerging evidential scholarship of his times, which is highlighted by the fact that he chose leading textual scholars to edit the topographical material for the geography project. Xu's appointment of Gu Zuyu, perhaps the most qualified student of historical geography in his time, indicates the high degree of expertise that went into the Comprehensive Geography project.[37]

Similarly, the late Qianlong compilers of the 1787 edition of the *Comprehensive Analysis of Civil and Military Institutions during the Qing Dynasty* (*Huangchao wenxian tongkao*), which included documents and materials covering the period 1644 to 1785, demoted the mention of Europe to a minor section on Italy within the category "Four Frontiers." Twenty-four chapters in the traditional category of "Geography and Lands" dealt with imperial domains, while only eight covered the borderlands. The compilers of "Four Frontiers" focused on Korea, the Ryukyu Islands, Vietnam, and other neighbouring tributary countries.

The section on Italy mentioned that "what the Italians [i.e., Matteo Ricci] had said about the division of the world into five continents followed from Zou Yan's Warring States theory of the Sacred Ocean [*Shenhai*], although the Italians dared to add that the land of China was but one of the five continents." Such claims infuriated the compilers, who dismissed the Italians as too grandiose. They could not be taken seriously because they were simply trying to impress Chinese with European customs, goods, governance, and education. By citing Zou Yan on the question of continents, the *Comprehensive Analysis* was drawing on a long tradition of classical interpretation that held that the ancient "nine regions" (*jiuzhou*) were surrounded by oceans, thus the geographic term for "regions" could also serve as a native term for "continent."[38]

Still, the *Comprehensive Analysis* included detailed geographic discussions of Europe and Russia. Moreover, the dramatic political impact that European surveying methods had in China early in the eighteenth century also piqued the interest of the Qianlong emperor and his court when the Kangxi map of the empire was updated using European surveying methods. European geographical content may have been overlooked, but European methods were still admired and copied in official geography as well as astronomy.[39]

Xue Fengzuo had studied astronomy and mathematics under the Jesuits. Xue then applied the techniques of spherical trigonometry and logarithms to surveying, which was appreciated by the Qianlong Imperial Library editors in their review of Xue's compendium on the Yellow River and Grand Canal. The editors noted that Xue's mathematical expertise was an invaluable aid in analyzing problems related to flood control and canal upkeep. His use of European trigonometry was recognized as a clear improvement over the native forms of trigonometry known as "double application of proportions" (*chongcha*, i.e., properties of right triangles expressed as a function of angles), which dominated traditional Chinese surveying techniques.[40]

Evidential Research and Geography

Literati scholars who compiled imperial gazetteers such as the *Comprehensive Geography* and its Yuan and Ming precursors prioritized geographical knowledge. Qing dynasty geographers increasingly presented the history of geography as the study of topographical change, and, as scholars, they tended to distance themselves from the moral correspondences between heaven and earth that still informed the traditional cosmography popular in unofficial life. The Imperial Library editors writing in the late eighteenth century, for instance, singled out a Ming dynasty study of West Lake in the Hangzhou area by Tian Rucheng (1500-63) to make a methodological point: "Because of the lack of corroborating evidence, no one can evaluate the accuracy of his claims. This [imprecision] is an error that Ming scholars in general all shared." Precision became a new feature informing evidential learning as a result of the overlaps between classicism, geography, and mathematical astronomy.[41]

Within the academic community that promoted evidential research, historical and physical geography took precedence over the application of the idealized geopolitical paradigms popular in Han, Tang, and Song classical cosmography. Recognition of the physical difficulties in using the ancient mensural order to demarcate existing mountains and rivers indicated that Qing scholars were challenging the traditional approach to the ordering of space. Evidential scholars, for instance, no longer accepted uncritically the portent astrology associated with the field allocation system (*fenye*, lit., "allotted countryside"). Specific celestial fields associated with the twenty-four lunar lodges (*xiu*) constituted the equatorial coordinate system and were used to indicate the positions of celestial objects on the celestial sphere, which corresponded to terrestrial regions presented in the *Documents Classic*, one of the five Confucian classics.[42]

Since the Former Han dynasty, the twenty-eight lunar lodges were associated with twelve ancient feudal states. Analogies were drawn between the celestial realm and the imperial court then based in northwestern capitals of Chang'an and Luoyang. Constellations and stars were considered celestial counterparts to governmental bureaus and their officials. Astrological prediction based on this theory of the continuity between the astronomical and geographical realms remained a common feature in official astronomy through the late Ming and early Qing, even after the Kangxi emperor charged that officials manipulated the major traditions in portent astrology to suit their political purposes.[43]

Although many had questioned the field allocation system, and although astrology itself had not interfered with the accumulation of geographical knowledge, the system was not attacked as an outdated notion until the seventeenth century. Some noted that the southern region, mentioned in the *Documents Classic* as Yangzhou, had comprised a large and important portion of current China. In antiquity, when the capital was in the northwest, Yangzhou was allotted only three of the twenty-eight stations in the heavens. Others pointed out that field allocation was bound to a time when the northwest had been the centre of the empire. Yan Ruoju (1636-1704) discussed the system and noted that it took no notice of "foreign" regions. He asked rhetorically: "How can it be that the sun and stars did not look out over the Man, Yi, Rong, and Di [peoples]?"[44]

Scholars recognized, since medieval times, the gradual impoverishment of the classical centre of ancient culture in the northwest. They also perceived the concomitant enrichment of the southeast, highlighted by the emergence of the Yangzi delta, as the cultural nexus of China since the Song dynasty. Gu Yanwu and Huang Zongxi considered this development the result of historical growth in which circumstance and human effort had helped bring about the geopolitical transformation of the Chinese Empire.

Hu Wei (1633-1714), writing in the second half of the seventeenth century, confirmed the recent rise of the Yangzi delta and saw in it sufficient cause to show that the ancient correspondence with the "nine regions" mentioned in the *Documents Classic* could no longer be taken literally to account for historical changes. The historicization of cultural geography meant that the old cosmograms (i.e., charts of symbolic correspondences between the natural world and human affairs) were no longer applicable. The enlargement of geographical horizons led to the discrediting of the idea of the local applicability of portents.

Such pioneering views were more critical than were those of the Jesuit Figurists, who tried to add the Bible to the cosmological correspondences Chinese literati had woven together for centuries. Such correspondences were also reworked by others to favour the priority of Chinese traditions and were included in the new mathematical collections. Evidential learning (based on a community of scholars who were literati) and imperial ideology (propagated in the court) had parted ways. Thereafter, imperial rhetoric based on the five Confucian *Classics* was ever more undercut by scholarly opinion.[45]

Scholars who used empirical methods in their geographical research during the Ming-Qing period rejected the symbolic geography in cosmograms and magic squares. They turned instead to precise fields of descriptive and historical geography. Criticism of the River Chart and Lo Writing was so acute that even champions of orthodox learning felt compelled to dissociate the mysterious charts from the teachings of their Song dynasty masters.

Embarrassed by the inclusion of the charts in Zhu Xi's (1130-1200) commentary on the *Change Classic*, a second of the five Confucian classics, those who remained orthodox scholars played down the importance of the charts. Huang Zongxi (1610-95) denied the cosmological significance of the charts and maintained instead that they were originally primeval geographical maps, charts, and registers, not cosmograms of transcendental significance. Continuing Huang's efforts to historicize the universal charts, Hu Wei demonstrated the Daoist origins and associations of the charts in the *Change* in his critique of their purported mystical correspondences. Their heterodox origins also placed into doubt the legitimacy of Song literati as rightful transmitters of the classical canon.[46]

These cosmograms were linked by Han and Song literati to the origins of Chinese writing and mathematics, which was affirmed in the mathematical works compiled in the Kangxi court. The Qing literati attack on the authenticity of these charts thus struck at the heart of the traditional cosmological ordering of the heavens and the earth and, unknowingly, at Jesuits who associated these cosmograms with the Biblical narrative.[47]

The leading Qing literati-scholars turned historical geography into a precise field of evidential inquiry. Place-names were now a sign of their time and specific location. They were employed by scholars as the empirical basis for discerning geographical anachronisms in forgeries. On the technical level, geography was an important element of concrete studies (*shixue*) and was always valued for help in land reclamation and hydraulic works – projects used to order physical space in the eighteenth century. Jesuit surveys of the empire completed in 1718 also encouraged this practical emphasis. Separated since the late Song period, the reunion of classical and technical studies during the Qing produced literati specialists who adopted an active, interventionist approach to problems in river and flood control. The empirical emphasis of evidential studies had implications for imperial statecraft that began to be felt in China a century before the forced introduction of European technology.[48]

More and more, diagrams (*tu*) and tables (*biao*) were used as aids in discussion, explanation, and classification. One of the most prominent features of eighteenth-century historical scholarship, for instance, was the use of tables of persons (*renwu biao*), supplements, and supplemental tables to help make the *Dynastic Histories* more accessible as research tools. Many evidential scholars produced important works in this genre. Interested in the organization of knowledge more than in evidential studies, Zhang Xuecheng (1738-1801), for instance, insisted that historical writing should include documentation tables and tables of persons, which would summarize the institutional forms and workings of central and local government.[49]

Gu Donggao's (1679-1759) *Table of Major Events in the Spring and Autumn Annals* (*Chunqiu dashi biao*, 1748) was a model for the collection of chronological, geographical, genealogical, and economic information concerning the late Zhou period from 722 to 481 BC. Gu arranged his work in tabular form under fifty topics, and he placed supplementary notes by other scholars after each topic whenever there was an element of dispute or doubt. Gu also attached maps that included explanations in which the ancient and present forms of place-names were given.

The use of diagrams as the first step in the graphic reconstruction of ancient relics by Dai Zhen (1724-77) and others indicates that leading Qing scholars changed the meaning and use of such diagrams from cosmogram to explanatory model. Geometrical diagrams were very abundant in Mei Wending's (1633-1721) writings because, through them, Mei was depicting the mathematical nature of astronomy. In their attempts to comprehend celestial motions, Chinese astronomers such as Wang Xichan (1628-82) shifted from strictly numerical procedures to geometric models of successive locations in space.

Rather than imago mundi, however, the epistemological status of diagrams became for evidential scholars such as Qian Daxin (1728-1804) simply ingenious calculations. Unlike Mei Wending, Qian Daxin would not accept abstract diagrams as possible keys to understanding natural phenomena. The mathematization of the world, which in Europe was dependent on the unique wedding of Newtonian mechanics and Leibnizian calculus in the latter half of the eighteenth century, was unavailable to evidential scholars in China until the aftermath of the Opium War.[50]

Although the internal turn in Qing evidential research did not produce a cartographic reconceptualization of foreign lands, we should not underestimate Jesuit and European cartographic influence in China. Through systematic gathering of materials that they would then critically scrutinize and in some cases quantify, Qing scholars combined evidential research methods with data collection and organization. As research pushed forward in the eighteenth century, Asian and Chinese continental geography became a key discipline.[51]

Despite the internal turn of this research away from concern with maritime lands far from China, achievements in geographical knowledge during this period were still evident in military defence and historical and descriptive geography, particularly along the Qing borders with Russia, Zungharia, and Kashgaria in Siberia and Central Asia. In addition, the cultural construction of Mukden (Shenyang) and its environs as the exclusive homeland of the Manchus was achieved in part through the mapping of the area under Jesuit direction. The mapping of Manchuria began circa 1690 in the aftermath of negotiations with the Russians to determine the boundaries of the Amur River in Northeast Asia.

Such achievements lent themselves to the accumulation of geographical knowledge. Cumulative progress was possible because evidential scholars, building on the efforts of their predecessors, stressed an empirical epistemology and focused on research topics that allowed for a continuity in geographical research. As a result, geography emerged as a precise discipline during the Ming-Qing transition period. Song-Yuan mathematics also became an important aspect of evidential studies and the revitalization of classical learning.[52]

To be sure, the Americas were still depicted as parts of the Asian land mass north of the Great Wall in a Chinese world map circa 1743, which was based on Liang Zhou's 1593 world map. Moreover, Phillipe Foret's account of the planning for the Manchu summer capital in Chengde and for other imperial sites demonstrates how European cartographic technologies coexisted with earlier Chinese geographic practices such as the geomancy informing cartography, landscape architecture, and urban arrangements. The geography of the Qing Empire was intertwined with Tibetan Buddhism, and this relationship was an essential component of Manchu expansion into Central Asia. That expansion also required a substantial investment in state-of-the-art mapping techniques from Europe to delineate accurately the Russo-Chinese border in the eighteenth century.[53]

Cartography, Sino-Russian Relations, and Qing Imperial Interests

Early Manchu rulers recognized the need for better records for land use and taxation. In 1646, a cadastral survey was undertaken, but its geographic inadequacies were recognized. When the Russians appeared in force along the northern frontier in the seventeenth century, the Manchu court and Chinese officials required more accurate geopolitical information to deal with the latest threats to the empire. After the Tungusic chief Gantimur defected from the Qing in 1670 to allegedly Russian territory, the Russians quickly took advantage.

A crisis in Sino-Russian relations ensued from the 1670s to 1690s, when the Manchus learned that the Russians had already built a fortress in 1654 along the Amur River at Nerchinsk in Gantimur's native region. The Kangxi emperor refused any further trade or diplomatic relations with Russia until the deadlock was resolved. Meanwhile, the Russians and Zunghar Mongols both expanded their interests in the northwest while the Qing was preoccupied in the south and southwest during the Revolt of Three Feudatories from 1673 to 1681. Much like late Ming calendar reform, Qing recognition of its geographic needs preceded the European contributions to Chinese cartography. The changing borders threatened the Manchu homeland.[54]

During the Rites Controversy, the Manchu court was embroiled simultaneously in military threats from Zunghars and Russians along the borders of the empire in Central Asia, which introduced new elements into the storm over the Jesuits and their loyalty to the Qing dynasty. For example, when the Russian mission was allowed into Beijing in 1676 to negotiate trading agreements and population movements, Ferdinand Verbiest was involved. The lack of a clear boundary in the Amur River area and the ambiguous claims to sovereignty in the area later led to the Treaty of Nerchinsk in 1689, negotiated by the French Jesuit Gerbillon, which demarcated the frontiers between the Qing and Russia.[55]

Jesuits and Mapping the Qing Empire

The Jesuits and others were commissioned to provide the necessary data that would enable Qing leaders to stem the tide of Russian infiltration into Manchu and Mongolian homelands. The geographical knowledge that accrued during this time was an important addition to earlier information on foreign lands. In the process, the Kangxi court's awareness of the actual geographical divisions of the Sino-Russian frontier slowly came apace of their long-standing knowledge of and interest in Southeast Asia.

In addition, the new mapping technique known as "trigonometric surveying," which both the Kangxi and Qianlong emperor mastered, became part of the political repertoire used by the dynasty in the eighteenth century to take stock of its dominions. Careful measurement of a base line, with one known location, was linked to determining latitudes using celestial observations. Precise longitudes were then calculated by the actual measurement of distances using a calibrated chain. When the exact location of the second end of the base line was known, the third point could be reckoned by triangulation. A series of triangles could then be extended trigonometrically for any distance. Additional positions could be determined in this manner (i.e., an entire area or region could be successfully "surveyed").[56]

The geographical ambitions of the empires of the Qing dynasty, Imperial Russia, and the Mongol Zunghars in Central Asia led to the redrawing of the frontier boundaries between Russia and the Qing as well as to the crushing of the autonomous state of Zungharia in 1760 by Qing armies. Peter Perdue has noted how eighteenth-century Central Asian borders were constructed in three stages: (1) military confrontation, (2) negotiated treaties, and (3) symbolic representation on maps and instantiation in imperial documents. Joanna Waley-Cohen adds stelae inscriptions, military pageants, and commemorative paintings to the repertoire of empire-building. The Qing dynasty, Zungharia, and Russia each produced important new maps of unprecedented scale and accuracy as political and ideological weapons in their struggle for control of Central Asia. In fact, however, these maps were the products of preliminary surveys that had preceded warfare and, moreover, often made it possible.[57]

Because Russian expansion in Siberia challenged Qing power, the Jesuits limited access to the most sensitive frontier areas of the Qing Empire when the survey for the *Kangxi Atlas* was carried out. Territorial claims and dynastic security compelled the Qing court to hire only those Jesuits who did not intend to return to their native lands. The dynasty avoided circulating such information too widely inside and outside China. Seeking to open an overland route from Rome to China via Russia, Verbiest, however, may have secretly provided Russian missions with maps and descriptions of the border region with Siberia, which included the locations of Manchu forces obtained from Russian deserters. By 1727, Qing knowledge of the region of Amuria was seen in light of the realities of Russian penetration into Siberia.[58]

When Russia and China defined their mutual borders in the Treaty of Nerchinsk in 1689 and the Treaty of Kiakhta in 1727, they both applied new cartographic surveying techniques to the newly defined borders. In addition, new classification systems and ethnographic atlases to control the movements of refugees, nomads, tribes, traders, soldiers, and other mobile groups across the borders were compiled. Both sides used tax and land registers, censuses, border patrols, passports, and visas to keep people from moving freely across the borders. Each also applied seventeenth-century European technical knowledge (transmitted through the Jesuits) to survey their new territories.[59]

The Kangxi emperor, like Louis XIV, mapped his entire empire out of strategic concern. The Jesuits produced their first survey of Beijing in 1700, which the emperor checked. Later, he asked for a survey of portions of the Great Wall in 1707. In 1710 further surveys along the Amur River helped mark the strategic bases on the border with Russia. The *Kangxi Atlas* attempted to systematize the Qing dynasty's knowledge of its imperial territories and rationalize its claims vis-à-vis the Zunghars and Russians. The Manchu homelands were surveyed between 1709 and 1712, and a complete map of greater Mukden (i.e., "Manchuria") was produced.

The text and maps that were included in the 1733 edition of the *Collected Statutes and Precedents of the Great Qing* (*Da-Qing huidian*) were concerned with military deployments and garrison towns. They were compiled under the auspices of the Ministry of Military Personnel. The maps that the Jesuits prepared for the Manchu homelands became the starting point for later Japanese and European maps of the region in the eighteenth and nineteenth centuries.[60]

The atlas and its subsequent Qianlong-era revisions shared features that were consistent with contemporary European maps. They left out pictorial elements and drew on astronomical observations to calculate longitude and latitude based on a precise scale. Hostetler interprets such developments in light of Qing evidential studies and the change in research epistemologies that affected scholarly views of geography in the late seventeenth century, a time when government interests increasingly focused on internal military defence and historical and descriptive geography. In the original maps, however, "China" and the "Qing Empire" were not coterminous. "China" was presented as one distinct part of the Qing Empire, and the Manchu homelands were another. Two other versions of the map from the same surveys, however, were entirely in Chinese with no Manchu script, perhaps to avoid offending Han Chinese cultural sensibilities. These Chinese language maps elided the Manchu view that the maps included distinct administrative and cultural spheres, to which Zungharia and Tibet would later be added.[61]

French and Russian Imperial Cartography

France was a leader in cartographic activity under Louis XIV after he appointed Jean-Baptiste Colbert as minister for home affairs. Colbert made France a centre for science and solidified that role in Europe by founding the Academy of Sciences in 1666. Louis XIV also promulgated topographical surveys for territories based on astronomical observations that were initiated under his chief of astronomy, the Italian Jean Dominique Cassini. While in the employ of Pope Clement IX, Cassini published a series of tables in

1668 based on the eclipses of Jupiter's moons. Colbert invited Cassini to France in 1669 in order to make astronomical observations that were crucial to improved navigation and mapping. Because Cassini communicated with the Jesuits in China, he sought such observations globally.[62]

Enlarged in 1676, Cassini's Ephemerides permitted astronomers to determine the latitude and longitude of the point from which they made their observations. In 1679, France began a national survey relying on Cassini's tables for accurate measurements. The French Academy required observations from around the globe, which, in part, led to Louis XIV sponsoring the French Jesuits in China under the Missions Etrangères in 1663. Once map-making became a vital component of imperial expansion, the cartographic technology to carry out accurate geodetic surveys spread quickly. France, Russia, and the Qing employed experts regardless of their origins. Colbert had recruited the Italian Cassini, Kangxi employed the French Jesuits, and Russia engaged the Swedish officer Philip Johan von Strahlenberg, who was taken prisoner by Russians in 1711, to collect information about Siberia, Mongolia, and neighbouring regions.

Peter the Great (r. 1682-1725), like the Kangxi emperor, used maps to measure the growth of the Russian Empire and to legitimate its claims. In 1698, Peter had already commissioned a survey of his new territories, and new maps for an atlas were completed in 1701, although full surveys of the empire were not formally initiated until 1727. For France, the Qing, and Russia, the requirement of better maps was tied to imperial expansion. New surveying and map-making techniques were essential. In the midst of Russian expansion into Siberia, the Qing Empire more than doubled in size between 1660 and 1760 within a global context of population growth and colonial exploration and expansion.[63]

The Kangxi surveys were completed by 1717, while French surveys took until 1744 to accomplish. The Qianlong revisions of the 1717 survey were finished in 1755, while the second edition of the French survey appeared in 1788. Similarly, the Russian imperial atlas, which followed the French national survey, appeared in 1745. Peter the Great used cartography and his European experts, who were also hired to explore the North Pacific, to put Russia on the map of eighteenth-century Europe. The *Kangxi Atlas*, for instance, had decisively changed European map-making when the Jesuit maps first arrived in France in 1725 and the new information was digested in Paris, London, and elsewhere.

Similarly, the latest mapping technology was effective for the Qing in legitimating and consolidating the empire, and it became the basis for China's modern territorial claims in the twentieth century. The Kangxi emperor's gift of his survey to Peter in 1721 indicated a desire to apprise Russia of Qing sovereignty and cartographic sophistication. It did not record all the strategic information the Qing had about the northern border areas, however.[64]

More important, the Kangxi emperor sought peace with the Russians to free his hand in wars with the Zunghar Mongols in Central Asia. By neutralizing Russia, the Qing court prevented a possible Russo-Zunghar alliance against them. Hence, when the Russians demanded the principle of equality at the Nerchinsk peace negotiations, the Manchus did not allow ceremonial difficulties to interfere with their primary diplomatic task. The emperor relented on the usual Qing ceremonial claim of imperial superiority when dealing with bordering states. The Treaty of Nerchinsk represented a compromise in which the marking out of the frontier was more favourable to the Manchus, while the Russians kept Nerchinsk. In addition, the Manchus conceded that trade could be initiated by either side, and each could cross the border with passports. Furthermore, the problem of the repatriation of fugitives was settled.

As instruments of diplomacy, the Qing government's economic concessions in the 1689 treaty proved their political worth when the leader of Zungharia, Galdan, proposed an alliance with the Russians in 1690. Joint military action against the Manchus was now impossible, however, because the Russians were bound by treaty with the Qing. The Kangxi emperor was left free to eliminate the Zunghar threat, arguably the "last nomadic empire," which he did in 1696. Galdan's death in 1697 reduced the Mongols as a potentially divisive third force in Central Asia.[65]

In 1718, the Russians contemplated full normalization of Sino-Russian relations during the Rites Controversy, which was damaging Jesuit and Roman Catholic interests in China. Peter the Great, for example, expelled the Jesuits from Russia in 1719 and tried to install a Russian "bishop" in Beijing in 1722. Russian authorities were not successful in keeping this effort secret from the Manchus and the Jesuit enemies of the Greek Orthodox Church in Beijing, but Qing suspicions prevented the appointment. Subsequently, in 1728, the Zunghar threat against the Manchus in Turkestan and Tibet revived. Again, the Manchus eliminated the threat through the Zunghar wars in the 1750s, which were facilitated by the Treaty of Kiakhta, which ended Russian interference.

Since 1727, the Treaty of Kiakhta had established officially supervised trade in Amuria, which stabilized the Russian-Qing frontier until the nineteenth century: The Qianlong reign brought a complete victory over the Zunghars, and the Qing incorporated Ili (in the far northwest) in 1755. Manchu military victories led to Qing overconfidence vis-à-vis the Russians, and this generated a ban on trade caravans to Beijing from Russia after 1755.

Qing success in Central Asia in the eighteenth century thus occurred within the context of Russian expansion into Amuria. Through compromise and accommodation, Russian interests in trade and Manchu interests in Central Asia were negotiated. Diplomacy, warfare, and timely mapping of strategic frontiers enabled the Qing dynasty to incorporate major portions of Amuria,

Zungharia, and Kashgaria at the expense of the Mongols, Uighurs, Kazaks, Tajiks, and Russians.[66]

Before the arrival of the Macartney mission in 1793, the inward turn among Qing scholars to native traditions of classical learning remained in place despite Jesuit influence in the arts and crafts. Moreover, during the Newtonian century in Europe, Chinese scholars simultaneously focused on restoring native medicine, mathematics, and astronomy to admired fields of classical learning worthy of the attention of literati. When Chinese had their first intellectual contacts with modern science as it appeared in Benjamin Hobson's *Treatise of Natural Philosophy* (*Bowu xinbian*, lit., "Broad learning of things newly compiled," 1851), they quickly realized how far beyond the Jesuits natural studies in Europe had gone. Their eighteenth-century predecessors in China, however, never knew what had transpired in Europe after the demise of the Jesuit order in the middle of the eighteenth century. They were content to domesticate the Western learning and geography that the Jesuits had introduced and to note its similarity to ancient astronomy, historical geography, and Song-Yuan mathematical innovations. Native geographical studies, however, grew apace with the eighteenth-century expansion of the Qing Empire in Central Asia and rarely addressed the maritime world again until the Opium War (1839-42).[67]

Notes

1 Henry Serruys, *Sino-Mongol Relations during the Ming*, in *Melanges Chinois et Bouddhiques*, vol. 1: *The Mongols in China during the Hung-wu Period, 1368-1398;* vol. 2: *The Tribute System and the Diplomatic Missions* (1967) (Brussels: Institut Belge des hautes études Chinoises, 1959), 8.

2 See Philip de Heer, *The Care-Taker Emperor: Aspects of the Imperial Institution in Fifteenth-Century China as Reflected in the Political History of the Reign of Chu Ch'i-yü* (Leiden: E.J. Brill, 1986); and Frederick W. Mote, "The T'u-mu Incident of 1449," in *Chinese Ways in Warfare,* edited by Frank Kierman, Jr. and John Fairbank, 243-72 (Cambridge: Harvard University Press, 1974).

3 Arthur Waldron, *The Great Wall of China: From History to Myth* (Cambridge: Cambridge University Press, 1990), 79-86. Waldron notes how Ming forces withdrew from steppe garrisons as early as 1403-10. See also Alastair Johnston, *Cultural Realism: Strategic Culture and Grand Strategy in Chinese History* (Princeton: Princeton University Press, 1995), 195-97.

4 On the Ming fleets and their forays into the Indian Ocean, see Joseph Needham, *Science and Civilisation in China,* vol. 4, pt. 3 (Cambridge: Cambridge University Press, 1954-), 477-553. On Ming relations with Southeast Asia, see Wang Gungwu, *Community and Nation: China, Southeast Asia and Australia* (St. Leonards, Australia: Allen and Unwin, 1992), 77-146.

5 See Jung-pang Lo, "The Decline of the Early Ming Navy," *Oriens Extremus* 5, 2 (1958): 147-68.

6 See Richard Smith, "Mapping China's World: Cultural Cartography in Late Imperial Times," in *Landscape, Culture and Power in Chinese Society*, edited by Yeh Wen-hsin, 62-68 (Berkeley: University of California, Center for East Asian Studies, 1998). See also Alexander Wylie, *Notes on Chinese Literature* (Taibei: Book Shop Limited, 1970 [Shanghai: American Presbyterian Press, 1867]), 43-67, for premodern works on geography.

7 Smith, "Mapping China's World," 67-68.

8 *Science and Civilisation in China*, vol. 3, 533-51 and vol. 4, pt. 3, 500-2; and L.C. Goodrich and Chaoying Fang, eds., *Dictionary of Ming Biography,* 2 vols. (New York: Columbia Univer-

sity Press, 1976), 982. Compare such speculations with the claims presented as facts to unsuspecting audiences in Gavin Menzies, *1421: The Year China Discovered America* (New York: HarperCollins, 2002), passim.

9 See Jan Julius Lodewijk Duyvendak, *Ma Huan Re-examined* (Amsterdam: Noord-Hollandsche uitgeversmaatschappij, 1933), 8-9.

10 See *Hsing-ch'a sheng-lun: The Overall Survey of the Star Raft by Fei Hsin*, translated by J.V.G. Mills, revised, annotated, and edited by Roderich Ptak (Amsterdam: Noord-Hollandsche uitgeversmaatschappij, 1933). See also Sir David Percival, trans., *Chinese Connoisseurship, the Ko Ku Yao Lun: The Essential Criteria of Antiquity* (London: Faber, 1971).

11 *Siku quanshu zongmu* [General catalog for the complete collection of the four treasuries] (Taipei: Commercial Press, 1983-86 [reprint]), 78.14b-19a.

12 *Siku quanshu zongmu*, 71.3b-4b, 78.14b-15a; *Science and Civilisation in China*, vol. 3, 511, 557-58. See also Ting Wen-chiang, "On Hsu Hsia-k'o (1586-1641): Explorer and Geographer," *New China Review* 3, 5 (1921): 325-37. Detailed discussion of Hsu Hsia-k'o's travels can be found in Li Chi, *The Travel Diaries of Hsu Hsia-k'o* (Hong Kong: Chinese University, 1974).

13 Originally completed in 1562, the *Maritime Survey* was reedited by Hu Zongxian's descendants and reissued in 1624. The editors of the later editions dropped Zheng Ruozeng's name as the author and replaced it with Hu Zongxian, their revered ancestor. Compare the account in *Siku quanshu zongmu*, 69.31a-32b.

14 *Science and Civilisation in China*, vol. 3, 514-17.

15 Cordell Yee, "Traditional Chinese Cartography and the Myth of Westernization," in *The History of Cartography*, vol. 2, book 2: *Cartography in the Traditional East and Southeast Asian Societies*, edited by J.B. Harley and David Woodward, 170-202 (Chicago: University of Chicago Press, 1994).

16 Ricci's world map is reproduced in *Science and Civilisation in China*, vol. 3, 582-83 (Plates XC and XCI). A 1608 colour version is included in *Symbols of Power: Masterpieces from the Nanjing Museum* (Anaheim, CA: Bowers Museum, 2002).

17 Helen Wallis, "The Influence of Father Ricci on Far Eastern Cartography," *Imago Mundi* 19 (1965): 35-45; and Kenneth Ch'en, "Matteo Ricci's Contribution to, and Influence on, Geographical Knowledge in China," *Journal of the American Oriental Society* 59, 3 (1939): 325-59. Compare Theodore Foss, "A Western Interpretation of China Jesuit Cartography," in *East Meets West: The Jesuits in China, 1582-1773*, edited by Charles Ronan S.J. and Bonnie Oh, 209-51 (Chicago: Loyola University Press, 1988).

18 Zhang Huang, *Tushu bian* [The compendium of maps and materials] (Taibei: Chengwen chuban she, 1971 [reprint]), 19.33a-40a. See also Ch'en, "Matteo Ricci's Contribution," 343-47. For the initial reaction of Chinese literati, see Pasquale M. d'Elia, "Recent Discoveries and New Studies (1938-60) on the World Map in Chinese of Father Matteo Ricci S.J.," *Monumenta Serica* 20 (1961): 82-164.

19 *The Library of Philip Robinson*, pt. 2 (London: Sotheby's Auction Catalogue, 1988), 77 95, especially 76-77, 78-79. The 1593 world map was engraved by Liang Zhou, an education official in Wuxi, and printed in Nanjing. See also John Day, "The Search for the Origins of the Chinese Manuscript Copies of Matteo Ricci's Maps," *Imago Mundi* 47 (1995): 94-117.

20 *The Library of Philip Robinson*, pt. 2, 79-80. See also Lionel Giles, "Translations from the World Map of Father Ricci," *Geographical Journal* 52, 6 (1918): 367-85; and ibid., 53, 1 (1919): 19-30.

21 Wylie, *Notes on Chinese Literature*, 58.

22 See Bernard Hung-kay Luk, "A Study of Giulio Aleni's *Chih-fang wai-chi*," *Bulletin of Oriental and African Studies* 40 (1977): 58-84; and Eugenio Menegon, *Un solo Cielo: Giulio Aleni S.J. (1582-1649)* (Rome: Grafo, 1994), 141-46. See also Richard Smith, *Chinese Maps: Images of All under Heaven* (Oxford: Oxford University Press, 1996), 49-54.

23 *The Library of Philip Robinson*, pt. 2, 83, 85-86, 89, 95. Martini had been in China from 1643 to 1646. See also Boleslaw Szczesniak, "The Seventeenth-Century Maps of China: An Inquiry into the Compilations of European Cartographers," *Imago Mundi* 13 (1956): 116-36.

24 Smith, "Mapping China's World," 71-83, usefully introduces the "Complete Maps" genre.

25 See Luk, "A Study of Giulio Aleni's *Chih-fang wai-chi*," 76-77. See also Chen Minsun, "Ferdinand Verbiest and the Geographical Works by Jesuits in Chinese 1584-1674," 123-64, and Lin Tongyang, "Ferdinand Verbiest's Contribution to Chinese Geography and Cartography," 135-164, both in *Ferdinand Verbiest, S.J. (1623-1688): Jesuit Missionary, Scientist, Engineer, and Diplomat*, edited by S.J. John Witek (Nettetal: Steyler Verlag, 1994).
26 Walter Fuchs, "Der Jesuiten-Atlas der Kanghsi-Zeit," *Monumenta Serica*, Monograph Series 4 (1943): 60-75. See also James A. Millward, *Beyond the Pass: Economy, Ethnicity, and Empire in Qing Central Asia, 1759-1864* (Stanford: Stanford University Press, 1998), 70-72.
27 Smith, "Mapping China's World," 77-81.
28 *Science and Civilisation in China*, vol. 3, 551-86. Maps based on latitudinal and longitudinal degrees were essential for ocean-going vessels (which the Chinese did not prioritize for their coastal fleet).
29 For the locus classicus, see Benjamin Elman, *From Philosophy to Philology: Social and Intellectual Aspects of Change in Late Imperial China*, 2nd ed. (Los Angeles: UCLA Asia Institute Monograph Series, 2001), 72-122.
30 Compare Frank Swetz, trans., *The Sea Island Mathematical Manual: Surveying and Mathematics in Ancient China* (University Park: Pennsylvania State University Press, 1992), 7-16.
31 See Kenneth Swope, "Crouching Tigers, Secret Weapons: Military Technology Employed in the Japanese Invasion of Korea, 1592-1598," *Journal of Military History* 69, 1 (2005): 11-41.
32 Cordell Yee, "A Cartography of Introspection: Chinese Maps as Other than European," *Asian Art* 5 (1992): 29-45. See also Tonio Andrade, "Commerce, Culture and Conflict: Taiwan under European Rule, 1623-1662" (PhD diss., Yale University, 2001).
33 Cheng K'o-ch'eng, "Cheng Ch'eng-kung's Maritime Expansion and Early Ch'ing Coastal Prohibition," in *Development and Decline of Fukien Province in the 17th and 18th Centuries*, edited by E.B. Vermeer, 228-44 (Leiden and New York: E.J. Brill, 1990).
34 John Wills, Jr., "Maritime China from Wang Chih to Shih Lang [Shi Lang]," in *From Ming to Ch'ing: Conquest, Region, and Continuity in Seventeenth-Century China*, edited by Jonathan Spence and John Wills, 228-34 (New Haven: Yale University Press, 1979).
35 Wills, Jr., "Maritime China," 233; and Peter Perdue, "Boundaries, Maps, and Movement: Chinese, Russian, and Mongolian Empires in Early Modern Central Eurasia," *International History Review* 20, 2 (1998): 263-86.
36 Ch'en, "Matteo Ricci's Contribution," 347-59.
37 Arthur Hummel, *Eminent Chinese of the Ch'ing Period* (Washington: US Printing Office, 1943), 522, 909.
38 *Huangchao wenxian tongkao* [Comprehensive analysis of civil and military institutions during the Qing dynasty], in *Shitong*, vol. 2 (Shanghai: Commercial Press, 1935-37), 298.7469-70.
39 *Huangchao wenxian tongkao*, vol. 2, 298.7469-74, 298.7481-89.
40 *Siku quanshu zongmu*, 69.22a-23a. See also *Science and Civilisation in China*, vol. 3, 569-79.
41 *Siku quanshu zongmu*, 70.4b. See also Minghui Hu, "Measuring the Cosmos: The Rise of Precision Narratives in Qing China," paper presented at the Colloquium sponsored by the Center for the Cultural Studies of Science, Medicine, and Technology, UCLA History Department, 6 May 2002.
42 On the *fenye* system, see Edward Schafer, *Pacing the Void: T'ang Approaches to the Stars* (Berkeley: University of California Press, 1977), 75-84. In unofficial life and popular culture, however, literati efforts to distance such correspondences and the mantic arts were unsuccessful. See Richard Smith, *Fortune-Tellers and Philosophers: Divination in Traditional Chinese Society* (Boulder, CO: Westview Press, 1991); and Elman, *A Cultural History*, 295-370.
43 See Schafer, *Pacing the Void*, 75-84; and John Major, "A Note on the Translation of Two Technical Terms in Chinese Science: *Wu-hsing* and *Hsiu*," *Early China* 2 (1976): 1-3.
44 See Yan Ruoju, *Qianqiu zhaji* [Assorted notes by Yan Ruoju] (Taibei: Commercial Press, 1973), 3.2a. See also *Science and Civilisation in China*, vol. 3, 231-52.
45 John Henderson, *The Development and Decline of Chinese Cosmology* (New York: Columbia University Press, 1984), 82-87, 219-25.
46 See Schuyler Cammann, "The Evolution of Magic Squares in China," *Journal of the American Oriental Society* 80 (1960): 116-24.

47 Michael Saso, "What Is the *Ho-t'u?" History of Religions* 17, 3 and 4 (1978): 399-416. See also *Science and Civilisation in China*, vol. 3, 55-59.

48 See Rong Zhaozu, "Yan Ruoju de kaozheng xue" [Yan Ruoju's evidential studies], *Lingnan xuebao* 1, 4 (1930): 90-91.

49 Du Weiyun, *Qing Qianjia shidai zhi shixue yu shijia* [Historians and historical studies during the Qing Qianlong and Jiaqing eras] (Taibei: Wenshi zongkan, 1962), 11-12, gives a comprehensive list of such supplements. See also David Nivison, *The Life and Thought of Chang Hsueh-ch'eng* (Stanford: Stanford University Press, 1966), 195, 216.

50 See Henderson, *The Development and Decline of Chinese Cosmology*, 231-53; and Nathan Sivin, "Wang Hsi-shan," in *Dictionary of Scientific Biography*, editor in chief, Charles Gillispie, 159-62 (New York: Scribner's Sons, 1970-78).

51 Smith, "Mapping China's World," 71-77, stresses Chinese disdain of "barbarians." For problems with this perspective, see Lydia Liu, "Legislating the Universal: The Circulation of International Law in the Nineteenth Century," in *Tokens of Exchange: The Problem of Translation in Global Circulations*, edited by Lydia Liu, 127-64 (Durham, NC: Duke University Press, 1999). Though frequently anti-foreign, Qing rhetoric about "barbarians" is a later European construction.

52 See Mark Elliot, "The Limits of Tartary: Manchuria in Imperial and National Geographies," *Journal of Asian Studies* 59, 3 (2000): 603-46.

53 See *The Library of Philip Robinson*, pt. 2, 95; and Smith, *Chinese Maps*, 54-59. Compare Phillipe Foret, *Mapping Chengde: The Qing Landscape Enterprise* (Honolulu: University of Hawai'i Press, 2000), chap. 6.

54 Peter Perdue, "Boundaries, Maps, and Movement: Chinese, Russian, and Mongolian Empires in Early Modern Central Eurasia," *International History Review* 20, 2 (1998): 263-86; and Laura Hostetler, "Qing Connections to the Early Modern World: Ethnography and Cartography in Eighteenth-Century China," *Modern Asian Studies* 34, 3 (2000): 623-62. Compare Elliot, "The Limits of Tartary," 619-20.

55 Vladimir Miasnikov, "Ferdinand Verbiest and His Role in the Formation of Sino-Russian Diplomatic Relations," in Witek, *Ferdinand Verbiest (1623-1688)*, 274-75.

56 See Sun Jiji, *Kang-Yong-Qian shiqi yutu cehui yu jiangyu xingcheng yanjiu* [Research on cartographic surveys and boundary formations during the Kangxi, Yungzheng, and Qianlong eras] (Beijing: Zhongguo renmin daxue chuban she, 2003).

57 Perdue, "Boundaries, Maps, and Movement," 263-86; and Perdue, "Military Mobilization in Seventeenth and Eighteenth-Century China, Russia and Mongolia," *Modern Asian Studies*, 30, 4 (1996): 782-90. Compare Joanna Waley-Cohen, "Commemorating War in Eighteenth-Century China," *Modern Asian Studies* 30, 4 (1996): 869-99.

58 Peter the Great later expelled the Jesuits from Russia because he thought they had betrayed Russian interests in the Treaty of Nerchinsk. See Miasnikov, "Ferdinand Verbiest," 273-79; and Hao Zhenhua, "Ferdinand Verbiest and Sino-Russian Relations," in Witek, *Ferdinand Verbiest (1623-1688)*, 282-96. Compare Mark Mancall, *Russia and China: Their Diplomatic Relations to 1728* (Cambridge: Harvard University Press, 1971), 98-109. See also Perdue, "Boundaries, Maps, and Movement," 269-71.

59 See Perdue, "Boundaries, Maps, and Movement," 263-86; and Laura Hostetler, "Qing Connections to the Early Modern World: Ethnography and Cartography in Eighteenth-Century China," *Modern Asian Studies* 34, 3 (2000): 623-62.

60 See Walter Fuchs, "Materialen zur Kartographie der Mandju-Zeit, part 1," *Monumenta Serica* 1 (1935-36): 395-96; and Fuchs, "Materialen zur Kartographie der Mandju-Zeit, part 2," *Monumenta Serica* 3 (1938): 189-231. Compare Elliot, "The Limits of Tartary," 621-32.

61 Perdue, "Boundaries, Maps, and Movement," 274-75; and Laura Hostetler, *Qing Colonial Enterprise: Ethnography and Cartography in Early Modern China* (Chicago: University of Chicago Press, 2001), 17-18, 76. Compare David Turnbull, "Cartography and Science in Early Modern Europe: Mapping and the Construction of Knowledge Spaces," *Imago Mundi* 48 (1996): 5-24.

62 See Roger Hahn, *The Anatomy of a Scientific Institution: The Paris Academy of Sciences, 1666-1803* (Berkeley: University of California Press, 1971), 66-67, 90, 96-97.

63 Hostetler, *Qing Colonial Enterprise*, 71-75. See also Perdue, "Military Mobilization," 757-93; and James Millward, "'Coming Onto the Map': Western Regions' Geography and

Cartographic Nomenclature in the Making of the Chinese Empire in Xinjiang," *Late Imperial China* 20, 2 (1999): 61-98.

64 Hostetler, *Qing Colonial Enterprise*, 74-79; and Elliot, "The Limits of Tartary," 626.

65 Thomas Barfield, *The Perilous Frontier: Nomadic Empires and China* (Cambridge, MA: B. Blackwell, 1989), 277-94.

66 Mancall, *Russia and China*, 149-59, 209-10. The translation of the treaty is on 280-83. See also Eric Widmer, *The Russian Ecclesiastical Mission in Peking during the Eighteenth Century* (Cambridge: Harvard University East Asian Research Center, 1976), 45-58, 174-78.

67 See Benjamin Elman, *On Their Own Terms: Science in China, 1550-1900* (Cambridge: Harvard University Press, 2005), chaps. 9 and 10.

3
Marital Politics on the Manchu-Mongol Frontier in the Early Seventeenth Century

Nicola Di Cosmo

The formative period of Manchu power, and especially the years that preceded the proclamation of the Qing dynasty in 1636, sits uneasily at the intersection between Chinese and Inner Asian history.[1] "Uneasily" in the sense that the focus on overcoming the strictures of a paradigm of sinicization that inserted the Manchus in the line of bona fide Chinese dynasties has not been counterbalanced by a comparable level of attention to the Inner Asian side of the equation. Over the past decade, an extended and at times heated debate has invested matters of identity and sinicization, ritual and representation, acculturation and assimilation, and change and continuity within the Chinese and Inner Asian cultures and traditions that converged in the formation of the Qing dynasty.[2] Yet the linkages between the Inner Asian "grand narrative" and the Manchu conquest remain anchored to notions that, not unlike the sinicization thesis, have a constraining effect on the way in which we tend to conceptualize the rise of an Inner Asian power such as the Manchu.

From the 1930s and 1940s to the present, Owen Lattimore's theoretical contribution has cast a large shadow on China's "frontier studies." Whether one agrees with it or not, Lattimore's analysis of the northern frontier, developed in his *Inner Asian Frontiers of China* and further expounded in a large production of essays and minor works, continues to be the chief single term of reference of current rationalizations of historical relations between China and Inner Asia.[3] The greatest appeal of Lattimore's theories possibly lies in the streamlined, neatly organized, and forcefully argued thesis that the frontier zone was the fountainhead of all Inner Asian "nomadic" dynasties and regimes that emerged as rivals or conquerors of China. Moving away from idealized notions of "civilization versus barbarism," the Great Wall was understood by Lattimore, mainly in geographical and ecological terms, as a transition zone between two mutually exclusive forms of human adaptation to the natural environment. The economic and social forces resulting from these forms of adaptation – agriculture and pastoralism, sedentary farmers, and horse-riding nomads – could not be integrated into a single system. Hence, the frontier became a contested place whose inherent instability accounted for the ebb and flow of nomadic cycles of power.

But it was on the frontier that ambitious Inner Asian leaders could emerge because it was there that they could muster the force needed to create a successful "supratribal" state.[4] To concentrate in one chieftain's hands the power to mobilize large numbers of people from outside one's natural body politic required access to resources from both the steppe and the sedentary areas: horses and riches. The cycle of nomadic power that Lattimore described as the central feature of Inner Asian history therefore could not have materialized without access to the frontier and the material opportunities that it offered.[5]

Lattimore's frontier thesis (or, better, theses) inspired broader studies on frontier relations and had considerable influence outside the fields of Chinese and Inner Asian studies, prompting historians to identify meanings that could be extended to a variety of other frontiers. Particularly appealing was the notion of frontier societies as bodies developing "their own interests quite different from those of the central government. They feel neither bound by the center nor binding the realm. Rather, they represent runaway elements and interests of the state's corporate body."[6] This definition describes well Frederick Wakeman's concepts of transfrontiersmen and frontiersmen as key social forces enabling the consolidation of Manchu power on the northeastern frontier. Frontier societies include both Chinese settlers and "barbarian tribesmen" that could be assimilated on both sides.[7] The Chinese frontiersmen's willingness to cross over to the Inner Asian side was essential to the Manchu conquest, and the possibility of assimilating people on either side of the frontier created the conditions for the expansion of the political space and ambitions of the founders of the Manchu dynasty.

This line of reasoning has notable advantages. For instance, it brings into question the historical circumstances under which the centrifugal pull of the periphery vis-à-vis the centre may be accelerated, thus implicitly working against near-deterministic views of a frontier largely explained in terms of deep ecological and socioeconomic dynamics. Yet, the frontiersmen thesis still needs to be taken with caution since it is essentially based on a representation of the frontier as a soft area between two separate and antagonistic worlds. The existence of a soft matter that can solidify in one form or another does not alter the notion of the Sino-Inner Asian frontier as bipolar and as shaped by opposite-pulling forces.

Clearly, Lattimore's thesis that Inner Asian dynastic founders use both worlds to forge their empires is compatible with Wakeman's frontiersmen thesis, which argues that people living on the frontiers could be easily persuaded to switch camps. But how do we explain the emergence of a

Manchu-Mongol conflict, as it unfolded in the 1620s and 1630s and whose resolution required years of war and diplomacy? The concept of a bipolar Sino-Inner Asian frontier tends to screen from the historian's view the existence of other frontiers, mainly because not much attention is paid to the identification of "lines of cleavage" (to borrow Lattimore's term) between Mongols and Manchus.[8] The political scene among the Mongols was perhaps too fluid to permit the formation of clearly demarcated political centres. Moreover, perceived differences in the basic characteristics of the Mongolian and Manchurian economies, the first being more pastoral and the latter more "mixed" (with agriculture and gathering being important elements), must not be exaggerated. The actual economic strength of both areas derived more from the political leaders' ability to exploit trading opportunities with China and to extract payments from border towns than from the intrinsic quality of native economies.[9] Finally, from the cultural point of view, we cannot say that Manchus and Mongols saw themselves as possessing entirely different "identities." There was, of course, awareness of difference, but this was often overcome by a language of commonality.[10] The Manchus were sometimes referred to as "the Mongol nation with red-tasselled hats," referring to the distinctive ornament on the Manchu nobles' hats.[11] In turn, the Manchus often stressed the similarities of customs and language that existed between the two peoples. The traditional political culture and the manner of conducting diplomatic relations, including alliance ceremonies and rituals, did not differ in any significant way.[12]

Failing to identify the characteristics that were specific to the Manchu-Mongol "frontier" prevents us from understanding the dynamic nature of this portion of the complex phenomenon that was the Manchu conquest, while analytical criteria such as Wakeman's "transfrontiemen's" thesis, or Lattimore's concept of "ecological" frontier, clearly do not extend to the study of Manchu-Mongol relations. This lacuna has led to the theoretical difficulty, when it comes to frontier politics, of integrating frontier relations internal to the Inner Asian camp into the analysis of the political culture of the Manchus and of the Qing dynasty in general. Studies in this direction usually stress the indebtedness of the Manchus to Mongol political culture or the Inner Asian "affinity" of the two peoples. Yet surely the Manchu "debt" to the Mongols (the extent of which is by no means clear) was not an instance of passive cultural reception, nor should affinity imply that Mongol and Manchu traditions and practices were entirely coterminous. My contention is that investigating the internal nature of Manchu-Mongol relations, and in particular the tensions between war and diplomacy that carried on intensely for about fifteen years (1619-34), is essential to understanding the formation of the Qing elite and its attitude to frontier management. A possible point of entry into this territory is the Manchu diplomacy towards the Mongols at a critical juncture of their relations – namely, at the time when the Manchu leadership intervened in the political crisis of the southern and eastern Mongols, which had been caused by the bid for imperial unification led by Ligdan Khan (1592-1634).

The facts are fairly well-established: as Nurhaci's (1559-1626) power increased after the establishment of the Jin (or Latter Jin) dynasty in 1616, and especially after the victory against overwhelming Ming forces at Mount Sarhū in 1619 followed by the Manchu move into Liaodong, the rising Mongol leader Ligdan Khan warned the Manchus to keep away from his territory or face punishment. In his long letter to Nurhaci of 27 November 1619, Ligdan Khan presented himself as the ruler of the "forty Mongol *tumens*."[13] Historians generally agree that Ligdan's project to reunify the Mongol tribes and to recreate a Mongol empire was under way by then and that it continued through more than ten years of wars and political upheaval. To explain its eventual failure, emphasis is usually placed on Ligdan's lack of popularity among the Mongol chiefs, which created disunity, favouring the Manchus' political and military intervention. This, ultimately, undermined Ligdan's hegemonic plan by luring various Mongol leaders to the Manchu side.[14]

Given that no accommodation could be found between Nurhaci and Ligdan Khan, hostilities ensued, but this was no ordinary confrontation. The period roughly between 1620 and 1634 deepened and finalized the Manchu strategy vis-à-vis the Southern Mongols, while shaping the political process along the northern frontier. It is difficult to explain in purely military terms why the Mongol tribes attacked by Ligdan, or simply caught in between the two emerging powers, would choose to submit to the Manchus while they had defended their independence against Ligdan.[15] A close analysis of Manchu and Mongol sources, such as the diplomatic correspondence between Mongol chieftains and Manchu leaders, reveals instead that the success of the Manchus was due to a skilful combination of marital arrangements and legal practices that allowed them to enter and eventually dominate the political world of the Mongol tribes.[16] Marital contracts in particular fulfilled a vital political function, whose implications in shaping the frontier strategy of the early Manchus has yet to be investigated properly. Here I present an attempt to glean from the Manchu-Mongol diplomatic correspondence the political meanings of marriage and how kinship relations (real, not fictive) affected the process that led to the expansion of Manchu hegemony into southern Mongolia and to the completion of a critical step towards the creation of the future Qing state.

Manchu-Mongol Marital Relations during the Chakhar Wars

In 1606, after Nurhaci's defeat of a hostile coalition of Jurchen-Mongol forces that included members of the five southern Khalkha tribes, a peace treaty was concluded whereby the defeated Khalkha leaders conferred upon Nurhaci the title of Kündülen Khaghan (Most Honoured Ruler).[17] This was a term of respect and political recognition that certainly did not lead to the submission of the Mongols or to a serious expansion of Nurhaci's power into Mongol territory, but it did greatly elevate the position of the Manchus among the Mongols.[18] More important, the higher status allowed the Manchu leaders to forge alliances with Mongol aristocrats and thus extend the range of their political and military reach. Indeed, Nurhaci's strategy in the early period of his rise to power (i.e., before 1616), was carefully conceived in terms of making alliances with faraway tribes while antagonizing the adjacent ones.[19] Within this logic, a series of marital alliances were forged that made it clear that the Manchus were pursuing a "Mongol strategy" that, albeit temporarily secondary to the "Manchurian strategy," was going to develop further after the consolidation of the Jianzhou Jurchen's power in southern Manchuria. It is therefore no surprise that Ligdan Khan, for all the bravado contained in his letter of 1619, appeared to be gravely concerned that Nurhaci, after having defeated the multinational force sent against him by the Ming in the same year (inclusive of Chinese, Korean, and Yehe troops), would turn his attention to "unifying" the Mongol tribes.[20]

The difficulties the Manchus met in their occupation of Liaodong, however, prevented any serious military action against the Mongols as ethnic strife between occupying forces and local population and economic strictures forced them to consolidate their hold on the peninsula before attempting further expansion.[21] Hence, Ligdan's anticipated competition from the Manchus did not materialize until a few years after 1619, allowing him to pursue unchallenged his own policy of forcibly uniting the southern Mongol tribes. Ligdan's heavy-handedness, however, alienated a large number of Mongol chiefs, fomenting opposition and generating widespread violence. It is against this backdrop of chaos and danger that we must situate Manchu diplomatic efforts and military involvement among the south Mongol tribes. The political advantages offered by marital relations was exploited with great skill by Nurhaci and by his son and successor Hong Taiji (1592-1643). Marriages soon became an essential element in their strategy to defeat Ligdan, while recruiting the Mongol aristocracy into the Manchu political project and placing the Mongol tribes under Manchu sovereignty.

As is customary in Inner Asian politics, intertribal alliances were marked by oaths, sacrifices, and marriages.[22] Diplomacy operated, broadly speaking, through a class system and a kinship system. The system of marriage alliances, known in Mongolian by the term *khuda*, was based on exogamous relations among patrilineal lineages. This had been current among the Mongols at the time of Chinggis Khan, although during the late Ming dynasty inter-Mongol marital alliances had shifted with the tendency of the Chinggisid aristocracy, descended from Dayan Khan (c. 1480-1517), to marry into prominent but subordinate families.[23] Still, the system offered Mongol and Manchu aristocracies the possibility of recognizing and co-opting each other into their respective political spheres, not unlike European royal families during the same period in time, and not unlike Chinese nobility during the "Springs and Autumns" period in preimperial Chinese history (770-481 BC).

Nurhaci's marriages with women of allied clans (or even rival ones) closely followed the twists and turns of his political ascent. His main consorts came from Manchurian (i.e., Jurchen) clans: Tunggiya, Fuca, and the Nara clan of the Yehe tribe.[24] Still, among the so-called "royal concubines," or *fei,* we find no less than thirteen Mongol women, one of whom, a *dafei* (or grand concubine) was the daughter of a Khorchin Mongol chief. Moreover, some of his daughters were married off to Mongols, such as Mangguji, who married first a Manchu from the Hada tribe in 1601 and then a Mongol in 1628.[25] The relationship between Khorchin Mongols and the Manchu royal clan became particularly close in 1614, when Hong Taiji and his two brothers, Haoge and Dorgon, married aristocratic women of the Khorchin Borjigid clan.[26] In the same year, Manggultai (1587-1633), fifth son of Nurhaci, also married a Mongol noblewoman from the Jarut tribe.[27]

Hong Taiji, more than any of his siblings, participated in this marriage diplomacy.[28] His first wife, daughter of the Khorchin chief Manggus, was later honoured with the title of Xiaoduan Wen Huanghou.[29] Altogether he married seven Mongol women, three of whom occupied the highest possible ranks in the hierarchy of his consorts.[30] On the other hand, ten out of fourteen daughters of Hong Taiji married Mongol aristocrats, including the son of Hong Taiji's arch-enemy Ligdan Khan, Erke Khonggor-eje (1622-41).[31] The following Mongol tribes were represented among the Manchus' "in-laws": Khorchin, Chakhar, Barin, Aukhan, and Abagha. Two of Nurhaci's daughters were married to Aukhan (a Chinggisid line of the Chakhar tribe) and Khalka noblemen, and a presumed sister of Hong Taiji was married to the chief of the Khorchin Tüsiyetü Khan.

This is "genetic engineering" on a grand scale, as a consequence of which the later generations of south Mongol leaders were to be, by virtue of their family affiliations created through the institution of the *efu* (Imperial Son-in-Law), very closely connected to the Manchu royal house. However, given that the outcome of the Manchu struggle for power was unknown at the time, the future of these marriage alliances does not explain, in itself, either why Mongol clans entered marriage alliances with the Manchus or what advantages either side hoped to gain from these relations. Looking at the political situation, the marital connection made it possible for one or the other party to use its "in-law" status to manipulate the political process and increase its leverage in political negotiation. In addition to the obvious advantage of securing a degree of protection against one's external enemies, we can identify several other uses of the marriage alliance: to gauge the trustworthiness of an alleged friend and ally, to enhance a leader's power vis-à-vis challenges coming from within his own family, and even to provoke war.

First, the presence of wives offered the option of ranking one's political allies or, conversely, gauging one's position in another tribe's estimation. Second, the in-law line ensured the continuance of the "genetic pool" of a clan or family in case military disaster led to the destruction of the patrilineal lineage. Third, marriage supported the internal politics of a given tribe, particularly with regard to securing assistance in the struggle among siblings – something that was all too frequent in steppe politics.

Alliances in the steppe could be fickle, and oaths of alliance, even when sworn with great pomp and gravity, were often short-lived.[32] The position of a given wife within the allied (and potentially adversarial) camp, then, could be a useful indicator of the political direction in which a given chief might be leaning. Since male aristocrats could have multiple consorts and concubines, and since these were "ranked," the Manchu bride could be given a lower position than the one originally desired or negotiated. These marital ranks, in addition to actual titles assigned to wives and concubines, were expressed by positioning the individual tent of the consort in a more or less honourable place within the encampment.

Prime locations reflected a high position in the hierarchy of the tribe's "foreign relations." If a Manchu bride did not attain a high rank, while consorts from some other tribe did, this was tantamount to a loss of Manchu political status. Since agreements were generally concluded on the understanding that the two parties were equal (even though, in reality, this may not have been true), the subsequent lowering of the status of one of the parties by "demoting" the acquired bride created a disconnect that could produce a series of unhappy consequences: trust could be compromised, mutual aid might no longer be expected, and, in the last instance, war could break out.

During the Chakhar wars, the close relationship between the Khorchin and the Manchus was subject to severe strain, and, in a public document, Hong Taiji decided to denounce his ally Oba (d. 1632, known by the title of Tüsiyetü Khan) for his "three crimes and nine sins." Among them, the crime of having showed little respect to the Manchu bride, is cited as one of the most serious offences:[33]

> You let the tent of your guilty wife[34] be set up in the front [of the encampment, i.e., the most honoured place], while you had the tent of our daughter set up in the back. Over and over again you have said that your guilty wife is the offspring of a great man; but what *qaγan* prepared [her for marriage] and married her to you? What kind of great princes are her relatives now?

> Have they not all become retainers? They [i.e., the Chakhar] killed your paternal uncle. Then you were afraid that they would kill you, and therefore you call her the offspring of a great man. Why would you make this woman higher [than ours] when her Chakhar family was going to kill you? Why would you make our daughter lower, when we always cherished you? This is the sixth instance in which you humiliated us. Bring our lowly man's offspring back to us, and live with the descendent of the great man!

Few documents reveal more openly the political dimension of the marital alliance. The position held by the wives reflected the standing of the wife's relatives and tribe in the hierarchy of relations that the husband established in his external politics. By asking Oba to return his daughter, Hong Taiji effectively threatened to cut off any relationship, thus leaving him and his tribe at the mercy of the Chakhars. If a wife was not given due respect by the clan into which she married, then obviously the in-laws could not be trusted.

The same Oba had communicated with Hong Taiji in a previous letter, in which he attempted to exculpate himself for not having gone in person to receive the Manchu bride Junje Gege, who was promised to him as a result of the compact concluded in 1626.[35] Here the marital relation – that is, the promise of marriage made to him by Nurhaci himself (Kündülen Khaghan) – is seemingly mentioned to confirm his trustworthiness as a relative. Since his claims that he could not attend in person – first, he was injured; second, he was unable to leave his territory lest it remained unprotected – came from an imperial son-in-law (*efu*), they were supposed to carry great weight and might, therefore, more easily elicit a pardon:[36]

> As I was loved by your good father Kündülen Qaγan, he let [me] become his ninth son after his eight sons, and gave me his daughter in marriage.
>
> If you say "come," then I shall go [to meet her]; if you say "don't come," then you Qaγan decide yourself how to send [her to me].
>
> If you let me go while I am lame, there is no question that I will not go. But if I stay home, there are no men [who can go] out, and if I go out, there are no men at home. I have met you at a time when I should not have met you.[37] Why should I not go at a time when you have [already] forgiven me? These words of mine are true. The Qaγan himself shall decide in what manner he himself shall forgive me.

A somewhat similar letter was sent to Hong Taiji by a Kharachin nobleman identified as Dügureng Güyeng, who justifies himself for not having attended the ceremony of the oath of alliance between Kharachin and Manchus.[38] Concerned that he may be marginalized in the political relationship between the two parties, he seems to imply that the reason he did not attend the ceremonies was that his wife, who was the daughter of the Khaghan of the Kharachin, was present. He invoked his status as an in-law of an important political person to justify his behaviour:[39]

> Ever since the Year of the Rabbit [1627] [we] have regularly sent each other messengers for the sake of political consultation. Because of [my waiting for] the arrival of Sečen Qaγan's messengers, I had [many] delays. The daughter of the Qaγan [of the Qaračin] is my [own] wife.[40] [Hence] I did not go to the ceremony for the oath of alliance.[41] In harmony with all [the other nobles] led by the Qaγan and Qong Tayiji [of the Qaračin], I shall not transgress Sečen Qaγan's commands. Although the messenger and the letter issued by [Sečen] Qaγan's authority reached everyone under the [Qaračin] Qaγan, Qong Tayiji, and all the high and low-ranking nobles, they did not come to me.

Second, a marriage alliance could also be used as leverage to curb the inappropriate or disruptive behaviour of an ally who needed to be kept in check. This is the case of the reprimand issued by Hong Taiji against Yeldeng, who was guilty of having pillaged people and property within his own tribe. The argument brought forward by Hong Taiji, which is quoted only partially below, makes it clear that the status of in-law had allowed Yeldeng to gain the confidence of the Manchus but that he was going to lose it if he did not reform this ways. His reference to the possibility that Yeldeng's victims might unite against him is a clear message that the Manchus would be withdrawing whatever protection they had so far provided for him. Clearly, the Manchus did not want their Mongol allies to begin fighting among themselves, and his status as a relative gave Hong Taiji the legitimacy to intervene politically in this dispute:[42]

> Initially you, who became a relative of us before any other person, behaved well ...
>
> The [Qorčin] people intend to carry on together with us and keep to their word, but if there is an enemy such as you in their own homes, how can they leave their homes and come to us? If you give back completely all and every person and head of livestock that you have seized, there will be no crime or fault. If you do not give them back, when all of them [i.e., the Qorčin chiefs] assemble and hold discussions according to the Mongol laws, we shall hold discussion together with them. Would it not be good if all of you *noyans* of the Naγun Qorčin lived happily embracing peace and law, settling where the grass and water are good, and breeding your own livestock? Would it not be bad if you acted in such a way as to destroy the political order and to stir up disorder and violence? ... If you do not stop your robberies and disorderly conduct, it would be easy for those who have

> been robbed to hold joint consultations and come to an agreement regarding you.
>
> I have openly expressed my thoughts because we have become relatives and have an alliance. You must know [what to do] reflecting by yourself. That you pillaged and seized the Jürced and the γoulčin[43] [indicates that] you were not pleased with [them] and were tormenting [them] for having come towards us and settled there. If the nobles of the right wing and you make a union with me, we will go on [war] expeditions in every direction. If Heaven shows mercy to me, these people and animals will be taken in by me. But if within a group somebody seizes the people and livestock of their own brothers, it would be very difficult to absorb [them].

Above all, a marriage alliance was a form of insurance against the worst possible outcome of steppe warfare – namely, that one's family could be wiped out entirely, with the consequent annihilation of the whole "genetic pool" of a given clan. This type of concern is made explicit in the oaths of alliance. Although the mode of expression of the oaths is formulaic and fairly standardized, such oaths refer to the importance of the preservation of progeny.[44]

In a piece of correspondence with the Naγun Khorchin probably dated between 1627 and 1628, Hong Taiji tried to persuade the chieftains to join the Manchus in a marital alliance. Here he alluded to the possibility that they might be annihilated by the Chakhar. Arguably, while Hong Taiji is overtly concerned about their survival as in-laws – and, on this account, he promises to extend his protection to them – there may be also an additional, hidden message. And that would be that the marital alliance itself would ensure the survival of at least some of their descendants should the main tribe be wiped out:[45] "In my opinion our two nations should marry each other's daughters and the marriage relationship should never be interrupted. If you were to be wiped out by the Chakhar, then with what nation would we keep marriage relations?" In-laws, in other words, could offer a way to prevent the extinction of a given lineage, an outcome not too uncommon given the ruthless wars that were current in the steppe region.

Marriages also allowed leaders to recover a common political ground after having had a falling out. In this letter written by a Khorchin leader, Erdeni Khong Tayiji (possibly Ukšan, son of Jayisang and grandson of Manggus), the in-law relationship is regarded as something that does not require the observance of normal diplomatic etiquette and, therefore, allows a special closeness, aptly described as a thrice-knotted rope:[46]

> Erdeni Qong Tayiji sent [this] letter to Hong Taiji: "I was your elder brother-in-law, you were the husband of my sister. From among the many, we were dear to each other; from among the few we were necessary [important] to

> each other. When you gave me a poor suit of armor [as a gift], did I stop sending my messengers? Why did you stop [sending] messengers saying that [I] gave [you] bad horses? But rather than sending gifts to each other, let us be united by strengthening at the utmost our own feelings. What if we came without gifts and [simply] inquired about one another's health? If we [just] considered getting good things, we would not be like relatives. People say that a robe with two layers does not feel cold, and a rope with three knots cannot be untied.

On the other hand, marriage did not provide ironclad security. The in-laws could easily become outlaws. The previously mentioned Jarut tribe, for instance, had intermarried with the Manchu royal clan in 1614, but in 1619 it broke the alliance. The betrayal and endless vexations caused by Jarut raids on Manchu-controlled land angered and exasperated Nurhaci, who continued to protest this behaviour for years. It is remarkable that, even in the midst of mounting violence, the Jarut envoys who had come to Nurhaci under the protection of a marital agreement would be given favourable treatment.[47] Eventually, when the Jarut came under attack from the Chakhar, they sought protection with the Khorchin Mongols and surrendered to the Manchus, who celebrated their submission in 1629.[48]

In the steppe world, sibling rivalry was common and was surely not limited to the struggle to succeed as khan. The famous episode of the young Temüjin (Chinggis Khan) slaying his half-brother Bekhter can be taken as a parable that conveys one of the most useful pieces of advice in steppe politics: do not trust your relatives. For a long time, Nurhaci himself had to contend with his uncles, brothers, and other relatives.[49] Likewise, Mongol chieftains would regard support from the Manchu in-laws as valuable in their own family feuds. Here are the words of a Mongol chieftain requesting Hong Taiji's support to persuade Nurhaci to protect him against his relatives – a request based on Hong Taiji's position as in-law:[50]

> If Kündülen Qaγan does not protect me mercifully, I will not have the strength to engage them in battle. Since older and younger brothers are in disagreement, and because our life is dear [to us], we shall become tributaries ... If we are not protected by you, we shall have no place to flee and no strength to fight. Do not think that there are ulterior motives in my words. Since you, Hong Taiji, are a relative of mine by marriage, I told you the truth.

Again, the word of a powerful in-law was worth something, and at times of crisis this was an asset that could mean the difference between life and death.

Resolution of hostilities and protection from enemies were not the only areas in which marital alliances were of use. Along with the ever-present obligation to right a perceived wrong, or to exact revenge for a hostile action, marriage diplomacy allowed a party to find pretexts for concocting accusations against an adversary without disclosing his or her real motives. The Manchus reacted fiercely when a marriage promise that had been made to them was broken – an act that could easily constitute a casus belli.

For instance, in the famous Seven Grievances included in Nurhaci's open declaration of war to the Ming, the fourth accusation refers to Ming intervention in Manchu territory, which – according to Nurhaci – resulted in a woman from another Jurchen tribe, who had been betrothed to him, being instead married to a Mongolian prince.[51] Another case in point is the already mentioned accusation levelled by the Manchus at their foremost ally, Tüsiyetü Khan, for having insulted his Manchu bride by placing a wife from the rival Chakhar tribe in the most honoured position.

Let us not forget, however, that the attention paid to the condition of the sisters and daughters married off to Mongol chieftains may not have been as sincere as it appears in some pronouncements. We have a document that reports the unhappiness of a Manchu princess who asks her "brother" Hong Taiji why he never writes to her:[52] "Your elder sister presents a letter to her own younger brother Sečen Qaγan. Previously, when we lived in a single home, we inquired after each other's health, and exchanged with one another our own wishes and requests. When I acquired a second home, my younger brother the Qaγan became estranged from me, and did not send any messenger to me. For this reason I sent an envoy with special instructions, wishing that you may think more of me." This rare testimony indicates that the bride's contacts with her original family had become extremely infrequent. Moreover, the situation of brides sent off to their Mongol in-laws, often as very young girls, was made more difficult by the fact that it was either hard or impossible to come back to their original families even for a short visit.[53]

Conclusion

After Nurhaci's unification of the Manchu tribes, the axis of marriage relations shifted dramatically from the Manchurian to the Mongol area. This shows the importance of the Mongol front in Manchu politics and the sustained efforts made by Nurhaci and Hong Taiji to position the Manchu royal clan favourably within the web of alliances that determined inter-Mongol relations. Through intermarriage, the Manchus fully inserted themselves into the Mongol political space, and this allowed them to take part in the power struggle triggered by Ligdan's bid for the creation of a unified Mongol regime. Both offensive and defensive marriage diplomacy expanded the manoeuvring and negotiating range of the contracting parties, ensured military protection, established a trusted diplomatic plane, and allowed the fabrication of pretexts for war as well as of opportunities for peace.

Nurhaci and Hong Taiji used in-law relations with great effectiveness to construct the skeletal structure of the Manchu-Mongol political relationship, and their policy is consistent with the politics of marital relations adopted by Nurhaci in the course of the wars to unify the various Jurchen tribes and confederations. However, the Manchu strategy towards the Mongol tribes cannot be regarded simply as an extension of the Jurchen-oriented one. Once on Mongol political turf, the Manchus had to compete with a rival force, the powerful Chakhar tribe, which was openly pursuing an analogous, if not identical, project of political centralization. While the oaths and marriage arrangements sucked the Manchus into the depths of treacherous Mongol politics, they also allowed them to subvert Ligdan's process of unification and to intervene with the Mongols from a position of higher status, which authorized the legitimate use of coercive measures in case of non-compliance.

Moreover, marital alliances helped the Manchus to co-opt Mongol political and military elites into a new "conquest elite" that, aimed explicitly at the conquest of China, promised to yield enormous returns. This prospect may not have been sufficient in itself to lure the Mongols to the Manchu side, but, at a time when Ligdan's project to forcibly unify the Mongol tribes promised only additional violence and insecurity, it made the traditional protection that marriage relations offered from the perils of steppe politics especially attractive. The wars among Mongol tribes also caused the widespread territorial displacement of individuals and families, who then had to flee their lands and seek a safer place elsewhere. In-laws could, and indeed were under an obligation to, provide refuge in case of need, and the Manchus were able to assist Mongol refugees who were otherwise entirely defenceless and devoid of the means to support themselves. From the Manchu point of view, anchoring the Mongol aristocracies to the Manchu polity was important in that it offered a way to limit the uncertainty that was implicit in the system of tribal alliances. It also offered, if needed, a ready cause for war against "in-laws" who strayed from the alliance, as a compact sealed by marriage carried a high moral burden and commanded great loyalty.

At the same time, marriage alliances were fluid and had limited currency, given that multiple marriage alliances could be made by the same person. And since mutual obligations could easily be reversed, these marital contracts were insufficient either to ensure loyalty or to force another party into submission. The incorporation of Mongol leaders – that is, powerful aristocratic families and their retainers – into the Manchu "conquest elite" required another and more complex level of coercion, which led to a layered approach that eventually comprised the introduction of legislative measures, the creation of administrative structures, and substantial changes in Mongol territorial allocation and distribution.

Military force had to be used against those Mongols who were openly hostile or repeatedly deceitful and untrustworthy. At the same time, armed intervention was of limited use since the Mongol fighters were just as good as were the Manchu fighters, making the outcome of military action uncertain and being potentially taxing for the thinly stretched Manchu forces. More important, the Manchus could not be indefinitely engaged in chronic intertribal wars lest they expend excessive time and resources trying to police Mongol political boundaries. Soon after the end of the Ligdan wars, the Manchu leadership made the restoration of order among the Mongol tribes a priority and, thus, introduced a series of laws and regulations meant, in essence, to bring the Mongols under the formal suzerainty of the Manchus and to ensure that the alliance would be transformed into an asymmetric partnership (with the Manchus being, of course, the senior partner), eventually resulting in Mongol submission.[54] The frontier policy of marriage and diplomacy was clearly essential to achieving this end, and any evaluation of the Qing conquest and, especially, of the Sino-Inner Asian frontier in the preconquest period has to consider the multifarious aspects of Manchu-Mongol relations. Indeed, this is a long-standing issue, and it is central to Manchu progress towards the formation of a power that was eventually able to challenge and to conquer China.

Notes

1 For the sake of consistency and simplicity, I use the term "Manchu" for both the Nurhaci and Hong Taiji periods, although strictly speaking this is anachronistic.

2 These issues have been discussed, most recently, in Joanna Waley-Cohen, "The New Qing History," *Radical History Review* 88 (2004): 193-206.

3 Arthur Waldron refers repeatedly to Lattimore's views in his *The Great Wall of China: From History to Myth* (Cambridge, Mass.: Cambridge University Press, 1990). Peter Perdue refers to Lattimore's theories on the origins of steppe nomads in *China Marches West* (Cambridge, MA: Harvard University Press, 2005), 30.

4 The concept of a "supra-tribal leadership" within the context of the Inner Asian monarchic tradition is partly dealt with in Joseph Fletcher, "Turco-Mongolian Monarchic tradition in the Ottoman Empire," *Harvard Ukrainian Studies* III/IV (1979-80): pt. 1, 236-51.

5 On the nomadic cycle, see Owen Lattimore, *Inner Asian Frontiers of China* (Boston: Beacon Press, 1967), 519-23. On the function of the frontier zone as the place of origin of Inner Asian dynasties, see Lattimore, *Inner Asian Frontiers of China*, 540-49.

6 Ladis K.D. Kristof, "The Nature of Frontiers and Boundaries," *Annals of the Association of American Geographers* 49, 3 (1959): 271-72.

7 Frederick Wakeman, *The Great Enterprise: The Manchu Reconstruction of Imperial Order in 17th-Century China* (Berkeley: University of California Press, 1985), 41.

8 Owen Lattimore, "Origins of the Great Wall of China: A Frontier Concept in Theory and Practice" in *Studies in Frontier History: Collected Papers, 1928-1958* (London: Oxford University Press, 1962), 114.

9 This is not to say that there were no differences in their economic products, which in fact lent themselves to different commercial uses. The Manchurian forest economy, in particular hunting and gathering, provided various items that were valued highly in the border markets (e.g., ginseng, pelts, and pearls). On the other hand, Mongolian horses and other pastoral products had long been an important item in frontier trade.

10 On the other hand, sometimes differences would be stressed, as in the communication between Nurhaci and the Jarut chiefs (See G. Kara, *Chants d'un Barde Mongol* [Budapest: Akadémiai Kiadó, 1970], 17-23, note 37). The rhetoric of cultural similarities and differences was often resorted to in order to support a particular political point.

11 Nicola Di Cosmo and Dalizhabu Bao, *Manchu-Mongol Relations on the Eve of the Qing Conquest: A Documentary History* (Leiden/Boston: Brill, 2003), 96.

12 The article by David M. Farquhar on early Manchu political concepts remains one of the few studies of this issue in English. See his "The Origins of the Manchus' Mongolian Policy," in *The Chinese World Order*, edited by John K. Fairbank, 198-205 (Cambridge, MA: Harvard University Press, 1968). On the other hand, we should stress that the similarities did not extend to some of the more specific features of Mongolian political thought, in particular the relationship established by the Mongol elites with Tibetan Buddhism and the Chinggisid principle of imperial inheritance.

13 Michael Weiers, "Die Kuang-Ning Affäre, Beginn des Zerwürfnisses zwischen den Mongolischen Tsakhar und den Mandschuren" [The Kuang-ning affair: The beginning of the hostility between Chakhar Mongols and Manchus], *Zentralasiatische Studien* 13 (1979): 73-91; Walter Heissig, *Die Zeit des letzten mongolischen Großkhans Ligdan (1604-1634)* [The time of the last Mongolian Great Khan Ligdan] (Opladen: Westdeutscher Verlag, 1979); Veronika Veit, "Die mongolischen Völkerschaften vom 15. Jahrhundert bis 1691" [The Mongolian tribes from the fifteenth century to 1691], in *Die Mongolen: Beiträge zu ihrer Geschichte und Kultur* [The Mongols: Contributions on their history and culture], edited by Michael Weiers (Darmstadt: Wissenschaftliche Buchgesellschaft, 1986), 397.

14 For instance, see Gertraude Roth li "State Building before 1644," in *The Cambridge History of China*, vol. 9.1: *The Ch'ing Dynasty to 1800*, edited by Willard J. Peterson (Cambridge: Cambridge University Press, 2002), 18; Morris Rossabi, *China and Inner Asia from 1368 to the Present* (London: Thames and Hudson, 1975), 113; Fred W. Bergholz, *The Partition of the Steppe. The Struggle of the Russians, Manchus and the Zunghar Mongols for Empire in Central Asia, 1619-1758: A Study in Power Politics* (New York: Peter Lang, 1993), 163.

15 On the military aspects of the war, see: "Military Aspects of the Manchu Wars against the Čaqars," in *Inner Asian Warfare (500-1800)*, edited by Nicola Di Cosmo, 337-67 (Leiden/Boston: Brill 2002).

16 For a detailed historical account of this period, see Dalizhabu, *Mingdai mo nan Menggu lishi yanjiu* [Studies on the history of the Southern Mongols in the Ming Dynasty] (Hailaer: Nei Menggu chubanshe, 1997), 251-335.

17 Nicola Di Cosmo, "Introduction: A Brief Survey of Manchu-Mongol Relations before the Qing Conquest," in *Manchu-Mongol Relations on the Eve of the Qing Conquest*, 8.

18 The Khalkha began to pay the tribute of the "Nine Whites" (eight white horses and a white camel) to the Manchus in 1636, with Secen Khan Šoloi; see Veronika Veit, "Die Mongolen: von der Clanföderation zur Volksrepublik" [The Mongols: From tribal confederation to people's republic], in *Die Mongolen: Beiträge zu ihrer Geschichte und Kultur* [The Mongols: Contributions to their history and culture], edited by Michael Weiers (Darmstadt: Wissenschaftliche Buchgesellschaft, 1986).

19 Wada Sei, "Some Problems Concerning the Rise of T'ai-tsu the Founder of Manchu Dynasty," *Memoirs of the Research Department of the Toyo Bunko* 16 (1957): 51-63.

20 Ray Huang, "The Liaotung Campaign of 1619," *Oriens Extremus* 28 (1981): 29-54.

21 Gertraude Roth, "The Manchu-Chinese Relationship, 1618-1636," in *From Ming to Ch'ing: Conquest, Region, and Continuity in Seventeenth-Century China*, edited by Jonathan D. Spence and John E. Wills, Jr., 1-38 (New Haven: Yale University Press, 1979).

22 On some aspects of Mongolian oaths, see Henry Serruys, "Oaths in the Qalqa Jirum," *Oriens Extremus* 19 (1972): 131-41.

23 Christopher Atwood, *Encyclopedia of Mongolia and the Mongol Empire* (New York: Facts on File, 2004), 460-61. Changes in patterns of marital alliances among the Mongol tribes may be attributed to the political and ideological changes that occurred within the "Mongol nation" at the time of Altan Khan (1507-83). According to Johan Elverskog, Altan Khan's political reform led to political fragmentation among the Mongols. See his *The Jewel*

Translucent Sūtra: Altan Khan and the Mongols in the Sixteenth Century (Leiden/Boston: Brill, 2003), 40.

24 On Nurhaci's marital alliances with Manchurian tribes, in particular the Hada and Yehe, see Wada Sei, "Some Problems Concerning the Rise of T'ai-tsu," 51-59.

25 Arthur Hummel, *Eminent Chinese of the Ch'ing Dynasty*, 2 vols. (Washington: Government Printing Office, 1943 [rpt Taipei: Ch'eng Wen, 1970]), 562.

26 For a list of marriages contracted between Mongols and Manchus, see Sechin Jagchid, "Mongolian-Manchu Intermarriange in the Ch'ing Period," *Zentralasiatische Studien* 19 (1986): 68-87.

27 Jagchid, "Mongolia-Manchu Intermarriage," 72. On Manggultai, see also Hummel, *Eminent Chinese*, 562-63.

28 Jun Matsumura, "The Queens and Royal Concubines of the Emperor Ch'ing T'ai-tsung," *Bulletin of the Institute of China Border Area Studies* 3 (1972): 55-76.

29 Wang Zhonghan, "Empress Xiao Duan Wen of the Borjigit Clan," in *Biographical Dictionary of Chinese Women: The Qing Period, 1644-1911*, edited by Lily Xiao Hong Lee, A.D. Stefanowska, and Clara Wing-Chung Ho, 336-37 (Armonk, NY: M.E. Sharpe, 1998). See also Hummel, *Eminent Chinese*, 304.

30 Di Cosmo, "Introduction: A Brief Survey," 8-9.

31 In 1636, after he surrendered to the Manchus, Erke Khonggor-eje married at the age of fourteen the Manchu Princess Makata, daughter of Hong Taiji and Empress Xiaoduan. See Hummel, *Eminent Chinese*, 304.

32 For instance, the Jarud, a south Qalqa tribe, began to plunder the Manchu people only a short while after a marriage alliance and a solemn oath had been sworn in 1614 and 1619, respectively. Nurhaci reacted fiercely to this betrayal, but there was relatively little he could do. See also Veit, "Die mongolischen Völkerschaften," 399.

33 Di Cosmo and Dalizhabu, *Manchu-Mongol Relations*, 57.

34 This "guilty wife" is one from the Chahar tribe, led by the Manchu's enemy Ligdan Khan.

35 Michael Weiers, "Der Manschu-Khortsin Bund von 1626," in *Documenta Barbarorum: Festschrift für Walter Heissig*, edited by Rudolf Kaschewsky, Klaus Sagaster, and Michael Weiers, 412-35 (Wiesbaden: Harrassowitz, 1983).

36 Di Cosmo and Dalizhabu, *Manchu-Mongol Relations*, 26-27.

37 This refers to the battle between Nurhaci's Manchurian forces and the enemy coalition of nine tribes, which took place in 1593 (twenty-first year of the Wanli emperor). This coalition also included the Qorčin Mongols headed by Mingγan. See Yan Chongnian, *Nuerhachi zhuan* [Biography of Nurhaci], Beijing: Beijing chubanshe, 1983), 103.

38 On this, see Michael Weiers, "Zum Mandschu-Kharatsin Bund des Jahres 1628" [On the Manchu-Qaračin alliance of the year 1628], *Zentralasiatische Studien* 26 (1996): 84-119.

39 Di Cosmo and Dalizhabu, *Manchu-Mongol Relations*, 125.

40 This is Donui Günji, daughter of the Qaračin Qaγan Lask'ib.

41 Literally, to the aspersion of libations.

42 Di Cosmo and Dalizhabu, *Manchu-Mongol Relations*, 101-2.

43 In Mongol, γoulčin is the Gūwalca clan of the Manchus. See *Manbun Rōtō: Tongki fuka sindaha hergen i dangse* [The secret chronicles of the Manchu Dynasty, 1607-1637 AD], edited by Nobuo Kanda, Keiji Okamoto, Hideo Ishibashi, Jun Matsumura, and Hidehiro Okada (Tokyo: Toyo Bunko, 1955-63), 1:37, 306-7; 2:900; 3:981, 1054-55, 1057-64.

44 A typical formula that concludes an oath is: "if we follow our own words sworn to Heaven and Earth, Heaven and Earth will bless us and our lives will be long, our descendants will follow us for a thousand eons and will live in peace and happiness."

45 Di Cosmo and Dalizhabu, *Manchu-Mongol Relations*, 37.

46 Ibid., 157.

47 The Manchu account of their relationship with the Jarut tribe is summarized in G. Kara, *Chants d'un Barde Mongol*, 17-23, note 37. The specific passage regarding the Jarut envoy whose life was spared because of the bridal connection can be found on page 21.

48 *Manbun Rōtō, Tongki fuka sindaha hergen i dangse*, vol. 4 (1959), 6, 129, 192.

49 Wada Sei, "Some Problems Concerning the Rise of T'ai-tsu," 41-51.

50 Di Cosmo and Dalizhabu, *Manchu-Mongol Relations*, 24.

51 On the Seven Grievances, see Meng Sen, "Qing Taizu gaotian qi da hen zhi zhenben yanjiu" in *Qingshi luncong* [Essays in Qing History] (Hong Kong: Dadong tushu gongsi, 1977), 62-76; Giovanni Stary, "La politica mancese delle 'sette accuse': Una costante per giustioficare la conquista della Cina e della Corea," in Giampiero Bellingeri and Giorgio Vercellin, eds., *Studi Eurasiatici in Onore di M. Grignaschi* [Eurasian studies in honour of M. Grignaschi] (Venezia: Libreria Universitaria Editrice, 1988), 43-55.

52 Di Cosmo and Dalizhabu, *Manchu-Mongol Relations,* 113.

53 Even later Qing regulations made it very difficult for the princesses and noblewomen married to Mongol aristocrats to come to the capital. See Sechin Jagchid, "Mongolian-Manchu Intermarriage," 80-81.

54 On this issue, see Dorothea Heuschert, "Legal Pluralism in the Qing Empire: Manchu Legislation for the Mongols," *International History Review* 20, 2 (1998): 310-24.

4
What Happens When Wang Yangming Crosses the Border?

Timothy Brook

The emperors of the Ming dynasty ruled a bounded territory. There might be occasional doubt as to where exactly the border ran in places where the terrain was rough and the state's ability to control local populations weak. But everyone understood that borders existed, and all who served the Ming understood that imperial sovereignty extended only that far and not an inch beyond. A border marked a clear break between the order that Chinese sovereignty was thought to create and the disorder that its absence must imply. Being at the edge of sovereignty, where one thing became another, borderlands were places where sovereignty was difficult to enforce, where control required more stringent enforcement than was necessary elsewhere, and where administrative operations had to permit innovations and compromises that were unacceptable in the heartland. Borderlands were troubling to rule-enforcers; they were also politically dangerous for those faced with adjusting heartland rules to conditions in the periphery. This chapter is about one instance of alleged border-crossing in a Ming borderland and the great political excitement that this allegation caused.

Wang Shouren (1472-1529), better known by his sobriquet Yangming, was not only the most innovative philosopher of the Ming dynasty but one of its leading field administrators. His experience of dealing with civil disturbance and armed revolt, notably his suppression in 1519 of the rebellion of the Prince of Ning, Zhu Chenhao (d. 1521), in Jiangxi province endowed him with a reputation as a trouble-shooter. Although being politically savvy was the key to his success in the field, it was his military genius that he was most known for. Political rivalry at court turned his accomplishments against him, however, and he was sidelined by the Zhengde emperor (r. 1506-21) for the remainder of that man's reign. The ascendancy of the Jiajing emperor (r. 1522-66) brought Wang out of retirement to serve as minister of war in Nanjing, but, in 1522, the obligation to mourn his father once again removed him from the corridors of power. He remained sidelined until June 1527, when the emperor ordered him to lead a campaign to quell a rebellion

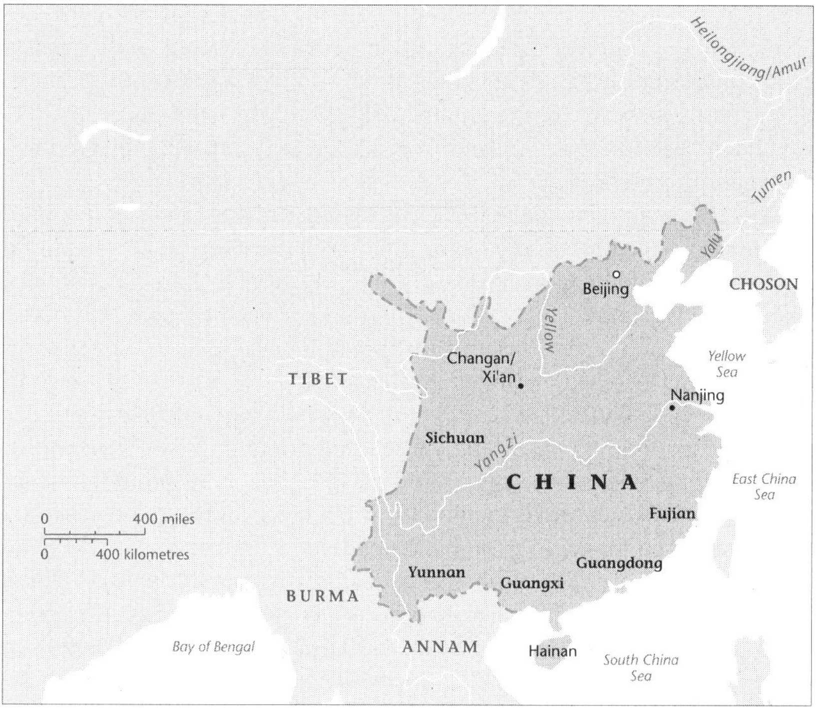

China in the Ming dynasty

in the borderlands of Guangxi province, where violence among aboriginal tribes and between aboriginals and settled agriculturalists was endemic. Reinstated as minister of war, Wang was additionally invested with the rank of left censor-in-chief; was appointed superintendent of military affairs for Guangdong, Guangxi, Jiangxi, and Huguang; and was given wide discretionary powers to bring the uprising to an end.[1]

Wang doubted his reputation as a military genius. He says as much in the memorial he sent back to the emperor, asking that he be excused from the commission to quell the southwest on the grounds that he was in poor health. Health aside, he insisted that the emperor should place his trust in the regional military leaders already on site as he himself was not the person best qualified for the job. "Your servant is only a student of books and is not skilled in military command," he insisted. "My service in years past in Jiangxi led happily to a successful outcome entirely because I happened to meet with fortunate circumstances."[2] The emperor denied his request, and so Wang had no choice but to proceed to Guangxi. There he was successful again, through the same combination of good fortune and an ability to see his assignment in relation to larger problems. After the leading insurgents, Lu Su and Wang Shou, surrendered without a fight, Wang extended his campaign to quell Yao raiders in central Guangxi and bring the entire region under state control. The pacification of Guangxi would be Wang's last great contribution to his dynasty. Too ill to wait for imperial authorization, Wang left his post and headed home, dying en route. Qing policy analysts would look back on this campaign as the last significant Ming intervention on the southern border.[3]

Wang's biography in the voluminous dynastic history gives only a brief account of the campaign and of the politics surrounding his service in the southwest.[4] While he was on the campaign, Wang came under attack from Minister of Personnel Gui E (d. 1531). Wang's biography provides a brief summary of Gui's charges, one of which was that he tried to capitalize on his success in Guangxi by using the surrendered rebel forces under this command to invade Jiaozhi (a classical term used for Vietnam, and sometimes Laos). It was a serious charge, and Wang's supporters at court were alarmed. Both Hanlin Academician Fang Xianfu (d. 1544) and Minister of Rites Huo Tao (1487-1540) submitted memorials in his defence. Fang's original memorial seems no longer to exist, but Huo's does. Huo rose to the charge by arguing: "An official may be permitted to cross the border [*chu jiang*, which might also be translated as 'proceed beyond a borderland'] when it is purely to do something that can bring peace to the *guojia* (nation) and benefit to the *sheji* [altars of soil and grain]."[5] Wang Yangming thus stood accused by one party of crossing a border without authorization and stood defended by another of doing so for a legitimate reason.

This chapter is an exegesis of Huo Tao's statement, which I have undertaken in order to answer these three questions: Why was border-crossing selected as the charge designed to ruin Wang Yangming's reputation? What was at stake in the charge? And what does this tell us about the understanding of borders and borderlands in Ming political theory and practice? To approach these questions, we need first to survey the contexts central to this story: (1) the politics at the Jiajing court, (2) the reputation and political status of Wang Yangming, and (3) the security situation in Guangxi province. That done, we can turn to the charge and the defence and, more particularly, the language of the defence, in order to assess why border-crossing was regarded as a politically vulnerable act as well as why it could be defended. None of this will reveal much about what went on in the borderland; but some of it should indicate what borders could be made to do through the process of being talked about as well as how the borderland could provide fodder for political struggles that had nothing whatsoever to do with borders.

Court Politics

Gui E's attack on Wang Yangming was part of a larger political campaign to discredit Wang at court. Wang Yangming's biographer in the *Ming shi* suggests that the person behind Gui's attack was Senior Grand Secretary Yang Yiqing (1454-1530). To judge from their prominence in the court's *Veritable Records* for 1527, Yang Yiqing and Gui E dominated the politics of the Jiajing court that year. Neither was indifferent to Wang's considerable talents nor averse to using him. Indeed, as I shall note later, it may even have been Gui who was responsible for bringing Wang back into government service. And yet, within a year of Wang's return to service, it was Gui who proposed that Wang was scheming to cross the border into Vietnam.

Yang and Gui were powerful in the 1527 court, but they did not enjoy a political monopoly. Another important group of courtiers had formed around Minister of Rites Xi Shu (1461-1527), who was a one-time political ally of Gui E. Xi was in poor health as the year dawned and would die that April, but he controlled a key ministry at the end of his life – the Ministry of Rites, where the difficult issues arising from the Jiajing emperor's succession had to get sorted out (see below). Xi was both a student and patron of Wang Yangming, and he surrounded himself with ardent supporters of Wang, among them Fang Xianfu and Huo Tao. Huo Tao, who would take over the Ministry of Rites in 1528 when Gui E was promoted to the position of grand guardian of the heir apparent, was politically most influential within this group. Another member of the group was Huang Wan (1480-1554), who moved up from Nanjing to Beijing in 1527 to assume the post of vice-minister of the Court of Imperial Entertainments and to take part in editing the *Minglun dadian* (Great precedents for clarifying morality) (again, see below). He would soon play an active role among the Huo Tao group as vice-minister of Rites.[6]

In 1528, whether to attack or support Wang Yangming became the wedge that drove a factional cleavage between the Yang/Gui group and the Fang/Huo/Huang group. Prior to this parting of ways, men on both sides of the cleavage shared a common admiration for Wang Yangming. All had been minor capital officials at the time the Jiajing emperor came to the throne in 1521, and all had come to notice and higher position by supporting the emperor in the struggle that dominated his first five years on the throne: seeking to have full posthumous imperial honours granted to his natural father. Jiajing had come to the throne as the successor of his cousin, the Zhengde emperor, and imperial convention required that he sacrifice to that cousin as though he were his father. He also wanted his mother to be elevated to the status of empress dowager. The issue divided the bureaucracy in what was known as the Great Rites Controversy.[7]

Those who supported the emperor would stay, and those who opposed him would go. All the men I have named submitted memorials within the first three years of Jiajing's reign backing his position. Their support for Jiajing placed them in conflict with senior grand secretary Yang Tinghe (1459-1529). Yang had held the senior secretaryship under Zhengde and had weathered the transition to Jiajing's reign, but he was not keen on the new emperor's demands that his father be given full imperial status. Yang encouraged the emperor to accept the precedent of investing his natural parents with the titles of imperial aunt and uncle rather than empress dowager and emperor, but Jiajing held out. Those who supported the emperor went on the attack against Yang Tinghe, among others.[8] Huo Tao had already gone on the offensive as early as 1522, declaring Yang unfit for the noble rank he might otherwise have expected to receive for his service to the throne. Others followed Huo's lead. Once Jiajing imposed his own settlement of the matter in 1524, Yang found himself completely politically outmanoeuvred and was "permitted to retire." The emperor then rewarded his supporters. Four months after Yang Tinghe's retirement, he made Gui E chancellor of the Hanlin Academy on the strength of Gui's attack on Yang.[9] Yang Yiqing, Xi Shu, Fang Xianfu, and Huang Wan also won political favour for siding against Yang Tinghe. Their joint support of the emperor reached its apogee in 1527, when the documents relating to the Great Rites Controversy were officially published as the *Minglun dadian*. When the book was issued in June 1528, Yang Yiqing, Gui E, Huo Tao, and Huang Wan were all prominently named at the beginning as its compilers. It was, however, a last gesture of unity among those who had come to power on the back of this controversy and who were now jockeying for control among themselves.

Fifteen twenty-eight would prove to be a pivotal year in the politics of the early Jiajing court. In the three or four years leading up to it, power at court had been controlled collectively by those who supported the emperor's ritual claims for his father. In 1528, when the emperor purged the last of Yang Tinghe's associates and punished all who had continued to oppose his wishes, that collective leadership collapsed. Thereafter, willingness to support the emperor's position in the Great Rites Controversy lost its salience as a base for political advancement. It also lost its capacity to ensure factional unity. What might be called the Great Rites leadership came apart, and one of the points of stress causing cracks to open was whether to support or to condemn Wang Yangming.

The Problem of Wang Yangming

Wang was a lightning rod for faction-formation in the mid-1520s for two reasons. One was his political reputation. His stature as a statesman capable of formulating comprehensive solutions to intractable problems was so great that many serving officials were offended by the political conniving that had turned his impressive defeat of the Prince of Ning into grounds for dismissal. They believed that the Zhengde court had acted shamefully and that Wang should be brought back into government service at the highest level. In a memorial in 1525, Minister of Rites Xi Shu went furthest by recommending that Wang be appointed to the Grand Secretariat. This proposal was not warmly received by the other grand secretaries, even those who recognized Wang's talents. Xi's comment that there was no one of Wang's ability currently serving at the grand secretarial or ministerial level offended other high officials as well as the emperor who had appointed them, though it is not clear that Xi intended to be quite so sweeping in his criticism.[10] The proposal opened factional rifts within the court. In the zero-sum political game played by those at the centre, an increase in Wang's reputation could only mean a decrease in theirs. Bringing the southwest under control could earn him political capital that might alter the balance of power in Beijing. Were Wang to stage a comeback and show up in Beijing as a grand secretary, Gui E and Yang Yiqing, among others, would certainly be eclipsed. They had to block this from happening.

The second reason that Wang was a lightning rod for faction formation was his intellectual posture. Although Wang himself was careful not to get entangled in the debates kicked up by the Great Rites Controversy,[11] his followers were sympathetic to Jiajing's desire to respect his filial obligations rather than to adhere to established precedents that required an emperor to place himself in ritual sequence to the previous emperor. In their view, although this is never explicitly stated, Jiajing was following his innate moral urging. This, in Wang Yangming's philosophy, was the necessary foundation for ethical action.[12] As James Geiss has noted in his history of the Jiajing era, the issue of whether to support the emperor's position was decisive in opening a split between those who accepted the authority of Song neo-Confucianism and its reverence for textual precedent, and those who believed that moral judgments had to arise from ethical promptings within the individual. Jiajing's desire to honour his father was not a self-contained constitutional issue, therefore; rather, it represented the first clear public declaration of Wang Yangming-style moral independence from narrow neo-Confucian ritual convention – and by none other than the emperor himself. Wang's innovative philosophy was thus no longer simply an academic project: it had found political footing, albeit by accident. As a result, Geiss points out, "Wang's teachings became known throughout the empire in a very short time and remained a subject of great interest and contention into the seventeenth century."[13]

Those who feared Wang's political re-emergence and disdained the subjectivist tendency of his philosophical position – a fear and a disdain that came to be held by the same people – were unwilling to allow his latest contribution to the military stability of the realm to alter the status quo within either court politics or neo-Confucian debates. Conversely, those among Wang Yangming's adherents who sought to weaken the grip on power that Yang Yiqing and Gui E were enjoying found it useful to champion their teacher as both a man of action, whose political morality placed him above all other office-holders, and as a man of wisdom whose unparalleled grasp of the essence of Confucius' teachings authorized his own actions as well as the emperor's decision. If you were not for Wang Yangming, you had to be against him.

The Problem of the Southern Borderland

Gui E charged Wang with seeking to capitalize on his military success in Guangxi by bringing the surrendered rebel forces under his personal command, crossing the southern border, and capturing Jiaozhi. The allegation that Wang was plotting to take Vietnam was consciously designed to cast the most threatening suspicion Gui could formulate, which was that Wang harboured great, possibly even dynastic, ambition. The capacity of military power to morph into political power, even in Chinese political theory, made this allegation the perennial sword of Damocles hanging over the head of every competent military commander, especially one in a borderland. A commander with his own army was vulnerable to the charge that he would go beyond the terms of his command and turn the personal loyalty of his troops into resources to remove the emperor from the throne. A commander who crossed a border without an order permitting him to do so was turning his back on the authority of his ruler. Gui did not dare voice that much on either count, given Wang's towering reputation for having served the dynasty during the troubled Zhengde reign. Yet by suggesting that Wang had overstepped his commission to the extent of crossing a border when explicit instructions to do so had not been issued, he could hint at this ambition.

There is no evidence that Wang actually crossed a border, as I shall note later, but let us set this question aside for the moment. More interesting is the charge itself, particularly as it came from someone who appears to have played a key role in getting the emperor to assign the task of quelling Guangxi to Wang in the first place. In the spring of 1527, the Ming faced heavy raiding on the northern border and endemic banditry in the south. The situation in the south was not a recent development. As Huo Tao put it in his memorial in 1528, southerners such as himself had a popular saying: "Of every ten Guangxi people, three are loyal subjects and seven are bandits." Some aboriginal tribes had been quelled in 1472, Huo noted, but those in the Eight Forts (Bazhai) region, right in the heart of Guangxi, had gone unchallenged by the Ming since the dynasty had been founded in 1368.[14] Huo uses an anatomical metaphor: the Eight Forts region is the heart of Guangdong and Guangxi, and when the heart is sick, the body – the south – is threatened.[15] A hugely expensive military campaign was undertaken in 1525-26 to deal with the problem. Victory was reported to the court in March 1527,[16] but it won barely fifty days of peace before Lu Su and Wang Shou rose against the Ming.[17] In early May, the emperor asked Gui E to submit a memorial suggesting how to resolve the situation in Guangxi.

In his review of the situation, Gui traced the troubles back to the 1440s, when aboriginal bands became sufficiently strong to assert independence from the chiefs whom the Ming had appointed, raiding other local communities and robbing travelling merchants with impunity. Gui observed that the intra-ethnic conflict among the aboriginals was worse than were their raids on Han Chinese, indicating that the problem went deeper than inadequate security around centres of population or along transportation routes. Recently the conflict had escalated to a level ten times what it had been during earlier reigns, in large part because military and civil officials were now in cahoots with the aboriginals. The solution Gui proposed was twofold: (1) dispatch a high-ranking military leader to the region to coordinate and focus the work needed to assert military control in the region and (2) establish a new system of civil administration by suspending the rule of avoidance and appointing local degree-holders to local leadership positions. Gui believed that, were these two proposals to be adopted, a comprehensive solution was feasible not just in theory but also in practice.[18]

Emperor Jiajing agreed to proceed as Gui proposed. Wang was chosen for the task, and on 9 June 1527 he was ordered to proceed to the prefectures of Sien and Tianzhou to suppress the Lu/Wang uprising.[19] It seems that Gui played a key role not just in having a new campaign mounted but also in getting Wang Yangming assigned to the job. No actual proposal naming Wang appears in the *Veritable Records* in the months prior to 9 June, but Gui's role is confirmed in a later entry for 19 July. This is the date upon which the emperor answered a memorial from Gui E, in which Gui pointed out the pressing dangers on the Ming's northern and southern borders and proposed that Wang Qiong (1459-1532) and Wang Yangming, respectively, be sent to deal with them.[20] The emperor notes in his reply that day that he had acted on the second part of the suggestion six weeks earlier.[21] If Gui E was indeed pivotal in bringing back Wang Yangming, it makes his later allegations all the more interesting.[22]

Wang Yangming's initial assessment of the Guangxi problem in his first full memorial to Jiajing, dated 23 December 1528, was similar to Gui's. He regarded Lu Su and Wang Shou as symptoms of deeper problems. The difficulty was not loss of military control but inadequate regional administration. The only hope for restabilizing the region was to introduce a comprehensive program linking local administrators to a larger network of civil, not military, control, of which the base consisted of the aboriginal chieftains (*tuguan*) upon whom the Ming had always relied, not officials sent in from outside. It would be much better to empower local leaders; doing otherwise meant that the state would have to bear the enormous military costs needed to keep the latter in place. In the course of explaining the capacity of aboriginals in the region to escape state control, Wang mentions in passing that Tianzhou prefecture "closely neighbours on Jiaozhi" and that locals were able to move unhindered through the region. The control needed to prevent this promiscuous mobility could only be imposed by local chieftains. "Were local [appointments] to be changed to rotating [appointments] (*gai tu wei liu*), the trouble in the borderland would only be cause for regret in the future."[23] The borderland needed reorganization, but it should not be hastily assimilated to the heartland model of appointing officials from the outside, as Wang's predecessors in Guangxi had tried to do.[24]

Soon after arriving in Guangxi, Wang proved the first part of his argument by negotiating with Lu Su and Wang Shou to bring their forces over to the dynasty's side.[25] Presumably Wang's reputation as a military genius preceded him as the matter was settled in a few short weeks without any battle. He then proceeded to operationalize the second stage of his analysis by mounting a larger campaign against the regional Yao insurgency in Liuzhou prefecture, which stretched from the Eight Forts on its west side, where it bordered with Sien prefecture, to Broken Rattan Gorge (*Duantengxia*) on its east side.[26] To underline the manageability of this project, he made the dramatic gesture of sending the soldiers who had been transferred from Huguang province for the original campaign back to their home province. In their place he used the 70,000 soldiers whom Lu Su and Wang Shou had turned over to the Ming. Using surrendered troops to attack other enemies was a time-honoured Chinese military expedient. It also promised to greatly reduce the costs of the campaign. But it could raise the question as to whether Wang had the authority to command an army that had not existed at the time he was given his command. His decision to suppress the Yao in Liuzhou also left him open to the charge that he was deploying his new force in an area for which he had not been given jurisdiction, thus enlarging his campaign beyond the terms of his appointment, which was restricted to Sien and Tianzhou prefectures.

Before these questions could boil up into a full-scale controversy, Wang was able to successfully conclude his campaign against the Yao.[27] He followed it up almost immediately by laying out a comprehensive overhaul of civil institutions following the model he had pioneered in rural Jiangxi a decade earlier: the formation of community compacts, the investiture of local elders, the revival of community rites, the promotion of schools, and the organizing of militia, among other programs.[28] It was, even by his competitors' accounts, a complete success. The problem of the southern borderland had been solved, at least for the time being.

The Crime of Border-Crossing

The comment that Wang made in his 23 December 1527 memorial – that aboriginal rebels in Tianzhou had moved down across the border into neighbouring Jiaozhi – appears to have been merely one item of information added to supply the larger picture rather than a telling detail.[29] In fact, Tianzhou and Vietnam did not share a border. Guangxi's border with Vietnam was over 100 kilometres further southwest, with half a dozen small prefectural and subprefectural jurisdictions lying between it and Tianzhou. The identification of Tianzhou as a border prefecture was apparently not to be taken literally: it simply highlighted the peripherality of the prefecture. There is no evidence that Wang crossed the Ming-Jiaozhi border, nor is there any evidence that his soldiers did. Indeed, the bulk of Wang's second-stage operations against the Yao were up in Liuzhou prefecture – to the *east* of Sien and Tianzhou (i.e., even further away from the border). Gui's charge that Wang intended to invade Vietnam thus seems to have been taken from a passing comment in his memorial rather than being a response to what he was actually reporting from the field.

The Ming Code is explicit on the matter of crossing national borders. The fourth chapter construes departure from one's home county as evasion of the service levy; the official compendium of substatutes of 1500 extends this article to include crossing a frontier border.[30] The fifteenth chapter, in the section on laws governing the military, specifies that neither soldiers nor military supplies are to be taken across a border, strangulation being the penalty for doing so. The stated reason for this rule was to prevent military supplies from being sold to an enemy, though the standard commentary goes on to declare that, even if the purpose of crossing a border was only to hunt or cut wood, these too must be judged as infractions.[31] The code's logic of closed borders is basically fiscal: crossing one implies a loss to state revenue or property. A military commander who crossed a border without explicit authorization, however, was committing a potentially more serious offence since the border marked the extent of the space within which the emperor enjoyed sovereignty. To step beyond it was to step outside that sovereignty. This seems to be what Gui E's charge of crossing into Vietnam was meant to imply. Entering Vietnam was not the issue: leaving the Ming was.

Gui E filed his charge well after his memorial in mid-May advising the emperor to give Wang a free hand to appoint either chieftains or graded officials as he deemed necessary. I suspect that it also postdates the clumsy attempt by an officer of the Embroidered Guard at the beginning of July to impeach Wang for having bribed his way back into office – a charge that the emperor had the good sense to dismiss as groundless.[32] The officer had probably been put up to this by his superiors. Huo Tao's defence of Wang appears in the *Veritable Records* on 6 December 1528.[33] Huo had no way of determining whether Wang had crossed a border, but he decided to play it safe and float an argument that accepted that he had, and that his border-crossing had been justified. Curiously, he makes no reference to Jiaozhi; rather, he enunciates the principle that "an official may be permitted to cross the border" in relation to a different charge – that Wang had overstepped his commission by extending his campaign beyond Sien and Tianzhou when he went into the Eight Forts and Broken Rattan Gorge regions (i.e., by crossing a prefectural, not a national, border).

To support his argument, Huo recounts a story from the Han dynasty. In 154 BC the principalities of Wu and Chu started a rebellion by attacking the principality of Liang. Emperor Jing ordered Zhou Yafu to go to Liang's defence. Huo says that Zhou ignored the literal order to proceed to Liang and instead went behind Wu and Chu to cut their supply lines. The result was the decisive defeat of Wu and Chu, the pacification of seven principalities, and the resecuring of the Han dynasty. Even though Zhou went against the emperor's directive, he was rewarded rather than criminalized.[34] The emperor recognized that Zhou acted on a higher principle and, therefore, should not be judged as having committed a treasonable act. "The way of the ancients" (*gu zhi dao*), which Huo cites from the *Zuozhuan*, was to leave domestic affairs (*nie yinei*, "that which is within the threshold") to the emperor and external affairs (*nie yiwai*, "that which is outside the threshold") to his generals. This was the sensible course for a trusted commander in the field to take.

The story sets out for Emperor Jiajing the precedent he should follow in judging this case by declaring that Wang had the right to make his own decisions in the field. But it is a muddy judgment because it points to many things at once. First of all, the order Zhou Yafu ignored had not restricted him to act within certain borders (the emperor had earlier given him carte blanche to do what he needed to do to cut supply lines). In the way Huo Tao presents it, however, Zhou went where he was not authorized to go in order to achieve victory for the emperor, though there is nothing about transgressing borders in the original story. Following it up with the adage about the emperor leaving what lies beyond the threshold to his generals is similarly ambiguous. Narrowly interpreted, it means that the emperor should not interfere in the command of ongoing military operations, but the explicit spatial reference manages to invoke the notion of the realm's periphery, its border, which lay at the point at which *nei* becomes *wai*. From this statement, Hou then segues to his assertion that a general in a borderland should be free to *chu jiang*, "cross the border." Up to this point, though, Huo has not given any example of crossing a border. He thus uses a story that is not explicitly about crossing borders to defend the concept of border-crossing. Why?

The implicit analogue for Wang's willingness to cross borders in the Ming would seem to be Zhou's indifference to interprincipality borders in the Han. The problem here, at least in terms of making sense of a Chinese political theory of borders, is that internal borders in the Han have no exact counterpart in the Ming. Was the issue that Wang went across the Sien border into Liuzhou, another prefecture? The analogy seems inapt, for the borders between Ming prefectures were much "lower" than were those between Han fiefdoms. On the other hand, the border between Guangxi and Vietnam was much "higher" than the border of a Han fiefdom. It is hard to think that Huo would have regarded Liang's position within the Han Empire as being the same as the Ming's position within the larger world – and yet that could be what his rhetoric was designed to imply.

If there seems to be ambiguity in Huo's declaration that "an official may be permitted to cross the border," that ambiguity was intentional. He was trying to formulate an evasive answer to a question that he did not want asked. That question – should a field commander be permitted to cross a border at will? – was an awkward one, given the legal restrictions on cross-border movement. Making it explicit could only go against the man he was trying to defend. Instead, he had to cast around for a higher principle that could acceptably trump such restrictions and then press the particularities of the case onto metaphorical ground so that the original charge would get overridden. The analogy to the Han dynasty did double duty, covering both overstepping marching orders and overstepping a border. Huo was not trying to get the emperor to accept a pan-China theory of borders that treated the Guangxi-Jiaozhi border as analogous to the Liang-Wu border; rather, he was interested in persuading the emperor to "lower" the Guangxi-Jiaozhi border, at least long enough to let Wang Yangming back across.

The Borders of the *Guojia* and the *Sheji*

Thus far we have concentrated on the front end of Huo Tao's declaration that border-crossing is defensible. Now we need to look more closely at how he phrases the back end: peace and security (*an*) for the guojia and benefits or advantage (*li*) for the sheji. Both terms are abstract concepts, slippery with connotations but well-weighted with an abundance of real-world correlatives.

Guojia may be said to describe the space coterminous with the sovereignty of the emperor (i.e., the national realm), although it could also be used to name the imperial line and even the emperor himself (i.e., the dynasty). The invocation works either way, depending on context. Both might apply here, for Wang Yangming acted to bring security to the dynasty and peace to the realm. Sheji, the altars to the spirits of soil and grain, is a more emotive piece of rhetoric, something to conjure with – neither the nation nor the dynasty but their spiritual vehicle or counterpart. Huo's decision to juxtapose guojia with sheji suggests that he wanted to evoke the sacred character of the dynasty and yet gesture towards something broader. Indeed, he had primed the emperor to respond in this fashion to the concept of sheji by using it to conclude the story from the Han dynasty of Zhou Yafu. Zhou's unauthorized actions, Huo declares in language he does *not* borrow from a Han source, brought *an* [peace/security] to the sheji of the

Han dynasty. To secure the continuing survival of a dynasty was the highest contribution an official could make to his ruler. There was nothing stronger that Huo could say in praise of Zhou Yafu.

Sheji was not just an abstraction in the Ming as every county had such an altar, where the magistrate was required to regularly perform sacrifices to alleviate local troubles or to sustain good fortune. Beijing, too, had its sheji altar, to which the emperor sent officials to pray in troubled times.[35] Prayers in times of natural disaster were particularly apposite, given that Chinese political theory read natural disasters as the worst of omens: that heaven was sending signs of changing the mandate to rule. The purpose of imperial prayers to the spirits of the soil and grain was not simply to ask that the realm survive into another year. Pacify the spirits, and the dynasty should continue for ever. Of more immediate concern to Jiajing in his first decade of rule was the role of the altar as the place where the ritual designation of empresses, heirs, and ancestors had to be carried out.[36] Huo's invocation of sheji and guojia together may seem innocuous, yet I suspect that it had a more specific referent. If Wang's bold actions could be described in terms of securing peace and benefits for the guojia/sheji, then his success could be taken as evidence that these spirits approved of Jiajing's rulership and, more particularly, of his judgment that full sacrificial rites were owed to his natural father and full dowager status to his natural mother. In other words, Huo Tao was implying that Wang's efforts not only pacified Guangxi but also confirmed the legitimacy of the emperor's ritual decisions.

It was a brilliant rhetorical move. By defending Wang Yangming in terms of guojia and sheji, Huo was mobilizing key constitutional language in Ming political theory. Gui could not now decouple Wang from this rhetoric, lest he risk casting doubt on Jiajing's position on the question of succession rites. It was always difficult to argue against the spirits, as anyone who invoked these terms understood.[37] In Wang's case, service to the state's security in Guangxi was also service to the emperor's ritual decisions in Beijing. It had nothing to do with crossing, or not crossing, the southern border and everything to do with assuring Jiajing of his right to determine imperial ritual. It could also protect Wang Yangming from his enemies.

Soft Concepts, Hard Boundaries

The accusation that Wang Yangming had crossed a border should not be taken as an instance of what happens when someone crossed a border in the Ming, since Wang did not; rather, it suggests what borders could be made to do in Chinese political theory. The immediate context of the accusation was the politics of the early Jiajing court, but context was everything. Those at court who feared Wang as a competitor for power could have invoked any number of other motifs that Chinese political theory made available to political discourse. They did not just happen to choose the matter of borders. Those who feared Wang's comeback needed something big enough to convince the emperor that Wang was a threat to his security. There was little, other than outright rebellion, with which someone this able and this senior could be charged. A crossed border would do.

Was Gui E's suggestion that Wang be moved down to a borderland a case of brilliant political strategy? Probably not. Wang, after all, was the best man for the job. Once he was there, however, Gui had him in a political periphery where he was vulnerable, especially should he turn out to be successful. What was important was not what Wang did in the borderland but, rather, what he could be imagined to be doing – that is, plotting with the rebels who populated borderlands, or even with the foreigners who inhabited the territory on the other side of the border, to take authority into his own hands. In that sense, a borderland was not just a liminal space: it was a politically dangerous space where any sign of loss of sovereignty or control could be taken as evidence that the existing political order was under threat and as proof that treason was brewing.

The theory of borders that this episode points to is a simple one: Ming Chinese had a clear understanding that a border was a hard break on the field of sovereignty. This is a notion more usually associated with the modern nation-state and its obsession with mapping, closing, and patrolling its outer edges. The border of the Ming emperor's realm was no different. It showed where sovereignty ended, not where something as vague and culturally comforting as civilizational influence continued to radiate its fading light. Despite the language of culture into which it might be braided, a border was a political, not a cultural, concept. Those who lived along the border, and who crossed it at will, may have imagined borders differently; but those at the centre knew that one step over the territorial limit of legitimate action was all that was needed to end a career, even Wang Yangming's.

Notes

1 The circumstances of Wang's return to power and his campaign are surveyed in Chang Yü-chüan, *Wang Shou-jen as a Statesman* (Peking: Chinese Social and Political Science Association, 1940), 52-67. The campaign is also examined in Leo Shin, *The Making of the Chinese State: Ethnicity and Expansion on the Ming Borderlands* (Cambridge: Cambridge University Press, 2006), 96-97.

2 Wang Shouren, "Ci mian zhongren qien yangbing shu" (1527, 6th month), *Wang Yangming quanji* [The complete works of Wang Yangming] (Shanghai: Shanghai guji chubanshe, 1992), 461; a summary is entered on 16 August in *Shizong shilu* [Veritable records of the Jiajing reign], 78.7a-b; a portion is translated in Chang, *Wang Shou-jen as a Statesman*, 53.

3 Zhao Yi's appreciation of Wang's success in imposing stability on the southern borderland without installing a vast standing army is noted in Alexander Woodside, "The Ch'ien-lung Reign," in *The Cambridge History of China*, vol. 9, edited by Willard Peterson (Cambridge: Cambridge University Press, 2002), 275. The success was temporary, however.

4 *Ming shi* [Dynastic history of the Ming] (Beijing: Zhonghua shuju, 1975), 195: 5166-68.

5 "Fu daifu chu jiang, you keyi an guojia, li sheji, zhuan zhi ke ye," *Ming shi*, 5167. Huo Tao's original memorial, entitled "Wei Xinjian bo song Liangguang gongshi shu" [Memorial defending Wang Yangming's record of accomplishments in Guangdong and Guangxi], is reproduced in *Ming jingshi wenbian* [Compendium of statecraft documents of the Ming], edited by Chen Zilong, 186.16b-23a (Beijing: Zhonghua shuju, 1980s [reprint]). Portions of this memorial are translated in Chang, *Wang Shou-jen as a Statesman*, 63-65. The *Veritable Records* lists Fang Xianfu as the co-author of this memorial (*Shizong shilu*, 94.14a), but the full text appears under Huo's name alone in *Ming jingshi wenbian*. For Fang's defence of Wang on another matter, see *Shizong shilu*, 80.12a.

6 In September 1527, Huang Wan argued that once Wang's assignment in Guangxi was completed, his defeat of the Prince of Ning should be re-evaluated along with Yang Yiqing's role in the matter; *Shizong shilu*, 79.5a-b.

7 The controversy is examined in Carney Fisher, *The Chosen One: Succession and Adoption in the Court of Ming Shizong* (Sydney: Allen and Unwin, 1990). On the roles of Gui E, Xi Shu, Fang Xianfu, Huo Tao, and Huang Wan in this dispute, see 72-80.

8 See, for example, Wang Bangqi's attack on Yang in *Shizong shilu*, 73.1b-2b (1527, 2nd month).

9 Chou Tao-chi, "Kuei O," in *Dictonary of Ming Biography*, edited by L. Carrington Goodrich and Chao-ying Fang (New York: Columbia University Press, 1976), 756; see also Chou's biography of Yang Yiqing, "Yang I-ch'ing," 1518.

10 Chou Tao-chi, "Hsi Shu," *Dictionary of Ming Biography*, (524. On Xi Shu's early association with Wang Yangming, see Wei-ming Tu, *Neo-Confucian Thought in Action: Wang Yang-ming's Youth (1472-1509)* (Berkeley: University of California Press, 1976), 147-48.

11 Wang never expressed a direct opinion on the subject, but he was sympathetic to Jiajing's position. See Fisher, *The Chosen One*, 163-67. He seems to be showing his hand in his third detailed memorial from Guangxi, in which he praises Jiajing as "the emperor who promotes perfect filial piety to rule the realm." See *Wang Yangming quanji*, 470. See also *Shizong shilu*, 88.2b, 4b.

12 On Wang's philosophy, see Wei-ming Tu, *Wang Yangming*.

13 James Geiss, "The Chia-ching Reign, 1522-1566," in *The Cambridge History of China*, vol. 7, edited by Frederick Mote and Denis Twitchett (Cambridge: Cambridge University Press, 1988), 450. Despite Geiss' sensitivity to the politics of the late 1520s, neither the campaign in Guangxi nor the struggle over Wang's reputation draws his attention. Oddly, volume 8 of *The Cambridge History of China* is equally silent on the campaign.

14 The Eight Forts were Siji, Zhouan, Gumao, Guteng, Gubo, Duzhe, Luomo, and Chating. In his memorial introducing the *Yudi tu* atlas to the emperor, Gui E explains in the section on Guangxi that the Eight Forts region lies within the prefectural boundaries of Liuzhou, which was contiguous with the east side of Sien prefecture, and that "it is known as a bandit zone." See his "Jin *yudi tu* shu" [Memorial presenting the *Atlas of the territories of Yu*], reprinted in *Ming jingshi wenbian*, 182.13b. See also Chang, *Wang Shou-jen as a Statesman*, 90-91.

15 Huo Tao, "Wei Xinjian bo song Liangguang gongshi shu," 186.18a (see note 5 above).

16 *Shizong shilu*, 73.3b.

17 The comment about fifty days comes from Huo Tao's memorial, 186.17a. The uprising of Lu Su and Wang Shou is first mentioned in *Shizong shilu*, 74.6a (see note 5).

18 Gui's memorial, "Lun Guangxi Tong Man shiyi shu" [Memorial on arrangements for dealing with the aborigines of Guangxi], *Ming jingshi wenbian*, 181.18a-20b. Gui suggested that the appointment of local degree-holders be handled within his ministry, the Ministry of Personnel, on a three-year trial basis.

19 *Shizong shilu*, 76.6a. Tianzhou was a prefecture until August 1528, when it was demoted to the status of subprefecture; it was made an independent subprefecture in November 1529. See *Ming shi*, 1164. The uprising in Tianzhou is described in Shin, *The Making of the Chinese State*, 86-88. Ch. 3.

20 *Shizong shilu*, 77.6b.

21 The emperor's delay in responding to the first part seems to have occurred because rehabilitating the exiled Wang Qiong was a more difficult problem than was clearing Wang Yangming for service. Wang Qiong had played a key role in the suppression of the Prince of

Ning and, as a result, like Wang Yangming, found himself in political disfavour at court. Unlike Wang Yangming, he was not just sidelined by Yang Tinghe when the Jiajing emperor came to power but, rather, was exiled to Shaanxi. Gui E's proposal to bring him back was yet another move on the part of the Great Rites clique to bring eminent opponents of Yang Tinghe back to office (though under their patronage). See Benjamin Wallacker, "Wang Ch'iung," *Dictionary of Ming Biography*, 1367-68.

22 Equally interesting is Gui E's posthumous dismissal of Wang's thought and conduct, cited in Tu, *Neo-Confucian Thought in Action*, 6.

23 *Wang Yangming quanji*, 465-66 (12th month, 1st day). The quoted passage appears verbatim in *Ming shi*, 5166.

24 Wang reiterates the importance of using local chieftains again and again in his Guangxi memorials (e.g., *Wang Yangming quanji*, 472, 477, 480-86, 495, 497). Contemporaries were pitching the same argument elsewhere in the southwest. For example, Hu Shining, who in April 1529 argued against installing appointed officials in areas of eastern Sichuan except where local chieftains were doing a conspicuously bad job. The Jiajing emperor agreed, and ordered that an edict go out to all local chieftains in Sichuan and Guizhou confirming their status so long as they maintained local order. See *Shizong shilu*, 96.6a-7a.

25 Wang's report of victory, dated 4 March 1528 (2nd month,13th day), appears in the *Veritable Records* on 29 May (5th month, 12th day). See *Shizong shilu*, 88.2b.

26 The history of the Rattan Gorge region, renamed Broken Rattan Gorge after the Ming conquered it in 1466, is provided in Leo Shin, *The Making of the Chinese State*, 117-22.

27 Wang's report of victory over the Eight Forts and Broken Rattan Gorge, dated 25 July 1528 (7th month, 10th day), appears in the *Veritable Records* on 1 December (10th intercalary month, 20th day). See *Shizong shilu*, 94.21a.

28 These proposals are outlined in a series of documents in *Wang Yangming quanji*, 626-55. These documents are significant for being the last administrative writings Wang would compose, yet they have received no attention from Yangming scholars.

29 Wang's point was to stress the impact of the close border on his suppression efforts. In another memorial two and a half months later, he rephrases Tianzhou's propinquity to Jiaozhi in terms of its "defending externally against Jiaozhi" (*Wang Yangming quanji*, 472).

30 *Da Ming lü* [The Ming Code], edited by Huai Xiaofeng (Beijing: Falü chubanshe, 1999), 49, 370, citing, *Wenxing tiaoli* [Substatutes on punishments]. One of the precedents for the substatute may have been the Hongwu emperor's ban on soldiers or civilians crossing the western border of Sichuan to trade; *Taizu shilu* [Veritable records of the Hongwu reign], 106.1a.

31 *Da Ming lü*, 119-20, 399.

32 *Shizong shilu*, 87.9a, 90.12a.

33 Ibid., 94.13b-15a.

34 *Ming jingshi wenbian*, 186.20a. On Zhou Yafu, see Sima Qian, *Shi ji* [Records of the historian] (Beijing: Zhonghua shuju, 1973), 2073 80. Sima Qian's version of the story says that Zhou already had the emperor's explicit permission to cut the Wu and Chu supply lines. The order he did not follow was the one calling on him to abandon his position and move into Liang when the prince of Liang begged for protection from Wu; by ignoring this order and remaining where he was, Zhou was able to cut the supply line that resulted in the defeat of both Wu and Chu, 2076.

35 For example, *Xiaozong shilu* [Veritable records of the Hongzhi reign], 160.5a.

36 None other than Gui E was involved in the designation of the empress at the *sheji* altar at the end of 1528. See *Shizong shilu*, 95.3b.

37 Officials later in the century more often used these terms to object to imperial innovation than to support it. For instance, the phrase "the root of the *guo*" (*guoben*, with "guojia" shortened for euphony to "guo") was used to remind emperors that they were not free to alter ritual precedents whenever they liked. Xia Yan uses this expression in 1534 to challenge Jiajing's request to change rites for a female relative (*Shizong shilu*, 180.5b). In 1586, when the Wanli emperor was refusing to follow precedent in selecting his heir apparent, an official argued that only the eldest son of the empress could be so named, since "rectifying names and fixing status is how the root of the *guo* is made right" (*Shenzong shilu* [Veritable

records of the Wanli reign], 171.5b). Seven years later, a lightning storm over the dynastic founder's tomb in Nanjing was the occasion for an official to prod the Wanli emperor on his failure to appoint the proper heir by speaking again of "the root (*ben*) of the guojia": "When the prince establishes (literally, "plants") the guo, this may be compared to planting a tree. A tree's branches and leaves may be luxuriant, yet if its core is hollow, it will burn; a guo's cultural and material achievements (*wenwu*) may be impressive, yet if its root wobbles, it will sicken. What is important is the root provided by the spirits of soil and grain (sheji)" (*Shenzong shilu* [Veritable records of the Wanli reign], 260.4a-b). By ignoring what the sheji spirits would accept as ritually proper, Wanli was undermining the stability of the dynasty. This distinction implies that the vitality of the dynasty depended not on the acts of the ruler but on the legitimacy of his emperorship, and so implicitly separates the monarch from his own person, even the country from the dynasty (though no Ming statesmen would have phrased it quite this way).

5
Ming China and Its Border with Annam

Leo K. Shin

Some time during the Chenghua reign (1465-87) of the Ming dynasty, a young man named Wu Rui was on his way from Hainan Island to the Chinese mainland when his boat was blown terribly off course. Found adrift near the shore of Annam (present-day northern Vietnam),[1] Wu Rui and his twelve companions were promptly captured by the coastal patrol and brought to the Annamese capital at Thang Long (now Hanoi). For their alleged transgression, Wu's fellow travellers were sentenced to set up agrarian colonies, while Wu Rui himself was ordered to be castrated. How Wu survived his years in the Annamese palace we can only guess, but his service was evidently deemed valuable. After the death of the king of Annam in 1497, Wu Rui was even offered a chance to serve as a military superintendent in the northern region. But just as he was finally in a position of power, Wu learned from one of his soldiers a way back to China. Determined to return home, Wu Rui trekked for nine days, often through mountainous terrain, and arrived in the native domain (*tu si*) of Long Zhou in the southern province of Guangxi. But Wu's ordeals would not end just yet. While Wu Rui was eager to make contact with Ming officials, Wei Chen, the native chief who had offered Wu shelter, was scheming to trade him back to Annam. Fortunately for Wu Rui, before Wei had a chance to strike a deal with the agents sent by the Annamese court, a chieftain from a nearby domain decided to seize Wu and turn him over to the local authorities. As a result, Wei Chen was ordered to be punished, and Wu Rui was brought to the Ming capital at Beijing where he was given a post in one of the eunuch offices in the palace.[2]

This intriguing if somewhat cryptic account found in the *Veritable Records of the Ming* (*Ming shi lu*) – the most important official record of the period we are concerned with – certainly raises more questions than it answers. What, for instance, prompted Wu Rui and his fellow Hainan natives to cross the south China strait? Did they indeed intend, as Wu claimed, to travel to Qin Zhou at the western end of the province of Guangdong to engage in regular trade? Or were they in fact involved, as in the cases of many who lived along China's southern coast, in prohibited dealings with foreign countries? How typical, or atypical, was Wu Rui's experience? Most mainland-bound travellers from Hainan, one suspects, would not consider the risk of being castrated as high (otherwise, most would probably stay home). But just as clearly, Wu and his companions were not the only ones who had ever been caught on the wrong side of the drift. To cite one example, not long before Wu Rui was captured by the Annamese patrol, according to another report in the *Veritable Records*, more than a hundred men from China who were suspected of having engaged in illicit trade had also been detained by Annam. Apart from questions related directly to Wu's ordeals, what types of strategic information was Wu Rui able to pass on to the Ming and how valuable were they? No doubt, it had been the practice of both the Ming and Annamese courts to dispatch agents to spy on each other. But how intensive were such cross-border activities? And how had such efforts shaped the relationships between the two states?[3]

For the purpose of this chapter, the most interesting set of questions raised by the experience of Wu Rui has to do with both the idea and the reality of the border. As it is well recognized, borders are almost never natural but, rather, are "constructed" in the broadest sense of the word. In northern China, as Arthur Waldron has demonstrated, even as seemingly timeless and permanent an edifice of border division as the Great Wall was, as it turned out, largely a product of political compromises of the fifteenth and sixteenth centuries. But if the construction of the northern border must be understood within the broader contexts of Ming-Mongol relations as well as of the internal dynamics of the Ming polity, how should one begin to tell the story of the making of China's southern boundary? This chapter does not attempt to offer a comprehensive answer; what it does attempt to do is to explain how Ming rulers and their agents defined and defended a particular southern border. To be sure, the boundary between China and Annam was never as serious a military concern for the Ming court as was that between the centralizing state and the Mongols. But though the border between China and Annam would continue to be permeable (in the early fifteenth century, the Ming sought but failed to colonize the southern kingdom), over time, as we will see, Ming emperors and their officials did try hard to demarcate China's southern boundary.[4]

Imagining the Border

Even though, almost right from the start, the Ming court had recognized Annam as a self-governing kingdom, Ming rulers did not at first appear to be especially concerned about demarcating and defending China's southern border. This neglect is not surprising for at least three reasons. First, although the Ming forces had managed to bring down the Yuan dynasty and beat the Mongol remnants back to the steppes, early Ming rulers such as the Hongwu (r. 1368-98) and Yongle (r. 1403-24) emperors were clearly far more concerned about the continual military threats from the north than about the potential troubles in the south. Second, even though Ming authorities would eventually extend to the southern border region their administrative and military apparatuses, given the inherent limits of the centralizing state, it actually took the Ming court some time before it could establish a semblance of order in its southern provinces. Third, in border areas where the Ming authorities were unable or unwilling to assert direct control, Ming rulers would come to rely on native domains – and the chieftains who ruled them – to maintain order. Not only would the Ming authorities increasingly depend on such *tu si* to provide soldiers for its military campaigns, but it would also come to regard such native domains as buffers between the centralizing state and its neighbouring kingdoms.[5]

To begin to understand how early Ming rulers conceived the southern border, let us consider the case of Siming and its territorial disputes with Annam. As was true for the institution of native chieftaincy in general, relations between the centralizing state and the Siming domain had, from the start, been founded on mutual benefits. In exchange for a degree of order in China's border regions, Ming emperors were willing to continue the Yuan dynasty practices of offering native chieftains official titles and letting them rule their domains with relative autonomy. The arrangement of native chieftaincy was no doubt a double-edged sword. When Huang Guangping (d. 1393), the teenage chieftain of Siming in southwest Guangxi (just across from Annam), was accused by Ming officials in 1392 of having first ordered and then covered up the killing of another chieftain, apparently the most the Hongwu emperor could do was to grant the young chief a pardon. Meanwhile, the institution of chieftaincy did allow Ming rulers to buffer themselves from the immediate problems of border control. As we will see, the Ming court would still be called upon to resolve disputes, but early Ming emperors were clearly willing to let native chieftains handle the task of defending the southern border.[6]

The case of Siming is interesting, in part, because it helps us understand what early Ming rulers and their agents saw as the major sources of tension in the southern border region. Consider the 1396 memorial submitted by the chieftain Huang Guangcheng (d. 1413), brother of Guangping, concerning the latest territorial disputes between Siming and Annam. Here, two main problems are laid out. The first and more immediate one, said the chieftain, had to do with the practice of the people of Annam to encroach on areas once under the control of Siming. In particular, by seizing control of the counties of Qiuwen, Ruao, Qingyuan, Yuan, and Tuo (all located in present-day northern Vietnam), not only had the people of Annam brought terror to Siming, but they had also deprived the Ming court of its tax revenues. The second and more general problem, according to Huang Guangcheng, had to do with the propensity of the people of Annam to disregard the boundary between China and the southern kingdom. To be sure, few people in the Ming period could actually say for certain where the "bronze pillar" that had long been thought to mark China's southern border had once lain. But if the physical pillar allegedly erected by the Han dynasty general Ma Yuan (14 BCE-49) could no longer be found, according to Huang, the people of Annam should still observe the boundary that had long been established in the southern region.[7]

The case of Siming is also interesting because it shows how Ming and Annamese rulers had rather distinct views about where the border between the two countries should lie. Despite his reluctance to intervene, by the winter of 1396-97, the Hongwu emperor did decide that it would be useful to dispatch two envoys – Chen Cheng (*jin shi* 1394) and Lü Rang (*jin shi* 1391) – to the southern kingdom to order its ruler to return the disputed territory to the Siming domain. The embassy would produce no concrete results, but the correspondence between Chen Cheng and the king of Annam (who was then in fact dominated by the regent Le Quy Ly) does offer us a glimpse of how each side approached the problem of border demarcation. From the Ming perspective, the basis for arbitration should be the vast corpus of Chinese historical records. According to Chen Cheng, not only was it evident that as early as the Han dynasty the general Ma Yuan had marked the southern border of China by erecting a bronze pillar, but it was also apparent that, over the course of the Tang, Song, and Yuan periods, the territory that would come under dispute had already been incorporated into the centralizing state. From the point of view of Annam, however, the basis for determination should not be the inconsistent historical records but the actual practices on the ground. From the Annamese perspective, not only was it impossible, given the distant and often faulty memories, to determine the location of the bronze pillar purportedly erected by Ma Yuan, but it was also disingenuous for Siming (and the Ming) to claim jurisdiction over the contested territory, especially when the five counties under dispute had long been submitting taxes to Annam.[8]

But from our perspective, what is most noteworthy about the case of Siming is clearly the reluctance of early Ming rulers to use force to defend and demarcate China's southern border. After the failed embassy of 1396-97, some court officials did suggest to the Ming ruler that he launch a military campaign against Annam. But the Hongwu emperor, following his own advice that the Ming should not expend its resources in exchange for "the military glories of the moment," decided in the end not to pursue the matter. As we have seen, this reluctance on the part of early Ming rulers to use force in the south must be understood within the broader context of Ming border relations. But this cautious approach, I argue, must also be set against the background of the often convoluted politics of native chieftaincy. In 1404, the chieftain of Siming would complain to the Ming court that the people of Annam had seized control of yet other areas of the native domain. For his part, the newly enthroned Yongle emperor would again order the ruler of Annam to return to Siming areas that did not belong to the kingdom. But while the Ming ruler would in his various pronouncements side with the domain of Siming, it is unclear to me that he was entirely convinced by the claims made by the native chieftain.[9]

The Yongle emperor did eventually decide in late 1406 to launch a war against Annam. But while the Ming ruler would cite the Annamese encroachment on Siming as one major reason for the attack, the war against Annam in the early fifteenth century was ultimately *not* about demarcating and defending China's southern border. For the Yongle emperor, who himself had usurped the Ming throne a few years earlier and who was no doubt particularly sensitive to any challenges to Ming authority, the war was about the continual deception of the Annamese regime. It was about how Ho (Le) Quy Ly – the one-time regent to the king of Annam – had deceived the Ming court by claiming that the original ruling house had died out, and it was about how the rulers of Annam had, despite periodic warnings from Ming rulers, repeatedly attacked the neighbouring kingdom of Champa. The war against Annam was no doubt about borders and boundaries. But in the early fifteenth century, the Yongle emperor was clearly less concerned about defending the physical boundary between China and Annam than about reinforcing the political hierarchy that had long characterized the relations between the centralizing state and its neighbours.[10]

Demarcating the Border

If the Hongwu and Yongle emperors had not been especially concerned about defending and demarcating the southern border, following the retreat of the Ming state from Annam in 1427-28, their successors were clearly much more conscious of doing so. This can be observed from the designation by the Ming court of the native domains of Pingxiang and Long Zhou (located just north of Siming) as the official contact zone between China and the southern kingdom, and it can also be noted in the increased efforts by Ming rulers and officials in the fifteenth and sixteenth centuries to resolve territorial disputes in the southern borderland.

To understand how later Ming rulers and officials sought to demarcate and defend the southern border, consider their efforts to control cross-border traffic. In time, not only would the Ming court require all Annamese envoys who wished to travel to the imperial capital to first pass through the domains of Pingxiang and Long Zhou – and not through other potential points of entry in the provinces of Yunnan and Guangdong – but it would also designate the Pass of Subduing the South (Zhennan Guan, now known as the Friendship Pass) in southwest Pingxiang as the official gateway. In 1539, for instance, when the Annamese ruler Mac Dang Doanh (r. 1530-40), son of Mac Dang Dung (1483-1541), who had overthrown the Le dynasty in 1527, decided to seek formal recognition from the centralizing state, it was at the Zhennan Pass that Ming officials would receive his envoys. Likewise, in 1563, when it was time for the Ming court to recognize a new Annamese ruler, it was made clear to the Mac ruling house that an official patent would only be issued if the new king would receive it in person at the Pass. And on occasions when Ming officials were required to accompany envoys from Annam back to the southern kingdom, it was at the Zhennan Pass that members of the travelling party would part ways.[11]

To see how Ming rulers and officials went about demarcating and defending the southern border, consider also some of the contemporary visual representations. No doubt, early Ming dynasty maps are in general relatively generic. For example, in the illustration of Guangxi found in the imperially sponsored *Union Gazetteer of the Great Ming* (*Da Ming yi tong zhi*, 1461), the border with Annam is simply indicated at the lower-left margin by the words "southwest to the border of Annam" (*xi nan di Annan jie*). Even in the 1531 edition of the *General Gazetteer of Guangxi*, the border with Annam (Jiaozhi) is identified in the provincial map simply by a small rectangular box labelled "border of Jiaozhi." By contrast, illustrations included in later Ming sources are often more detailed. In the map of Long Zhou (which covers Pingxiang as well) in the *Essential Information for Governing Guangxi* (see figure), not only do the compilers of the early seventeenth-century military handbook identify many of the strategic passes that marked the border between Guangxi and Annam (see the rows of rectangles at the top and left-hand parts of the illustration), but they also indicate, in the lower left-hand corner, the official gateway between the centralizing state and the southern kingdom (an earlier version of the map found in a sixteenth-century handbook would clearly identify the gateway as the Pass of Subduing the South). The illustration of Long Zhou in question is of course far from "accurate," but it does demonstrate the level of attention late Ming officials paid to demarcating the southern border.[12]

In addition to more consciously demarcating the southern border, rulers and officials in the fifteenth and sixteenth centuries evidently also found it necessary to pay more attention to the territorial disputes at the borderlands. Consider the case concerning the native domains of Ha Tu Lang (Chinese: Xiasilang) and Anping. According to reports found in the *Veritable Records*, by 1438, not only had people from the domain of Ha Tu Lang (in northern Annam) snatched a good number of men, women, and livestock from the Anping domain (just north of Long Zhou in Guangxi), but they had also taken control of part of the Anping territory. The initial response of the Zhengtong emperor (r. 1436-49) was predictable: in an edict delivered by

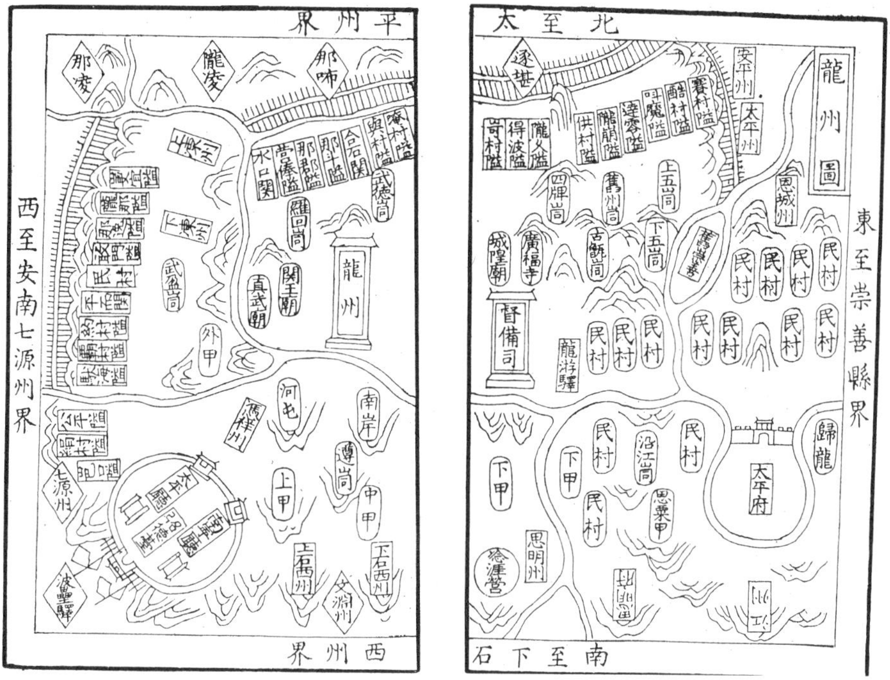

The Ming border with Annam

Source: Yang Fang (*jin shi* 1577) et al., eds., *Dian Yue yao zuan* [Essential information for governing Guangxi] (1602) (reprint; Beijing: Shu mu wen xian chu ban she, [1988]), *juan* 4, before *ye* 19. Annamese areas are identified by diamonds.

two special envoys, the Ming ruler demanded that the ruler of Annam order the chieftain of Ha Tu Lang to immediately return to Anping all the ill-gotten gains. But two aspects of the way the Ming approached the case are worth noting. First, the Ming emperor made it clear – albeit in the subtlest of language – that this time the fight was not between the centralizing state and the southern kingdom but between two borderland native domains. This distinction was significant because the focus now was less on punishing Annam than it was on restoring order on the southern border. Second, despite their rhetoric, Ming rulers and officials seemed to realize that the faults might not have lain entirely with the native domain in Annam. For the Ming court, what was important was to have the chieftains of Ha Tu Lang and Anping agree again on a common border.[13]

Consider also the case involving Ha Tu Lang and Long Zhou. According to reports found in the *Veritable Records*, disputes between the two native domains could be traced to at least 1448. That year, the king of Annam, no doubt in response to the troubles at the border as well as to the pressure from the Ming court, reported that he had succeeded in restoring order in the region by handing back eleven villages to Long Zhou and six to Ha Tu

Lang. But territorial disputes between the two domains would apparently persist. At issue, by 1472, was the alleged continual occupation of part of Long Zhou by the people of Ha Tu Lang. But while the Ming court would again order the ruler of Annam to rein in the chieftains at the border, as in the case concerning Anping, what seemed important to the Ming emperor was to have officials from both the centralizing state and the southern kingdom determine anew the proper boundary between the two native domains.[14]

Consider, as our last example, the case involving the native domains of Xialei and Guishun just to the northwest of Anping in southwest Guangxi. According to the records, by the early 1580s, frequent complaints had been filed by the ruler of Annam, Mac Hau Hop (r. 1562-92), concerning the alleged periodic encroachment on Annamese territory by the people of Xialei and Guishun. While such claims are impossible for us to verify, what is noteworthy are the responses by the Longqing (r. 1567-72) and Wanli (r. 1573-1620) emperors. To restore order in the southern border region, the Ming rulers and their officials decided it would be better for the centralizing state to "cede" to Annam more than 120 villages from the domains of Xialei and Guishun. Thus, if in the fifteenth century Ming rulers and officials still found it beneficial and credible to adopt the rhetoric – if not the practice – of an omnipotent state, by the late-sixteenth century, the Ming court would seem almost eager to rid itself of unnecessary troubles by redrawing the boundary between China and the southern kingdom.[15]

As we have seen, in the fifteenth and sixteenth centuries, Ming rulers and officials could be quite practical in how they demarcated the southern border. But just as the Ming court was willing to let native domains serve as buffers between the centralizing state and Annam, it could also be markedly uncompromising, especially when the population or territory under dispute was, in theory, under the direct control of the Ming authorities. For instance, in the early 1440s, when it was brought to the attention of the court that nearly three hundred households from the area of Qin Zhou in western Guangdong had, since the start of the Xuande reign (1426-35), submitted themselves to Annam, it was decided that the Ming must insist that all such households be brought back under the control of the centralizing state. Similarly, in the early 1540s, when the Mac ruling house was seeking formal recognition from the Ming court, it was made explicit to the Annamese ruler that he must first return to Ming control four particular settlements that were deemed to have long been part of the Qin Zhou area.[16]

Crossing the Border

Despite attempts by later Ming rulers and officials to demarcate and defend the border with Annam, efforts to deter unauthorized traffic had only limited success. To be sure, not all unofficial border crossings were deemed undesirable. Especially after the retreat of the Ming forces from the southern kingdom in 1427-28, chieftains who chose to cross the border to pledge allegiance to the centralizing state were particularly welcome. In 1434, in response to the news that two Annamese native officials, along with more than three hundred of their family members and followers, had crossed into the Ming territory to submit to the state, the Xuande emperor was notably accommodating. Not only should the chieftains and their followers be allowed to settle where they desired, the Ming ruler decreed, but they should also be supplied with whatever provisions they might need. Similarly, in 1437, in response to a recommendation that yet other newly arrived chieftains from Annam be given land to cultivate, the Xuande emperor was careful to note that such chieftains should be exempted from corvée labour and taxes and that, to help them settle down, they should be provided with two years' worth of food grain.[17]

Most unauthorized border crossings, of course, were not only undesirable but were also seen as threats to the Ming order. As can be seen from the cases concerning Siming and other domains in Guangxi discussed earlier, the threats were most apparent when people from Annam decided to cross the border to attack or seize control of Ming settlements. But the threats were evident also, from the perspective of the centralizing state, when people from the Ming ventured illegally into Annam. The troubles associated with the domain of Long Zhou in the 1470s are a case in point. Even though people from Long Zhou had complained to the Ming court about being encroached upon by their Annamese neighbours, according to a memorial submitted by the minister of war, Yu Zijun (1429-89), it was the residents of Long Zhou who had in fact first travelled across the river to take up farming in the Annamese territory. It was only after they had been forced by the villagers on the other side of the border to give up their newly acquired land, Yu claimed, that the people of Long Zhou began to accuse their Annamese neighbours for encroachment. From the point of view of the Ming authorities, the threats associated with unauthorized border crossings were not limited to encroachment. To judge from the records, what Ming rulers and their officials were most concerned about was actually the prospect of collaboration between unscrupulous elements from both sides of the border. Though the Ming court would issue repeated warnings against unauthorized border crossings, such frequent exhortations only serve to remind us how ineffective the injunctions must have been.[18]

One reason the Ming court had difficulties deterring unauthorized border traffic had to do with the lure of profits. Although Ming rulers had from early on forbidden their subjects to deal privately with foreign countries, cross-border trade, whether overland or maritime, would continue to thrive throughout the period. In the case of south China, a major source of illicit trade, especially in the fifteenth century, were the pearl-beds located off the coast of Guangdong province. While the records offer only a glimpse of the goings-on, it is evident from the reports by officials that a complex trading network had evolved over time. And though it is hard to gauge the scale of the illicit pearl trade – a report dated to 1457 notes that pirates sailing in ships with masts could be seen daily plundering areas where pearl-beds could be found – it is clear that people from both Annam and China were involved in this network. To be sure, Ming rulers and officials did try to put a halt to the cross-border traffic. But as the king of Annam acknowledged in 1471 in a rare moment of candour, given the need for people along the coast to go out to the sea to make a living, it was simply impossible for government authorities to impose firm control.[19]

Another reason the Ming court had difficulties securing its border with Annam had to do with the institution of chieftaincy. The *tu si* system (here I will leave aside the institution as it was practised in Annam), as we have seen, was a double-edged sword. Just as it allowed the Ming authorities to claim a degree of order in the southern border region without having to expend the limited military resources of the state, it also helped undermine that very stability by fostering both inter-domain and cross-border rivalries. As a result, even though the native domains did in general serve as buffers between the centralizing state and the southern kingdom, over time the desire of chieftains and their subjects to extend the boundaries of their domains had clearly led to much tension and violence in the border region.

To understand the dynamics and extent of such tension and violence, especially in the late-Ming period, let us examine a few episodes of cross-border turmoil as they were reported by the indefatigable traveller Xu Hongzu (Xu Xiake, 1586-1641). Consider first the case of the native domain of Guishun not far northwest of Pingxiang and Long Zhou. According to Xu Hongzu, troubles linked to the domain of Guishun could be traced to as early as the 1620s. At the time, in Annam, the Le ruling house had been back in power and the Mac clan had, as a result, been pushed further and further up the highlands of Cao Bang (Chinese: Gao Ping) just across the border from Guishun. Troubles for the domain of Guishun began when its chieftain decided to offer a refuge for the leader of the Mac clan in exchange for a handsome payment. The plan backfired, however, when troops sent by the Le ruling house descended upon Guishun and forced its chieftain to hand over the wife of the Mac leader (the leader himself had fled earlier). Angered by the perceived betrayal, the Mac leader returned and launched an attack against Guishun. The chieftain of Guishun was eventually killed. At the end, according to Xu Hongzu, even though the Ming authorities would decide to intervene on behalf of the native domain, half of the territory of Guishun would fall under the control of the Mac leader.[20]

Consider also the case of the domain of Longying, which was located not far north of Pingxiang and Long Zhou. Unlike the case of Guishun, the troubles in Longying began not from outside but, rather, from inside the native domain. According to Xu Hongzu, it was in 1634, three years before he began his travel in Guangxi, that a power struggle erupted in Longying. It happened that Zhao Zhengjin, brother of the chieftain Zhao Zhengli, had long had his eyes set on the chieftaincy. When Zhengli finally died without a son of his own, Zhengjin took it as his cue to seize power. Not only did he conspire with the widow of Zhengli to conceal the truth from the Ming court, he also brought in military reinforcements from the Mac clan of Cao Bang to help suppress any dissent. Even though Zhengjin's deed would eventually be exposed and punished by the Ming authorities, the domain of Longying, according to Xu, was devastated as a result.[21]

Finally, consider the case concerning Guishun and the domain of Tianzhou. The problem in this case, according to Xu Hongzu, had to do with the desire of the chieftains of both Guishun and Tianzhou to seize control of yet another domain whose chieftain had just died without leaving an heir. But since neither Guishun nor Tianzhou had a clear military advantage over the other, both decided to seek help from the Mac clan of Cao Bang. What this and other cases discussed show is not only how wide the gap had become between the theory and the reality of the "chieftain system" but also how fluid boundaries in the southern border region had become in the late Ming.[22]

Borders Hard and Soft

After all, how "hard" or "soft" was China's southern border? To answer this question, it is worth remembering that, as early as 1373, the Hongwu emperor had already included in the original version of his *Ancestral Injunctions* an explicit instruction forbidding future rulers from invading Annam or other similar countries. Although the wording of the injunction would be modified in subsequent editions, it is evident that, right from the start, the Ming founder had recognized Annam as a politically and territorially distinct entity. It is also worth noting that, in addition to the perceived physical boundary between China and Annam, it was also part of the official discourse, especially from the mid-fifteenth century on, to emphasize the inherent or "natural" distinctions between "Chinese" (*hua*) and "non-Chinese" (*yi*). In a memorial submitted in 1537 by Vice-Minister Tang Zhou (*jin shi* 1502), for instance, while Tang, a Hainan native, offers a list of seven reasons the Ming should not again go to war against Annam, one of the most compelling ones, according to the vice minister, is the fact that, as in the case of heaven and earth, there exists a "natural boundary" (*zi ran zhi xian*) between hua and yi. Although Tang Zhou does not find it necessary to explain further in his memorial the idea of "natural boundary," it is clear from other writings of the time that he had in mind not just the physical separation between "Chinese" and "non-Chinese" people but also the distinct "nature" of hua and yi.[23]

At the same time, one may consider the southern border "soft" for at least two reasons. First, even though Ming officials would emphasize the distinctions between hua and yi, most would never retreat from the rhetoric of the civilizing influence of the centralizing state. To many an observer, given the right conditions, it was possible for any "non-Chinese" to adopt the practices of the "Chinese." Second, although well-meaning Ming officials would, from time to time, recommend strengthening the border defence in the south, having long depended on native chieftains and their domains to serve as buffers, the Ming court was simply unprepared to commit its own regular military forces to defending the southern border. What this study of the Ming construction of its border with Annam shows is that, even though Chinese rulers and their agents had a fairly firm notion of a political-cum-cultural boundary, it was not always possible for them to define it clearly or to defend it effectively.

Notes

1 Since my primary concern here is the Ming construction of the southern border, I have, for the sake of consistency, followed the Ming convention of referring to the southern kingdom as Annam (or Jiaozhi) rather than as Dai Viet. To avoid cluttering the text, I have left out the diacritical marks in my transliteration of Vietnamese names. Research for this chapter has been greatly facilitated by Geoff Wade, trans., *Southeast Asia in the Ming Shi-lu: An Open Access Resource* (Singapore: Asia Research Institute and the Singapore E-Press, National University of Singapore, 2005), available from http://epress.nus.edu.sg/msl/. Although specialists should always check the translations against the original texts, Wade's impressive undertaking has made the most important official record of the Ming period much more accessible and useful.

2 For the ordeals of Wu Rui, see *Ming shi lu* [Veritable records of the Ming] (1418 to mid-17th century) (Taipei: Zhong yang yan jiu yuan li shi yu yan yan jiu suo, 1961-66), *Xiaozong shi lu*, 153:1b-2a (10 September 1499).

3 For the report on the Chinese detainees in Annam, see *Ming shi lu, Xianzong shi lu*, 106:7-8a (1 September 1472). For the use of spies, see, for example, *Ming shi lu, Xianzong shi lu*, 138:3b (9 March 1479).

4 For the Great Wall, see Arthur Waldron, *The Great Wall of China: From History to Myth* (Cambridge: Cambridge University Press, 1990). For an introduction to the relations between Ming China and Annam, see Wang Gungwu, "Ming Foreign Relations: Southeast Asia," in *The Cambridge History of China*, edited by Denis Twitchett and Frederick W. Mote, vol. 8, *The Ming Dynasty, 1368-1644*, pt. 2, 301-32 (Cambridge: Cambridge University Press, 1998). For a Vietnamese perspective, see Keith W. Taylor, "The Early Kingdoms," in *The Cambridge History of Southeast Asia*, edited by Nicholas Tarling, vol. 1, pt. 1: *From Early Times to c. 1500* (Cambridge: Cambridge University Press, 1999), esp. 149-52. For more systematic studies, see the chapters by Yamamoto Tatsurō, Fujiwara Riichirō, and Ōsawa Kazuo in Yamamoto Tatsurō, ed., *Betonamu Chūgoku Kankeishi* [History of international relations between Vietnam and China] (Tokyo: Yamakawa Shuppansha, 1975). For a useful but far from comprehensive source book, see Xiao Dehao and Huang Zheng, eds., *Zhong Yue bian jie li shi zi liao xuan bian* [Selective documents on the border history of China and

Vietnam] (Beijing: She hui ke xue wen xian chu ban she, 1993). One of the first major studies in English of the Ming colonization of Annam is of course Alexander Woodside, "Early Ming Expansionism (1406-1427): China's Abortive Conquest of Vietnam," *Papers on China* 17 (1963): 1-37. For a recent study of the history of Sino-Vietnamese relations, see Brantly Womack, *China and Vietnam: The Politics of Asymmetry* (Cambridge: Cambridge University Press, 2006).

5 For the official recognition of the kingdom of Annam, see *Ming shi lu, Taizu shi lu*, 43:3 (23 July 1369). For the Ming-Mongol relations, see Morris Rossabi, "The Ming and Inner Asia," in Twitchett and Mote, *The Cambridge History of China*, 224-41.

6 For Siming and the institution of native chieftaincy, see Leo K. Shin, *The Making of the Chinese State: Ethnicity and Expansion on the Ming Borderlands* (Cambridge: Cambridge University Press, 2006), chap. 3. For Huang Guangping, see *Ming shi lu, Taizu shi lu*, 221:3 (12 October 1392).

7 For the disputes between Siming and Annam, see *Ming shi lu, Taizu shi lu*, 137:5b-6a (24 June 1381), 249:2b-3a (31 December 1396). For the myths surrounding the "bronze pillar," see Edward H. Schafer, *The Vermilion Bird: T'ang Images of the South* (Berkeley and Los Angeles: University of California Press, 1967), 98. For Ma Yuan and his cult, see Donald S. Sutton, "A Case of Literati Piety: The Ma Yuan Cult from High-Tang to High-Qing," *Chinese Literature: Essays, Articles, Reviews* 11 (1989): 79-114. For an early reference to the pillar by the Ming founding emperor, see *Ming shi lu, Taizu shi lu*, 51:8b-9a (10 May 1370). For confusions over the location of the pillar(s), see, for example, Li Xian (1408-66), *Da Ming yi tong zhi* [Union gazetteer of the Great Ming] (Taipei: Wen hai chu ban she, 1965 [1461]), 85:23b, 90:6a; Wei Jun (*jin shi* 1604), *Qiao nan suo ji* [Miscellaneous notes on Guangxi] (pref. 1612), Bai bu cong shu ji cheng ed. (Taipei: Yi wen yin shu guan, 1966 [reprint]), *shang*:15-16a.

8 For the Ming embassy, see *Ming shi lu, Taizu shi lu*, 250:3b-7a (20 March 1397). For Chen Cheng (Ch'en Ch'eng), see L. Carrington Goodrich and Chaoying Fang, eds., *Dictionary of Ming Biography, 1368-1644* (New York: Columbia University Press, 1976), 144-45. For his correspondence with the king of Annam, see Chen Cheng, *Chen Zhushan xian sheng wen ji* [Collected writings of Chen Cheng] (Jinan: Qi Lu shu she chu ban she, 1997 [reprint]), *juan* 1. For a transcription of the letters exchanged, see Wang Jiguang, "Hongwu san shi nian Zhong Yue ling tu jiao she de yuan shi wen jian" [Primary documents concerning the border disputes between China and Vietnam during the thirtieth year of the Hongwu reign (1397)], *Zhongguo bian jian shi di yan jiu* 14.4 (2004), 119-23.

9 For the injunction by the Hongwu emperor against invading Annam and other countries, see Zhu Guozhen (1557-1632), comp., *Huang Ming da xun ji* [Imperial instructions of the Great Ming], 1:3-4, collected in *Huang Ming shi gai* [General history of the Great Ming] (Yangzhou: Jiangsu guang ling gu ji ke yin she, 1992 [1632]). For the complaint by Siming and the reaction of the Yongle emperor, see *Ming shi lu, Taizong shi lu*, 30:3b (11 May 1404), 32:3a (25 July 1404). According to an official history of Dai Viet, perhaps to appease the Yongle emperor, in 1405 the southern kingdom did "cede" to the Ming a total of fifty-nine villages. See Ngo Si Lien, *Dai Viet su ky toan thu* [Complete history of the Great Viet], edited by Chen Jinghe [Ch'en Ching-ho] (Tokyo: Tokyo Daigaku Tōyō Bunka Kenkyūjo Fuzoku Tōyōgaku Bunken Sentaa, 1984-86 [pref. 1479, 1665, 1697, 1884]), *ban ky*, 8.485.

10 For the official rationale for invading Annam, see *Ming shi lu, Taizong shi lu*, 60:1-4a (19 November 1406). For background, see John K. Whitmore, *Vietnam, Ho Quy Ly, and the Ming (1371-1421)* (New Haven: Yale Center for International and Area Studies, 1985); Wang Gungwu, "Ming Foreign Relations," 307-17.

11 For the importance of the Zhennan Pass, see *Ming shi lu, Shizong shi lu*, 221:16-17a (14 March 1539), 521:3b (3 June 1563); *Shenzong shi lu*, 47:4a (3 March 1576); *Xizong shi lu*, 17:13a (27 January 1622). For a Vietnamese perspective, see Ngo Si Lien, *Dai Viet su ky toan shu, ban ky*, 17.909-10. For visual depictions of the Pass, see Feng Shiyang (fl. 1541), ed., *Annan lai wei tu ce* [Album concerning the submission of Annam] (Beijing: Shu mu wen xian chu ban she, 1988 [1571]). For Mac Dang Dung (Mac Dang-dung), see *Dictionary of Ming Biography*, 1029-35.

12 Li Xian, *Da Ming yi tong zhi, juan* 83, before page 1; Huang Zuo, ed., *Guangxi tong zhi* [General gazetteer of Guangxi] (Beijing: Shu mu wen xian chu ban she, 1988 [1531]),

1:1b-2a. For an early version of the map of Long Zhou discussed, see Ying Jia (1494-1554), Ling Yunyi (*jin shi* 1547), and Liu Yaohui (1522-85), eds., *Cangwu zong du jun men zhi* [Record of the Office of the Supreme Commander at Cangwu] (Beijing: Quan guo tu shu guan wen xian shu wei fu zhi zhong xin, 1991 [1581]), 4:57.

13 For the case of Ha Tu Lang and Anping, see *Ming shi lu, Yingzong shi lu*, 43:2a (25 June 1438), 54:1 (13 May, 1439), 54:3b (22 May 1439), 95:1b (7 September 1442).

14 For the case of Ha Tu Lang and Long Zhou, see *Ming shi lu, Yingzong shi lu*, 166:3b-4b (15 June 1448); *Xianzong shi lu*, 104:9b-10a (28 June 1472).

15 For the case of Xialei and Guishun, see *Ming shi lu, Shenzong shi lu*, 145:4a (22 February 1584), 162:6 (22 July 1585), 178:2 (12 October 1586); Qu Jiusi (1546-1617), *Wanli wu gong lu* [Record of the military accomplishments during the Wanli reign] (Taipei: Yi wen yin shu guan, 1980 [1612]), 4.400-26.

16 For the case of the 1440s, see *Ming shi lu, Yingzong shi lu*, 72:5 (9 November 1440), 90:2 (18 April 1442). For the case of the 1540s, see *Ming shi lu, Shizong shi lu*, 236:2-3a (11 May 1540), 248:1b-5a (29 April 1541), 268:3 (16 December 1542).

17 For the border crossings of Annamese chieftains, see *Ming shi lu, Xuanzong shi lu*, 109:3b-4a (17 April 1434); *Ming shi lu, Yingzong shi lu* 36:2a (3 December 1437).

18 For the memorial by Yu Zijun, see Wang Sen (1653-1726), ed., *Yuexi wen zhai* [Anthology of belle-lettres of Guangxi] (ca. 1704), Ying yin Wen yuan ge Si ku quan shu ed. (Taipei: Taiwan Shang wu yin shu guan, 1986 [reprint]), 5:23b-27a.

19 For pronouncements against private dealings, see, for example, *Ming shi lu, Taizu shi lu*, 205:4a (3 December 1390), 252:2b (30 April 1397); *Xuanzong shi lu*, 78:6a (2 June 1431). For reports of illicit trade between people from China and Annam, see *Ming shi lu, Yingzong shi lu*, 163:2a (8 March 1448), 279:7b-8a (6 July 1457), 317:4b-5a (1 August 1460); *Xianzong shi lu*, 92:1b-2a (26 June 1471). For a discussion, see Fujiwara Riichirō, "Reichō zenki no Min to no kankei (1428-1527)" [Early relations between the Le dynasty and the Ming], in Yamamoto, *Betonamu Chūgoku kankeishi*, esp. 281-85. For the pearl-beds in Guangdong, see Zhang Tingyu, ed., *Ming shi* [History of the Ming] (Beijing: Zhonghua shu ju, 1974 [1739]), 82.1996-97.

20 For his travels in Guangxi, see Xu Hongzu, *Xu Xiake you ji* (ca. 1641) (Shanghai: Shanghai gu ji chu ban she, 1995 [1987]), *juan* 3A-4A. For the case of Guishun, see 4A.467, 478-79, 496-97. For a recent study of Xu's travel writings, see Julian Ward, *Xu Xiake (1587-1641): The Art of Travel Writing* (Richmond: Curzon, 2001). For background on the Macs of Cao Bang, see *Dictionary of Ming Biography*, 1035; Wang Gungwu, "Ming Foreign Relations," 330.

21 For the case of Longying, see Xu Hongzu, *Xu Xiake you ji*, 4A.477-78.

22 For the case of Guishun and Tianzhou, see Xu Hongzu, *Xu Xiake you ji*, 4A.478-79, 485-88, 496-97.

23 For a discussion of the injunction of the Hongwu emperor, see Wang Gungwu, "Ming Foreign Relations," 311-13. For Tang Zhou's memorial, see *Ming shi lu, Shizong shi lu* 195:1-2a (12 January 1537). For the context, see Jung-pang Lo, "Policy Formulation and Decision-Making on Issues Respecting Peace and War," in *Chinese Government in Ming Times: Seven Studies*, edited by Charles O. Hucker, 63-66 (New York: Columbia University Press, 1969). For a mid-Ming perspective on the "nature" (*xing*) of hua and yi, see Leo K. Shin, "The Last Campaigns of Wang Yangming," *T'oung Pao* 92.1-3 (2006): 101-28.

6

Embracing Victory, Effacing Defeat: Rewriting the Qing Frontier Campaigns

Peter C. Perdue

The writing and rewriting of history never ends. Not only among scholars, but in popular memory, events constantly change and link up in different forms as new experiences alter our perspectives on the past. Paul Cohen, in his study of the historiography of the Boxers, separates forms of history into three "keys": (1) events as the historian constructs them, (2) immediate collective experience, and (3) myths created by ideologues who use the past as a political weapon. His categories are useful, but artificial, because we cannot neatly divide immediate experience from later "mythological" construction. Right after any event occurs, popular memories and official historians write it into texts and oral accounts. Experience, event, and myth interdigitate and interact dialectically without end.[1]

Here I discuss one example of this kind of historical self-fashioning: Qing efforts to set down definitive histories of the major military campaigns of the eighteenth century. Very soon after the wars ended, the emperors commissioned campaign histories that moulded the flux of events into monuments of Heaven's will. Military history, the oldest form of historical writing, seems to fit well into stereotyped narratives of heroism, strategic planning, dramatic conflict, and ultimate victory or defeat. Yet even the most successful campaigns of the eighteenth century in Qing terms – the extermination of the Zunghar Mongols of the northwestern frontier (1756-60) – contained many difficult reverses and uncertain prospects. The much less dramatic campaigns against Burma (1769-70) and Vietnam (1788-89) illustrate even more sharply how hard it is to disguise defeat as victory. Qing historians, however, smoothed out the rocky course of imperial expansion into a confident demonstration of imperial sagacity backed by Heaven. They left a strong legacy to the nationalist historians of the twentieth century.

The French literary scholar Louis Marin, discussing a seventeenth-century proposal for a history of Louis XIV's reign, argues that historians and rulers write each other into existence. The ruler commissions an official account

China in the Qing dynasty

in order to make the historian a royal mouthpiece, but the historian has the last laugh. His narrative creates the royal persona, reproducing the ruler's power and transmitting it beyond the temporal limits of his reign. In both France and China, narrative and imperial authority shaped each other, both when they were created and for centuries thereafter.[2]

Qing and French rulers tried to dominate their historical terrain as they encompassed their territory by producing authoritative accounts of their frontier conquests. Imperially commissioned histories supported the broader projects of the high Qing elite: normalization, standardization, and classification. Institutionalized practices aimed to constrain the boundaries of interpretation, construct a carefully defined archive, and develop routine, predictable categories for incorporating new experiences. Since the empire had expanded vastly from its early days, these techniques helped to filter the incoming flood of new data. After the end of Ming loyalist resistance in the mid-seventeenth century, nearly all of the scholar intellectuals enthusiastically joined the imperial enterprise. Imperial norms were not imposed by force on a dissident elite but, rather, were developed in collaboration with it. The *Siku quanshu* project, as Kent Guy has shown, built on the methods of textual criticism developed by Qing scholars, using their talents to make a comprehensive archive of what was known, while excluding anti-Manchu literature.[3]

When it came to recounting war, however, the goals of a Manchu elite devoted to conquest clashed with those of a Confucian-trained scholarly class for whom war was only a necessary evil. Emperors repeatedly had to defend military campaigning against critique. The Kangxi emperor denounced close advisors who warned about the dangers of leaving the capital for extended military campaigns. They feared both the expense he inflicted on wealthy southern regions and social unrest when he left the Forbidden City. (Riots, in fact, did break out in Beijing after Kangxi left on his personal campaigns.) The Yongzheng emperor had to insist that he would not *qiongbing duwu* (exhaust soldiers in useless manoeuvres), so he stressed low-cost defence measures over aggressive expansion, the use of trade levers instead of coercion, and reliance on Mongol allies to carry out many of the most difficult steppe campaigns. Even so, he suffered an embarrassing defeat in 1731 when his trusted general fell into an ambush.

Qianlong's great northwestern campaigns of 1756 to 1760, however, appeared to prove that Heaven had made the Qing superior to all previous dynasties because only the Qing had finally eliminated the Mongolian menace on the steppe frontier. The "return" of the Torghuts to the Qing border in 1776 brought all the Mongols under the emperor's benevolent gaze. By admitting them to the empire, and settling them under close control, Qianlong ended the epic story of interactions with steppe nomadism that had opened in the first millennium BCE.

The northwestern campaigns thus allowed imperial historians to write a unified, closed narrative of the frontier. The historians put the difficult, ill-understood, fluctuating border under a predictable gaze. The mobile nomads, formerly incomprehensible, even animal-like beings, now had accepted gratefully the protection of the Qing ruler, who embraced Manchus, Mongols, Han, Hui, and Tibetans alike with equal benevolence. Even these campaigns, however, only succeeded because of many contingencies. They were by no means a foregone conclusion. The imperial historians had to gloss over uncertainties, mistakes, and difficulties in order to portray an inexorable drive towards victory. Careful study of the documentary evidence shows that the outcome could well have been different.

Kangxi's Campaign History

The *fanglue*, or military campaign history, was a new Qing genre. The Kangxi emperor, conscious of his place in history, revised the historical record as he created it. In August 1696, shortly after returning to the capital from his personal expedition against the Zunghar leader Galdan, the emperor ordered three grand secretaries and the Hanlin academy to compile a detailed history of his campaigns, the *Records of the Personal Military Expedition to*

Pacify and Fix the Northwest Regions (*Qinzheng pingding shuomo fanglue*).[4] These histories inscribed the dynasty's military achievements into the literary tradition that was its ultimate judge.

Qing historians and the emperor together constructed the primary myths of the campaigns: that Heaven's will had doomed Galdan to defeat, that the emperor had foreseen his death, and that Galdan had committed suicide out of despair.[5] They also suppressed inconvenient facts and anomalies, and exempted the emperor from the dramatic irony that Lionel Gossman has called the "essential condition" of historical writing.[6] Although the generals who opposed the expeditions – Galdan and his followers, and the other Mongols who submitted to the Qing – could not know the consequences of their actions, retrospectively the historians gave the Son of Heaven power to foresee everything.

Since the fanglue is a halfway-house of historical reconstruction, neither archival compilation nor fully smoothed-out narrative, modern scholars have found significant discrepancies between the archival record and the published texts. These alterations reinforce the emperor's authority by removing embarrassing or contradictory details, elevating his personal role, and denigrating the capacity of his enemies. The compilers omitted and manipulated documentary evidence so as to give the impression that the emperor was always engaged in active military strategic planning, not merely feasting and hunting. They also falsified and distorted documentary evidence about significant decisions made by the emperor during his campaign. Original sources in Manchu reveal clearly the uncertainties and constraints that limited the Son of Heaven's vision, but the fanglue makes him consistently omniscient.

The Chinese edition not only created a uniform evaluation of the emperor's achievements but also placed them within the classical Chinese literary tradition. Chinese terminology added moral and spatially centred perspectives to neutral Manchu vocabulary. For example, where the Manchu text describes envoys and tribes as "coming here" (*jidere*), the Chinese has them "coming to the interior" (*xiang nei er lai*). Armies that "moved against Galdan" (*galdan-i baru ibehe*) become "punishment expeditions" (*jintao*). Chinese terms like "within the borders" (*jingnei*), or "the multiple Frontier-Subject Mongols" (*zhufan menggu*),[7] reflect a new Qing border consciousness seen in its extensive cartographic projects and in institutions such as the *Lifanyuan* (Court for Management of the Outer Dependencies), which was established in 1638 to incorporate frontier Mongols as a separate unit of the Qing administration.

The changes in the fanglue text show that, as the Qing Empire embraced more territories and peoples, it also framed the story of the conquest itself in an encompassing narrative. Later writers drew on the manufactured documentary record laid down by Kangxi's editors to create ever more stereotyped depictions of the complex process of imperial expansion.

Qianlong's Account of the Zunghar Mongols

The Qianlong emperor, unlike his grandfather, never personally led a military campaign in the field. Yet he was "a man obsessed by war."[8] At the end of his life, he liked to call himself "the old man of ten complete victories" (*shiquan laoren*). He wrote many poems celebrating his armies' conquests, and he plastered the country with steles boasting of his Heaven-sent victories. He had portraits of successful generals hung in a special pavilion behind the Forbidden City. But the real wars fought by Qianlong's armies did not fit too well with the image of total victory. So the emperor had to rewrite the history books. Even better than rewriting them, he pre-empted interpretation by commissioning official histories and controlling the documentary record. His projects strongly affected how the Qing conquests have been viewed ever since. The imperial histories produced in the eighteenth and early nineteenth centuries formed the pattern on which later nationalist histories were built.

Qianlong's three northwestern campaigns looked like a cakewalk by comparison with those of Kangxi and Yongzheng. In the mid-eighteenth century, the Zunghar Mongols invited Qing armies into their territory to settle a succession dispute; then the Khoit prince Amursana, who expected to be made khan with Qing support, rebelled when he discovered that the victorious Qing intended to limit his power. Eliminating Amursana's scattered followers took time but few casualties or major battles. The main challenges were logistic, not military. The conquest of Turkestan faced even less serious military resistance, only the temporary uprisings of the Khojas of the oases of the Tarim basin. But these three campaigns generated a larger volume of commemorative material than was ever produced by the Kangxi or Yongzheng emperors.

In 1763, the Qianlong emperor ordered the compilation of a general history of the Zunghar Mongols based on all available Mongolian genealogies and Chinese official documents. None of the Mongolian genealogies collected by the emperor's orders appears to have survived. Once again, the victorious rulers have nearly succeeded in erasing alternative views from the record.

The history of the Zunghars was the first of a series of imperially commissioned compilations about the newly conquered territories, which provided information for nineteenth-century officials and scholars. It uses classical Chinese categories of lineage and administrative hierarchy to fit the turbulent history of the Zunghar state into a static model. Native Mongolian clan divisions, transmuted through the Chinese classifying lens, become fixed relations of subordination and kinship connections. Mongolian chronicles, by contrast, do not give populations for each clan and do not order them in a consistent hierarchy. Even though the Zunghars had disappeared, the Qing historians needed to embrace them as peoples who followed the universal laws of history.

The *Campaign History of the Pacification and Delimitation of the Zunghars* (*pingding zhungar fanglue*), edited by General Fu Heng, commissioned in 1755 and completed in 1770 in 172 *juan* (volumes) was the largest official campaign history produced in the Qing. It is one of the series of monumental scholarly products of the Qianlong reign, which culminated in the 36,000 *juan* of the *Complete Record of the Four Treasuries* (*Siku quanshu*) in 1783. The emperor wrote the introduction to the text, giving a brief summary of the Zunghar state. First he established a legitimate succession to the title of khan from the Yuan dynasty to the Qing Khan of Kokonor. Then the "crafty and arrogant" Galdan caused disorder until he was defeated by Kangxi, after which he took poison and killed himself. Galdan's nephew, Zewang Rabdan, because of his "wild wolf's ambition" (*langzi yexin*), attacked Hami and Tibet. His son Galdan Tseren continued his evil practices until the Yongzheng emperor crushed him. Then the Zunghar chiefs, terrified into submission, agreed to pay tribute, allowing the emperor to fix the border and withdraw his troops. But the violent Tsewang Dorji Namjar, who succeeded Galdan Tseren, caused further "internal disorder" (*neiluan*). The emperor describes his military expedition against Amursana and Amursana's flight and death in Russia. Once Russia, honouring its treaty to send back fugitives, returned Amursana's bones, peace returned to the border.

The emperor and his historians presume that Mongol tribes will inexorably submit to Qing benevolence, except for the violent, aggressive Zunghars, who only create disorder. Qing military campaigns are depicted as reluctant responses to the turmoil of the frontier. The official account erases evidence of Qing instigation of conflict and Qing military defeats. Explicitly designed as a sequel to the Kangxi emperor's personal campaign history, it insists that the Qianlong emperor has surpassed the achievements of all his predecessors.

The emperor's introduction, and his compliant scholars' prefaces, give the simplest possible account of the victories, but the massive compendium itself undermines their complacency. Although they tampered with some original documents and did not record all important events, the compilers did provide enormous quantities of contradictory and valuable evidence. Later historians can still use this collection to write a different history than the compilers intended.

Zhao Yi, Gong Zizhen, and Wei Yuan Carry on the Imperial Project

In the late eighteenth to mid-nineteenth centuries, Qing historians continued to invoke the eighteenth-century expansion as a model for foreign policy and domestic reform. The best known of these are the statecraft writers Wei Yuan (1794-1856) and Gong Zizhen (1792-1841), but in 1792, the Han official Zhao Yi (1727-1814) had anticipated much of Wei Yuan's project.[9]

Zhao, as a secretary of the Grand Council, wrote many of the communications to the northwest during the Turkestan campaigns, served on the southwest frontier for much of his life, and helped to compile the Pingding zhungar fanglue. His *Glorious Record of the Imperial Dynasty's Military Accomplishments* (*Huangchao Wugong Jisheng*), published in 1792 in four *juan*, bridged the imperial historiographical projects of Qianlong and the private accounts of Wei Yuan and his successors.[10] He discussed seven Qing campaigns, including two, in Burma and Taiwan, in which he had personally participated. Zhao Yi shared Wei Yuan's interest in both military history and in the historical evolution of imperial institutions. Zhao Yi did not write his history out of anxieties over domestic upheaval and foreign incursions, but he prepared the way for Wei Yuan as his historical approach "stressed the role of environment and continuous, cumulative institutional change, instead of looking back to a static and absolute utopian antiquity."[11]

Zhao boasted that "our dynasty's military might exceeds all previous dynasties." He knew that Qing armies had achieved unprecedented feats, exceeding even those of the Han and Tang. He wrote his short book in order to widely publicize the dynasty's achievements. Even though the fanglue had compiled detailed records on the campaigns, and the *Siku quanshu* had placed these accounts in the literary tradition, Zhao aimed for a wider readership than the official elite. He gives a concise, twelve-page account of the Zunghar wars, covering the main events from 1717 to 1760. He does not omit the catastrophic defeat of General Furdan in the ambush at Hoton Nor in 1731, noting that "out of 20,000 troops, only 2,000 returned."[12] Zhao, however, partly redeems the defeat by stressing the heroism of General Yue Zhongqi, who vainly tried to rescue Furdan from his encirclement.

Zhao also has to defend the campaigns against charges of wastefulness and excessive ambition. After describing the negotiations that led to a truce in 1734, and a peace treaty in 1739, he notes: "Our emperor's policy of cherishing [barbarians] follows circumstances and will not in the slightest damage the state's authority. The emperor does not want to use troops recklessly. If Galdan Tseren and his successors had respected the borders and treated us as friendly neighbours, our emperor would have devoted all his efforts to peace. Why would he want to mow them down or hunt them? But by rebelling they brought on their own destruction."[13]

Zhao portrays the emperor as a man of peace, anxious to avoid the costs of war but reluctantly drawn into battle by aggressive, unreliable enemies who brought on their own destruction. His account of the final war against the Zunghars, however, reveals another motivation. After the Mongol prince Amursana sought an alliance with the Qing in order to overthrow his rival

Dawaci in 1754, the emperor realized that "now is the chance to destroy Zunghars, when previous emperors could not eliminate (*tianmie*) them. This shows Heaven has given the Zunghars to us. We cannot miss the opportunity."[14] The miraculous success of the campaign against Dawaci, which crushed the Zunghar Khan in one hundred days "without losing any soldiers or breaking any arrows," seemed to bear out the claim of Heavenly support. A slightly sceptical reader might, however, conclude that the emperor, who had previously sworn that he only sought peaceful relations, had in 1754 grasped an irresistible opportunity to get what he really wanted from the beginning: the extermination of the rival Mongol state.

Zhao Yi's brief account contains traces of the imperial historiography of the past and the germs of the nationalist histories to come. He does not flinch from describing defeats but redeems disaster by stressing individual heroism. This trope fits both the classical ideals of finding moral exemplars in the past and the romantic narrative that encapsulates the history of a nation in its heroes. Zhao Yi shares the Confucian reluctance to endorse war and a sensitivity to its costs, but he exults in cheap victories as signs of Heavenly favour. He gives one of the highest estimates of the total cost of the northwestern campaigns (over 70 million taels), but for him the unprecedented achievement of eliminating the Mongol menace in the end justified the price.

By writing a concise account for a large audience, instead of a huge, definitive documentary compilation, Zhao reached out to a broader public. New historians like Zhao Yi, Gong Zizhen, and Wei Yuan addressed not just the sages of the past and the literati of the future but all the literate subjects of the empire, who needed to take pride in their ruler's victories. Yet Zhao Yi is on the cusp of nationalist history, without quite having crossed over. What is missing is a broader spatial reference. He compares the Qing only to previous regimes in the dynastic tradition without placing it in the geopolitical frame occupied by other states beyond the Central Kingdom. Wei Yuan and Gong Zizhen made this decisive step, building on Zhao Yi's foundation.

All three historians defended costly frontier expansion by claiming that the Qianlong emperor had successfully resolved the security dilemmas of the northwest frontier, which had plagued every dynasty since the Han first fought the Xiongnu. Wei Yuan and Gong Zizhen went further than Zhao Yi, arguing that China now needed to integrate the frontier regions closely with the interior. Like the emperor's official historians, they thought that the victories exhibited Heaven's will, but they also knew of a wider world beyond the frontiers. Wei Yuan and Gong Zizhen brought the eighteenth-century project into the nineteenth-century world of international geopolitics.

Although Western scholars know them best as advocates of resisting Western maritime incursions and of extending China's knowledge of European nations,[15] Gong and Wei drew lessons from dynastic history that closely linked continental and maritime security. They also tied security issues to domestic political reform. Security for the state meant both defence of its boundaries and maintenance of internal order.

Gong Zizhen was only twenty-nine years old when he wrote his prophetic essay arguing that Turkestan should be made into a province.[16] Like the Qianlong emperor, he justified the conquest in terms of Heaven's mandate, but unlike the emperor, he located China not in the centre of the civilized realm but, rather, at the eastern end of the Asian continent. China's rulers had expanded first to the east, then to the south coast, but by dominating the Mongols, the Qing had made the northwest safe, no longer remote or dangerous. Gong rejected the "shallow views of ignorant weaklings and vile writers" (*yuru bisheng*) who said that supporting the conquest was "wasting the resources of the interior to support the frontier" (*haozhong shibian*).[17]

Gong wanted to round up the landless, roaming populations of North and Northwest China and send them west. The region would be systematically divided into prefectures and subprefectures; Chinese names would replace the native ones; and the begs, jasaks, and other frontier authorities would come under the regular administration. Eighteenth-century policies had already promoted immigration and created a hybrid civil and military administrative structure, but the Manchu rulers kept Turkestan separate from the rest of the empire and continued to insist that it should pay for its own support. Gong rejected the idea of self-sufficiency, arguing for subsidizing the new province with subventions from wealthier provinces. Carefully controlled border trade would keep out corrupting "luxuries." The Han Chinese population could make a new start here, uncontaminated by the social tension and commercial seductions of the interior. Even the exiled criminals in the region, and other "wicked people" from the interior, could redeem themselves there by working hard on their own lands.

Wei Yuan supported his colleague by stressing what James Millward calls the "forward defense dividend": transferring troops to the frontier relieved the interior provinces of the expense of supporting them at home.[18] Wei argued that the cost of frontier expansion was fully justified, and, furthermore, the region could relieve population pressure in the interior. "Heaven has left us this vast wilderness," he exclaimed, to accommodate the floating population of the "flourishing age."[19]

Wei Yuan's most popular work, the *Record of Sacred Military Campaigns* (*Shengwuji*) synthesized all the Qing conquests into an accessible form.[20] During the Opium War, as a clerk in the office of the Liangjiang governor general, Wei had observed China's humiliating loss to the "sea barbarians," and he used the "sea of documents" available to him to create this comprehensive account of the Qing's military achievements, which would instruct later generations.[21]

Wei Yuan's preface argues for the radical proposition that "fighting war is superior to worshipping at ancestral temples" (*zhan shengyu miaotang*). In other words, border defence should take precedence over spreading civilized culture through the world; ethical universalism must yield to national security. Yet Wei Yuan also stresses that material resources cannot replace human will. Only the "dynamism" (*jing*) of "human talent" (*rencai*) will make the state strong. Wei, like Gong, focused his efforts on strengthening control within the borders achieved in the eighteenth century. The state should not promote culture beyond its borders but, rather, ensure obedience within them. We have crossed the blurred boundary separating nationalist ideology from classical norms.

Wei derived this proto-militarist ideology primarily from the historical record of Qing conquests, not from his knowledge of Western powers. Although foreign ideas made some contribution, the classical tradition and its official history contained enough intellectual material to support all three of Wei Yuan's most striking proposals: military defence, global geographic knowledge, and public participation in state affairs.

Wei Yuan's writings linked military conquest, foreign relations, and internal reform within a comprehensive historical vision. He put the capstone on the succession of imperial efforts to construct a fixed interpretation of the wars of expansion. His version of the Qing expansion has served as the almost unquestioned basis for subsequent accounts, and even his errors have been perpetuated by twentieth-century writers. Xiao Yishan's *Comprehensive History of the Qing* (*Qingdai tongshi*) of 1923, for example, incorporates verbatim, without citation, whole passages from the Shengwuji.[22]

Nevertheless, PRC historians criticize Wei for committing two grave "errors." He favoured the repression of popular rebellion, but, even worse, he questioned the permanence of China's boundaries. He wrote that much of the territory of China defined by the Nerchinsk treaty was "waste land" newly entered on the registers, and he noted that Taiwan "from ancient times was not part of China." The editors of the 1984 Beijing edition of the Shengwuji insist that "these are undoubtedly completely mistaken assertions, which do not accord with historical truth."[23] The PRC official histories of the Qing have to remove even a hint that the borders of the contemporary state have changed over time.

Nationalists must claim the Qing boundaries as eternally fixed, endowed by Heaven or by the course of history with natural legitimacy. The Qianlong emperor would smile to realize how successfully he had instilled this myth in the modern Chinese mind. Nationalist historians took the parameters of interpretation begun by the imperial historians and narrowed them even further, filtering out awkward implications of refractory facts.

Effacing Defeat: A Comparison with the South

Historians have more trouble massaging defeats than manipulating victories. As we know, Qianlong's other campaigns have less obvious claims to divine favour. The Taiwan intervention faced minimal opposition from peasants with primitive arms. The two Jinchuan campaigns, by contrast, cost an enormous amount and had great difficulty prevailing over tough Tibetan rebels in mountain fortresses. The two Nepal campaigns, which inspired Qianlong to boast of his ten great victories, were great logistical achievements, but they were essentially defensive actions: driving out invaders from Tibet, which appealed for Qing aid. Most questionable of all are the two southern campaigns: the Burma wars and the intervention in Vietnam. Qing armies clearly lost to the Burmese, and they did not do well against the Vietnamese either. Both campaigns showed the costs of excessive ambitions, overextended supply lines, and fighting in unfamiliar environments.

In the northwestern campaigns, the armies travelled enormous distances through barren terrain to confront the supreme warriors of the continent, who had threatened the borders of Chinese dynasties for millennia. Their victories were epochal. In the southern campaigns, by contrast, the commanders, at very high cost, put down localized rebellions at best, or withdrew with heavy losses from conflicts with regional states who posed only minimal security threats. Yet in the emperor's eyes, and in those of his chroniclers, all campaigns counted equally as complete victories over rebels, aided by Heaven's irresistible will. How did the imperial historians account, in the two cases, for the vast discrepancy between announced goals, costs, and real achievements?

Costs of major Qing campaigns

Name	Time	Cost [1,000 taels]
First Jinchuan	1747-49	10,000
Zunghar: Turkestan	1754-61	33,000
Burma	1767-69	13,000
Second Jinchuan	1771-76	70,000
Taiwan	1787-88	10,000
Vietnam	1788-89	1,300
First Gurkha	1788-89	1,000
Second Gurkha	1791-92	11,000
White Lotus	1797-1804	150,000

Source: Chen Feng, *Qingdai Junfei Yanjiu* [Military expenses in the Qing dynasty] (Wuhan: Wuhan Daxue Chubanshe, 1991).

Zhao Yi's account of the Burma campaign illustrates the imperial method of redeeming defeat by stressing heroic dedication.[24] On the face of it, the Burma campaigns of 1767-69 do not look particularly heroic or epochal. Except for the Yuan dynasty, Burma had always been separate from China, and it had no tributary relations with the Qing until the eighteenth century. When the last emperor of the Southern Ming regime escaped into Burma, the Burmese king briefly gave him refuge but handed him back in 1662 when threatened with invasion by a large Qing army. Burma and the Qing had no official relations for a century after that. Yunnan, a remote, poor province of no particular strategic value also received little attention from the court in Beijing, and the borders remained undefined and loosely patrolled.

Two new factors brought the Qing and Burmese states into conflict: (1) the influx of Chinese miners into the Shan states on the Yunnan-Burmese border and (2) political upheaval in Burma. After Aung Zeya (Ch. *Yongjiya*) subdued his rivals and set up the new Alaungpaya dynasty, he insisted on tighter control over the peoples on his northern border. When several local chieftains on the border of Pu'er prefecture of Yunnan refused to pay him tribute, he sent military forces from Ava to enforce payment. This intervention touched off conflict with Qing garrisons in Pu'er.

Qianlong, emboldened by his successes in the northwest, then pushed his provincial officials into war. He escalated a small border conflict into a great plan for "regime change." The Yunnan governor general, Liu Zao, did not see the border conflicts as particularly significant: severely rebuked by the emperor, he committed suicide. His replacement, Yang Yingju, a vigorous Chinese bannerman who served as commander in the northwest, sent false reports of victory. When his lies were exposed, he was fired and condemned to execution in Beijing. Then the emperor sent a real Manchu – Mingrui, a valiant fighter from the northwest – to take charge. Mingrui also committed suicide after a humiliating defeat. Finally, he sent his best general, Fuheng, with the Manchus Agui and Aligun under him, fresh from his victories in Zungharia, into Burma, expecting an easy victory. Qing troops, however, suffered heavily from malaria, repeatedly failed to break through tough Burmese resistance, and had to withdraw with heavy casualties. The emperor strongly resisted peace talks but eventually had to agree to an unsatisfactory truce in 1769.

Rather than discuss the details of the war, I will only comment here on how Zhao Yi and Wei Yuan portray it.[25] (Wei Yuan's account of the Burma campaigns follows Zhao Yi's very closely, and it even reproduces numerous passages verbatim.) Zhao Yi, arriving in Burma several months after General Mingrui had committed suicide, was fully aware of the fiascos of the campaign. He also recognized the difficulties of fighting in the tropical environment, describing vividly the impact of malaria, jungles, mountains, and thick forests on the Qing troops. The Burmese resisted invasion by building sturdy wooden palisades on the mountains, which held out against repeated assaults even by Qing artillery. The Burmese themselves also had cannon, mounted on elephants, with which to return fire. When one palisade fell, they retreated and built others. Initially, Qing soldiers climbed up the mountains and battered down the palisades, advancing far into the country. The Burmese then withdrew and conducted a guerrilla war. Eventually, decimated by disease, completely exhausted, and lacking any food supplies, the Qing troops had to withdraw.

Zhao later wrote an essay insisting on the need for military forces to obtain local knowledge about the regions they entered. This meant depending heavily on local ethnic minority informants and military formations, and avoiding heavily bureaucratized structures ignorant of ecological realities. He implicitly critiqued the policies of "defeudalization" (*gaitu guiliu*) and sinicization that alienated native headmen on the frontiers. Zhao Yi had learned that it was very costly to ignore the impact of different terrain on military strategy.[26]

In his description of the Burma war itself, however, Zhao Yi partially balances the fact of retreat by describing the well-coordinated Qing rear-guard manoeuvres: half of the army held off Burmese attacks while the other half retreated. Then the rear guard moved behind the forward force, which held off the advancing Burmese. Zhao Yi admits that the Qing retreat was slow and painful: it took sixty days to cover two thousand *li*. Even so, he claims, "in 60 days we did not suffer one defeat."[27]

The most moving part of Zhao Yi's account is his description of the death of Mingrui. This essay was republished in the *Collected Essays on Imperial Statecraft* (*Huangchao jingshi wenbian*), edited by Wei Yuan under He Changling's supervision in 1826.[28] In Zhao Yi's view, Mingrui was a man who "truly understood people's feelings" (*de renxin*). When he realized that his starving troops had completely exhausted their rations, he decided to retreat, even though he knew that it meant his death. He told his soldiers to attempt to escape across the border, while he remained behind with his trusted officers and a few hundred troops. They fought desperately to hold off more than ten thousand Burmese troops while the army fled: "Each Qing soldier killed one hundred Burmese."[29] Heavily wounded, with all hope gone, Mingrui dismounted his horse, cut off his queue, and hanged himself from a tree.

Zhao Yi recounts a speech that Mingrui is said to have given to his troops to inspire them: "The enemy knows that we are exhausted, but we must fight to the death, in order to show the enemy our country's awesome power (*guojia weiling*). If we demonstrate that our warriors will give up their lives even when they are totally worn out, and every man does his utmost, the enemy will respect us, and future generations will have the will to carry on our struggle." Zhao then comments, "This shows how deeply he was committed to the state. Those who lament useless loss in battle cannot stand up to him."[30]

By stressing noble dedication to a cause, and the lessons future generations could learn from it, rather than the justice of the cause itself, Zhao Yi partially redeemed the expedition from disaster. Zhao Yi's main goal was to broadcast the merits of Mingrui, to earn respect for his tragic death. In this, he succeeded. Mingrui had a special temple erected in Beijing in his memory, and the generals who failed to come to his rescue were executed.[31]

When Zhao compared the Zunghar and Burmese campaigns, both of which he knew intimately, he recognized that they differed greatly. In the northwest, the Qing armies faced little organized resistance: "wherever our troops went the rebels were in disorder, no one resisted our troops ... there was no single day of mutual killing. In Burma the rebels constantly engaged us; there was no day without an attack ... Bandits (*zei*) could choose the place to fight, but we had no rear base; the rebels could get supplies anywhere, but we had no supply line transport. Rebels could carry one cannon per elephant, while our gunpowder decreased daily; during battle we suffered from lack of gunpowder, but their guns thundered so loud you couldn't hear conversation."[32]

Thus Zhao Yi used similar techniques to narrate the Burmese defeat and the Zunghar victory. He did not cover up defeat in battle but, rather, balanced it against other features: personal heroism, the difficulties of terrain, and the importance of historical memory. On the other hand, he did not claim great Heavenly backing for the Burmese campaign. He only states: "Burma returned to peace."[33] Qianlong himself realized the modest results of the campaign. He did not celebrate the troops' return, and he did not have a campaign history compiled.

By stressing his personal experience in Burma and concluding with a moving eulogy to Mingrui, Zhao reinforces his readers' personal involvement with the fate of the distant Yunnan border. As an "embedded" participant, Zhao portrays the thrill and horror of battle in close-up. Instead of endorsing the campaign strategy, he highlights the everyday experience of the emperor's men who fought there. Wei Yuan adds more emotional force to Zhao's account, exclaiming, "Unfortunately, when the general died, his military glory was not known by his superiors, and the world did not know it. Alas! Alas!"[34] Zhao and Wei's emotional accounts draw on readers' sympathies with tragic death, while evading the issue of the importance of the campaign itself.

The Vietnam Campaigns

As in Burma, Qing intervention in Vietnam in 1788-89 led to less than glorious military results. Alexander Woodside has discussed the implications of the Vietnam intervention for the Qianlong emperor's perception of his state and his neighbours.[35] Qing and modern Chinese accounts of the intervention differ substantially from those of Vietnamese historians. For most Qing historians, the Vietnam intervention was only a minor event. Many textbooks on modern Chinese history curiously neglect both the Vietnam and Burma misadventures or mention them only briefly.[36] For Vietnam, Qianlong's expedition was part of nearly twenty years of military conflict that began with the Tây-sơn rebellion of 1773. The Tây-sơn rebellion, intimately connected to the fall of the Lê and the rise of the Nguyễn dynasty, in Alexander Woodside's words, "inaugurates modern Vietnamese history."[37]

I only examine Wei Yuan's account of the Vietnam expedition here (Zhao Yi does not discuss it). Wei Yuan's perspective reflects the limited information of Qing officials about conditions across the border to the south and is strongly influenced by the slanted version of events provided to the Qing by the exiled Lê royal family. Wei Yuan first notes that the Lê family had controlled Annam (the archaic term used by the Qing for northern Vietnam) under the Ming dynasty. In 1666, the Lê king was enfeoffed by the Qing as king of Annam, but the Mạc lords controlled Cao Bang on the Guangxi border. The Mạc forces fled into Yunnan when attacked by Lê, and the Qing court told Lê to return Cao Bang to the Mạc, but the Lê king took advantage of the chaos of the Wu Sangui rebellion in 1674 to take Cao Bang and then offered to pay tribute to the Qing. For the next hundred years, Annam and the Qing had peaceful relations. In this early period, the Qing accepted refugees who crossed the border, but in the end it refused to back the Mạc lords' efforts to recover their frontier territory.

The power of the Lê kings weakened over the eighteenth century as the rival Trịnh and Nguyễn families contested for power. Wei Yuan does not mention the outbreak of the Tây Sơn rebellion, which was instigated by the three brothers Nguyễn Huệ, Nguyễn Nhạc, and Nguyễn Lữ when they attacked the Nguyễn prince ruling in the south and seized his capital at Phú Xuân, modern Huế. Qing officials clearly knew little about events in Vietnam at this time.

Nguyễn Huệ, the strongest general, restored the Lê king to power in the north but withdrew and made his base in Quảng Nam in central Vietnam. In 1787, on the death of the Lê king, Nguyễn Huệ attacked the Lê capital (modern Hanoi), taking away elephants loaded with gold and jewels. Nguyễn Huệ tried to place the king's son on the throne under his protection, but he refused. In retaliation, Nguyễn Huệ again looted the palace, taking the heir's son and daughter with him back to the south. The Lê king fled across the border to Guangxi and requested Qing aid to restore him to the throne. The emperor responded that, since the Lê had paid tribute and "protected the frontier" (*shoufan*) faithfully for centuries, they deserved Qing attention, but he was already concerned that the Lê king disdained to make efforts to recover his own territory. He gave the king refuge in Guangxi, while sending Sun Shiyi to mobilize troops and investigate the military situation. Wei Yuan makes sure to note that Annam used to be part of the Tang dynasty, and he gives a detailed breakdown of its administrative organization in the Tang and in the eighteenth century. Annam looked familiar to Qing eyes because its administrative structure used the same terms for "counties and districts" (*junxian*) as did the Qing bureaucracy.

Sun Shiyi collected a ten-thousand-man army to cross the border, while over 100,000 Annamese militia joined his force under Lê leadership. Three armies prepared to advance on the Lê capital – one from Yunnan, one from Guangxi, and one by sea from Guangdong – but only Sun Shiyi's troops actually marched all the way. Because of famine in Annam, the Qing troops had to bring nearly all supplies with them, building over seventy storage posts. Crossing the border in November, the Qing troops and their local militia fought several fierce battles at river crossings, but they dispersed the Nguyễn "bandits" (zei) easily because of their superior discipline and tactics. In less than a month, Sun Shiyi had taken the capital, and on 19 December he once again bestowed the title of king of Annam upon the Lê king, who now joined the Qing troops from his hiding place in a nearby village. Wei gives credit for the victory to the enthusiastic Annamese support of the Lê king and the military experience of Sun and his generals in the Taiwan campaigns, which had taught them how to move large numbers of troops quickly through difficult terrain.

Nguyễn Huệ, however, did not surrender but, rather, retreated to his base in the south. Sun Shiyi prepared to pursue him, asking to build a fleet of boats and recruit over 100,000 porters to carry supplies further south. In Wei's account, the emperor warned Sun that the country was already devastated, that the Lê king had shown himself to be pusillanimous, that the Nguyễn base was far away from Qing supply lines, and that victory was by no means assured. He told Sun to withdraw to the border, but Sun, ambitious for military glory, defied the emperor's warning and underestimated the enemy. He disbanded the local militia and remained in the capital for a month without making defensive preparations. Meanwhile, Nguyễn Huệ secretly assembled troops to surround the capital while lulling Sun's suspicions with spurious offers of negotiation. Suddenly, during the New Year celebrations, while Sun's troops were drinking, Nguyễn Huệ attacked in force, using elephants to bring heavy cannon to bear on the city. The Lê king fled immediately, while the Qing troops scattered in disorder. Sun straggled back to Guangxi, but he left many of his best generals and at least ten thousand troops to drown in river crossings. The emperor summoned Sun to the capital to answer for his crimes and replaced him with Fu Kang'an.

Wei works hard to deflect blame from the emperor by placing primary responsibility for the disaster on Sun's lust for military glory and the cowardice of the Lê king. In fact, the emperor took responsibility for the disaster because he had not directly ordered Sun to withdraw but had left it up to him. Only after the fact did Sun's decisions appear unwise. The emperor gave Sun remarkably lenient treatment, in recognition of his own responsibility. His grandfather, the Kangxi emperor, had warned against premature celebrations of victory as they led to complacency: "By rejoicing and not having concerns, did I not disobey the warnings? So I do not blame Sun for coveting glory ... but only blame myself for failing to heed my grandfather's lessons."[38]

Subsequently, in Wei's words, Nguyễn Huệ realized that he had brought calamity on himself (*zizhi guhuo*).[39] Fearing an attack by Siam in his rear, he changed the name he used in addressing Qing officials to Nguyễn Quang Bình, "knocked on the border gate, confessed his crimes, and begged to submit" (*kouguan xiezui qixiang*) to the Qing, arguing that he had only sought to defeat Annam, and would not attempt to cross the border. The emperor concluded that "Heaven had tired of the Lê" because they had abandoned their lands and their titles when threatened, and Annam had been disorderly for a century because of their weakness. The Qing had no need to concern itself with petty quarrels in this distant land. The emperor sent Fukang'an to negotiate peace terms and agreed to Nguyễn Quang Bình's request for a personal audience. In 1790, Nguyễn Quang Bình, or his double, attended an imperial banquet in the villa at Rehe and formally received from the Qianlong emperor his title of enfeoffment.[40]

Wei's account cleverly tracks the details of the campaigns, making sure to exempt the emperor himself from any error. Like the earlier imperial historians, he cannot afford any dramatic irony at the emperor's expense. Other actors have limited visions, blinded by pursuit of glory or negligence, but for Wei, the Qing emperor alone sees the whole picture. As Louis Marin noted for Louis XIV, Wei wrote into existence an imperial persona that transcended the ambivalences of the real emperor himself.

Despite his imperial hagiography, Wei is in some ways more revealing than are either his nationalist successors in China or certain modern Western scholars. He openly uses the term "conquest" (*zhengfu*, literally "pacification with a punishment expedition") for the campaigns against Annam, Burma, Korea, and the Zunghars rather than euphemisms like "unification" and "development," which are required phrases in PRC historiography. Wei Yuan also does not endorse the concept of a "tributary system" popularized by John King Fairbank and his disciples in the 1960s. The Taiwan scholar Li Guangtao's study of this campaign is entitled *The Sino-Vietnam War, 1788-1790: War and Peace under the Tributary System*, but the term "tributary system" does not appear in the Chinese title of his book, in any of the contemporary documents, or in Wei Yuan's account. Truong Buu Lam argues that "it was in the Chinese interest to keep Vietnam within the tributary system" and that "the investiture of a tributary ruler was apparently viewed by the Chinese emperor as similar to the appointment of an official within the empire."[41] But the Qianlong emperor was well aware that his control of Vietnam was purely nominal. He stated openly that, despite Sun Shiyi's catastrophic losses, "Yet in Annam to have the name of victory is the same as having real victory: have I not obtained a nominal victory?"[42] This was indeed a form of "pragmatism" ratified by myth, as Truong Buu Lam writes, but it was not disguised as the true subordination of a tributary king. A number of scholars have pointed to the inadequacies of the concept of "tributary system" developed in John K. Fairbank's pathbreaking 1968 book, *The Chinese World Order*, but they have mainly relied on postcolonial theory and non-Chinese sources to support their critique. Even if we look at the canonical Chinese writers of this period, we can still find glaring contradictions between the idealized "tributary system" and the facts on the ground.

None of the Qing materials mentions the Tây-sơn rebellion, the most significant aspect of these years for Vietnamese historians. The Qing writers view the Vietnamese conflict as purely a struggle for succession between rival dynastic lineages; they never link the Nguyễn to mass support. They do, however, note repeatedly the support of militia troops for the Lê king, a fact that Vietnamese writers tend to suppress. Ultimately, Qianlong accepted the dynastic transition in Vietnam by placing it within a context he knew: the transfer of a Heavenly mandate from one lineage to another. The fiascos in Vietnam and Burma, however, did not stimulate a drastic reform of Qing military institutions. Shifting the blame to vainglorious generals and vacillating allies diverted attention from the need for structural change. Comforting accommodation of defeat spared Qing pride but delayed recognition of serious weakness in military and foreign policy.

Conclusion

Eric Hobsbawm has commented that, just as the opium poppy is the essential ingredient for heroin, so history is the essential ingredient for nationalist ideology.[43] Nationalist histories close collective minds and excite collective emotions. They stimulate mass identification with imagined communities, defining who belongs and who does not, praising heroes and demonizing enemies, giving a clear shape to collective human experience. Powerful and addictive, they connect people to a conventional past at the cost of suppressing its other possibilities.

Dipesh Chakrabarty argues that the secular, "empty, homogeneous time" of modern history writing effaces other potential paths found in the "heterogeneous present," which contains in it many pasts at once. He aims to "provincialize Europe" by undercutting its claim to embody the single authoritative narrative of modernity. He looks to marginal figures and hidden voices in elite non-Western texts to find a more open-ended view of where history can go.

Yet we may also look at even the most stereotyped imperial, or imperialist, histories of war and still find there signs of alternative futures. Even official histories betray tensions that undermine simple classifications. By looking carefully at how they tell the story and what they include and exclude, we can show how Qing historians began to construct a fixed version of the frontier conquests. Their narratives are not mere propaganda but, rather, complex interpretations. They leave open more questions than they appear to solve. The gap between imperially constructed "mythistory" and the facts on the ground yawns wider in some cases than in others. Looking at this gap, however, may lead us to reflect on the inability of any historical account, including our own, to capture the full experience of the past. It may also remind readers that the modern world, defined by histories of the nation, did not begin simply or sharply at one well-defined place or time.

Most theorists portray nationalism as a distinctly modern creation, beginning in Europe in the early nineteenth century. Concepts like "invention of tradition" and "print capitalism" tie nationalist ideologies closely to new projects of elite intellectuals aiming to draw in masses of citizens to their movements. Theorists are suspicious of tying nationalism too closely to earlier periods because they fear endorsing the "primordialism" of nationalist ideologies themselves. But just because nationalists (falsely) claim to find their nations deeply embedded in misty antiquity does not mean that they create nations out of nothing. China, as a nation that has taken over most of the territory of an empire, clearly draws on its imperial past to define its current national goals and identities. Even though twentieth-century nationalists rejected the Manchu regime wholesale, they took over half-consciously the territorial and narrative definitions that the Qing had already refined out of its nearly two centuries of continuous expansion. As more elements of old China reappear with the fading of the Communist interlude, we realize that China's past never really passed away. Exposing hidden links between past and present may help us to imagine other futures.

Notes

1 Paul A. Cohen, *History in Three Keys: The Boxers as Event, Experience, and Myth* (New York: Columbia University Press, 1997)

2 This section draws on Chapter 13 of my book, *China Marches West: The Qing Conquest of Central Eurasia* (Cambridge, MA: Harvard University Press, 2005).

3 R. Kent Guy, *The Emperor's Four Treasuries: Scholars and the State in the Late Ch'ien-lung Era* (Cambridge, MA: Harvard University Press, 1987).

4 *Da Qing Lichao Shilu (Shengzu)* [Kangxi reign] (Taibei: Huawen Shuju, 1970), *juan* 174, dated 1696/7/*wuwu*; Jaqa Cimeddorji, *Die Briefe des Kang-Hsi-Kaisers aus den Jahren 1696-97 an den Kronprinzen Yin-Cheng aus mandschurischen Geheimdokumenten: Ein Beitrag zum ersten Dsungarenkrieg der Ching 1690-1697* [The letters of the Kangxi emperor from the years

1696-1697 to the crown prince Yinzheng, from secret Manchu documents: A contribution to the study of the first Qing Zunghar war] (Wiesbaden: Otto Harrassowitz 1991), 21; Borjigidai Oyunbilig, *Zur überlieferungsgeschichte des Berichts über den persönlichen Feldzug des Kangxi Kaisers gegen Galdan* [The compilation of the personal campaign history of the Kangxi Emperor against Galdan]*(1696-1697)* (Wiesbaden: Harrassowitz, 1999), 35; Arthur W. Hummel, ed. *Eminent Chinese of the Ch'ing Period* (Washington DC: US Government Printing Office, 1943-44), 66, 309, 489.

5 This section draws on Peter C. Perdue, "The Qing Empire in Eurasian Time and Space," in *The Qing Formation in World-Historical Time*, edited by Lynne A. Struve, 57-91 (Cambridge, MA: Harvard University Press, 2004).

6 Lionel Gossman, *The Empire Unpossess'd: An Essay on Gibbon's "Decline and Fall"* (Cambridge: Cambridge University Press, 1981), 75.

7 Oyunbilig, *Zur überlieferungsgeschichte*, 109.

8 Joanna Waley-Cohen, "Commemorating War in 18th Century China," *Modern Asian Studies* 30 (1996): 869-99. Joanna Waley-Cohen, *The Culture of War in China: Empire and Military under the Qing Dynasty* (London: I.B. Tauris, 2006).

9 For further discussion, see Chapter 14 of Perdue, *China Marches West*.

10 Zhao Yi, *Huangchao Wugong Jisheng*, Wenhai reprint, n.d.

11 Quotation from Quinton G. Priest, "Portraying Central Government Institutions: Historiography and Intellectual Accommodation in the High Ching," *Late Imperial China* 7 (1986): 39. On "historical analogism," see Robert M. Hartwell, "Historical Analogism, Public Policy, and Social Science in 11-12th Century China," *American Historical Review* 76 (1971): 690-728.

12 Zhao Yi, *Huangchao Wugong*, 60.

13 Ibid., 64.

14 Ibid.

15 Jane Leonard, "Qing History, Wei Yuan and Contemporary Political Dialogue," in *New Directions in the Social Sciences and Humanities in China*, edited by Michael B. Yahuda, 28-45 (London: Macmillan, 1987); Jane Kate Leonard, *Wei Yuan and China's Rediscovery of the Maritime World* (Cambridge, MA: Harvard University Press, 1984); Judith Whitbeck, "Kung Tzu-chen and the Redirection of Literati Commitment in Early Nineteenth-Century China," *Ch'ing-shih Wen't'i* 4 (1983): 1-32; Shirleen S. Wong, *Kung Tzu-chen* (Boston: Twayne, 1975).

16 "Xiyu zhi xingsheng yi" [On making the Western regions a province], in Gong Zizhen, *Gong Ding'an Quanji Leibian* [Complete works of Gong Zizhen], edited by Gong [Zizhen], 164-72 (Shanghai: Shijie shuju, 1937); He Changling, *Huangchao Jingshi Wenbian* [Collected essays on statecraft] (Shanghai: Zhongxi shuju, 1899), Perdue, *China Marches West*, 500-4, 80, 17a-23a. See also James A. Millward, *Beyond the Pass: Economy, Ethnicity, and Empire in Qing Central Asia, 1759-1864* (Stanford: Stanford University Press, 1998), 241-43.

17 Gong Zizhen, "Xiyu zhi xingsheng yi," 165.

18 Millward, *Beyond the Pass*, 41-42.

19 Wei Yuan, *Shengwuji*, 3b

20 Philip A. Kuhn, "Ideas behind China's Modern State," *Harvard Journal of Asiatic Studies* 55 (1995): 301; Wei Yuan, *Shengwuji* [Record of sacred military victories] (Beijing: Zhonghua Shuju, 1984), preface.

21 Hummel, *Eminent Chinese,* 851.

22 Xiao Yishan, *Qingdai Tongshi* [Comprehensive history of the Qing dynasty] (Beijing: Zhonghua shuju, 1986). Millward, *Beyond the Pass*, 41-2. Earlier, Naitô Konan also exposed inaccuracies in Wei Yuan's account. See Naitô Konan, "'Qinbian Jilue' no 'Gardan zhuan,'" *Naitô Konan Zenshû* [The biography of Galdan in the Records of the Northwest Border] (Tokyo: Chikuma Shobo, 1970), 7:380-425.

23 Wei Yuan, *Shengwuji*, 3.

24 Zhao Yi, *Huangchao Wugong, juan* 3.

25 There is a short account in Hummel, ed., *Eminent Chinese*, 7, 578. See discussion by Alexander Woodside, "The Ch'ien-lung Reign"; and the excellent article by Dai Yingcong, "A Disguised Defeat: The Myanmar Campaign of the Qing Dynasty," *Modern Asian Studies* 38, 1 (2004): 145-88, with extensive bibliography. See also C. Patterson Giersch, *Chinese*

Borderlands: Indigenes, Migrants, and Empires on Qing China's Yunnan Frontier (Cambridge, MA: Harvard University Press, 2005). On Qianlong's ten campaigns, see Zhuang Jifa, *Qing Gaozong Shiquan Wugong Yanjiu* [Studies on the Qianlong emperor's ten military campaigns] (Taibei: Guoli gugong bowuyuan, 1982).

26 Zhao Yi, "Ming biansheng gongjiao bingshu" [The number of offensive troops stationed on the Ming borders], He Changling, *Huangchao Jingshi Wenbian* [Qing dynasty essays on statecraft], *juan* 71, 21-22.

27 Zhao Yi, *Huangchao Wugong*, 12a, 119.

28 He Changling, *Huangchao Jingshi wenbian, juan* 3.12a, 119, *juan* 87, 19-31.

29 Zhao Yi, *Huangchao Wugong*, 108.

30 Zhao Yi, *Huangchao Wugong, juan* 3.8a, 111.

31 Hummel, *Eminent Chinese*, 578.

32 Zhao Yi, *Huangchao Wugong*, 119.

33 Ibid., 118.

34 Wei Yuan, *Shengwuji*, 267.

35 Alexander Woodside, "The Ch'ien-lung Reign," in *The Cambridge History of China*, vol. 9, pt. 1: *The Ch'ing Empire to 1800*, edited by Willard J. Peterson, 276-78 (Cambridge, MA: Cambridge University Press 2002).

36 Jonathan Spence, *The Search for Modern China* (New York: Norton 1999), 111, gives a one-paragraph summary of the Vietnam campaign, with a small map. F.W. Mote, *Imperial China: 900-1800* (Cambridge, MA: Harvard University Press, 1999), and Dai Yi, *Jianming Qingshi*, 2 vols. (Beijing: Renmin Chubanshe, 1984) do not mention the campaigns at all. The most extended study in English is Truong Buu Lam, "Intervention versus Tribute in Sino-Vietnamese Relations, 1788-1790," in *The Chinese World Order: Traditional China's Foreign Relations*, edited by John King Fairbank, 165-79 (Cambridge, MA: Harvard University Press, 1968). In Japanese, see Suzuki Chûsei, "Kenryû Annan ensei kô" [A study of the Qianlong expedition to Annam], *Tôyô gakuhô* 50, 2 (September 1967): 1-23; 50, 3 (December 1967): 79-106; and Suzuki Chûsei, "Reichô Kôki No Shin to No Kankei [Relations of the late Lê dynasty with the Qing] (1682-1804)," in *Betonamu-Chûgoku Kankeishi* [History of Sino-Vietnamese relations], edited by Yamamoto Tatsurô, 405-92 (Tokyo: Yamakawa Shuppansha, 1975). Li Guangtao, *Ji Qianlong Nian Pingding Annan Zhi Yi* [A Record of the Qianlong military expedition against Vietnam] (Taibei: Zhongyang yanjiuyuan lishi yuyan yanjiusuo, 1976) collects materials from the *Qingshilu* on the Vietnam campaign.

37 Alexander B. Woodside, *Vietnam and the Chinese Model: A Comparative Study of Nguyễn and Ch'ing Civil Government in the First Half of the Nineteenth Century* (Cambridge, MA: Harvard University Press, 1971), 3; Trương Hữu Quýnh, Bùi Quý Lộ, and Đào Tố Uyên, *Lịch Sử Việt Nam Tự Thế Kỉ X – 1858: Giáo Trình Dào Tạo Giáo Viên Trung Học Cơ Sở Hệ Cao Dẳng Sư Phạm* [History of Vietnam from the tenth century to 1858: A basic curriculum for middle school students] (Hà Noi: Nhà xuât bản Giáo dục, 1998), 85-95.

38 Li Guangtao, *Ji Qianlong Nian Pingding Annan*, 94.

39 Wei Yuan, *Shengwuji* (Beijing: Zhonghua Shuju, 1984), 279.

40 Truong Buu Lam and Suzuki Chûsei argue that Nguyễn Quang Bình, fearing upheaval if he left his realm for China, may well have sent a stand-in. See Truong Buu Lam, "Intervention versus Tribute," 176; Suzuki Chûsei, "Kenryû Annan ensei kô."

41 Truong Buu Lam, "Intervention Versus Tribute," 179.

42 Li Guangtao, *Ji Qianlong Nian Pingding Annan* , 94.

43 Eric J. Hobsbawm, "The New Threat to History" (Address to the Central European University, Budapest), *New York Review of Books*, 16 December 1993.

7
Tributary Relations and the Qing-Chosŏn Frontier on Mount Paektu

Andre Schmid

This chapter discusses tributary relations, the limits of the Qing Empire in East Asia, and murder. In the middle of the night in August 1710, Yi Mangŏn, together with eight associates, crossed the Yalu River from Chosŏn into Qing territory in search of ginseng. Finding it easier to thieve than to dig, they jumped a group of six Qing subjects, murdering five of them and stripping their victims of medicinal roots and deer pelts before retreating back into Chosŏn territory. Yi, who was later to lose his head over what Chosŏn documents labelled this "illegal crossing," would have been surprised at the subsequent brouhaha, which eventually reached the ears of the Kangxi emperor and embroiled the Chosŏn court in a series of debates about how to deal with Qing investigators. He would likely have been even more surprised that, three centuries later, his knavishness would offer historians an avenue for reconsidering what, in contemporary Qing documents and recent historiography, has often been presented as the exemplar of tributary relations – Qing-Chosŏn relations.

This chapter is, in part, an old-fashioned yarn. The four years from 1710 to 1713 were an unusually active time along what today is understood as the Sino-Korean border. I would like to suggest that, by following the tribulations of an imperially appointed Manchu detective-cum-surveyor in his quest to reach the top of Mount Paektu, a very different picture of tributary relations emerges. Rather than the supposedly harmonious relations between the two courts, as is so often captured in references to the performance of the kowtow in Beijing by emissaries from Seoul, there is murder and what essentially amounts to at least a modicum of mayhem in a remote area under the dubious control of these two authorities. By shifting away from the ideological redoubts of the imperial centre – the imperial palace, the Board of Rites, the rituals surrounding the kowtow, and, most important, the historical records generated by these institutions – I argue that we can begin to see not only how conflicting interests could be contested within the elder brother-younger brother ideology of tribute but also how often startling different understandings of the relationship could be held by the two neighbours. This is a picture of tribute where shared cultural vision and notions of a larger East Asian culture are *not* the issue. Instead, the tributary relation is seen as marked by tension and conflict, as a medium through which self-interests were pursued and through which some highly political and sophisticated subterfuge were conducted – all of this occurring through the same institutions and ideology about which we have heard so much in the past.

That these two countries were immediate neighbours, with adjacent lands, is a feature of the relationship often overlooked in the literature on tribute. The Qing and Chosŏn were both centralized, bureaucratic states – unusual at this point in world history. Yet this very propinquity became a source of tension as both courts sought to control the transfrontier movement of their subjects in efforts that reveal to us the importance given to the location and demarcation of territory in the early eighteenth century, well before such matters concerned European nation-states.[1] This murder along the frontier brings questions of territory, its demarcation and control, into the purview of both bureaucracies, enabling us to examine the territorial limits of the Qing empire together with the rather ambiguous, and contested, position of the Chosŏn within that empire.

Finally, this chapter also suggests that, as the Qing dynasty is historiographically recast as a multiethnic empire, voices from other peoples – in this instance Koreans – will further broaden our understanding of the variety of relationships that constituted this empire. No reader of late Chosŏn dynasty documents, with their frequent pejorative anti-Manchu comments, would ever accept the proposition that the Manchus had been sinicized to the point of being considered the inheritors of a long Chinese tradition. Yet the rereading of the Qing dynasty as a distinctly Manchu empire, together with all that this entails, tends to overlook the fact that, despite their multiple ways of ruling the various peoples of their vast lands, Manchu understanding of empire was not necessarily shared by peoples subject to their power. This was certainly true of Chosŏn, a dynasty that had been conquered and coerced into tributary status under the Qing. The rise of the Manchus had been met with nothing but enmity by the Chosŏn court, a hostility that, while hidden from Beijing beneath the gifts and rituals of tribute, continued to animate attitudes towards the Qing Empire and coloured the intellectual environment in Chosŏn right down to the nineteenth century. My strategy is to examine a particular moment in the conduct of tributary relations in a particular locality so as to problematize any attempt to understand tributary relations that is based solely on studies coming out of Beijing. By comparing the rival versions of these moments, as produced in Beijing and Seoul, respectively, it becomes clear that the historical record produced in Beijing functioned to fit Chosŏn into the category of loyal tribute while glossing over any instances – murder, recalcitrant behaviour, and the like – that may have ruffled the assumptions underlying the use of tributary ideology to support imperial legitimacy. It is upon these central Qing documents, I argue, that our understanding of tributary relations has largely been developed – a process that has oversimplified our understanding of the Qing's relations with this "ideal" tributary and has insinuated a type of Sinocentrism into our understanding of the relationship between Beijing and Seoul. The view from the south of the Yalu River offers a very different vision of empire. The ideal tributary was perhaps not so ideal after all.

Conquest and Antagonism

Our understanding of tributary relations has come a long way since being famously formulated as a "system" by John King Fairbank. As has been well noted, in Fairbank's approach to East Asia, the tribute system served the historiographical purpose of explaining China's response to the West in terms of traditional diplomatic behaviour, or, as he more colourfully put it, the way it used "old bottles for new wine."[2] A number of critics have pointed out many of the problematic assumptions of this approach – in particular its culturalism, reliance on modernization theory, and benign approach to Western imperialism[3] – and Fairbank himself, in his last major contribution, downplayed its significance.[4] Wider empirical research has broadened our understanding of the role and function of tribute, showing that it did not represent traditional attitudes "inbred with the Chinese ways of life"[5] but that it was, in fact, a policy option, one of the many ways that Chinese elites flexibly pursued foreign policy objectives at various times, depending on the period, location, and contact peoples. This newer understanding, derived largely from research on various dynastic ties with the peoples of Central and Inner Asia, has taken new directions with the recent emphasis on the distinctive Manchu nature of the Qing dynasty as well as with the surge in studies concerning relations with minority peoples along the frontiers.[6] Most provocatively, in his study of Anglo-Chinese relations, James Hevia has emphasized how the various institutions and rituals of tribute were used by the Qing to achieve and protect the shifting interests of its own empire.[7] Whereas in the past, tribute represented a cultural difference distinct to China, for Hevia it represents an equivalence between two empires, just one of the tools in a litany available for the management of imperial interests, their forms less important than their service to the relations that enabled central power. Little, it would seem, is left of the Fairbankian approach to tribute.

Yet this might be too quick of an assessment. The subjects of this newer research – Miao, British, or Zunghary – were all barbarians according to the classical ritual categories. And as barbarians, after all, the proprieties of tribute were not *supposed* to apply to them, at least not until they had risen within the hierarchy of acculturated peoples. The recent spate of studies of imperial dealings with the various peoples of empire, while greatly changing our understanding of the technologies and institutions of rule at play in the premodern period, has shifted attention to these other peoples; however, in so doing, it has essentially accepted older arguments about how tribute works. To use Fairbank's terminology – a lexicon that adopted, if not the exact categories, certainly the spirit of the Ministry of Rites and Lifanyuan – the recent focus has certainly challenged conventional approaches to the Inner Asian and Outer. But what about the third of Fairbank's categories, the Sinic?[8]

Korea during the Chosŏn dynasty, more than any other country, gained a reputation as the pre-eminent tributary, the nation that showed how tribute was supposed to "work." This image of China's peninsular neighbour can be found in many documents, ranging from contemporary sources from the Ming and Qing dynasties (if not earlier), the work of Fairbank and his defenders, and even the work of his most recent critics.[9] This shared image is arguably one of the most consistent strains in these vast, at times discordant, works. Here was a student who had reputedly superseded the teacher, a country supposedly more Confucian than China itself, and, in an ultimate affirmation of sinicization theories, a country that had become, in one famous articulation, "the perfected Chinese pattern."[10]

Yet there is every reason to question the ease with which representations of Chosŏn from the Chinese and Manchu imperial dynasties have found their way into twentieth-century English – and Chinese – historiography.[11] For proponents of the sinicization thesis, such an image of the more than five-hundred-year-old Chosŏn dynasty had its obvious uses. It served to weave the complex history of East Asia into the unifying cultural category of a "Sinic zone," where the Chosŏn court's dispatch of missions to Beijing – on average more than four times a year and occasionally so frequent as to become an irritant to their less than welcoming hosts – affirmed the centrality of Beijing. It also functioned to provide East Asia with a unified cultural realm that offered the region as a legitimate subject for historical inquiry and for institution building. But this focus on tribute conduct – how often did envoys arrive? how well did they perform the rituals? – not only reproduces the concerns of the Beijing court with regard to its uses of ritual but also neglects to consider the fact that tribute was the medium for negotiating a plethora of issues that, though deeply embedded in the concerns of empire did not necessarily manifest themselves solely in the rituals conducted in Beijing.

Before turning to one of these neglected areas – territorial jurisdiction – it is important to note that the function of Chosŏn as the paragon of Qing tribute nations overlooks the tempestuous start of this relationship. It was hardly the charm or allure of Qing culture that led the Chosŏn court to dispatch its envoys to Beijing; rather, it was the brute force of two successive invasions. In 1627, because of Seoul's support for the Ming cause, the Manchus invaded. Only when the court agreed to subordinate itself to the rule of the now "Later Jin," as the aspiring dynasty was called, did the Manchus agree to withdraw. But ten years later, when the new dynastic name of "Qing" was adopted, the Chosŏn court refused to receive Manchu emissaries requesting Chosŏn observance of Manchu suzerainty. A second invasion followed. Led this time by Nurhaci himself, the intrusion reached deep into the peninsula, capturing Seoul and forcing King Injo to prostrate himself before the Manchu aspirant to the Mandate of Heaven. A stele, with inscriptions in Manchu and Chinese, was erected on this spot at Samjŏndo on the Han River, south of the royal capital, to commemorate the victory. The crown prince, spirited off to Jehol, became a prisoner to ensure the court would not return to its recalcitrant ways. Thus began the history of a relationship often portrayed as the harmonious ideal for other tributaries. Only after the two invasions did a more submissive policy begin, marked most famously by the dispatch of tribute missions. Yet, in many ways, this shift remained an outward show.

The anti-Manchu policy prevalent in these early years continued to dominate the court and intellectual circles and, as Jahyun Kim Haboush has argued, continued to have repercussions for the meaning and position of the monarchy in Chosŏn.[12] Most remarkably, under the reign of King Hyojong (1649-59), leading officials initiated preparations for what was openly called a "northern expedition." Hyojong, as crown prince, had been a hostage in Jehol, where he developed an antipathy towards his captors that, when he returned home to assume the throne, manifested itself in a variety of anti-Manchu policies. Enormous expenditures were made on the military, with the vain goal of invading the Qing in order to restore the Ming. Famous officials such as Song Siyŏl made their careers, in part, by advocating an unbridled antipathy towards the Qing.[13] Ming studies scholars will be entertained by the fact that, unbeknown to the Manchus, refugee Ming loyalists continued to offer sacrifices to the imperial house in the peninsula well after the defeat of the Three Feudatory Rebellion – rituals that, in fact, have been conducted until recently.[14] Aversion to the Qing dynasty led to a wistfulness for the Ming dynasty. This wistfulness emphasized the generosity of Ming assistance consequent upon Beijing's defeat of Hideoyoshi to such an extent that many problematic features of this defeat were swept aside in favour of a rosy nostalgia.[15] In 1704, more than six decades after the second Manchu invasion, a shrine was erected to the memory of the

Wanli emperor, eventually becoming the centrepiece of one of Korea's most famous academies. By the end of the nineteenth century, this shrine emerged as the object of a power struggle as the monarchy and the yangban aristocracy struggled to control what had become a powerful symbol in the distribution of political power in the peninsula.[16] Thus, the meaning of the Ming dynasty continued to be debated and remained politically resonant in the Korean peninsula long after it had faded from memory in China.

Indeed, when the Western powers and Japan began demanding trading privileges from Chosŏn in the 1860s, the Manchu invasions of the early seventeenth century served to provide historical allusions for scholars who argued against concluding any treaties. Just as the Manchus had threatened the moral integrity of the dynasty, so now did Western nations and Japan. In 1881 Hong Chaehak was executed for an especially adamant anti-Japanese memorial, one that used an image that, throughout the peninsula, had long referred to the Manchu occupation of China: the "stench of mutton that pervaded the Four Seas" (*sihai xingshan*).[17] As the famous scholar Yi Hangno argued, the conclusion of commercial treaties threatened the teachings of Confucius, which, he believed, since the Manchu conquest of the Qing, had their last bastion in the peninsula.[18] In 1895, shortly after the signing of the Treaty of Shimonoseki had formally ended this long tributary relationship, Korean nationalists razed the stele erected by Nurhaci in 1637 on the banks of the Han River at Samjŏndo.[19] Even at this point, contemporary, Korean observers could still comment that this long overdue action had finally erased the shame of all the intervening reigns.[20]

A more comprehensive history recounting the consequences of the rise of the Qing for Chosŏn has yet to be written. My point in briefly relating these various episodes is to show how this history of conflict and tension – whether military or intellectual, between the Qing and Chosŏn, or between Chosŏn elites – has been erased from Sinocentric English language histories of tribute relations. With memories of the double Manchu invasion always fresh, the Chosŏn court had every reason to hide its hostility, be it in the form of a pejorative reference to the less than worthy barbarians, possible (if self-delusional) military plans, or the use of Ming and Chosŏn reign dates. None of these manifestations of anti-Qing sentiment, however important for the distribution of power or intellectual debates within the peninsula, ever interfered with the regular dispatch of tribute missions to Beijing. From the Manchu perspective, the Ministry of Rites hosted more missions from Chosŏn than from any other tributary. Read in terms of frequency of missions alone, this most regular of tribute bearers understandably – but most one-sidedly – came to be represented in dynastic documents as the ideal tributary. This perspective from the centre has insinuated itself into twentieth-century approaches to the Qing-Chosŏn relationship.

Crossing Frontiers

The neglect of the history of conflict is not the only historiographical consequence of this tendency to represent Chosŏn as the ideal tributary. Perhaps most important, there has been little consideration of the way spatial issues between these two adjacent states, in particular issues over territorial jurisdiction, were mediated through tributary language and institutions. That the frontier was a critical issue to both courts can be seen from the *Tongmun hwigo* (A Compendium of Diplomatic Documents), a compilation of official documents exchanged between the Chosŏn court and its Ming and Qing counterparts.[21] In its many categories of documents, one of the single largest sections is devoted to what was called *pŏmwŏl* (*fanyue*), or "illegal crossings."

The documents in this categoy all concern the handling of individuals or groups arrested when unlawfully traversing the frontier. From accounts of motivations for crossing – more often than not, gathering ginseng or hunting, and, occasionally, more serious criminal activity – to descriptions of capture and summaries of the final disposition, these documents detail the concern on the part of both courts to observe boundaries and to limit local flows of population. This was no light offence: violators were in most cases beheaded, their corpses laid out on the frontier to deter others, while their families were often cast into slavery. Local Chosŏn officials who failed to prevent these illegal crossings were often banished to remote southern islands in internal exile.

Though the recorded cases of pŏmwŏl begin in the Ming dynasty, the rise of the Manchus did not change the way in which these issues were treated. Territory was considered sufficiently important that, after their invasion of the Korean peninsula in 1627, the Manchus included a statement of territorial division in the "joint oath" declared by the two courts. As the agreement read, "We two nations have now established a peace. From today onward, let us each respect this agreement, each observe our territories [*fengjiang*], and refrain from disputing small matters." Only then, it asserted, would both sovereigns "jointly enjoy everlasting peace."[22] Mutual repect of the frontier may have been seen as a condition for "everlasting peace," but such statements clearly presumed a mutual sense of a delineated frontier. How, then, was this division of space understood? And did both parties share the same understanding?

Along parts of the frontier, long-standing conventions stretching back to the mid-Ming and Chosŏn dynasties had established what were tantamount to boundaries. By the late Chosŏn dynasty, travellers to China were quite conscious that, in the words of the famous scholar Pak Chiwŏn, "This river [the Yalu River] is the point of contact and the boundary between them and us." To cross the Yalu River was to enter into Qing territory. Parts of the frontier, especially the lowest sections of the Yalu River, had long been defined by means of social and administrative practices, creating what Marion Eggert has called a "ritualized space."[23] But, along other stretches, particularly the remote depopulated sections of the upper Yalu and Tumen Rivers, just where the territory of the two dynastyies began or ended was less clear.

This situation began to change with the maturation of Qing rule. In the early years of their reign, the Manchus devoted their energy towards separating Manchuria from China proper through the construction of the willow palisade. Their southern frontier with Korea was a less pressing concern, reflecting just how strongly their orientation had turned to the central plains since their conquest of Beijing. The new rulers were not intent on challenging the boundary conventions that had already developed and exhibited little interest in clarifying territorial claims in more ambiguous areas. But this was to change with the growing presence of Russians in the northeast. By the reign of Kangxi, more attention was directed towards the northeast.[24] Moreover, once the Qing had defeated the Sanfan rebellion and had begun to consolidate its rule in China proper, a nostalgic eye began to be cast back onto the homelands of the Changbai mountain region as questions of Manchu identity gradually gained significance.[25] So too was Kangxi interested, for administrative reasons, in producing maps for his entire empire and compiling the information to be used in the *Daming yitongzhi*. In response to these needs and impulses, Kangxi strengthened the dynasty's administrative presence in Manchuria, particularily in Jilin, and sent a number of survey expeditions into the frontier area. The Korean court, however, establishing a pattern of behaviour that would underline much of its interaction with the Qing on this issue, proved to be less than cooperative. In 1692, Korean officials refused to assist one of the teams that had been sent to inspect the sources of the Yalu and Tumen rivers.[26] When ordered seven years later, in 1699, to provide topographic information about the eight provinces of the peninsula, Korean officials again declined.[27] But, in 1710, Kangxi was presented with a new opportunity.

This opportunity came in the form of a particularly egregious case of illegal crossing – the case of Yi Mangŏn and associates described at the outset of this chapter. After killing five of the six Qing subjects they encountered and stealing their ginseng and deer pelts, Yi retreated to the Chosŏn village of Wiwŏn. Unusually, this illegal crossing did not end at this point. The sole survivor of the attack, upon returning home to Wuliaoliang, organized a group of more than twenty people, who, the following month, crossed over to Wiwŏn to demand an accounting. Standing outside the northern gate, they shouted out the names of the culprits, accusing them of murdering five people. Nor did they restrict their actions to demands that the murderers be turned over. They quickly captured a minor official, Ko Yŏgang, holding him hostage. The local magistrate, confounded by this novel situation, at first merely locked the gates to keep the mob out. But soon he adopted a more time-tested strategy – plying the group with wine and treats while offering them "gifts" of silver, silk, cattle, and rice. Having perhaps overly enjoyed the libations, the demonstrators failed to maintain a vigilant watch, and, as they slept off the effects of the wine, Ko managed to slip away. With no hostage and perhaps satiated by the bribes, the members of the group of twenty returned to their homes. Quelled at the local level, the incident now entered the purview of the bureaucracy.[28]

As news of the event spread, Governor Yi Cheyŏng ordered the arrest of Yi Mangŏn and his fellow transgressors. Though all were quickly brought into custody, a few escaped. The extreme measure of issuing a reward for their capture was taken, and the governor went so far as to offer manumission for any slave that turned the escapees over to authorities. Anybody who concealed them would share the same punishment as the culprits themselves.[29] News of the events was conveyed to the Board of Rites in Beijing.[30]

When informed of the disruption at the frontier, Kangxi ordered two officials to Fenghuang to investigate the murders rather than leave the matter to Chosŏn officials. Punishing the perpetrators was not the only thing Kangxi had on his mind, however, for the illegal crossing offered him an opportunity to get his officials into the frontier area to conduct a survey. This would also allow him finally to get the topographical information he had long been seeking. The leading role in the murder investigation was assigned to a Manchu official, the "Master of the Hunt" (*Hulie Zongguan*),[31] Mukedeng. To him a second, secret task was also assigned: after the meeting at Fenghuang, he was to proceed to Wiwŏn to investigate the site of the execution and then travel up to the Mount Paektu area to investigate and clarify the border region.[32]

These supposedly secret orders were not so secret, however. No official notice had been conveyed to the Chosŏn court, but word of Kangxi's intent had reached it even before Mukedeng had reached Fenghuang. The advance notice gave Chosŏn officials a chance to plan just how they would deal with a Manchu official seeking to journey up the Yalu River. Their chief concern was security. This was expressed in court at a later date by Yi Kangjwa, the second minister of the Board of Personnel. He invoked a common saying – "barbarians do not have one hundred years of fortune" – to suggest that the Manchus, in power for over six decades, would soon be defeated. In such a scenario, he predicted, they would have to escape into the northeast, perhaps even into Chosŏn territory. A mission to survey the frontier, he warned, only provided them with a chance to inspect the terrain and measure the roads.[33]

From the very beginning, a general policy of what might be called unproductive cooperation was undertaken. Featuring half-truths and outright deception, the approach pursued by Chosŏn officials sought to corral the

Manchu envoy so as to prevent him from obtaining information about the frontier region while still meeting the most minimal expectations of tributary status. Just where those minimal expectations lay was open to interpretation from both the Chosŏn and Manchu sides – and Chosŏn officials were more than willing to push the limits of these commitments.

For the next few weeks, Mukedeng sought to fulfill his imperial mission. Communication between local Chosŏn officials and Seoul was constant, providing information to Seoul, where court officials, with the full support and participation of the king, devised strategies to confound Mukedeng. Mukedeng arrived in Fenghuang in April to be greeted by the third minister of the Board of Punishments, Song Chŏngmyŏng, the Seoul court's front man. At first, Mukedeng merely inquired about the incident itself, asking about the murderers and the way they had been handled. Song reported back to court that he did not believe any problems would arise from the investigation, but he did sound a warning. One of the translators had suggested that the mission would next head towards Mount Paektu, though Song admitted he could not confirm the report. During another deliberation, Mukedeng decided that he must personally inspect the corpses of the murderers, which he had learned were along the frontier near Wiwŏn. Song demurred. He pointed out that the orders of neither the Qing emperor nor his own king went beyond the meeting in Fenghuang. Arguing they could not recklessly proceed on their own initiative, Song suggested memorializing for permission. Mukedeng refused, protesting that he had been assigned the task of preventing any further such incidents. To fulfill this goal, he must go to the site. They argued heatedly over this point until Mukedeng, losing his temper, departed in a huff.[34]

Unable to convince Mukedeng, Song turned to subterfuge. That night he had his translator approach one of the Korean officials accompanying Mukedeng to plant the idea that the latter could travel on the north side of the river while the Chosŏn party headed along the southern shore. A bribe was even offered to make this option more appealing, but, as the official responded, the northern side was especially treacherous so even a bribe of ten thousand pieces of gold would not work.[35]

When the Seoul court received Song's report of these events, King Sukchong gathered his officials to decide how to best deal with this turn of events. Officials such as the second state councillor, Kim Changjip, argued that, following the precedent of 1692, a memorial should be sent to the Board of Rites, requesting a halt to the mission on account of the dangers in the mountains. Others rejected this option as too slow, urging instead that accompaying officials should interfere with Mukedeng's mission. Minister of War Ch'oe Sŏkhŭng warned that Mukedeng must be kept from learning of, much less entering, strategic mountain passes and roads. All agreed that

Song should use every means at his disposal to wrangle, negotiate, and argue with Mukedeng. He could not be permitted to cross the river.[36]

At the frontier, every time Song suggested they travel on separate sides of the river, Mukedeng heatedly protested. The matter finally came to a head when Song informed Mukedeng that the Chosŏn court was memorializing the Board of Rites in Beijing to inform them that the route was far too dangerous for the mission to be allowed. Until a response was received, Mukedeng would not be allowed to cross the river. In effect, the Chosŏn officials were going over Mukedeng's head in the vain hope that the board would recall the mission. Even if they were not successful, they would at least gain time to prepare. At this point, Mukedeng confronted Song, "If your small country [*xiaoguo; soguk*] has no faith, then I have a secret edict to show." From a yellow box he pulled out a piece of paper that was clearly an imperial edict. No doubt pleased finally to confront his recalcitrant counterparts, Mukedeng challenged them to question his privileged position. "Fabricating an Imperial order is a capital offense, so is there anything to doubt?" he asked.[37] Clearly there was no doubt. Nor was there much that Song could do. In the face of a direct imperial command, the decision to circumvent Mukedeng by appealing to the emperor through the Board of Rites lost all legitimacy.

Mukedeng could not be stopped outright, but Song could still create problems for him. Mukedeng had expected Song to follow him to Wiwŏn, but Song, claiming he could not proceed without permission from the court, refused. Again, Mukedeng is reported to have lost his temper.[38] Song may have relented in the face of an imperial command regarding Mukedeng's right to venture to Wiwŏn, but he did not need to agree to just any route. The imperial command did not detail the path of the journey, so again Song refused Mukedeng access to Ŭiju, insisting that the imperial envoy travel on the northern bank while the Chosŏn retinue proceeded on the southern side.[39]

Back in Seoul, court officials sought to stay one step ahead, offering opinions on how to interfere further with Mukedeng's mission. Yu Chibil, appointed to meet up with Mukedeng's retinue in Wiwŏn, gained the king's approval to steer Mukedeng away from the pass at the Sŏrhan mountains should he cross into Korean territory. Instead, Mukedeng should be guided to the steep passes of what was literally called the "Four Abandoned County Region" (*pyesagun*). As the king explained, at first he should be obstructed, but if he persisted with the imperial command, then he should be guided to these steep passes. Seeing that they are impassable, he will then have no choice but to return to their side of the river.[40] In short, he was to be steered into a dead end.

The next confrontation occured at Hansudong, a small town on the Yalu River. Here Mukedeng wanted to cross the river so as to proceed on the southern side, but Song again insisted that they continue on their respective sides until they reached the vicinity of Wiwŏn. After two days of wrangling, Mukedeng finally relented, agreeing to cross when they reached this location.[41]

Before heading into Wiwŏn, Mukedeng announced that, after inspecting the corpses and the border-crossing site, he would head upriver through the Kanggye region, travelling all the way to Kyongwon on the lower reaches of the Tumen River. By this time, Yu Chibil had met up with the group and was ready to put into action the plan for obfuscation that had been decided upon by officials at court. There was, he admitted, a route as far as Manp'o, but beyond that there was no route. Mukedeng was told that over a thousand *li* of tall mountains stood in the way and that "since the earth was formed [they had] been impassable."[42] So he suggested an alternative route: cross over to the north side and proceed. By this time, Mukedeng was clearly skeptical. Insisting that he must complete his survey mission in order to prevent future problems along the frontier, he tried to point out a contradiction in an earlier communication that had spoken of barren lands in the area. "How can there not be another route?" he demanded. To this the Chosŏn officials responded quite simply that the barren land that had been referred to was on the northern side. If he was worried about future problems along the frontier, then all he needed to do was to inspect his own side of the border. To continue to insist that there must be a route, he was told, would be to suggest that he did not believe that the king was sincere in his duties of serving the great (*shida*; *sadae*).[43]

In Wiwŏn, Mukedeng inspected the site of the murder, but he seemed less interested in the murder investigation than in the rest of his journey, passing the responsibility for the final resolution of the case over to the Chosŏn authorities. He quickly turned his attention back to haggling over the route ahead. For two days, both parties repeated their positions. Eventually, Mukedeng ceded, agreeing to travel as far as Manp'o, where he would determine whether, as he had been repeatedly told, one could proceed any further. Mukedeng next tried to get more information on the frontier by ordering some minor local officials to write a detailed description of all they knew about the geography between Uiju and the Pyesagun as far as Kapsan, even including the six commanderies in the lower stretches of the Yalu River. One of these officials merely listed some place-names and indicated that the northern route was "far away," explaining that, because this information referred to "inside the country," he would not discuss it with Mukedeng, thus providing the Manchu envoy with yet another reason for losing his temper.[44]

Mukedeng, no doubt out of frustration with all the delays and interference, decided not to cross to the north side as urged by his Chosŏn counterparts but, rather, to continue his voyage by boat. Ignoring the entreaties of the Chosŏn officals and rejecting the warnings that the waters were too dangerous, Mukedeng and his retinue scrounged up four small boats. Immediately upon embarkation, they ran into problems navigating upstream against the turbulent waters. When attempting to dock at a small outpost named Chŏktong, Mukdeng's own boat nearly capsized. One of the Korean translators fell overboard, the swift current sweeping him to his death. Mukedeng himself was more fortunate, avoiding the water but falling into the boat – a fall that broke his front teeth.[45] This accident did not weaken Mukedeng's resolve, however. After a rest of two days, the journey upstream continued. The next report back to the Seoul court described Mukedeng's frustration with the boatmen, whom he felt were not applying themselves. His reaction was to strip off his clothes, enter the water, and begin pulling on the boat's hawser. Much to the consternation of the other officials who pleaded vainly for him to return to the boat, Mukedeng, while still in the water, rope in hand, announced his determination to fulfill his mission.[46]

Only when he received a report that Kangxi had ordered another official to Fenghuang to begin a second investigation into the border incident did he agree to abandon his assignment and return to Fenghuang. But his exasperating experience with Chosŏn officials was not yet over. These same officials who had interfered with his journey upriver intended to keep him out of Korean territory for his return trip. The king, perhaps worried that their treatment had been overly harsh, suggested allowing the Manchu to return via the easier southern route, but officials on the scene did not relent. To their pressure to retrace his steps and cross over at Wiwŏn, Mukedeng is reported to have responded angrily, "This, then, is sending me to my grave!" The next day Mukedeng was told of the king's wish that he return through Ŭiju – a piece of generosity for which, according to the Chosŏn records, he expressed deep gratitude.[47] Not long after, Mukdedeng had exited Korean territory, ending his first but not his last mission to the frontier.

Throughout the mission, the conduct of Chosŏn officials accompanying Mukedeng had hardly followed the norms attributed to tributary status by either Chinese ideological utterances or more recent English language historiographical representations. Rather than the type of submissiveness reputedly granted a recognized superior, Chosŏn officials manifested a kind of obstreporous non-cooperation. Instead of the servility expected of a vassal state, Chosŏn officals displayed a subdued defiance of the wishes of Kangxi's personal envoy. The vaunted humility and sincerity of the tribute subordinate was replaced with a willingness on the part of officials at the frontier, officials at the court in Seoul, and even the king himself to deceive, beguile, and subvert. Indeed, the decision-making circles at the top together with the implementers at the frontier staged an elaborate drama for Mukedeng, leading him up impassable valleys, refusing him guides, wrangling over access to specific areas, forcing him into physically dangerous situations – in one case at the cost of his front teeth – and generally interfering with the smooth progression of his journey. All this from the state that supposedly most closely honoured the ideals of tribute status. It was certainly not without reason that the records of these days show Mukedeng repeatedly losing his temper.

Yet, despite these frustrations and heated arguments, Mukedeng chose not to report the less than ideal behaviour of the Chosŏn officials to his superiors. In his memorial to the emperor, Mukedeng expressed regret that he had not been able to reach the headwaters of the two rivers, yet he did not blame this on Chosŏn interference but, rather, on the poor transportation in the region and the swollen river.[48] In what amounts to a memorial of little more than a few sentences as captured in Beijing court records, there is no mention of his mission's treatment at the hands of the Chosŏn officials. This was no doubt deliberate. From Mukedeng's perspective, there was likely little to be gained from detailing his exasperating experience. As the Kangxi's personal envoy, Mukedeng was expected to impress Chosŏn officials with the imperial aura and to command their respect. In the rhetoric of the imperial court, his presence beyond the pale of civilized culture was to be edifying, his behaviour hortatory. To suggest otherwise was to call into question the ideologies of the "Middle Kingdom." That Chosŏn officials obstructed an imperially appointed mission, then, would suggest, according to the legitmizing devices used by the court, that the virtue of the emperor was less than assured across his realm. Moreover, at a personal level, such revelations were likely to be risky for a Qing official. Any discrepancy between an official's actions and the ideology of the imperial centre would more likely than not be interpreted as reflecting less on the emperor himself than on his personal envoy. Such an account would open Mukedeng to charges of improper or ineffectual conduct – especially since Chosŏn envoys continued to journey to Beijing and abide by the strictures of tribute in front of the emperor. It was much easier for Mukedeng to excuse the lack of results on the heavy spring waters of the Yalu River. As a result, Chinese court documents do not include any information concerning Mukedeng's tribulations along the frontier.

In fact, these records leave quite the opposite impression of his mission: shortly after his return to Beijing, Qing court records show Kangxi reducing the amount of tribute required of the Chosŏn court. The edict announcing this reduction was typical of the type of document issued on matters concerning tribute relations. There were references to the emperor's magnanimous rule of "ten thousand kingdoms" and how the middle and the outer constitute a single united body. The bounty of everlasting peace, it announced, reached out as far as the vassal states. Every year, since being enfeoffed, the Chosŏn king – as befits a subordinate, the edict cited his personal name, Yi Ton – had submitted tribute, never relaxing for over forty years. In recognition, and perhaps in reward for this loyalty, Kangxi eliminated in perpetuity two items from the annual tribute list, 1000 *liang* of gold and 142 leopard pelts.[49] Here was the benevolent ruler at his best, reducing the tribute of his most loyal vassal. The historical record from Beijing is perfectly in keeping with the legitimizing myths of the imperial centre. The reticence of the Manchu envoy effectively silenced any dissonance between tribute ideology and the actual interactions of the two courts' representatives along the frontier. Kangxi's edict affirmed that relations fit the ideal. The benevolent will of the imperial court was respected by all, with the perhaps understandable exception of the waters of the Yalu River. The dilemmas of the frontier were glossed over.

The Qing historical record creates a number of problems for twenty-first century readers. Just as Beijing's ideology of tribute was not disturbed by Mukedeng's politic decision, so the resultant silence in Qing court records creates little reason to query standard accounts of the workings of tribute. Central Qing documents from these years reveal little about the negotiations conducted along the frontier, while the grandiose statements of imperial benevolence and the kowtows of Chosŏn missions are chronicled for posterity. These are the very type of court records that, more than two centuries after these events, historians have used to develop theories concerning the conduct of premodern East Asian relations. As a result, just as the Qing bureaucracy and record keepers worked to preserve the ideological pretensions of the Middle Kingdom, so have histories of premodern East Asian relations tended to reproduce Sinocentric assumptions and, again like their earlier counterparts, to neglect the many instances that ruffle a complacent tribute ideology. It is hardly coincedental that many of the ideological tenets of tribute have thus become sublimated into twenty-first-century representations of the "tribute system."

It is only when we shift to documents produced outside the imperial bureaucracy that the flexibile, even contestatary, workings of tribute are divulged. Chosŏn dynastic records are still central state-generated documents, and they do not provide a ground-level perspective on frontier life. But they do provide access to events that have otherwise been erased from the Chinese historical record.

Yet, if Qing court records on issues of tribute preserved a self-serving imperial ideology, it is equally true that Chosŏn court historians selectively embellished their own records. Reports back to the throne from officials on the frontier seem to highlight efforts to obstruct Mukedeng while underplaying any progress the Manchu emissary achieved. On his return trip, Mukedeng was permitted, at the behest of the benevolent king, to follow the very trail along the south shore that, on his journey upwards, Chosŏn officials had adamantly refused him. No detailed reports concerning this latter leg of Mukedeng's journey were entered into the records. The silence is quite a departure from the detailed accounts provided of the constant wrangling and haggling during the first half of the trip. In contrast to Mukedeng, who appears to have wanted to conceal from the court his troubles on the Yalu River, Chosŏn officials energetically detailed how their actions exasperated their Manchu visitor and prevented him from reaching his goal while they nevertheless conducted themselves with the utmost decorum. Unlike the Qing records, the Chosŏn records display little attempt to hide any dissonance between the tribute ideology and conduct. The historiographic slant of these records stresses the creativity of Chosŏn officials to manipulate the conventions of tribute, never quite defying them yet being able, in at least this initial case, to achieve a goal that ran counter to the wishes of the imperial centre. Thus, whether we uncritically accept the accounts of Korean treatment of Mukedeng or simply consider the way these dealings were recorded for posterity by Seoul court scribes, the events of the spring of 1711 hardly fit the Sinocentric image of a dependent and loyal vassal state that the Qing imperial records assiduously cultivated.

Bordering the Frontier

Mukedeng's failure to reach the summit of Mount Paektu did not signal the end of Kangxi's quest for information about the frontier. Having first set out to obtain information on the frontier region in the early 1670s, Kangxi was not about to be stymied by what Mukedeng had characterized as the rough roads and heavy waters of the region. Indeed, as Yang Zhaoquan and Sun Yumei have suggested, it is possible that Kangxi's lowering of Chosŏn tribute requirements may have been a clever attempt to place moral pressure on the Chosŏn court in order to elicit more cooperation for his next planned mission.[50] As may be seen in the first mission, however, convincing the Chosŏn court was a delicate matter. If Mukedeng's first mission demonstrated the ways Chosŏn officials could circumvent the desires of the centre, then the second mission revealed that consistent pressure, combined with careful orchestration on the part of Beijing, could limit the Chosŏn court's ability to resist.

By August, the decision to send Mukedeng back up to Mount Paektu the following spring had already been made.[51] The Board of Rites dutifully notified the Seoul court in February that Mukedeng would be returning in the spring, departing from Fenghuang and heading for the mountain. Only this time the communication specified the route. He would travel by small boat from Uiju up the Yalu River as far as possible, then switch to the easiest land route. The trip, it said, was expressly designed to investigate "our frontier" (*bianjie*) and did not concern any other country (*biguo*). Yet, because the terrain was rough and the roads far, if any obstacles were encountered Chosŏn officials were "to lend a bit of assistance" (*shaowei zhaoguan*).[52] The prerogative of the Qing as the Middle Kingdom was manifest: a Manchu was to be in charge of a mission that, despite its significance to Chosŏn officials, had been unilaterally defined as of no concern to them. The latter was instructed to play – and then only if nececessary – a secondary role. As in the previous year, the Seoul court could not directly refuse this instruction, but it could explore other options.

As soon as this notice was received, officials at court debated how best to deal with the second coming of Mukedeng. Following similar lines to the 1711 deliberations, the first option raised suggested emphasizing the danger of the route as a means of getting the Board of Rites to reverse its decision. Others argued this option had been played before, was hardly convincing, and may simply cause problems. It was in this context that the second minister to the Board of Personnel, Yi Kangjwa, made clear his fears about the security threat presented by the mission, accusing Mukedeng of seeking intelligence in case the Manchus were forced to retreat from China proper. They could not be allowed into the Sorhan pass, he concluded.[53] Kwŏn Sangyu drew attention to the wording of the communication, pointing out that in the previous year, Mukedeng had not had imperial instructions specifying his route and so did not dare cross the river into Chosŏn territory. This year, Kwŏn pointed out, not only did he have such permission but the Chosŏn court had also received instructions to help him overcome any difficulties. In the end, after listening to the disputes, the king decided obstruction was the best tactic. Mukedeng would be told by the official receiving him that people and horses could not make it up river; if he insisted, there was little to do but let him proceed.[54] Two officials, the governor of Hamgyŏng, Yi Sŏnmu, and Pak Kwŏn were appointed this task. The Chosŏn king and his officials had, up to this point, succeeded in keeping Chinese missions out of the area, but now, due to the insistence of the Qing court, it was becoming difficult to stave off further missions. And so attention shifted towards controlling the conduct and the results of the investigation.

By the following month, Seoul court officials were already deliberating the possible consequences of a mission investigating the frontier. What concerned Chosŏn officials, despite the fact that the original Board of Rites document gave no hint in this direction, was that Mukedeng would be demarcating the bounds of the frontier. How this would be determined – and how the decision could be influenced – became a matter of much consideration in the Seoul palace. Keenly aware of the vulnerability of the Chosŏn position, officials sought to devise strategies for concealing their own weaknesses while exploiting Mukedeng's ignorance of the region.

Much of the strategizing centred on the lands just south of Mount Paektu. Court discussions show Chosŏn officials worrying about how to substantiate their claim on these lands to the Manchu emissary. As Ch'oe Sŏkhang, an official in the Office of Royal Lectures, advised, it was necessary to make preparations in advance of his arrival. The Yalu and Tumen rivers could serve as the basis of the demarcation, he pointed out, but the problem was that there were too many rivers flowing in various directions for one to be able to adequately identify the sources of these two rivers. He recommended that officials be sent immediately to the area to gather information.[55] As Yi Sunmyŏng noted, there were no traces of people in the region between Kapsan and Mount Paektu, a six- or seven-day journey. As a result, all fortresses and embattlements had been erected a five- or six-day journey south of the mountains. Moreover, he warned, the *Daming yitongzhi* (Comprehensive Gazeteer of the Ming Dynasty) recorded that Mount Paektu belonged to the Jurchens. If Mukedeng came to the area and chose Chosŏn fortresses as the marker of the border (*kye*), it would be difficult to argue with him. Instead, Yi recommended that officials accompanying Mukedeng should impress on the Manchu visitor that the Yalu and Tumen rivers served as the borders of Chosŏn country. "Everything south of the rivers is 'our land' (*aji*)," he stated, and our officals must argue this point.[56]

The official ultimately responsible for implementing this strategy, however, was less than confident. Pak Kwŏn, in an appearance before the throne, expressed his concern that "establishing the bounds" (*chŏnggye*) would be complicated by the absence of inhabitants in the region. Not only were there no people there, but he had no documents that he could use to counter a claim by Mukedeng that these lands belonged to the realm of the Qing. In response, the second minister without portfolio, Yi Yu, could only repeat the decision to use the two rivers as a divide. For the area between the two rivers, he urged that a horizontal line between the two sources of the rivers be used as a demarcation (*han*; *xian*). The king made sure that Pak understood the urgency of this matter. "Territory (*kangyŏk*) is of the utmost significance," he said, "so you must make great efforts." [57]

The next day, in a parting memorial before embarking for the frontier, Pak offered a possible solution to his concern about lack of documents. He had discovered a source that could be used to counter the claims of the *Daming yitongzhi*. It was, most significantly, a Qing book, the *Shengjing Gazeteer* (*Shengjingzhi*). According to this book, the lands south of Mount Paektu belonged not to the Jurchen but to Chosŏn. By the next day, numerous remonstrations were received by the court, each arguing that the *Shengjing Gazeteer* could not be used because it was a forbidden book. Since it was not supposed to be in the hands of Chosŏn officials, using it in negotiations with Mukedeng might simply instigate further problems.[58] In the end, that this Chinese book could not be used to negotiate with the Qing official did not matter for, despite the strategizing of the Seoul court, the issue ended up being determined by the officials on the spot – the ones who were rendering the "assistance" requested.

Mukedeng arrived in Huzhou at the end of April, to be greeted by Pak Kwŏn and Yi Sŏnbu. After some preliminary negotiations about supplies and guides for the journey, Mukedeng broached the subject of his trip. Pak's report on this conversation addressed all the concerns first aired at the court. Mukedeng began by directly asking Pak and Yi whether they clearly knew the border (*kukkye*) between the two countries. The two officials put into play the basic strategy devised at court. "We have not seen it with our own eyes," they responded, "however there is a great lake in the Changbai mountains, from which the Yalu river flows west and the Tumen river runs east. To the south of that great lake is our national land [*kukkye*]." Mukedeng next did what Pak had feared: he asked for documentary evidence of this border. In what must have been a well-rehearsed response, Pak dismissed the need for this, privileging convention over writing. "Since the country was first established until today, [this understanding] has been passed down, so why rely on written words and books?" The question was side-stepped, and in his report Pak does not show Mukedeng pressing this line of inquiry. Instead, the Manchu official switched to the topic of military defences south of Mount Paektu. Again, Pak went on the defensive. "The area is extremely steep and dangerous," he began, "People do not venture there. As a result, it is barren and abandoned and there are no forts." Next, going on the offensive, he drew a comparison with Manchu defences, suggesting the Manchu defences were no different from Chosŏn's: "This is just like the lands outside the willow pallisade of your great country." His report of the conversation demonstrated to court officials that Pak had fulfilled his duties. As he confidently reported, the Chosŏn claim on all the land south of Mount Paektu did not elicit a strong response, let alone close scrutiny, from the Manchu official. "There is no great worry," he reassured the throne.[59]

The trek towards Mount Paektu began the next day, with the retinue splitting into two groups, one proceeding by boat, the other, which included Mukedeng, travelling on the southern shore. By the fourth of May, they had reached Hyesan, just south of Mount Paektu, where they made ready to reach the mountain summit. Three local guides were acquired and provisions were prepared. Most of the retinue was dispatched to Musan, a village to the east of the mountain, where they were ordered to wait for Mukedeng to complete his ascent. Not long after setting off on their upward trek, Pak and Li tried to dissuade Mukedeng from pressing forward. Employing a warning that had been used many times before, they cautioned him about the dangerous mountains and urged him to order some lower officials to complete the task. Mukedeng refused, saying he had an imperial mission to fulfill regardless of the dangers and difficulties. Instead, he suggested that Pak and Li, given their old age, would do better to remain behind. Since they were riding in sedan chairs, Mukedeng wondered whether they would be able to walk on their own when they came to steeper grades. If they were to fall, he concluded, the journey would be delayed.[60] Pak and Li, probably eager to avoid the arduous climb and now given an excuse to do so, acquiesed.

Only translators and guides remained on the Chosŏn side to complete the mission. Mukedeng led the group up at a torrid pace, crossing the river several times a day in an attempt to find the easiest path. At times they braved heavy rains. Parts of their route took them through woods so thick they could not even see the noon-day sun and had to hack out a path with axes.[61] Throughout the journey, Mukedeng asked questions about places and the terrain, frequently using his telescope to check the contours of the land and his sextant to gauge the lay of the land so that others could draw rough maps.[62] Finally, on the eleventh and twelve days after leaving Huju, they made it to the summit.

Once on top, the retinue turned its energies to the problem of ascertaining the watershed. On the Yalu side, where they began, the task was quite simple. A few *li* down the summit, a stream gushed out from an opening in the mountainface, entering a deep gulley a few hundred steps further along. This was the source of the Yalu.[63] But on the Tumen side, no such single obvious source existed. With multiple streams heading in various directions, merging and diverging, identification presented a greater problem.

Mukedeng never challenged the basis of the Chosŏn strategy for division. Indeed, at times, his comments even suggested a larger stake for the south. When one of the Korean translators asked Mukedeng for a copy of the map of Mount Paektu that he had been preparing, the Manchu responded, "I can't give you [information on] the mountains and rivers of the Great Country, but Mt. Paektu is your country's, so why should there be any problems in giving it to you?" This may have been a slip by Mukedeng, yet it confirmed the hopes of the Chosŏn officials on the frontier. When these comments reached the court in Seoul, they were accompanied by yet another reassurance that there was little worry of a dispute breaking out over the lands to the south of Mount Paektu.[64]

The next day, after a great deal of searching, Mukedeng finally identified what he believed to be the source of the Tumen River. As one report back to the Seoul court recounted, Mukedeng announced that "to set the border and erect a [marking] stone was [his] imperial order."[65] He then ordered the engraving of a stele, which was erected three days later. Two large characters proclaiming the Great Qing stood at its head. The "Master of the Hunt, Mukedeng" (*Hulie Zongguan*), the text began, "received an imperial order to survey the frontier. The examination was carried out to this point, where to the west flows the Yalu and to the east flows the Tumen. So on this mountain watershed this stone has been engraved as a marker."[66]

His mission to the top of the mountain complete, Mukedeng descended, heading east to Musan to rendezvous with the rest of his staff and continue the investigation of the frontier. On the 21st of May, he was greeted by Pak Kwŏn and Yi Sŏnbu. Immediately upon hearing about Mukedeng's placement of the stele, Pak expressed doubt, unsure whether Mukedeng had mistaken an upper tributary of the Dahongdan River for the Tumen River. Mukedeng refused to accept this possibility, showing Pak the map and saying that, together with a number of Koreans, he had carefully examined the area. "Besides," he assured Pak, "there was certainly no other river." Still less than convinced, Pak urged Mukedeng to retrace his steps about ten li to a point where the mistake would be clear. The Manchu refused, asserting the accuracy of his decision. Mukedeng had already sent a memorial to Beijing describing his success, so "if the river source was mistakenly identified, then only after your King memorializes the Emperor will [the area] be resurveyed."[67]

Mukedeng next raised the issue of distinguishing those portions of the newly defined border that were not obviously demarcated by natural features by laying out some type of marking system. This problem had been raised at the summit, but now Mukedeng wrote a formal communication to Pak. As in so many of the documents exhanged over the frontier issue, Mukedeng stated that the two rivers formed the division between the Great Country and Chosŏn. His task had been to find the source of the two rivers, which he had done. But a number of li downstream from the stele, he wrote that all signs of water disappeared as the stream headed underground, not to emerge again for about one hundred li. Much of this stretch was grass-covered and flat, so that people did not recognise the border (*pyŏngye*). "To make the people realize that a border exists," he suggested erecting a sturdy barrier, one over which they "will not dare cross over and create problems."[68] Pak responded in the affirmative, accepting the task of building a fence – of stone, trees, or mud, depending on what was available.[69] Moreover, the task was to be carried out by Chosŏn officials alone.

The building of a barrier proved more complicated than expected, however, for, in the process of preparing to do so, it was discovered that Mukedeng had indeed erred. The stele, as Pak Kwŏn had suspected, had been positioned in the wrong location. As a number of Chosŏn officials reported, Mukedeng had confused the four different streams located on the eastern face of the mountain. When descending from the top of the mountain – no doubt being "in a hurry," as one person generously excused him[70] – Mukedeng did not follow the streams all the way down the mountain. As one of the builders of the fence described it, "as one walks downstream [from the stele], after about thirty li the stream continues downwards as another river from the north merges. Slowly it curves towards the northeast. It doesn't belong to the Tumen River." It headed deep into the "barbarous lands" (*hoji*), a common Chosŏn term for territory under the control of the Manchus. Mukedeng, he concluded, did not go beyond the fork of these two rivers, assuming that, from this point on, the stream eventually made its way to the Tumen River. It did not.[71]

Another important debate concerning this territorial issue ensued at court. If the marker was in the wrong place, what should be done? Advice to the king was varied. Some officials, believing they should take the initiative, wanted to resurvey the area then inform the Qing. Others suggested a more cautious route: approach Mukedeng individually to see whether the marker could be changed. This would put Mukedeng in a difficult position, some argued, and in any case, since territory was a national concern, it should not be the responsibility of a single person.[72] If they notified the Qing, then a new survey team would be sent out, a mission that some officials feared might not be conducted as "smoothly" (*sunp'yŏn*) as was Mukedeng's. It could even lead to the calamity of a changed demarcation, reducing the territory of Chosŏn.[73] More investigations of the site were ordered.

The following year, Kim Changjip, who had been involved in various stages of the court deliberations on Mukedeng's investigation, travelled to Beijing as the head of a tribute mission. He met Mukedeng to ask him whether Qing officials would be inspecting the fence, without ever mentioning the concern with its positioning. Mukedeng replied in the negative, saying it was up to Chosŏn officials to complete it.[74] He was taken at his word, and construction continued along the lines that he had originally indicated.

This was the last Chosŏn-Qing interaction over demarcation questions for the next 150 years. Inside Korea, however, grumbling over the positioning of the border soon emerged. Once the problem over the stele's position became apparent, Pak Kwŏn and Yi Sŏnbu were relieved of their official positions. That they had not proceeded to the summit of Mount Paektu and had allowed Mukedeng to decide about the the disposition of the stele was considered a dereliction of duty. Others, however, were to object strenuously, targeting instead the basic policy adopted by the court to propose the Yalu and Tumen rivers as demarcation lines. These individuals, largely scholars alienated from positions of power, complained that the claim to lands on the northern side of the Tumen River had been too readily abandoned. Sin Kyŏngbok, in his "Treatise on Territory" (*Kanggye chi*), wrote: "Setting territorial boundaries is a matter of great importance for the nation ... so how is it that one can just listen to another's words, withdraw and sit quietly?" Pointedly criticizing the two officials, he complained that they had allowed Mukedeng to single-handedly erect the stele "without a single word of argument" and, thus, lost over three hundred li of land.[75] Such opinions, commonly found in scholarly writings, gained greater attention at the end of the nineteenth century.

The demarcation of the watershed, the erection of a stele, and the construction of a fence did little to stem "illegal crossings." During both his missions, Mukedeng had stated that marking the border would put an end to the type of incidents that had him investigating murders along the frontier. But, of course, people continued to cross. The *Tongmun hwigo,* which records only those people unfortunate enough to get caught, shows no slowdown in the rate of apprehension: and these incidents occurred along the entire frontier, not just in the upper reaches of the Tumen River. Nor were these merely cases of an odd individual slipping across the frontier. In one case, over 460 people crossed the Yalu River by boat from Manchuria to get into Chosŏn territory.[76] Clearly the spatial definitions of the central bureaucracy – whether Manchu or Korean – did not delimit the social and economic activities of local frontier life. The limits to the extension of central rule in these remote areas is apparent.

More than 150 years passed before the Qing and Chosŏn states again officially took up the issue of their joint border. By this time, new incidents were picked up by the central states as a means of raising the question of the frontier. But new conceptions of territorial sovereignty, together with the growth of nationalism on both sides of the border, were to give these talks a very different dynamic than is found in the early eighteenth-century efforts of Mukedeng.[77] Nevertheless, the question of Mukedeng's stele arose in these discussions, and the efforts of this Manchu surveyor were heatedly contested. By the end of the nineteenth century, the erection of the stele, which revealed much about premodern conceptions of space and the exigencies of tributary relations, emerged as a central moment in the construction of competing historical narratives, which continue to support divergent understandings of a border that remains in dispute today.

Notes

I would like to thank Prof. Gari Ledyard for first bringing the excitement of the frontier to my attention.

1 For the European case, see Peter Sahlins, *Boundaries: The Making of France and Spain in the Pyrenees* (Berkeley: University of California Press, 1989).

2 J.K. Fairbank and S.Y. Teng, "On the Ch'ing Tributary System," *Harvard Journal of Asiatic Studies* 6 (1941): 161.

3 Paul Cohen, *Discovering History in China: American Historical Writings on the Recent Chinese Past* (New York: Columbia University Press, 1984); Robert Marks, "The State of the China Field, or the China Field and State," *Modern China* 11, 4 (1985): 461-509; Judith B. Farquhar and James L. Hevia, "Culture and Postwar American historiography of China," *Positions* 1, 2 (1993): 486-525.

4 John King Fairbank, *China: A New History* (Cambridge: Harvard University Press, 1992).

5 John King Fairbank, *Trade and Diplomacy on the China Coast: The Opening of the Treaty Ports, 1842-1854* (Cambridge: Harvard University Press, 1953), Introduction.

6 P.K. Crossley, *A Translucent Mirror: History and Identity in Qing Imperial Ideology* (Berkeley: University of California Press, 1999); M. Elliot, *The Manchu Way: The Eight Banners and Ethnic Identity in Late Imperial China* (Stanford: Stanford University Press, 2001); L. Hostetler, *Qing Colonial Enterprise: Ethnography and Cartography in Early Modern China* (Chicago: University of Chicago Press, 2001); J. Millward, *Beyond the Pass: Economy, Ethnicity, and Empire in Qing Central Asia, 1759-1864* (Stanford: Stanford University Press, 1998); E. Rawski, *The Last Emperors: A Social History of Qing Imperial Institutions* (Berkeley: University of California Press, 1998).

7 James Hevia, *Cherishing Men from Afar: Qing Guest Ritual and the Macartney Mission of 1793* (Durham, NC: Duke University Press, 1995).

8 John King Fairbank, ed., *The Chinese World Order: Traditional China's Foreign Relations* (Cambridge: Harvard University Press, 1968), preface.

9 Hevia, *Cherishing Men from Afar*, 50, for example, uses the Chosŏn dynasty for the way tribute ideally functioned.

10 J.K. Fairbank, E.O. Reischauer, and A.M. Craig, *East Asia: Tradition and Transformation* (Boston: Houghton Mifflin Press, 1973), 300.

11 Zhang Cunwu, for example, has traced the vagaries of Qing-Chosŏn relations quite closely yet tends to fashion his arguments on Beijing-centred ideology. See Zhang Cunwu, *QingHan zongfan maoyi, 1637-1894* [Qing-Korean tributary trade, 1637-1894] (Taibei: Zhongyang yanjiuyuan jindaishi yanjiusuo, 1978); and *Qingdai ZhongHan guanxi wenji* [Essays on Sino-Korean relations during the Qing dynasty) (Taibei: Shangwu yinshuguan, 1986].

12 Jahyun Kim Haboush, "Constructing the Center: The Ritual Controversy and the Search for a New Identity in Seventeenth-Century Korea," in *Culture and State in Late Chosŏn Korea*, ed. J. Haboush and M. Deuchler, 46-90 (Cambridge, MA: Harvard University Press, 1999).

13 This antipathy was deeply rooted in his devotion to orthodox interpretations of Zhu Xi. For one English language piece on Song's intellectual background, see Miura Kunio, "Orthodoxy and Heterodoxy in Seventeenth Century Korea: Song Siyŏl and Yun Hyu," in *The Rise of Neo-Confucianism in Korea*, ed. William Theodore de Bary and Jahyun Kim Haboush, 411-44 (New York: Columbia University Press, 1985).

14 Interestingly, at least until 1993, these rituals were annually attended by an official representative, usually the ambassador of the Republic of China. I do not know whether, after the South Korean recognition of the People's Republic of China and the rupture of ties with Taiwan, a representative of the PRC embassy attended.

15 For a consideration of the politicking that took place between the Ming and Chosŏn at the time of the Hideoyoshi invasion, see Gari Ledyard, "Confucianism and War: The Korean Security Crisis of 1598," *Journal of Korean Studies* 6 (1988-89): 81-119. This romanticized nostalgia was first pointed out to me by Milan Hetjmanek.

16 James Palais, *Politics and Policy in Traditional Korea* (Cambridge, MA: Harvard University Press, 1975), 119-24.

17 See Hong's memorial, as quoted in *DaiNippon Gaiko Bansho* [Documents of Japan's Foreign Relations] 14, 378-79.

18 Chai-sik Chung, *A Korean Confucian Encounter with the Modern World: Yi Hang-no and the West* (Berkeley: Institute of East Asian Studies, 1995), chap. 4. See the memorial by Ch'oe Ikhyŏn, as translated in Peter Lee, ed., *Sourcebook of Korean Civilization*, vol. 2 (New York: Columbia University Press, 1996), 333.

19 For a treatment of shifting attitudes towards China after 1895, see Andre Schmid, *Korea between Empires* (New York: Columbia University Press, 2002), chap. 2.

20 As recorded in Hwang Hyŏn, *Maech'ŏn yarok* [Maech'on's unofficial history] (Seoul: Kuksa p'yŏnch'anwiwŏnhoe, 1961), 171.

21 This was a Chosŏn compendium, but it has also been republished in Taiwan. For the Korean version, see Kuksa p'yŏnch'an wiwŏnhoe, *Tongmun hwigo* [A compendium of dipolomatic documents], 4 vols. (Seoul: Kuksa p'yonch'an wiwonhoe, 1978).

22 *Injo sillok*, [Veritable records of King Injo] 15:50a, b.

23 Marion Eggert, "A Borderline Case: Korean Travelers' Views of the Chinese Border (Eighteenth to Nineteenth Century)," in *China and Her Neighbours: Borders, Visions of the other, Foreign Policy, 10th to 19th Century*, edited by Sabine Sabringhaus and Roderich Ptak (Wiesbaden: Harrossowitx Verlag, 1997), 76.

24 Gari Ledyard, "Cartography in Korea," in *The History of Cartography*, ed. J.B. Hartley and David Woodward, vol. 2, no. 2, 298-99 (Chicago: University of Chicago Press, 1994).

25 Crossley, *A Translucent Mirror*.

26 Yang Zhaoquan and Sun Yumei, *Zhong Chao bianjie shi* [A history of the Sino-Korean border]. (Changchun: Jilin wenshi chubanshe, 1993), 169.

27 Zhang, *QingHan zongfan maoyi*, 474.

28 Kuksa p'yŏnch'anwiwŏnhoe, ed., *Sukchong sillok* [Veritable records of King Sukjong] (Seoul: Tamgudang, 1978), 49, 27b-28a.
29 *Chosŏn wangjo sillok, Sukchong sillok,* 49:28a.
30 *Tongmun hwigo,* 53:28-29a.
31 This title as translated by Ledyard, *Cartography of Korea.*
32 *Kangxi shilu,* juan 246:10.
33 *Chosŏn wangjo sillok, Sukchong sillok,* 51:13a.
34 Ibid., 50:20b-21a.
35 Ibid., 50:21a.
36 Ibid., 50:21-22
37 Ibid., 50:24b.
38 *Chosŏn wangjo sillok, Sukchong sillok,* 51:24b.
39 Ibid.
40 *Chosŏn wangjo sillok, Sukchong sillok,* 50:25a.
41 Ibid., 50:27b.
42 Ibid., 50:28a.
43 Ibid.
44 *Chosŏn wangjo sillok, Sukchong sillok,* 50:30b-31a.
45 Ibid., 50:35b.
46 Ibid., 50:36b-37a.
47 Ibid., 50:39b.
48 *Kanggxi shilu, juan* 247:9.
49 Ibid., 248:13
50 Yang and Sun, *Zhong Chao bianjie shi,* 175.
51 *Kangxi shilu, juan* 247; *Tongmun hwigo,* 48:1.
52 *Tongmun hwigo,* 48:5b-48:6a; *Chosŏn wangjo sillok, Sukchong sillok,* 51:11b
53 *Chosŏn wangjo sillok, Sukchong sillok,* 51:12b-13a.
54 Ibid., 51:14a, 17b.
55 Ibid., 51:15b.
56 Ibid., 51:16a.
57 Ibid., 51:17b.
58 Ibid., 51:17b, 18a.
59 Ibid., 51:22a,b.
60 Hong Set'ae, "Paektusan'gi," in *Kando yŏngyu'gwŏn wan'gye charyojip* [Materials relating to the rights of possession of Kando], edited by No Yakhyon (Seoul: Paeksan charyowŏn, 1993), 2:35; see also, *Tongmun hwigo* 48:8a.
61 Hong Set'ae, "Paektusan'gi," 35.
62 *Chosŏn wangjo sillok, Sukchong sillok,* 51:26a.
63 Hong Set'ae, "Paektusan'gi," 37.
64 *Chosŏn wangjo sillok, Sukchong sillok,* 51:26b.
65 Ibid., 51:29a.
66 As quoted in Yang and Sun, *Zhong Chao bianjie shi,* 103.
67 *Chosŏn wangjo sillok, Sukchong sillok,* 51:30a.
68 *Tongmun hwigo,* 48:8b.
69 Ibid., 48:9a.
70 *Chosŏn wangjo sillok, Sukchong sillok,* 52:37b.
71 Ibid.
72 *Chosŏn wangjo sillok, Sukchong sillok,* 52:38b.
73 Ibid., 52:38b-39a.
74 *Chosŏn wangjo sillok, Sukchong sillok,* 53.
75 As quoted in Cho Kwang, "Chosŏn hugi ŭi py'ŏngy'ŏng ŭisik" [Border consciousness in late Chosŏn], *Paeksan hakpo* 16 (1974): 164.
76 Yang and Sun, *Zhong Chao bianjie shi,* 58-59.
77 Andre Schmid, *Korea between Empires, 1895-1919* (New York: Columbia University Press, 2002), chap. 6.

8
The Amur: As River, as Border

Victor Zatsepine

An occasional visitor to the border town of Heihe finds the Amur River its main attraction. In summer, Chinese residents swim or bathe in it. The shallow waters form islands in the middle of the river that children can easily walk to. Across the river, in the Russian town of Blagoveshchensk, rough-looking village youths stroll along the embankment sipping bottled beer. While Heihe is a city typical of China's northeast, Blagoveshchensk's solid old buildings are unmistakably European. The river at this junction separates two distinct cultural worlds.

The Amur River's role as a political divide is even more pronounced. The Aigun Treaty (1858) and the Peking (1860) Treaty established the river as the Sino-Russian border, one that has endured for more than 150 years. Twentieth-century writings about the Amur River portray it as a line of tension between Qing China and Tsarist Russia. The general trend in scholarship has been to demonstrate that the early expansionist foreign policies of Russia and China survived into the twentieth century. Diplomatic historians see hostilities between the USSR and China along the Amur River in the 1920s, 1960s, and 1970s as a natural outcome of earlier colonial practices and events.

Did the Amur River really function as a line separating the two empires? The focus on cultural and political divides overlooks the role of this river as a system of arteries connecting people and facilitating the flow of goods. For indigenous peoples, migrants, and traders, this boundary either did not exist or was extremely porous. The diverse topography and constantly changing natural conditions of the frontier always interfered with imperial colonization policies. Even when the Qing and Russian governments made claims over navigation rights and disputed sections of the river, they could never draw the line as accurately as it appeared on political maps.

Geography

The vastness of the Amur River Basin contradicts the twentieth-century view of the river as a margin of two empires. The river system runs through a basin of 1.85 million square kilometres, larger than the river systems of the Yangzi or the Volga. The Amur, with its two major tributaries, the Shilka and the Onon, is about 4,350 kilometres long, making it one of the longest rivers in the world. More than two hundred tributaries join the Amur from Mongolia, the Russian Far East, and Northeastern China. These tributaries are linked to sixty thousand small lakes, of which the Khanka, or Xingkaihu, is the biggest.[1]

For centuries, the Amur River system facilitated the movement of indigenous peoples who joined the main current from one of its tributaries. The Shilka River rises in Siberia; the Argun River rises in present-day Mongolia, about 1,600 kilometres from the Amur's confluence with the Shilka; and the Songhua River comes in from China. The lower and middle Amur connects its Siberian tributaries – the Zeya, Bureya, and Amgun – with the Ussuri (Wusuli) River, running from the present-day Primorsky Krai (Maritime Region). The Amur's main artery enters the Okhotsk Sea and the Sea of Japan through a wide estuary resembling the roots of a massive tree. Those roots linked a rich array of cultures and lifestyles, stretching from Mongolia to Korea, and from China to Siberia.

The multiple names of the river reflect the presence of different cultures. The main stream is known in Chinese either as the *Heilongjiang* (Black Dragon River) or *Heihe* (Black River). The dragon symbolized imperial power for the Chinese emperors, and the colour black referred to the river's black soil and its dark, clean water. The Manchus called it the *Sakhalian-Ula* (Black River), the Mongols the *Hara Muren'* (Big Black River). The river's English name was adopted from the Russian *Amur*. Amur is not a Russian word. There is no agreement about the origin of this word, but one popular theory attributes the name to a small tributary, the *Emuri/Emura*, near the first Russian settlement on the river at Albazin. Other theories link it either to the Mongolian name of the Amur River's upper stream Hara-Muren' or to a Tungus greeting, meaning "kind peace." A late imperial Russian geographic dictionary explains it as a corruption of the Gold, or Hezhe, name for Amur's lower stream *Mamu*. A Soviet encyclopaedia traces its origin to the Gyliak and Evenk words meaning "big river."[2] These diverse names suggest a strong link between the Amur and its indigenous peoples – a link preceding Qing or Russian claims to rights over the river.

The Amur River is navigable by riverboat all the way from its confluence with the Shilka to its estuary. It has no major falls or disruptions. In summer and fall, native people navigated it in light canoes, while early Russian settlers used barges or rafts to transport people, animals, and goods. In winter, in the deep cold, sections of the Amur and its tributaries functioned as the only available transport route, especially in the mountainous areas. In addition, minimal snowfall in the region between Lake Baikal and Khabarovsk turned the frozen Amur into a sledge-friendly highway in the winter.

The Amur varies in depth and width as it runs through different geographic zones. The shallow Shilka is a mountainous river, while the Argun runs through a valley. Both rivers are narrow up to their confluence with the Amur. The river gathers strength and becomes wider after the waters of the major tributaries Zeya and Bureya join the river. The middle section of the Amur cuts deeply through the Little Xinggan mountain range. The lower section of the Amur, enriched by the waters of the Sunghua and the Wusuli, is wide and moves slowly to the ocean through valleys and flat lands covered with high grasses. At its estuary, the river is more than twenty-five kilometres wide. Sea-going vessels can navigate the lower Amur up to Khabarovsk at high water, but Sakhalin island blocks entry to the Amur's estuary. The entry to the shallow Tatar Strait from the Sea of Okhotsk is deeper than the entry from the Sea of Japan and is therefore more convenient for ships with deep draft.[3]

The waters of the Amur River and its tributaries run relatively slowly. The Shilka is the fastest, flowing with a maximum current velocity of sixteen kilometres per hour. However, strong storms and winds make navigation of the river from Shilka to the Ussuri a dangerous enterprise. In 1863, the Russian anarchist Peter Kropotkin travelled 320 kilometres accompanying a fleet of barges with provisions for new Russian settlers. He recalled:

> When the rainy season, due to monsoons, comes in July, the Sungari, the Ussuri, and the Amur are swollen by unimaginable qualities of water; thousands of low islands, usually covered with willow thickets, are torn away, and the width of the river attains in places two, three or five miles; water rushes into hundreds of branches and lakes which spread in the lowlands along the main channel; and when a fresh wind blows from an eastern quarter, against the current, tremendous waves, higher than those which one sees in the estuary of the St. Lawrence, roll up the main channel as well as up its branches. Still worse is it when a typhoon blows from the China Sea and spreads over the Amur region.[4]

The environment makes life along the Amur River seem full of potential, however miserable it might be. The climate is better than that in Siberia; the land is fertile and rich in gold, other minerals, and coal. The river is rich in beluga, sturgeon, and salmon. The surrounding forests are home to tigers, bears, foxes, sable, wild boar, deer, wild chicken, and rare birds. The Amur's flora contains precious herbs and plants, of which ginseng is the most valued.

The Russian explorer Arseniev linked the exceptional variety of the Amur's flora and fauna to the existence of three distinct climatic zones: continental in the west, subtropical in the middle, and subarctic in the north.[5]

Despite its diversity, the Amur's land is not good for rice or cotton cultivation. Only migratory people like the Golds, equipped with light birch-bark canoes, could deal with the Amur's seasonal floods. Floods regularly inundate the valleys, destroying villages and forcing people to move away from the river. Indigenous people handled these floods better than anybody else because their hunting and fishing skills made it easier for them to avoid flood epicentres. The Golds made their homes in the marshy areas between the lower Songhua and the Ussuri, demonstrating their ability to adjust to harsh natural conditions – something they were able to do much better than were new settlers. Nonetheless, all had to deal with the daily challenge of taiga, harsh winters, heavy rains, mosquitoes, and deadly diseases like scurvy and bubonic plague.

Amur winters are bitterly cold. The farther west one goes, the colder the winter. The contrast between winter and summer temperatures in the northwest of China's northeast is equally striking. In places like Barga, the temperature in January can be as low as –50°C, while in July it can be as high as 35°C.[6] The spring and autumn are both very short, which means that the winters are long; this makes it difficult for people without adequate housing to survive. Native people survive winter by engaging in hunting and fishing. This climate is suitable only to people who are familiar with cold weather, such as the native people or Russians coming from Siberia or from central Russia.

Overall, the influence of nature on Amur Basin societies was always stronger than was the impact of military and political conflicts or of colonization. The Amur River runs through a landscape divided by mountains, forests, and marshes, complicating communication between sparsely populated villages and towns. Most of the settlements along the Amur started out as tiny, bleak villages, and they have remained like this to the present. No major urban settlement along the river developed into commercial hubs, with the exception of Harbin on the Songhua River. Harbin started as a railway town, the administrative centre of the Chinese Eastern Railway, and became a thriving commercial centre, the major city in the Sino-Russian frontier region. The city's prosperity owed little to its proximity to the river. The Songhua provided water but was also a seasonal challenge. Harbin and its surrounding areas witnessed at least one natural calamity every two years, such as heavy thunderstorms, floods, premature freezing, and epidemic diseases.[7] Thus, the history of human settlement along the Amur River and its tributaries is also a story of the human battle with nature – a battle that nature often wins.

The Sino-Russian Quest for the Amur

The Amur River was long a site of clashes between subjects of the Russian and Qing empires. After the Russian conquest of Siberia, Cossack groups from Siberian settlements, or *ostrogs,* crossed the river in search of furs and of new places for agricultural settlement. Far away from the political centre, these settlements, led by Poyarkov (1644) and Khabarov (1649-1951), ruled their own affairs and took their own initiative. In 1650, Khabarov established the outpost Albazin on the left bank of the Amur, near the confluence of the Shilka and Argun rivers. Manchu forces attacked the fort in 1685 and 1686, forcing the Russians to withdraw from the Amur. The Treaty of Nerchinsk (1689) fixed the Argun and Gorbitsa rivers as the new border between Russia and the Qing empire, making the entire Amur River system east of Albazin a Chinese territory.[8]

Nearly a century later, knowledge of the Amur River in Russia and in Europe was still sparse. The French sailor Le Perouse (1785-88) and the Russian explorer Kruzenstern (1805) erroneously believed that navigation along the Amur by seagoing vessels was impossible because the island of Sakhalin blocked the Amur estuary and the entry to the Amur at Okhotsk was too shallow (contemporary Russian maps showed Sakhalin as a peninsula, not as an island).[9] In 1846, Russian tsar Nicholas I showed that he also believed that the Amur did not have the capacity to carry seagoing vessels and, therefore, had no real strategic value. He wrote: "I regret that the question of Amur needs to be abandoned as it is a useless river. Those who explored it should be rewarded."[10]

The Qing government had more reason to be familiar with the area since the Manchu founders of the dynasty regarded the Songhua and Ussuri rivers, together with the Changbai Mountains, as their traditional homeland. After signing the Treaty of Nerchinsk, the Qing government kept a close eye on its new Amur frontier. It maintained military patrols along three routes, one along the lower bank of the Amur and two parallel ones from Nongjiang to the Argun River.[11] Moreover, in 1709-10 the Manchu emperor Kangxi sent Jesuit missionaries to survey the lands north of Korea. They travelled as far as the estuary of the Amur but did not reach Sakhalin Island.[12]

The westward expansion of the Qing empire during the eighteenth and nineteenth centuries weakened Manchu attention to the Amur frontier. Qing emperors isolated their ancestral lands from China proper by imposing a ban on Chinese immigration. Qing emperors were not interested in the lands beyond the Imperial Hunting grounds in Jehol or near present-day Chengde.[13] The northern edge of the Willow Palisade was separated from the main artery of the Amur River by hundreds of kilometres of forests, hills, and marshes. No emperor travelled there, and this frontier remained neglected and sparsely populated.

The Drive to Colonize the Amur

The strategic necessity of establishing Russian sea power in the Far East and the search for navigation routes through the Siberian interior forced Nikolai Nikolaevich Muraviev, the governor general of East Siberia from 1847 to 1861, to continue further explorations of the Amur River. In 1849, Admiral Gennady Ivanovich Nevelskoy's expeditions to the estuary of the Amur and to Sakhalin led to the discovery that Sakhalin was an island. This discovery opened up the idea that the Amur might be accessible for ship navigation not only from the Sea of Okhotsk but also from the Sea of Japan.[14]

A series of explorations by Russian sailors, military officers, and scientists, known as the Nevelskoi Amur Expeditions (1849-55), meticulously studied the river system. These people came into contact with the indigenous populations and, from the knowledge they gained from them, initiated the Russian policy of colonizing the upper reaches of the Amur and Sakhalin. Nevelskoi's expeditions included more than a dozen voyages on different ships under various commands. Their routes indicated Russia's strong interest in establishing transport links with a year-round port on the Pacific Ocean.

Financial support for these expeditions came from the Russo-American Company, a colonial enterprise founded by Russian merchants in 1799, with headquarters in St. Petersburg and Irkutsk. Deeper exploration into the interior required more people and a supply of money, equipment, and food, making contributions from the Russo-American Company inadequate. Struggling with shortages of food, these expeditions relied on the initiatives of Count Muraviev, the main proponent of the Amur's colonization.[15]

These expeditions resulted in Russian occupation of the sparsely populated right bank of the Amur River and the east bank of the Ussuri River. Since the signing of the Treaty of Aigun (1858) and the Treaty of Peking (1860), the Amur River and its tributaries acquired political significance, marking the eastern border between the two empires. Imperial Russia joined the Western powers in a drive for territorial and commercial gain in China. No battles accompanied the Qing loss of its northern lands. No efforts were made on the part of Manchu emperors to secure military posts in Sanxing and Aigun. The main negotiator on the Russian side, Count Muraviev, later became a national hero in Russia, and the name of the river was added to his family name, making him Count Muraviev-Amursky. Qing negotiator Prince I-Shan enraged the court by handing over to Russia a huge tract of land, and he was deprived of his rank. As a member of the Imperial Clan, he remained in service to the court, though in less important positions, for another fifteen years.[16]

Occupation of the lower section of the Amur River afforded Russia exclusive rights to continue surveying the river. The Nevelskoi Expeditions were only a small proportion of travels to come. Starting in 1855, for the next fifteen years, the upper bank of the Amur and the coast of the Sea of Japan and the Sea of Okhotsk became home to at least fifty scientific and military expeditions, which studied topography, climate, ethnography, and which brought with them Russian settlers.[17] During seven years of government-sponsored agricultural migration after 1850, about sixty settlements were established along the Amur and Ussuri Rivers. In 1858, Muraviev established the Amur region, stretching from the Amur's confluence with the Shilka to its confluence with the Bureya. Blagoveshchensk and Khabarovsk were established during the same year, serving as major military posts and springboards to eastward expansion along the Amur.[18]

The Qing's weak presence on the Amur frontier continued for at least two decades after the loss of its northeastern territory to Russia. Garrison towns along the Songhua and Nonni rivers were poorly funded, while local banner troops were dispatched from the region to fight the Taiping, Nien, and Muslim rebellions in China proper.[19] In the 1880s, the Qing government turned its attention to this frontier. In 1885, the Chinese official and explorer Cao Tingjie went along the same route as did the Russian Amur Expeditions thirty years earlier. He departed from Sanxing, went all the way to the mouth of the Amur River, and travelled the main artery and the Ussuri River, visiting Russian settlements on his way. He returned with detailed descriptions of the places he saw. His accounts of China's northeast and of Russian territories combine historical and geographic narrative. His maps of Russian and Chinese settlements along the border provided invaluable military intelligence to the Qing court.[20] Cao Tingjie's efforts helped the Qing government negotiate demarcation of the border with Russia along the Ussuri River and below Lake Khanka.

River as a Border

The Treaty of Peking (1860) fixed on paper the eastern boundary between Russia and China. Article I states:

> The eastern frontier between two states, starting from the confluence of the rivers Shilka and Argun will follow the course of the Amur River to the confluence of the latter with the Ussuri River. The lands located on the left bank (to the north) of the Amur River, belong to the Russian state, and the lands located on the right bank (to the south), to the confluence of the Ussuri River, belong to the Chinese state. Furthermore, from the confluence of the Ussuri to Lake Khanka, the boundary goes along the rivers Ussuri and Sungacha. The lands located on the eastern (right) bank of these rivers belong to the Russian state, and on the west bank (left) to the Chinese state.[21]

This treaty produced the first official map of the Amur border. This map was a result of mostly Russian surveys and efforts at defining the borderline.

The boundary on this map was marked by a red line with letters of the Russian alphabet, from A to U. The borderland of the upper Amur and would-be boundary south of Lake Khanka were not yet properly surveyed as part of it ran through the mountains and taiga. This treaty obliged both sides to establish a joint commission to further survey and install border signs along this river.[22]

After the Amur River and its tributaries were turned into a nominal boundary, it proved difficult if not impossible to enforce the border. The treaty is unclear as to whether the borderline ran along the centre of the main channel. According to the treaty, both Russia and China attained equal navigation rights along the border rivers, but the details of this navigation were not discussed. Moreover, the river does not behave as a fixed border; it moves when not frozen. The Amur changes shape at least twice each year during spring floods and summer drought. The river flows to the rules of nature, not the rules of empires. Demarcating and monitoring the Amur became a constant source of confusion for border authorities and for political centres.

Numerous islands complicated the drawing of a precise line of division in the navigable streams. One of these islands, known in Chinese as Heixiazi, was located near the Russian town of Khabarovsk, on the convergence of the Amur and Ussuri rivers. This island exemplifies what the Aigun and Peking treaties, as well as early maps, failed to resolve. The Qing government considered the boundary to run through the meeting point of the main streams of the Amur and Ussuri rivers, claiming the Heixiazi as Qing territory. The Russians considered the state boundary to be drawn along the Chinese banks of the river and claimed the island as Russian. The dispute over this and other islands was a constant friction in late nineteenth- and twentieth-century Sino-Russian border negotiations.[23]

The Amur River's islands could also not function as a border. Seasonal floods changed the number, location, and size of islands, destroying settlements and fortifications along the banks of the river. Summer drought made the upper Amur and Shilka rivers shallow. As a result, river islands increased in size and number, blocking navigation. The Russian merchant writer Dmitrii Stakheev, who lived in the border town of Blagoveshchensk and travelled the region from 1862 to 1863, recalled that during summer months chickens easily walked the waters of Shilka and women commuted from one bank to another.[24]

Over time, the channel of the Argun River moved west, became shallower, and created new islands. This caused territorial disputes over the eastern section of the northeastern border, where it was defined by the Argun River. Since the signing of the Treaty of Nerchinsk in 1689, a 1,200-kilometre-long border existed along the Argun River. In 1909-10, joint surveys by border commissions discovered that the Qing and Russian records of these islands did not match and that several islands were missing from contemporary maps. The Qiqihaer Protocol, signed in October 1911, divided the islands along the Argun border between Russia and China, recognizing nature's effect on the border.[25]

Natural complications demanded constant supervision, and the presence of substantial border patrols, at the Amur frontier, which neither empire was ready to commission. British consul Alexander Hosie, passing from Khabarovsk to Blagoveshchensk by boat in summer 1900, wrote:

> The Amur and the Shilka are marked, lighted, and in some places buoyed by the Russian government, and two vessels are constantly employed during the open season in surveying the river, and, as the channel changes, in altering marks. At all difficult crossings there are leading marks fixed on poles surmounted by oil lamps, red on the right bank, white on the left, which have to be kept in line to avoid grounding, for the shallowness of both rivers is remarkable and necessitates the employment of paddle or stern steamers only.[26]

The length of the Amur and the difficult access left most of its sectors unattended.

The chaotic movement of people across the Amur River was another factor beyond the control of border authorities. Indigenous people did not recognize the new, artificial boundaries; they continued to hunt and fish wherever nature allowed. New Russian, Chinese, and Korean settlers and traders did not respect the borders, making illegal trade a constant feature of life there. As a result, all the major territorial treaties between Russia and China during the late Qing and Early Republican periods were concerned with illegal border-crossing, if only on paper. The Amur River defied the imposition of rules external to itself.

Conclusion

Nature has been a dominant factor in the social history of the Amur River, constantly interfering with colonization efforts. Mapping the frontier was a gargantuan task. Not until surrounding territories became settled in the second half of the twentieth century were the Amur River and its tributaries properly surveyed and monitored. During the late Qing period, the Amur sector accounted for only a fraction of the Qing-Russian border making. The Qing government negotiated its western border with Imperial Russia along the Tianshan Mountains during the decades of the Amur border formation. Negotiations proved to be time-consuming as both sides lacked sufficient peoplepower to survey and maintain their common borders.

Mapping and demarcating the Amur River allowed for human manipulation: words and locations on maps could be changed, omitted, renamed, or wrongly translated. With secrecy surrounding the strategic maps of both sides of the border, they could easily be fabricated, replaced, or destroyed. On the ground, stone markers replaced wooden ones; the disappearance of wooden markers was often blamed on nature. Markers showing latitude could simply be removed. In times of peace, control over the Amur frontier was lax. But even in times of confrontation, the borderland was not nearly as clearly drawn as were Russia's borders with Europe.

Official maps showing the details of the Amur River have never been available to the public. Sino-Russian territorial agreements of the nineteenth and early twentieth centuries, published in either country, do not provide maps. In the fall of 2004, centuries-old border disputes over islands at the confluence of the Amur and Ussuri rivers were officially announced as resolved. But to date little information has surfaced regarding negotiations over these disputed islands. While the political border is seemingly "finally" fixed, the river maintains its prerogative to change yet again.

Notes

1 S.I. Pavlov, ed. *Bol'shaya Sovetskaya Entsiklopedia* [Great Soviet Encyclopaedia], vol. 2 (Moscow: State Scientific Society "Bol'shaya Sovetskaya Entsiklopedia," 1950), 307; N.K. Shulman, ed. *Amurskaya oblast': Opyt entsiklopedicheskogo slovaria* [Amur region: Encyclopaedic dictionary] (Blagoveshchensk: Khabarovskoye knizhnoye izdatel'stvo, 1989), 40.

2 P. Semenov, ed. *Geograficheskо-statisticheskii slovar' Rossiiskoi Imperii* [Geographic-statistical dictionary of the Russian Empire], vol. 1 (St. Petersburg: Tip. Bezobrazova, 1863), 88; A. Kirillov, ed. *Geografichesko-statisticheskii slovar' Amurskoi I Primorskoi oblastei s vkluchеniem nekotorykh punktov sopredel'nykh s nimi stran* [Geographic-statistical dictionary of the Amur and Maritime regions including selected parts of the neighbouring countries] (Blagoveshchensk: D.O. Mokin and Co., 1894), 48-49; N.K. Shul'man, ed. *Amurskaia Oblast'* [Amur Region] (Blagoveshchensk: Khabarovskoe knizhnoe izdatel'stvo, 1989), 42.

3 A.A. Bolotov, *Amur I ego Bassein* [Amur and its basin] (Khabrin, 1925), 18-23.

4 Petr Kropotkin, *Memoirs of a Revolutionist* (New York and Montreal: Black Rose Books, 1898), 178.

5 See V.K. Arseniev, "Kraikii fiziko-geograficheskii ocherk basseina reki Amura" [Protokol of public meeting of the Russian Geographic Society], 6 June 1916.

6 V.A. Anuchin, *Geograficheskie ocherki Manchzhurii* [Essays on geography of Manchuria] (Moscow: Gosudstvennoe Izdatelstvo Geograficheskoi Literatury, 1948), 151.

7 Shi Fang and Gao Ling, *Chuantong yu biange* [Tradition and change] (Haerbin: Heilongjiang renmin chubanshe, 1995), 37-39.

8 Jonathan D. Spence, *The Search for Modern China* (New York: W.W. Norton, 1990), 66-67; Mark Mancall, *Russia and China: Their Diplomatic Relations to 1728* (Cambridge, MA: Harvard University Press, 1971), 28-31.

9 A.I. Alekseev, *Amurskaya Ekspeditsiya 1849-1855 gg.* [Amur expedition, 1849-1855] (Moscow: Mysl', 1974), 5-8.

10 Ibid., 14.

11 Liu Yuantu, ed., *Zaoqi Zhong-E dongduan bianjie yanjiu* [Research on the early period of the eastern section of the Sino-Russian border] (Beijing: Zhongguo shehui kexue chubanshe, 1993), vol. 1, no. 38, 267-68.

12 Leo Bargow, "A Few Remarks on Maps of the Amur, the Tartar Strait and Sakhalin," *Imago Mundi* 12 (1955): 129-30.

13 See Richard L. Edmonds, "The Willow Palisade," *Annals of the Association of American Geographers* 69, 4 (1979): 611-21.

14 A.I. Alekseev, *Russkie geographicheskie issledovaniia na Dal'nem Vostoke I v Severnoi Amerike: XIX – nachalo XX v.* [Russian Geographic Explorations in the Far East and in North America, from nineteenth century to the beginning of twentieth century] (Moscow: Nauka, 1976), 8.

15 Nevelskoi, on many occasions, complained to Count Muraviev about the Russo-American Company's indifference to the needs of expeditions, and this worsened his relations with the high command. See Alekseev, *Amurskaya Ekspeditsiya* (1974), 161-63.

16 A.W. Hummel, ed., *Eminent Chinese of the Ch'ing Period,* 1644-1912, vol. 1 (Washington: Government Publication Office, 1944), 392-93.

17 G.F. Starkov and A.A. Stepanov, "Important Monument to Far Eastern Cartography," in *Voprosy Geografii Dal'nego Vostoka,* vol. 6 (Khabarovsk: Geograficheskoe obshchestvo SSSR, Priamurskii filial, 1963), 292.

18 P. Semenov, *Geographic-Statistical Dictionary of the Russian Empire* (St. Petersburg: Tip. Bezobrazova, 1863), 87-91.

19 Robert H.G. Lee, *The Manchurian Frontier in Ch'ing History* (Cambridge, MA: Harvard University Press, 1970), 116-17.

20 Peiyuan Cong and Mingqi Zhao, eds. *Cao Tingjie ji* [Collected works by Cao Tingjie)], vol. 2 (Beijing: Zhonghua shuji, 1985), 508-10.

21 V.S. Myasnikov, *Russko-Kitaiskie Dogovorno-Pravovye Akty* [Sino-Russian treaties and legal acts] *(1689-1916)* (Moscow: Pamyatniki Istoricheskoi Mysli, 2004), 71.

22 V.S. Myasnikov and Ye. D. Stepanov, eds. *Granitsy Kitaya: Istoriya Formirovaniya* [China's borders: history of their development] (Moskva: Pamyatniki Istoricheskoi Mysli, 2001), 113.

23 Neville Maxwell, "A Note on the Amur/Ussuri Sector of the Sino-Soviet Boundaries," *Modern China* 1, 1 (1975): 116-26.

24 Dmitrii Stakheev, *Za Baikalom I na Amure: Putevye kartiny* [Beyond the Baikal Lake and along the Amur River: Images of travel] (St. Petersburg: Tip. K. Vul'fa, 1869), 281.

25 V.S, Myasnikov, *Russko-Kitaiskie Dogovorno-Pravovye Akty* [Sino-Russian Treaties and Legal acts] *(1689-1916)* (Moscow: "Pamyatniki Istoricheskoi Mysli," 2004), 371.

26 Alexander Hosie, *Manchuria: Its People, Resources and Recent History* (Boston: J.B. Millet Co., 1910), 274.

9

The Ethics of Benevolence in French Colonial Vietnam: A Sino-Franco-Vietnamese Cultural Borderland

Van Nguyen-Marshall

In this chapter, borders are viewed as being more metaphorical than literal. Rather than exploring the historical interaction between the Chinese state and its borderland, I examine a group of Vietnamese intellectuals who stand on the border between the old and new, between the Classical Chinese and the Western worldviews, and, more specifically, between Confucian and Western ideas on social responsibility. My focus is on the organizational activities of non-revolutionary Vietnamese. On the whole, these people were not openly hostile to French colonial rule, and some may have even been supportive of the French colonial agenda in Indochina. These politically moderate men and women filled the memberships of mutual-aid societies and participated enthusiastically in state-endorsed relief organizations and activities. Both the state and the Vietnamese participants often regarded mutual-aid and charity organizations as modern and new. However, on closer scrutiny, it is clear that the values embodied in these discourses, institutions, and organizations were still recognizably Confucian, exhibiting deep concerns for cultivating ethical behaviour and instilling a sense of social responsibility.

My argument reinforces the continuity thesis in Vietnamese modern history that is famously associated with Professor Alexander Woodside. While it was never my intention to confirm or challenge my own supervisor's important contribution to Vietnamese historiography, my doctoral research on poor relief, along with my newest research project on mutual-aid societies, has shored up the idea that what appear to be "modern" ideas, organizations, and social forms might well be Confucian. This cultural "borderland" position can be seen as a cultural "hybrid," or cultural *métissage*, as suggested by Françoise Lionnet.[1] Rejecting the ideas of acculturation and assimilation, Lionnet prefers to use the notion of cultural métissage, or transculturation, as a way of viewing cultural interactions. In this perspective, the interaction of cultures can be seen as a dynamic, two-way process. Lionnet explains that in this cultural process, or in the "border zones" of cultural interaction, "all of our academic preconceptions about cultural, linguistic, or stylistic norms are constantly being put to the test by creative practices that make visible and set off the processes of adaptation, appropriation, and contestation that govern the construction of identity in colonial and postcolonial contexts."[2] Lionnet was writing about postcolonial Caribbean and African female writers who were appropriating the French language in order to create a space in which cultural identities could be negotiated and reformulated. For the Vietnamese case, the cultural interaction was, in fact, a three-way intersection, with the Vietnamese appropriating and transforming Western ideas and institutions within an indigenous ethical system, in which Chinese influence remained important and persistent. This argument for a three-way hybridity can be made in relation to two areas of activity: charity and mutual-aid organizations.

Northern Vietnamese Villages and the Ethics of Mutual Aid

The ethics of mutual aid and charity had deep roots in premodern Vietnamese villages, particularly those in the Red River Delta in Northern Vietnam. Mutual-help and charitable institutions generally serve useful functions, particularly in preindustrialized agricultural societies. It is not surprising to see mutual-aid or benevolent organizations in various communities, and there is no reason to think that they did not arise in response to local needs. What I would like to suggest here, however, is that mutual-aid sentiments and practices in Vietnam were encouraged by Confucianism and became institutionalized according to Chinese models. The Confucian influence remained important even in the French colonial period.

Both the granary systems and the ethic of benevolence in Vietnam, which contributed to equalization of wealth and provided food security during disasters, were inspired by their Chinese counterparts. The granary systems were created in both China and Vietnam in order to regulate grain price as well as to feed the population in time of food shortages. In the eighteenth century, the Qing dynasty played an important role in promoting people's welfare. In addition to ensuring people's access to their livelihood, the Qing administration played a significant role in food distribution.[3] At this time, the Chinese granary system was at the height of its efficiency with regard to both stabilizing the price of rice and responding to famines.[4] According to R. Bin Wong, the various spheres of grain circulation (commercial, state, and customary) were effective in ensuring a staple supply of grain for the market, in providing loans to those in need, and in feeding state officials and the military.[5] In times of food shortages, however, the ever-normal (*changpingcang*) and community granary (*shecang*) reserves also allowed the state to respond quickly to food shortages.[6]

Granaries on the Chinese model were also built in Vietnam. In 1834, a Vietnamese official petitioned King Minh Mang to build communal granaries, stating that Vietnam "should imitate the communal granary law of the Sung Confucian scholar Chu Hsi."[7] Under the reign of Tu Duc (r. 1848-83) there were a variety of granaries. The *thuong binh* granaries were managed by the central government, while the *nghia thuong* granaries were provincially controlled and the *xa thuong* were administered by the communes.[8] Imperial records for the Nguyen dynasty indicate that these granaries were in frequent use.[9] In 1820, for example, King Minh Mang ordered the granary in Quang Tri to sell paddy at a reduced price and to lend paddy to the local population.[10] When the French colonized Vietnam in the mid-1860s, granaries still existed, particularly in the north. The French administration, however, did not support the granary system and tried to dismantle it on the grounds that the granaries were corrupt and ineffective institutions.[11] Despite colonial discouragement, some granaries still existed in the early twentieth century. As of 1906, Sinh Lien commune (Ha Dong province) still maintained its granary. [12] As late as the 1920s, there were still local mutual-aid societies that organized their own granaries to protect themselves from food shortages.[13]

For the colonial administration at large, the Chinese-inspired granary system was symbolic of the Vietnamese ancien régime and was thus allegedly predisposed to corruption and inefficiency. Nevertheless, during subsistence crises, various French and Vietnamese officials had suggested resurrecting the granary system as a model for food security. During the 1906 famine, Paul Beau, the governor general of Indochina, requested that the provinces examine ways to help prevent famine. Beau suggested that the idea of a granary system could be revisited as a possible method of famine prevention.[14] Beau's idea was considered and subsequently rejected by French and Vietnamese provincial officials for a number of reasons; some were logistical concerns, but some no doubt had to do with the tie that the granary system had to the Vietnamese precolonial political and ethical system. As one provincial official pointed out, reviving an institution that the French had destroyed would provide ammunition for critics of French colonial rule.[15]

While granaries performed a crucial role in regulating the price of rice and in relieving famine, the granary system in Vietnam, as in China, was one component of a broader community welfare system. The notion of community welfare and, more specifically, the ethics of mutual-aid and benevolence were enshrined in village life through their incorporation into the *huong uoc* (village code or covenants). Huong uoc were written laws that set out the traditions, customs, and regulations of a particular village.[16] A similar institution existed in China, known as the *xiangyue*, or community covenant/compact, which was "a concept of subcounty organization, stressing the harmony of social relations, resolution of disputes, moral education, and mutual aid."[17] The first xiangyue was written in 1077 by Lu Dajun in Shanxi province. His xiangyue, the "Lu family community covenant," was an attempt to strengthen local control over village administration vis-à-vis the central government as well as an attempt to put Confucian ideals regarding communal organization into practice.[18] Around the 1170s, Zhu Xi (1130-1200) modified and added to Lu's covenant, making it famous but also changing the spirit of the xiangyue. According to Monika Ubelhor, Zhu Xi added many minute details regarding etiquette and decorum.[19] Comparing Lu's to Zhu Xi's xiangyue, Ubelhor writes: "Whereas Lu Ta-chun's community compact seems to be a device for smoothing daily life in the local community, Chu Hsi's version seems to be more of a device to regulate the social life of the educated elite."[20]

According to Kandice Hauf, central to the Lu xiangyue as well as subsequent covenants that were proposed or put into practice during the sixteenth century were concerns for moral education and mutual-aid.[21] Xiangyue of the early Ming period, for example, included the establishment of charitable schools, charitable fields, and granaries.[22] When Wang Yangming (1472-1529) was sent to put down rebellions in southern Jiangxi, he created a xiangyue for the newly subdued community. His covenant emphasized, first and foremost, mutual assistance for burials and disasters and, second, moral education.[23] Wang's xiangyue was imposed upon the local community by an official from the central state rather than by a local leader. Nevertheless, the covenant was aimed at providing the community with a mechanism for self-regulation. The xiangyue of Chinese communities, therefore, not only provided local leaders with a mandate for self-administration but also provided opportunities for the central government to impose some social control through encouraging a particular type of behaviour and ideals. In either case, ideas of mutual-aid, communal welfare, and charity were important aspects of these community covenants.

Vietnamese huong uoc had histories and relationships to the central state that were similar to those of the xiangyue. While huong uoc has been around at least since the fifteenth century and seems to have flourished in the mid- to late seventeenth century, some historians suggest that their roots can be dated back to the period when Vietnamese society first originated. According to Vu Duy Men, huong uoc evolved from the earlier community-bonding activities of "oath-taking societies" (*hoi the*), in which members of the village would swear oaths of allegiance to the village and promise to follow certain communal rules.[24] Vu Duy Men suggests that the oath-taking societies, which existed as far back as the fifth century, slowly gave rise to the written village laws.[25] He also maintains that, while huong uoc arose from these oath-taking societies, the emergence of written laws reflected the increasing influence and demands of the central state on villages. Similarly, Bui Xuan Dinh suggests that huong uoc, while still mirroring local practices and priorities, only emerged once central authority became stronger and more imposing. According to Dinh, in order for the village laws to be written in Chinese script, a class of scholars versed in Chinese learning needed to exist.[26] Thus as Confucian ideology became important during the Le dynasty (1428-1777), Confucianism became more important in state as well as in village life.[27]

The regulations and laws set out in the huong uoc were meant to ensure the smooth functioning of village life. According to Bui Xuan Dinh, while each village had its own particular set of laws, common among them were regulations relating to these main categories: territorial integrity of the village; agricultural production; social organization and relationship; culture, education, and religion; and the individual's obligation towards the state (e.g., paying taxes and performing military duty).[28] With regard to social organization, voluntary associations, such as rice- or money-lending societies, were specified in village laws, which indicates that these organizations existed in the precolonial period.[29]

Prominent among these articles regulating the function of the village were articles stressing an individual's obligation to the community, especially to the poor. Vu Duy Men's study of the huong uoc of Quynh Doi village demonstrates this point clearly. Quynh Doi village wrote its first huong uoc in 1638. In 1750, an article was appended to the huong uoc, stating that those who are sent to help the poor with funerals should not make any demands on the grieving family.[30] Later, in 1773, another article was added: "When a poor household has a funeral, the village must send thirty people to help."[31] Bui Xuan Dinh also indicates that some huong uoc have articles that deal directly with poor and famine relief, such as the granary system.[32]

During the French colonial period, the French administration attempted to impose control over village life. Beginning in 1908, the colonial administration attempted to introduce a series of village reforms, which would supposedly modernize the villages, making their governance more effective and their socio-economic life more efficient.[33] In fact, the colonial government probably also saw these reforms as ways to replace the older and more Confucian echelon of leadership who had dominated village politics with a crop of younger, Western educated men (who presumably were more easily persuaded to see the advantages of the French "civilizing" mission).

Connected with the French reform attempts was the colonial administration's 1923 call for revision of the huong uoc.[34] The reformed huong uoc shared a formula set out by the state. In general, the first halves of the reformed huong uoc are almost identical to each other in that they address the administrative and fiscal reforms stipulated by the state.[35] The second halves, however, address issues and customs particular to the individual villages.[36] These reformed huong uoc, however, still retained the emphasis on communal welfare, mutual aid, and charity. The 1936 revised huong uoc of La Doi village (Hai Duong Province), for example, contains articles stipulating village members' obligation to help each other during emergencies (articles 38 and 39) and mentions the formation of mutual-aid associations (article 62).[37]

The ethic of mutual help and benevolence was still alive in the early twentieth century under French colonialism, manifesting itself in the organization of mutual-aid societies and charitable activities. While these early twentieth-century organizations tended to wrap themselves in the language and trappings of modernity and Western efficiency, their inspirations, values, and concerns were still tied to Confucian morality. Therefore, within the manifestations of the mutual-aid ethic was the interplay between the modernist portrayal of the organization by the participants and the Confucian values that were at the core of these participants' concerns.

Mutual-Aid Societies in French Colonial Vietnam

Vietnamese mutual-aid societies of the early twentieth century exhibited hybridized values and worldviews. Mutual-aid societies were couched in the language of modernity while, at the same time, reinforcing traditional customs and social relations. Mutual-aid associations have been defined as "non-profit making, non-governmental, private groups which individuals join by choice; members are not born into them, nor drafted into them, nor are they obliged to join in order to make a living."[38] Historians writing about mutual-aid societies in France agree that their basic aim is to protect members who are not able to work because of illness, injury, or death.[39] In reviewing the scholarship on eighteenth- and nineteenth-century mutual-aid societies in France, Alan Baker highlights some of the "orthodox" characterizations of these organizations, one of which is the view of mutual-aid associations as forerunners of modern trades unions. According to Baker, the orthodox scholarship "continues to emphasize their [i.e., mutual-aid associations] modernity as fundamentally urban, industrial organisations which played a role in the formation and development of class consciousness among the better-paid craftsmen and male workers."[40]

This view can also be found in research on mutual-aid societies elsewhere. Ronaldo Munck's study on Argentina, for example, credits mutual-aid societies for laying the roots for Argentina's labour movement.[41] Baker's research on rural France, however, challenges this image of mutual-aid societies as "'voluntary associations of like-minded wage earners' in urban centres of commerce and manufacturing."[42] Other research on mutual-aid associations suggests that these associations, which were often organized along ethnic or regional lines, tended to reinforce local and cultural identities rather than help to create national or class consciousness.[43]

In a *Pacific Affairs* article published over thirty years ago, Alexander Woodside had already discovered this ambiguous, or métissage, nature of Vietnamese urban organizations.[44] Examining a few urban mutual-aid societies as part of social organizations in general, Woodside argued that seemingly modern organizations such as the Association of the Industrial and Commercial Employees of Tonkin were, in practice, hierarchically organized and built around a powerful patron. Furthermore, they reinforced elitism rather than equal participation.[45] Of a women's charitable organization, Woodside wrote: "The structure of this major urban organization was modern ... but the motives of its members were traditionalistic."[46] A similar comment can be made of many of the mutual-aid organizations that sprang up in Northern Vietnam in the 1920s and 1930s under the encouragement of French colonial officials.

As was shown earlier, mutual-aid societies had their roots in village ethics, particularly those of the north. At the village and neighbourhood levels there were many types of voluntary, privately organized mutual-aid societies that afforded members financial and spiritual support. These societies might be organized as labour-exchanges, as organizations offering rotating-credit, or as ceremony-assistance societies. Labour-exchange societies were usually organized among people of the same trade (e.g., guilds of farmers, specialty-crop growers, or artisans). Members would help each other prepare their fields, look after each other's water buffaloes, perform night watch over crops, or share equipment and work animals.[47] In addition to work exchange, trade societies might organize ritual feasts and group celebrations.[48] These occasions could be religious and/or social events, where ritual offerings would secure favours of the appropriate deities while, at the same time, bonding members together to facilitate future cooperation. Rotating-credit societies were usually organized among people of the same hamlet, neighbourhood, or street. Members might pool their money, with each member taking a turn to use a relatively large sum for a business investment or to finance an important family ritual or celebration.[49] Ceremony-assistance societies were organized specifically for helping members finance funerals, weddings, or Lunar New Year celebration expenses. These societies functioned in a similar fashion to the rotating-credit societies in that they required members to regularly contribute small amounts over time, which made them eligible to borrow a lump sum when it was their turn or when they needed it (such as for funerals).

While Vietnamese village ethics encouraged, and peasants' financial and spiritual needs necessitated, various forms of mutual-aid organizations, the colonial government was also keen on the proliferation of self-help societies. The existence of village mutual-aid organizations would ease the pressure on colonial state resources. During one famine in 1915, the resident superior of Tonkin, for example, wrote to the famine-afflicted provinces of the north that the administration of Tonkin was not prepared to provide relief to the population beyond setting up a few work camps.[50] Looking after the famine victims was under the purview of the communal administration, which presumably had some sort of welfare organization in place.

In addition to the financial and political expediency, mutual-aid societies also corresponded to a contemporary ideological trend. In late nineteenth-century France, the solidarité movement was influential among French socialists. Advocated by leftist radical politician Leon Bourgeois, the solidarité movement stood for "human interdependence and mutual responsibility, echoing from the Revolutionary triad the ideal of fraternity."[51] One manifestation of the ideas of solidarité was the promotion of mutual-aid societies, which grew in numbers in the mid-nineteenth century. By 1863, there were 4,721 mutual-aid societies with 676,000 members in France.[52] According to Robert Tombs, in late nineteenth-century France, these mutual-aid societies dominated the area of social provision.[53] Self-help organizations, which encouraged people to rely on each other as opposed to the state, were clearly a compromise between "liberal laissez-faire and radical state action" with regard to the issue of welfare.[54] While they addressed social and poverty issues, mutual-aid societies did not require the state to assume responsibility for these issues itself.

Highly enthusiastic about the benefits of mutual-aid societies, French officials saw mutual-aid societies as the solution to Vietnam's poverty and frequent subsistence crises. In 1906, for example, the mayor of Hai Phong suggested that mutual-aid societies such as Kien An's Dong Loi (Mutual Benefit) be set up to help with famine prevention.[55] Established by the former resident of Kien An province, Charles Prêtre, the Dong Loi Society was a producers' mutual-aid organization that helped farmers get a fair price for their produce. French officials represented Dong Loi and other such provident and mutual-aid societies as beneficial organizations that could help the Vietnamese cope with periodic food shortages. Moreover, French officials believed that such organizations, particularly rotating credit societies or mutual-savings organizations, would help "habituate" the natives to providence and frugality, an appreciation of which, according to the French colonial view, was supposedly lacking in Indochinese natives.[56]

French colonial officials at various levels of government wrote frequently about the need to teach the Vietnamese the value of mutual-aid organization. In 1907, Hanoi mayor Félix Hausser proposed that provident societies, like those that existed in Algeria, be set up in Indochina.[57] At the Colonial Exposition in Marseille, Hausser learned about the success of Algeria's Sociétés Indigènes de Prévoyance, de Prêts et de Secours Mutuels des Communes (the Indigenous Society of Providence, Loans, and Mutual-Aid of the Communes). He wrote a lengthy description of this society in the hope that the Vietnamese might be encouraged to organize their own. As Hausser stated, the Arabs were no more provident than were the "Annamites," and there was nothing to say that, in a short time, the Annamites would understand and appreciate the importance of such mutual-aid organizations.[58]

Some French officials, however, were not so generous in their views of the Vietnamese people's social capability. For example, in 1906, the resident of Ha Nam noted that Vietnamese people were selfish and lacked any sort of altruistic sentiments with which to organize mutual-aid groups.[59] According to the views of the French officials and a number of Vietnamese elite (such as those who wrote for the pro-French newspapers), forming mutual-aid organizations required modern attitudes and values, something that they considered sorely lacking in the Vietnamese population. The military commander of Ha Giang province opined that Vietnamese society was not ready for mutual-aid organizations: "They [the indigenous people] do not understand the function of financial societies and can only see one thing – that they are obligated to contribute money without a certainty of receiving some of it."[60]

Similarly, the resident of Ninh Binh wrote in 1906 that only when the Vietnamese have assimilated the French ideas of humanitarianism could they put into practice the idea of "all for one and one for all."[61] As it stood, the resident of Ninh Binh felt the indigenous mentality was not ready for solidarity and mutual-aid activities. These opinions clearly did not take into account the practice of mutual-aid and benevolence that had long existed in Vietnamese villages.

Some of the mutual-aid organizations that were formed in the 1920s and 1930s were large and "modern" enough to seek the colonial government's permission to operate. The statutes sent to the resident superior's office for approval were carefully typed or were handwritten in a professional manner, stating the goals of the society, its regulations, its fees structure, and its membership requirements as well as providing a list of founding members. Mutual-aid statutes were sometimes accompanied by *Sûreté* reports that identified members who might have communist or anti-colonial connections.

Many of the statutes held in the resident superior's archival collection pertained to the ceremonial mutual-aid societies. The statute of the Hop Thien (Philanthropic) Association of Hai Ninh province was typical of these statutes.[62] With fifty-three members, the Hop Thien Association applied for permission to function in 1938. It stated that its main goal was to provide mutual aid and to help the poor with funeral ceremonies. The founder and president was Ngo Kieu, the district chief of Moncay, the capital city of the military territory of Hai Ninh. Membership was open to men of eighteen years of age and over, who had good reputations, and whose ethnicity was either Viet, Nung, Tho, or Man. There were four different types of memberships: founding, honorary, beneficiary (those who contributed more than fifty piastres to the association), and regular. Regular members paid an entrance fee of two piastres and had to have their applications examined by the board of directors before being admitted. Membership fees would allow the association to purchase a number of funeral objects, such as a hearse, ceremonial drum and robes, and funerary musical instruments.

Articles eleven to nineteen of the Association's statute outline the procedures during a funeral. When there was a death of a member, the member's wife, his parents, or his wife's parents and all society members had to contribute forty cents each to buy funeral offerings (consisting of a funeral banner, two bottles of Vietnamese wine, incense, and candles) and to help the family with its mourning. The family of the deceased could also ask the association to help with the funeral rituals, to dig the grave, or to assist in transporting the coffin to the gravesite. If the family in mourning required the association's help, a member of the family had to come with a tray of betel nuts and meet with the association president. The association could offer assistance only in the above-mentioned ways; for other kinds of help, the family in mourning had to hire other people.

Members who shirked their responsibility towards the association, or whose behaviour at association functions and funerals was inappropriate, would be fined and, after six consecutive fines, would be expelled. In addition to helping members with funerals, the association also asked the government for a piece of land to be used as its cemetery. Members could be buried there for no charge, while non-members would be charged a fee, the cost depending on the plot in question. If the association's funds allowed it, the association would waive funeral outfit rental fees for poor families and would allow them to be buried in the cemetery at no cost.

What is striking about this association's statute are the minute details regarding the protocol and etiquette surrounding association business and funeral rituals. For instance, to approach the association president, one must bring along a tray of betel nuts (a customary gift). Association members' behaviour at funerals was also outlined. In short, while the association provided financial, labour, and moral support to its members, enabling them to carry out proper funerals following local customs, it was, at the same time, helping to preserve these customs. In other words, protocols associated with social status and rituals connected with funerals and ancestor worship were maintained and strengthened by these supposedly modern mutual-aid associations.

There were many other associations organized along similar lines to the Hop Thien Society of Hai Ninh. They existed in both the highland provinces and the densely populated Red River Delta provinces. Some examples are: Quang Thien Hoi (The Great Charity Society, Quang Yen, 1921); Bac Te (The Encompassing Assistance Society, Nam Dinh, 1926); Hoi Hieu (Mourning

Society, Bac Ninh, 1937); Tap Phuc Hoi (Collective Fortune Society, Hongay, 1939); Lien-Son Quang Thien Hoi (The Great Charity Society of Lien-Son, Vinh Yen Province, 1939).[63]

There were mutual-aid groups that attended to needs other than those associated with funerals. Hoi Chi Thien (Goodwill Society) of Bac Kan, for example, was founded not only to help members with funerals but also to provide charity. The association's statute states the following goals: to distribute charity, celebrate funerals, help indigents and victims of disasters, and bury deceased indigents.[64] Centred in Am-Hon pagoda, this society was open to both men and women, old and young, who wanted to participate in charity work. Thus it was not only a mutual-aid society but also a philanthropic and religious society. While there were provisions for helping its members with funerals and with other life celebrations (such as weddings), the society also set aside money for helping to bury the deceased poor (five piastres maximum per burial) and for helping the poor in general as well as those struck by disasters (three piastres per disaster). The association also carried out many ceremonies at the pagoda and accepted those who wanted to buy *hau,* an arrangement according to which people – usually those who did not have children – would pay the association to carry out the necessary rituals on their death anniversaries. The cost for buying hau was sixty piastres for members and eighty piastres for non-members.

Another type of mutual-aid association established granaries to store paddy for times of shortages, much like the granaries that were built and encouraged by the Nguyen kings in the nineteenth century. The Quang Hue (Great Kindness) Society, formed in Quang Uyen district of Cao Bang province in 1908, is an example of this type.[65] Quang Uyen was composed of four cantons and twenty-seven communes/villages, thus requiring intravillage coordination and linkages. The society's goal was to build a granary, and as soon as its resources reached either ten thousand piastres or 1 million kilograms of paddy, it would distribute aid to members as follows:

- In case of house fires, each member would receive six piastres.
- In the event of total loss of harvest, each family would receive four hundred kilograms of paddy or six piastres; if the loss of harvest were only partial, families would receive half the amount of aid.
- The society would provide help to poor families in the district (e.g., a group of Chinese families who had recently settled in the area). A family of five would receive two cows or two buffalos. The calves from these animals would belong to the society.
- The society would also support fifteen students at the Franco-Vietnamese school. The students had to be intelligent and studious and had to be chosen from the poorest families.[66]

A similar society was created in Nam Dinh province. As of 1926, this society, the Tu Ich (Personal Benefit) Society, functioned in Ninh Cuong village (Truc Ninh district). According to the Vietnamese governor of the province, the Tu Ich Society was the only one of its kind in the province's rural area.[67] Its objective was to buy and stock up on paddy in order to come to the assistance of members during periods of shortage. There were twenty members, and they had accumulated two hundred barrels of paddy in 1926.

Phu Tho province had a similar society with the same name: Tu Ich. There were branches of this organization in many of the villages, and they collected cash or grain donations from village members to be distributed as low interest loans during food shortages.[68] In the village of Sinh Lien in Ha Dong province, the villagers established a granary that was used to store paddy in case of such shortages. All landowners of the village were required to contribute approximately half a litre of paddy for every *sao* (360 square metres) of rice field they cultivated.[69]

From this brief sketch of the various mutual-aid societies in early twentieth-century Northern Vietnam, one thing is clear: there were active voluntary self-help societies throughout that region. The exact number and the length of time that these associations lasted are unknown. In a report to the resident superior of Tonkin in 1926, the resident of Hung Yen province listed eighteen mutual-aid societies functioning in this province.[70] Seven of the eighteen societies were funeral associations, like the Hop Thien Society, while eight were societies whose purpose was to help with both marriages and funerals. Of the other societies, one was devoted to "work of general interest," one was a credit society (Dong Loi), and one was formed to help members buy livestock and ploughing equipment. Membership ranged from ten to thirty-nine people. The report stated that, in addition to the listed societies, there were ceremony assistance societies in the villages of Khoa Chau district. Presumably, these societies were not considered to be formal or large enough to be included in the report. Two districts, Yen My and Van Lau, did not have any mutual-aid societies.

In addition to the associations that were formally recognized in written constitutions, there were many that escaped the government's scrutiny. The French administrators for Hai Duong and Cao Bang, for example, reported that, in their respective provinces, there were groups of people who helped each other during marriages and funerals.[71] These groups were small and functioned according to oral conventions. The military commander of Hai Ninh made reference to small rotating credit associations that were usually composed of ten to fifteen people.[72] It appears that even the colonial administration of that time did not keep track of all mutual-aid societies, particularly if they were small and informal.

Philanthropy and Charity in French Colonial Vietnam

In addition to mutual-aid associations, another manifestation of the ethic of benevolence during the French colonial period was intense activism in the areas of famine and poor relief, which seemed to have emerged in the early 1920s and, particularly, in the late 1930s. The boom in the publishing industry did much to help facilitate this increase in relief activities. One result of Governor Albert Sarraut's "association" policy, which tried to convince the politically moderate Vietnamese elites of the superior nature of French civilization, was the proliferation of *quoc ngu* (Romanized Vietnamese language) newspapers and journals. In the north, a number of important politically conservative, pro-French publications came into being. Some, such as *Nam Phong Tap Chi* (Southern Wind Review, 1917-34), *Trung Bac Tan Van* (Central and Northern News, 1915-45), and *Bao Dong Phap* (Indochina-France News, 1925-45), were subsidized by the colonial state, which saw these publications as vehicles for propagating "enlightened" French ideas and as a means of persuading the native elite to collaborate with the colonial state.

It was in the pages of these collaborative newspapers and journals that the supposed apolitical discussion of charity and poor relief played out. Elsewhere, I have argued that this discourse on charity could be seen as a stand-in for the discussion on national independence among the non-revolutionary intellectuals.[73] Here I would like to focus on the interesting discrepancy between the representation and the meaning of philanthropy in the writings of these intellectuals. While Vietnamese activists and writers portrayed philanthropy and charity as new, modern, and Western, they at the same time confirmed Confucian values and ideas.

One important writer for the daily *Trung Bac Tan Van*, who signed with only his initials (H.T.B.), wrote frequently on poverty and charity. H.T.B. was probably the penname/initials of Hoang Tang Bi, who had formerly been involved in the Reform Movement (an anti-colonial movement led by Vietnam's last Confucian scholar-rebels – Phan Boi Chau and Phan Chu Trinh). A prolific writer for *Trung Bac Tan Van* until his death in 1939, H.T.B. argued strenuously for the Vietnamese elite to build charitable institutions and societies and to organize poor relief activities. H.T.B. – as well as other writers for *Trung Bac Tan Van*, *Dong Phap*, and *Nam Phong* -- believed that these pursuits were essential to the survival of Vietnam as a country.

Vietnam's survival depended on organized charity because, according to H.T.B., caring for the poor was a modern (*duy tan*) way to behave. Becoming modern, he argued, was the only chance Vietnam had to gain independence and to survive on the competitive international stage:

> In these past few decades since our people have been excited by the movement of Westernization (*phong-trao Au-My*), many people have been

> awakened from their dream. They now know what it is to be a nation, and what it is to be a race. They now know what it is to be a country and the duty of a people toward the country. They know how to treat each other with some measure of sentiments, rather than being indifferent and treating each other like unrelated strangers as they had done three or four decades ago.[74]

H.T.B. continued to argue that the foundation of a modern society had to build upon national awareness and the acceptance of one's responsibility towards the nation and one's compatriots. He connected the strength of the country to the people's enthusiasm for charitable work, collective responsibility, and social cohesion. In H.T.B.'s belief that there is an intrinsic link between social responsibility and national strength, we hear the unmistakable echoes of Confucian moral and social ethics. These Confucian values, however, were decked out in a new discourse of nationhood and citizenship and were propelled by the urgency of social Darwinist imperatives. Early twentieth-century Vietnamese writers were deeply influenced by social Darwinism,[75] which depicted nations as being in life and death competitions with one another. Consequently, Vietnamese intellectuals believed that it was crucial for Vietnam to become strong in order to compete for a place in the world. Failing this task would mean the death of the nation.

Like mutual-aid societies, the message of H.T.B. and other writers regarding social responsibility was welcomed by the colonial administration. The discourse on charity resonated with Republican-minded colonial officials (such as Paul Beau) as it advocated similar ideas found in the solidarité movement. Vietnamese themselves seemed well aware of the important role that mutual-aid and private charity played in the mother country. Writers, for example, alluded to the many benevolent societies and institutions that existed in France.[76] Vietnamese writers were also conscious of the various trendy charitable activities that would attract the rising Western-educated class. In the late 1920s and early 1930s, for example, fund-raising activities included such Westernized activities as soccer matches, film and theatrical presentations, and variety shows and bazaars.[77] Furthermore, models for charitable institutions were sometimes inspired by Western examples. For instance, in 1926, H.T.B. called for the establishment of a poorhouse (*so te ban*).[78] Inspired by a recent article by Yves le Gadec published in a local French newspaper, H.T.B. suggested that the colonial government build poorhouses for beggars. Noting that the practice of sending beggars back to their native villages was not working, H.T.B. suggested that these paupers should be kept in poorhouses, where they would be cared for as well as taught new skills. Here, according to him, the "lazy" beggars could also be punished. While his opinion in this instance was in line with that of European advocates of poor relief (i.e., the poor must be reformed), his overall advocacy of modern poor relief was less on transforming the poor than it was on transforming the elite.

Indeed, even while charity advocates borrowed the language and activities of the new and Western model, at the core of their concerns one finds Confucian values and morality. According to H.T.B. and other writers for *Bao Dong Phap* and for *Trung Bac tan van*, it was not the behaviour of the poor that was in need of modification so much as it was that of the wealthy and educated elite. These writers were focussing their advocacy towards the elite – those with money and education – in order to remind them of their responsibility towards their unfortunate compatriots. The elite class was encouraged to be frugal and socially responsible.[79] Although the prescribed duty of the elite is a basic feature of Confucian teachings, it was presented in these articles as modern, as how one behaves in a *van minh* (civilized) society. In one article under the heading of "Opinions of the Readers" published in *Bao Dong Phap*, the "nouveaux riches" were criticized for squandering their money on gambling, alcohol, and drugs.[80] Others were criticized for being too tight-fisted, refusing to give any money to charity. Another article in the "Opinions of the Readers" section blamed high unemployment among the educated class on Vietnamese society's contemptuous attitude towards trade and commerce.[81] In another instance, an article written by a Mlle. Mo-Trung berated upper-class women for their selfishness.[82] According to Mo-Trung, in contrast to rural women and urban middle-class women, who spent all their time working and worrying about family finances, wealthy women had no worries and thus were in the best position to be socially useful. Mo-Trung lamented that these wealthy women, however, were poorly educated and were preoccupied only with face powder, mirrors, and combs.

The thrust of propaganda on charity and of the writings on poverty in general was to remind the rich and the middle class of their responsibility towards the poor. Accepting such responsibility was not only a moral but also a social duty. Thus, while writers were using the tools of the French colonizers – the state-subsidized newspapers and rhetoric about modernity, progress, and solidarité – their vision of a *van minh* society was not a Western one but, rather, was a métissage of Confucian and modern values. In their perspective, a *van minh* Vietnamese nation would be modern but would draw strength from the mythical Kinh ethnic unity, and it would exhibit a social harmony in which hierarchy and social responsibility functioned simultaneously.

In the area of charity and poor relief, Vietnamese non-revolutionary writers and activists were anxious to exhort the wider society to participate in what they saw as modern philanthropic activities. I suggest that these urbanites of the intellectual and wealthy classes wanted to adopt the modern trappings of poor relief institutions and charitable associations in order to show that they were capable of performing the role proper to a modern elite class. Their underlying concerns and their motivations, however, appeared to be similar to those found in Confucianism. Similarly, while some of the mutual-aid societies in Northern Vietnam appeared to be modern in their organizational structure, many of the values they reinforced were those associated with traditional rituals and hierarchical social relations. These non-revolutionary intellectuals and activists were in the "border zone" of cultural interaction. Clinging to Confucian morality, they were also attracted to, and were the beneficiaries of, Western education and culture. The three-way métissage of cultures in early twentieth-century Vietnam blurs the borders between the old and the new, between tradition and modernity, and between East and West.

Notes

1 Françoise Lionnet, "'Logiques métissage': Cultural Appropriation and Postcolonial Representations," in *Order and Partialities: Theory, Pedagogy and the "Postcolonial,"* edited by Kostas Myrsiades and Jerry McGuire, 111-36 (New York: State University of New York Press, 1995).

2 Ibid., 111.

3 Lilian Li, "Introduction: Food, Famine, and the Chinese State," *Journal of Asian Studies* 41, 4 (1982): 696.

4 Ibid., 696-97.

5 R. Bin Wong, "Food Riots in the Qing Dynasty," *Journal of Asian Studies* 12, 4 (1983): 768-69.

6 Ibid., 769. See also Pierre-Etienne Will, *Bureaucracy and Famine in Eighteenth Century China* (Stanford: Stanford University Press, 1990).

7 Nguyen Dang Giai, as quoted by Alexander Woodside, *Vietnam and the Chinese Model* (Cambridge: Harvard University Press, 1988), 78, 162.

8 Nguyen The Anh, *Kinh te va xa hoi Viet Nam duoi cac vua trieu Nguyen* [Economy and society in Vietnam during the Nguyen dynasty] (Saigon: Lua-Thieng, 1970 [2nd printing]), 139.

9 *Khâm định Đại Nam hội điển sự lệ* [Official compendium of institution and usages of imperial Vietnam] vol. 5, sec. 63 (Hue: Thuan Hoa, 1993), 373-416.

10 Ibid., 374.

11 Resident of Cao Bang to the Resident Superior of Tonkin, no. 176R, 1 August 1906, "A.S. de la création d'un Caisse de Prévoyance dans le 2e Territoire Militaire," Fonds de la Résidence Supérieure du Tonkin [hereafter RST] 75.780, Commission chargés d'etudier les mesures préventives contre les disettes après d'insuffisants du riz au Tonkin, Vietnam's National Archives, no. 1, Hanoi.

12 Report No. 878 of Thanh Oai district, 19 May 1906, Fonds de la province de Ha Dong 3484, "Disettes: Mesures préventives à prendre en cas des nouvelles disettes, 1906."

13 The Governor of Nam Dinh to the Resident of Nam Dinh, no. 3743, 22 October 1926, ND 1203.

14 Paul Beau to the Residents Superior of Indochina, no. 512, 29 May 1906, RST 75.780.

15 Resident of Cao Bang to the Resident Superior of Tonkin, no. 176R, 1 August 1906, "A.S. de la création d'un Caisse de Prévoyance dans le 2e Territoire Militaire," RST 75.780.

16 Vu Duy Men and Bui Xuan Dinh, "Huong uoc: Khoan uoc trong lang xa" [Huong uoc: Khoan uoc in the villages], *Nghien cuu lich su* 4 (1982): 45.

17 Kandice Hauf, "The Community Covenant in Sixteenth-Century Ji'an Prefecture, Jiangxi," *Late Imperial China* 17, 2 (1996): 1.

18 Ibid., 3.
19 Monika Ubelhor, "The Community Compact (*Hsiang-yueh*) of the Sung and Its Educational Significance," in *Neo-Confucian Education: The Formative Stage*, edited by William Theodore de Bary and John Chaffee (Berkeley: University of California Press, 1989), 376-77.
20 Ibid., 378.
21 Hauf, "The Community Covenant," 6.
22 Ibid.
23 Ibid., Table 1.
24 Vu Duy Men, "Nguon goc va dieu kien xuat hien huong uoc trong lang xa o vung Dong Bang-Trung Du Bac Bo" [The origin and condition for the appearance of huong uoc in villages of the Northern Delta and Midland regions], *Nghien cuu lich su* 1, 1 and 2 (1999): 49-50.
25 Ibid.
26 Bui Xuan Dinh, *Le Lang Phep Nuoc* [Village customs and state law] (Hanoi: Phap Ly, 1985), 17.
27 Ibid., 25-26.
28 Ibid., chap. 2.
29 Ibid., 45.
30 Vu Duy Men, "Vai net ve qua trinh dieu chinh va bo sung huong uoc Quynh Doi" [Modifications and popularization of Quynh Doi's huong uoc], *Nghien cuu lich su* 6 (Nov./Dec. 1985), 49.
31 Ibid.
32 Bui Xuan Dinh, *Le Lang Phep Nuoc*, 57.
33 Martin Grossheim, "Village Laws (*huong uoc*) as Source for Vietnamese Studies," in *Vietnam: Sources and Approaches* (Proceedings of the 2nd EuroViet Conference), edited by Philippe le Failler and Jean Marie Mancini (Aix-en-Provence: Publications de l'Université de Provence, 1996), 108.
34 Ibid., 109.
35 Ibid.
36 Ibid., 110.
37 Huong Uoc cua lang La Doi, Tong La Doi, Phu Nam Sach, Tinh Hai Duong [The community convention of La Doi Village, in La Doi Hamlet, Nam Sach Prefecture, Hai Duong Province] (Hanoi: Thong Tin Khoa Hoc Xa Hoi [Institute of Social Sciences Information] HU #1443, 1936).
38 Alan Baker, *Fraternity among the French Peasantry: Sociability and Voluntary Associations in the Loire Valley, 1815-1914* (Cambridge: Cambridge University Press, 1999), 49.
39 Ibid., 143.
40 Ibid.
41 Ronaldo Munck, "Mutual Benefit Societies in Argentina: Workers, Nationality, Social Security, and Trade Unionism," *Journal of Latin American Studies* 30 (1998): 573-90.
42 Ibid., 144.
43 Lori Weintrob, "From 'Petite Patrie' to National 'Solidarité: Regionalism and Inter-Class Alliances in Mutual Aid Societies," in *Proceedings of the Western Society for French History* (1999), edited by Barry Rothaus (Greeley: University Press of Colorado, 2001), 27.
44 Alexander Woodside, "The Development of Social Organizations in Vietnamese Cities in the Late Colonial Period," *Pacific Affairs* 44 (1971): 39-64.
45 Ibid., 49.
46 Ibid., 54.
47 Nguyen Dong Chi, "Vai net ve bien phap cuu te tuong tro trong lang xa Viet Nam" [Some aspects of mutual-aid relief in Vietnamese villages before the revolution], in *Nong thon Viet Nam trong lich su* [Vietnamese countryside in history], vol. 2, edited by Vien Lich Su [Institute of History] (Hanoi: Khoa Hoc Xa Hoi, 1978), 223-25.
48 Phan Ke Binh, *Viet Nam phong tuc* [Vietnamese customs], reprint (Ho Chi Minh City: Tong Hop Dong Thap, 1990), 202.
49 Ibid., 225.
50 Le Gallen, Resident Superior of Tonkin, no. 4580, 22 August 1915, RST 20.550 A/S de l'Assistance par le travail en faveur des inondés.

51 Orville Menard, "Leon Bourgeois, Antoine de Saint-Exupery and Solidarité," *International Social Sciences Review* 68, 1 (1993): 4.
52 Robert Tombs, *France, 1814-1914* (New York: Longman, 1996), 180.
53 Ibid.
54 Ibid., 179.
55 Mayor of Hai Phong, no. 336Z, 17 July 1906, RST 75.780. 3-4.
56 *Felix Hausser to the Governor General of Indochina*, Fonds de la province de Ha Dong, 31 January 1907, 3490 A/S de la Création des sociétés indigenes de prévoyance de secours et de prêts mutuels agricoles dans les provinces du Tonkin, 1907-11.
57 Ibid.
58 Ibid.
59 Resident of Ha Nam to the Resident Superior of Tonkin, no. 150, c. 28 July 1906, RST 75.780, 3.
60 Tétart, Resident of Ha Giang to the Resident Superior of Tonkin, no. 219, 17 July 1906, "A/S des measures à prendre en cas de disette," RST 75.780.
61 Resident of Ninh Binh to the Resident Superior of Tonkin, 16 August 1906, A/S des measures prendre contre disette, RST 75.780.
62 Le Bo-Chanh de Hai Ninh, "Hoi Hop Thien Thanh Pho Moncay, Dieu Le" [The Philanthropic Association of Moncay City: Regulations] 28 December 1938, RST 79.879, A/S des subventions sur le budget local à des oeuvres deverses on à des particuliers, 1925-27.
63 Le Dinh Diem, President of Hoi Hieu to the Resident of Bac Ninh, 24 February 1937, RST 79.879; Le Ba Khai, People's Representative, to the Resident of Quang Yen, 12 October 1921, RST 79.879; Statutes de la sociétéde bienfaisance dite Tap-Phuc-Hoi, Hongay, 20 July 1939, RST 79.879; Statutes [of Lien-Son Quang Thien Hoi], Vinh Yen, 1939, RST 79.879; Governor of Nam Dinh to the Resident of Nam Dinh, no. 3743, Objet: Viec cac hoi cua nguoi ban xu [Associations of the indigenous people], 22 October 1926, Fonds de la Résident du Nam Dinh (ND) 1203.
64 Status de l'association "Chi Thien," Bac Kan, 17 July 1939, RST 79.879.
65 Réglement de la Société de secours mutuels "Quang-Hue," Cao Bang, 28 March 1908, RST 75.788, Sociétés de secours mutuels à Cao Bang, 1908.
66 Ibid.
67 The Governor of Nam Dinh to the Resident of Nam Dinh, no. 3743, 22 October 1926, ND 1203.
68 The Resident of Phu Tho to the Resident Superior of Tonkin, no. 489, 17 July 1906, RST 75.780, 7.
69 Report No. 878 of Thanh Oai District, 19 May 1906, Fonds de la Province de Province de Ha Dong (HD) 3484, Dissettes: Mesures preventives à prendre en cas des nouvelles disettes, 1906.
70 Servoise, Resident of Hung Yen, to the Resident Superior of Tonkin, no. 3176, 29 October 1926, a/s organisations mutualistes indigenes, RST 74.542, Renseignements necessaries pour le rapport au Ve congrès de la mutualité colonale et des pays protetorat à Paris, 1926.
71 Military Commander of Cao Bang to the Resident Superior of Tonkin, 9 September 1926; Resident of Hai Duong to the Resident Superior of Tonkin (n.d.), RST 74.542.
72 Military Commander of Hai Ninh to the Resident Superior of Tonkin, 28 September 1926, RST 74.542.
73 Van Nguyen-Marshall, "Issues of Poverty and Poor Relief in Colonial Northern Vietnam" (PhD diss., University of British Columbia, 2002), chap. 5.
74 H.T.B., "Cai long tuong ai tuong tro nguoi trong nuoc voi nhau" [The feeling of mutual love and mutual help among people of a country], *Trung Bac Tan Van*, 5 August 1925, 1.
75 Hue-Tam Ho Tai, *Radicalism and the Origins of the Vietnamese Revolution* (Cambridge: Harvard University Press, 1992), 20-22.
76 H.T.B., "Cac cong-cuoc tu-thien o nuoc Phap" [Bevevolent work in France], *Trung Bac Tan Van*, 17 January 1924, 1.
77 See issues of *Phu Nu Thoi Dam* [Women's Herald] (Hanoi: 1930-32); *Bao Dong Phap* (Hanoi: 1928-30).
78 H.T.B., "O xu Bac-ky nen lap nhung so te-ban" [Need to set up poorhouses in the Northern region], *Trung Bac Tan Van*, 25 and 26 1 January 1926.

79 Calls for frugality were voiced in the following articles: Tung Phong, "Tinh hinh kinh-te nam 1931" [The economic situation in 1931], *Bao Dong Phap*, 3 January 1932, 1; Luong Nhat Tuan, "Quoc dan ta voi quan-niem kinh-te" [Our people and views of the economy], *Bao Dong Phap*, 30 January 1932, 2.

80 T., "Mot hang giau o nuoc ta" [A category of wealthy people in our country], *Bao Dong Phap*, 30 and 31 May 1931, 1.

81 Ng, V. Thuoc, "Nguyen nhan cai nan tri-thuc that nghiep" [The cause for unemployment problem among intellectuals], *Bao Dong Phap*, 28 May 1932, 1.

82 Mlle. Mo-Trung, "Tinh hinh sinh hoat cua chi em nuoc ta ngay nay" [The living situation of our sisters today], *Bao Dong Phap*, 6 January 1932, 1.

10
A Zone of Nebulous Menace: The Guangxi/Indochina Border in the Republican Period

Diana Lary

The Zhennanguan, The Pass that Guards the South, was from ancient times bridged by a modest gate, the only formal marker of the border between China and Vietnam, between Guangxi and Tongkin. It was the symbolic southern end of China, as Shanhaiguan was of the northern end.

A border between two states is often a nebulous and vague construct. A border need not be demarcated, either by a line on an agreed map or by a physical frontier. So long as a border runs through impassable terrain, or attracts little interest from the polities on either side, it can remain imprecise; it is not a fixed frontier but a zone in which one polity ceases and another begins. This type of border is porous and is often ignored by the people who live on either side of it, in the border zone. It does not transmute into a frontier until a line is drawn on a map and that line is transformed into a physical reality, demarcated by barriers and defended on both sides.

In the modern world, most borders between states have been demarcated; a line marks the place where one state ends and another begins. But until quite recent times most borders were not marked. Even when the border was a natural feature such as a mountain range or a sea, there was no actual line. In China, the most remarkable formal barrier ever built, the Great Wall, was not a frontier between states but a defensive system that marked the end of the agricultural world and the beginning of the grasslands.

The premodern borders of China were often vague, border regions rather than formal frontiers. There was a de facto recognition of the end of the known world and the beginning of the great beyond. Chinese living near such a border had little sense that a border existed; they saw themselves not as living on the Chinese side of a state border, with another state on the other side, but as inhabiting the outermost element of a self-contained world. The reality of non-Han peoples who were already integrated into social and economic ties beyond the Chinese world was ignored, even though these

Modern China

ties continued long after the claims of Chinese sovereignty were established. The Chinese world stopped well before the borderlands. The Chinese inhabitants of Guangxi turned their backs on the border, and on their "neighbours," and looked towards the distant centre. The indigenous inhabitants, meanwhile, lived in a world in which neither the Chinese nor the rulers of the state that is now Vietnam mattered very much.

The Precolonial Guangxi Border

Guangxi was China's southernmost province for much of China's history as a state, until the creation of the province of Hainan in the mid-1980s. Guangxi was the southern outpost of the Chinese world. It looked north to the distant capital and turned its back on the south. Beyond Guangxi lay the Extreme South (*Yuenan*, not coincidentally the Chinese name for Vietnam), a land inhabited by wild people (*man*), as the indigenous inhabitants were known until the modern age, a hot, sticky, dangerous place that Han Chinese should avoid at all costs.[1] The Far South actually began well before the limits of Chinese rule were reached, in the zones ruled for the Chinese government by local officials (*tusi*). Imperial Chinese administrations were not keen on hands-on administration of the southern border zone; sophisticated, even effete Chinese mandarins could not stomach life in turbulent, tropical areas occupied by fierce people and even fiercer insects and animals. In the Ming and Qing, the imperial government used the *tusi* system to administer the northern and western parts of Guangxi.[2] There was no formal line to mark the end of Chinese rule and the beginning of a non-Chinese administration, and, until the late nineteenth century, there was not even an agreement between the two polities as to where a frontier might lie.

The lack of a formal line did not inhibit successive Chinese governments from asserting that there had once been one – an assertion that relied on the records of the Han dynasty and their claim that the "Wave-Quelling" General Ma Yuan had demarcated a border between the Han and the barbarian regions and had established the limit of the Han Empire by erecting a bronze pillar. The pillar, if it ever existed, has long since disappeared.[3]

Instead of a formal borderline there was an extensive and unruly border zone, in which the larger political affiliation of the peoples living there was notional if not irrelevant. The line that appears today on Chinese and Vietnamese maps (including, anachronistically, maps for ancient periods) was not there until the late nineteenth century. The extrapolation of a fixed border line into the past has been critical for both the present-day states; both have interpreted their histories as though there had always been a line, and the line is essential for compiling indignant lists of invasions, incursions, and interferences. In both the modern states, the recitation of past aggression is part of the national mythology. And, in the case of Vietnam, it is a particularly compelling one since the history of Vietnam's resistance to Chinese invasion over two millennia gives the modern defiance of France and of the United States a long and illustrious historical pedigree. The Guangxi take was quite different – a reminder that the Vietnamese had succumbed to the French and let them come right up to the Guangxi border.[4]

The insistence on the line is ironic since, in fact, the intercourse (invasions, incursions, trade) across the land border between China and Vietnam, recorded for over two thousand years, was only occasional and irregular. The real intercourse between China and its southern neighbours took place via maritime routes, not via a land border.

The Sino-Indochina Border: Early Days

The concept of a remote, almost impenetrable, southern border zone best governed indirectly lasted well, surviving until almost the end of the Qing dynasty. Then the menacing French presence in Indochina forced Beijing to take notice of China's far south, especially after the French invasion of Guangxi in 1885.

In the land battles along the China/Indochina border the French were much less successful than they had been in their naval attacks on Fuzhou and Taiwan. On land, they were driven back by military irregulars and bandits, some of them Taiping remnants still on the run two decades after the end of the Taiping Rebellion, holed up in the untracked hills of the border zone. The most famous of the irregular military groups was the Black Flags, led by the intrepid Liu Yongfu. Liu was a martial arts specialist who had started his military activities in the Nanlu region (then in Guangdong) in the mid-1860s, during the vacuum caused by the Taipings, and he had been harassing French exploration groups for over a decade before actual war broke out.[5]

For the most part, Liu and his men acted independently of the Chinese central government. All the fulminations and negotiations going on in Beijing between Chinese and French authorities meant little to him. He saw the need for resistance and leapt into the breach, continuing the local tradition of turning to violence to deal with situations rather than waiting for political solutions.

Though the French were thrown back from southern China, they were not dislodged from Indochina, and it gradually became clear, over the decade after the end of the war, that they were there to stay and that a frontier had to be formally demarcated. This was done in 1894, with the implementation of the Sino-French Guangxi/Vietnam Border Treaty (*Zhongfa guiyue jieyu)* negotiated between Paris and Beijing. The borderline was about 1,300 li long, and eventually over one hundred small forts and watchtowers were built along its length.[6]

The formal establishment of the border did not improve the Sino-Indochinese relationship, whatever its proponents on the French side had expected, though the settlement did achieve one purpose, that of maintaining an uneasy peace. There was no warfare across the border – though fighting threatened several times in 1900 with the overflow of the Boxer troubles in the north and again in 1911 with the XinHai Revolution – but there was no real security. The border was still only a line through a border zone, which was insecure both for the Chinese and for the French because the endemic and rampant banditry in the zone took no account of an international frontier.

The establishment of the physical border did not lead to any serious growth in trade or other traffic. Preparations were made for the trade to come. An Imperial Maritime Customs post was set up in Longzhou, the nearest town to the border on the Chinese side, to manage trade, but there was very little trade to manage and no new trade developed. There were few products to trade. Western Guangxi was poor, and its people could not afford imported products. Nor did the region have many products that the much wealthier

Indochina might want. The slimness of the prospects for trade was pointed up by the absence in the city of both foreign traders and foreign consulates. The French opened a consulate in 1889, but no other countries followed suit. The Belgians, Austrians, and Italians each kept a notional presence in Longzhou for brief periods, but the Longzhou consul for each country was resident in Hong Kong.[7]

One of the reasons for this lack of foreign interest in trade was that the approaches to the border zone were almost impenetrable on the Chinese side. Longzhou could be reached from Nanning only in small vessels, which had to make their way upstream through the bandit-ridden upper reaches of the Left River. The level of water in the river fluctuated, sometimes being so low that even small boats could not get up the river. After Longzhou, the trip to the actual border was about 140 li, along narrow tracks, through a region of wild hills,[8] the *Shiwan dashan* (Hundred Thousand Hills), which were full of deserters, bandits, and smugglers who lived in places so hard to find and control that pre-Communist governments did not bother with them at all. Even the Communist armies were unable to subdue them until 1953.[9]

In the late nineteenth century, French visions of France's role in Asia were sometimes grandiose. Georges Famin, an energetic young French official writing in the early 1890s, saw France as "the dominant power on all questions which concern the southeastern part of Asia." He believed that France must "take advantage of the serious events which will be produced in the future in the state of decomposition of the old Asiatic world."[10] But these visions did not transfer well on the ground, where French ambitions had to be localized. French interest in the border provinces of China had to be limited and focused, and the focus was on the province of Yunnan, which was directly north of Hanoi and accessible only by land. The province was even more remote from central Chinese control, and considerably richer than Guangxi. The prospects for trade and investment in Yunnan looked much better than did those in Guangxi. The French began building the Hanoi/Kunming Railway in 1903 and completed it in 1910.

In contrast to their efforts in Yunnan, the French made only desultory attempts to establish a real presence in the province of Guangxi. There were few serious official efforts to develop commerce or communication between Indochina and Guangxi. This lack of activity was reflected in the reports of French officials stationed on the border, whose hopes for trade were negligible. In 1901, Joseph Dautremer, the consul in Longzhou, stated: "Can the French hope to find there [in Guangxi] an outlet for their commerce? We do not hesitate to reply: no."[11] The consul's gloom must have been reinforced every day as he woke in the rather makeshift French consulate – a building that had originally been intended for quite a different purpose.

Dautremer may have been speaking out of his own chronic dissatisfaction, bordering on despair, at being condemned to bring a member of the tiny European community in Longzhou, which must have been one of the most dismal outposts of empire anywhere in the world. He described it in these terms: "Long-tcheou [Longzhou] is an absolutely dead town, where one finds nothing. Everything has to be brought in from Hanoi ... life unfolds there in an excessively monotonous manner, and is terribly depressing. Every day, the five Europeans (the French consul, a missionary and three Imperial Maritime Customs representatives) play tennis at five o'clock, and that is all."[12]

Dautremer's translator at the consulate, Jean Beauvais, took a different view of his "exile" in Longzhou. He developed a great fascination for the Longzhou region, and he used his time there to produce an extraordinary work of scholarship, *Documents geographiques, historiques et linguistiques sur la ville at la region de Long-tcheou.*[13] The basis of this work was Dautremer's translation of Longzhou's 1801 gazetteer, annotated with scholarly notes and commentaries.

Beauvais and Dautremer were the mirror images of French (and, for that matter, other European) consular officials, one type sunk in misery, their lives dominated by a sense of personal failure often accentuated by alcohol, the other type resourceful, engaged, and deeply scholarly, grateful for the time that the lack of official duties gave them to conduct their academic work. Another romantic Frenchman who spent some time at the Longzhou consulate was Auguste Francois; he was an amateur filmmaker and used his copious free time in Longzhou and in Kunming to film the life he saw around him: "Auguste Francois' life is like an adventure novel. Lovable hero, funny, cultivated, he applies for a position in Asia after he has read Salumbo by Flaubert ... and he had the genius idea to bring in his luggage a little camera lent by the Lumiere brothers and that he used heavily ... leaving a complex and lively testimony of China at the beginning of the century."[14]

The situation of French civilians was bad enough, but the Roman Catholic missionaries had an even more challenging time in western Guangxi than did their secular compatriots. For one thing, their postings were for life; they knew that Guangxi would be where they would die. For another, though they saw themselves as serving the Lord, at the official Chinese level they were regarded as emissaries of the French government and were treated with a considerable degree of suspicion. At the popular level, they were, like missionaries of other denominations in the province, almost entirely without success. The Guangxi people were extremely resistant to conversion; the province held one of the lowest places on the Missions Etrangeres de Paris league table of conversions, lower than any other part of China except Tibet.[15]

The missionaries might well have abandoned their efforts at conversion in Guangxi had it not been for a great pressure put on them by the French church hierarchy, who insisted that they commemorate the memories of the French priest Father Auguste Chapdelaine and a group of his converts, who were martyred in the northwest of the province in 1856. These deaths gave the French missionaries a sacred cause: they had to serve in Guangxi to keep the mission there going so that the case for the canonization of the Chapdelaine and the other martyrs, which had started winding slowly through the labyrinths of the church bureaucracy in Rome soon after their deaths, could be kept alive. This even though the missionaries on the ground knew well that there was little chance that there would be major conversions in the province.[16]

The Guangxi/Indochina border was marked as much by what did not happen as by what did. The early interest (in the 1890s) on the French side in getting a railway line from Hanoi through to Nanning petered out, though only after the French had built their section of the line. There were major problems with the financing of the Guangxi section, and it was not built. The railway line in Tonking went up to the border and stopped. French authorities recognized how unlikely it was that the line would be built: the building under construction as the future railway station in Longzhou was converted into the French consulate.[17]

The notional railway was a symbol of the lack of activity on the border. No further work was done on the line on the Chinese side until the Anti-Japanese War in the late 1930s. Work started early in the war but, given the Vichy government's support of Japan, was soon aborted. In the end, what work was done on the railway was a disaster for China because the construction of the road bed facilitated the movement of Japanese troops into the province. The railway inside Guangxi was not finally finished until the 1950s.

The Sino-Indochinese Border: The Early Republic

The Sino-Indochinese border was a desolate place during the late Qing, and it became even more so in the early Republic. Even the pretence of a formal cross-border connection between Guangxi and Indochina disappeared. Guangxi came under the control of the local military and turned its back on the border and on Indochina, just as the Indochinese authorities lost their remaining patience with what they saw as a turbulent and ungrateful place, essentially giving up on it. Only the long suffering missionaries remained.[18] This caused little if any anguish in Guangxi; in fact, the French withdrawal may not even have been noticed. It was certainly never referred to by the provincial warlords who, when they were not fighting amongst themselves, focused their attention on Guangzhou or even on northern parts of China but almost never on the west of the province.

The major warlord in postrevolutionary Guangxi was a man from Wuming in the west of the province, near Nanning. Lu Rongting started life as a penniless, illiterate street child; after an early career as a bandit and petty thief, he moved into the Qing provincial army and, just before the 1911 Revolution, became the leading military figure in Guangxi. He was a tough, driving figure, unpretentious, warlike, and ambitious. Lu showed little interest in Indochina or in the French. For Lu, and for other warlords who ruled Guangdong and Guangxi during the Republic, the French could be ignored as they neither brought any benefit nor posed any threat.

This was not the case with the British. The southern warlords liked to maintain cordial relations with the British in Hong Kong, to provide themselves with access to arms, with facilities for conducting shady financial deals – and with a bolt hole in case they should ever lose the warlord wars and need to seek sanctuary in Hong Kong. Lu needed British approval quite badly, since, from 1917 to 1921, he managed to take over large parts of Guangdong.

Given the powerful position of Hong Kong in southern China, there was little if any reason for local warlords to look for other foreign connections. This periodically frustrated the French, whose efforts to build up a base on the China coast at Guangzhouwan, from which to challenge Britain in Hong Kong, never got off the ground. During the early Republic, the French in Indochina increasingly focused their attention on Yunnan.

The Border in the Middle Republic

Lu's successors, the new Guangxi Clique (Li Zongren, Bai Chongxi, and Huang Shaoxiong), which ran Guangxi from 1925 to 1949, showed as little interest in promoting any relationship with the French in Indochina as did Lu. They focused their attention on Guangdong and on central and northern China, where they had considerable ambitions.

During the first decades of the Republic, there was no pressure on Guangxi from the Chinese state to develop cross-frontier connections with Indochina. This was because, until 1936, the province was essentially independent of the centre. Neither the early Republican government in Beijing nor the Guomindang government in Nanjing had much control over Guangxi. The French representatives in China had no interest in dealing with a succession of what they regarded as provincial satraps in Guangxi, maintaining their significant presence in China far away, in Beijing. The French religious presence was centred in the huge Jesuit compounds in Xujiahui (Siccawei) in Shanghai, with important outposts in Beijing. The Missions Etrangeres de Paris maintained a string of missions in Guangxi, but these were only a small part of the French Catholic efforts in China, and the least successful.

The substantial overseas Chinese community in Indochina had almost nothing to do with Guangxi. Its members were drawn overwhelmingly from

Guangdong, and they fit neatly into an overseas Chinese world that had nothing to do with Guangxi or the land border.[19] They travelled to and from Hanoi by boat from Hong Kong or Beihai and would never have dreamt of using the overland route through Guangxi.

During the 1920s and 1930s, there was virtually no political relationship between Guangxi and Indochina. The border existed as the back door to the province, the route by which warlords fled when they had been defeated and went into exile in Hong Kong. When Lu Rongting lost out in 1924, he fled from Guangxi via Indochina. Later, the route was used in the other direction. In 1930, Bai Chongxi and his close comrades, who had been thrown out of the province the year before, returned to the province through the back door and were soon able to oust the group of Communists that had ousted them. This group (which included the young Deng Xiaoping) had set up a soviet in the Right River Valley of Guangxi, which leads through to Yunnan. The small band of Communists, who had given themselves the name of Eighth Red Army, had great difficulty in fleeing from Guangxi; they had to trek through the mountains in the north and east of the province, en route to the Central Soviet in Jiangxi, a nightmare journey sometimes referred to as the Little Long March. They took with them some of the fierce local fighters, including a man who would later play a central role in Guangxi – Wei Guoqing.

The fierceness of the local fighters in the west of the province was another reason that the Guangxi Clique leaders showed little interest in the frontier with Indochina; for them, the west of the province (i.e., the border zone) hardly counted as part of the province. Guangxi has never been either ethnically or linguistically homogenous. In the north and east, most of the population is Han (Mandarin-speaking in the north, Cantonese-speaking in the south). The west of the province is largely inhabited by people first known as *man* (southern barbarians), then, in the more polite Republic, as *turen* (local people), and now, as the Zhuang. Though the Guangxi Clique kept the provincial capital in Nanning for most of their rule (as opposed to Guilin, the previous location of the provincial capital), they were not interested in areas further west and northwest of Nanning or in the people who lived there. They regarded them as difficult and rebellious (a mirror image of how they themselves were viewed by national leaders in Nanjing).

The Guangxi leaders did have one interest in the west of the province – the Right River Valley, the route by which opium from Yunnan reached Nanning for transhipment to Guangzhou and Hong Kong. The tax on this opium was a vital source of revenue for a poor province, accounting for up to 50 percent of government revenues. By contrast, the Left River, which led through to Indochina, produced almost no revenue.

Most of the Clique leaders were from the Guilin region. When they looked out of the province they looked to the north, the locus of their political ambitions, or to the east, to Guangzhou and Hong Kong, where they found their alliances and their commercial and financial connections. They saw themselves as part of the modernizing movement that was going to transform China into a strong nation. Their anti-imperialist sentiments, which grew significantly in the 1930s, were aimed at the remote Japanese, not at the French just across the border to the west. This was a reflection of their own sense of destiny, their belief that they had a role to play in China – a role that played itself out in the Resistance War. Other Chinese might think of Guangxi as a remote place at the outer edges of civilization, but this was not a view that would have occurred to the Guangxi leaders; they saw their province as an integral part of China, a region that has special characteristics to offer to the nation.

Scholarly Explorations in the Border Region

The Guangxi Clique leaders were modern minded. They commissioned scholars to investigate every aspect of the province and to draw up plans for a new society. The French authorities meanwhile set up a major research institution in Hanoi. This was one of the finest academic institutions created by the French empire. Scholars worked there in lavish and refined conditions, focusing not on immediate issues of practical use to the colonial administration but, rather, on the pursuit of knowledge, no matter how esoteric. Their writings were published in a beautifully produced journal, the *Bulletin de l'école française d'extreme orient,* which continued publication through all the vicissitudes of warfare and political upheaval, such as the arrival of the Japanese in Indochina.

The Guangxi intellectuals were not really interested in the west of the province, but several of the French scholars at the école française were. They worked on a range of subjects, from the anthropology of the region to its languages and religious customs, and produced one of the largest single bodies of work on Guangxi. They were helped in their work by some of the Catholic missionaries stationed in the border regions, who developed strong local knowledge in the areas of language, ethnology, local history, flora and fauna, and archaeology. They dealt with almost any conceivable topic, except one, which had become the preserve of another nationality. German scholars took it upon themselves to investigate the mysteries of the great bronze drums found in the border region and further south. They wrote many highly academic studies of the drums and helped to bring together a huge collection of them, which they transported to Berlin.[20] This collection of drums disappeared from Berlin at the end of the War; they may have been destroyed in the bombing of Berlin, or they may have been moved further east, but either way they have never been seen again.

What was striking about the research conducted on the Guangxi/Indochinese border region during the late Qing and the early Republic was how restricted it was along national lines. There seems to have been no common ground between French and Chinese scholars, no collaboration or even awareness of each other's work. The French scholars were highly academic, disinclined to conduct fieldwork across the border from Indochina or to work on contemporary subjects. Chinese scholars, such as the economist Qian Jiaju and the geographer Ding Wenjiang, who worked in Guangxi, concentrated on modern subjects. The only French scholar who worked seriously with a Chinese scholar was Pierre Teilhard de Chardin, the great Jesuit paeleontographer who collaborated with the young Chinese scholar Pei Wenzhong – a collaboration that had started with work on Peking Man. They looked at potential sites for early humans in Guangxi but without any significant results.

There was a major language barrier between most Chinese intellectuals and the French: very few Chinese scholars knew French because few Chinese intellectuals who had studied abroad had been educated in France. After a group of worker/students, many of them Communists, went to France in the early 1920s, few other Chinese students followed. One of the few Chinese scholars who did study in France was the linguist Wang Li, whose *doctorat d'etat* for l'universite de Paris was written on the dialect of his hometown in southern Guangxi.

This lack of common ground between French scholars in Indochina and Chinese scholars is reflected in the way in which the histories of the border region diverged. There was no common history, each side claiming a vision of history that excluded or denigrated the other. The French view of Vietnamese history (until the colonial period) fitted the native Vietnamese view. The Chinese and Vietnamese views diverged so strongly (and still do) that each side claims the same hero as their own. For example, the Song rebel Nong Zhigao is either a Vietnamese or Chinese hero but never simply a local man living in a border region between states.

The Sino-Vichy Border

The lack of political and military interest in the border region and in the lands across the notional border, which characterized the early and middle Republic, was replaced by an acute awareness of a border once the Resistance War began in 1937, after the Japanese invasion. The eight years of war was a time of confusion across the frontier, which suddenly became real and, from time to time, very important.

One reason for the increase in importance of the frontier had to do with the change of the status of Guangxi within China; after 1937, the province was no longer autonomous but was brought back into the Nanjing fold. The responsibility for China's relations with Indochina was now firmly in Nanjing (later in Wuhan, when it was capital, and then in Chongqing). Guangxi was not only part of China again, but it was a key part, sending hundreds of thousands of troops north to fight the Japanese and winning great glory for the province in the Battle of Taierzhuang (April 1938).

The political change in China came just before a major change in the position of the French administration in Hanoi and of French nationals in China. This new position was now highly equivocal, not as a consequence of local events but, rather, as a consequence of the fate of the French state in Europe. After the Nazi invasion of northern France, France's colonial territories came under the administration of the collaborationist regime in southern France, headquartered at Vichy.

French Dilemmas: Collaboration, Resistance, Self-Preservation

French diplomats, businessmen, and missionaries living in China and in Indochina as the Resistance War ground on found themselves facing the same dilemma that Chinese and their compatriots in France were facing: should they resist or collaborate? The official representatives of France – diplomats, consuls, and soldiers – were presented with an especially stark dilemma. After the fall of France, they had to choose between continuing in their current positions, which meant associating with the collaborationist Vichy regime, or leaving their positions and going out into the void – morally correct but perhaps destitute.

From the beginning of 1942 on, the French were isolated in Occupied China. Most other foreigners living in China – British, American, Canadian, Australian – were rounded up by the Japanese and moved into internment camps. Even the Quebec Jesuit missionaries, who were in China under the aegis of the French, were put under house arrest. The only "free" foreigners in China in significant numbers were Germans, not the best friends of the French only two decades after the Great War.

The dilemma of allegiance affected over two thousand French citizens living in Japanese-occupied China, the majority of them missionaries. These people staffed France's interests in China, from the political and commercial interests in the French concessions in Shanghai, Tianjin, and Hankou to the missionary establishments throughout the country to the business interests throughout Occupied China.[21]

Many of the people who were faced with the awful decisions about whether to side with Vichy or Free France knew each other well: they were products of the same elite French colleges, had served as colleagues, and were even related to each other. These connections made the question of collaboration or resistance very personal, and often deeply painful. The anguish of decision making is brought out in the memoirs of Jacques Guillermaz, *Une vie pour la Chine*.[22] Guillermaz was the French military attaché in China at the beginning of the war and was stationed in Beijing. He was profoundly sympathetic to the Chinese cause, and this sympathy eventually led him to break with the Vichy French in China and in Indochina, even though this rupture cost him his connection to his wife and children, who stayed in Hanoi. Guillermaz, like other French people who threw in their lot with the Free French, faced a future of complete insecurity: they had to abandon their careers, their incomes, their pensions, and, often, as in Guillermaz' case, their families.

In the short run, Guillermaz was isolated. Most of the French officials in China, like the administrators in Indochina, took a sanguine, not to say self-serving, view of their situation. They had no confidence in Chiang Kai-shek and Free China, no sense that the war might end with a Chinese victory. They had even less confidence in de Gaulle and Free France. They threw their support behind Vichy, making Indochina an ally of the Japanese. Japanese troops were stationed in Indochina, virtually independent of the French authorities, as a result of the agreement signed between Tokyo and Vichy in September 1940. The French ambassador in China, Henri Cosme, was strongly pro-Japanese and a partisan of the Wang Jingwei regime. He saw no purpose in staying in touch with the Chinese regime in Chongqing. When he started the move to recognize Wang's regime, Chongqing responded to Vichy's new policy by recognizing the Free French, at first by accepting the establishment of a Free French mission in Chongqing and then, in 1943, by breaking relations with Vichy altogether.[23] This move meant almost nothing in a world at war, but in retrospect it was quite prescient – a sign of the coming downfall of Vichy.

The Consequences of Vichy for Guangxi

France, Vichy or Free, was not a major concern of the wartime Chinese government in Chongqing. Other countries were far more important – China's allies and her enemies. But the ups and downs of the Sino-French relationship did have a major impact on the southern and southwestern border provinces. Yunnan, the key route from Chongqing through to Burma, was on the front line of resistance to Japan as well as being one of the centres of wartime cultural resistance, through the Southwest United University in the provincial capital, Kunming.[24] This university housed one of the greatest collections of academic brilliance the world has ever known. Guangxi, meanwhile, had become a centre of cultural resistance. The province's capital, Guilin, became a major centre of Chinese culture, the temporary home of many actors, artists, and writers, especially those from the occupied parts of southern China.

Once Japanese troops arrived in Indochina, Guangxi was on the front line – a new and unanticipated front line, from the Chinese and Allied point of view. Japan had opened a new front against China, which, to strategists who did not know the topography of the border region, was quite threatening: they saw the nightmare scenario of Japan connecting its holdings on Mainland China with its holdings in Southeast Asia, which would mean that Japan would control a continuous swathe of land from Manchuria in the north to Indonesia in the south. As it turned out, the front was inactive for much of the war, but, as the province was poorly defended (most of the Guangxi armies being stationed in the hills of Central China), there was always a possibility that Japanese troops in Indochina would invade China across the Guangxi border. To underline this possibility, Japanese planes stationed in Indochina regularly bombed the main towns of Guangxi and any other targets that seemed strategic, such as the crews working on the railway from Nanning to the west.

For the first time in a long while, the border felt like a place of menace. On a trip to Guangxi in 1941, Guillermaz reported that "the local insecurity [due to threat of banditry in the border region] was exacerbated by the presence of a Japanese army in Indochina and another in the Canton region, from which they could, at any moment, launch combined operations against the south of Guangxi, which they did at least twice. In between times Japanese aerial reconnaissance planes flew up the [Yong] River quite often, machine gunning anything that moved."[25]

Twice during the war, the Japanese threat to the province proved to be a reality. The first invasion took place in 1940, when southern parts of Guangxi were invaded by Japanese troops who landed from the sea in southwestern Guangdong and then moved north into the Nanning region. This invasion, which was a diversionary tactic whose purpose was to draw Chinese troops away from Central China, lasted only a few months, but it underlined the vulnerability of the province to Japanese attack.

The second invasion took place in 1944 and came from the north, along the railway line from Hunan. It was the last part of Operation Ichigo, and it was much more serious than the first invasion. By now, there were several US air bases in Guangxi, built at huge expense to allow for attacks on Japanese shipping and possibly on Japan itself.[26] The Japanese mounted the largest army of any campaign – fifteen divisions. Guangxi was the southernmost point of the attack and was reached in November. The US air bases were destroyed just ahead of the Japanese arrival. All the major cities in the province were occupied, the province was thrown into panic and much of its infrastructure devastated, including the newly constructed railway lines. Guilin was fired by the defenders just before the Japanese arrived.

Neither of these invasions involved Japanese forces in Indochina. The reasons for the absence of an attack from Indochina were strictly tactical: it would have been extremely difficult to attack Guangxi from Indochina as there was no railway in the area and no real road. A mechanized Japanese army would have found it almost impossible to move through this region.

There is another, more arcane explanation for the fact that the border was never crossed, and that is that some members of the French administration in Indochina were able to block any Japanese incursion into China.

This explanation relies on the claim that, although Hanoi was technically pro-Vichy and pro-Japanese, many French officials and soldiers were tacitly anti-Japanese and believed, at least during the last two years of the war, that the Vichy regime would not last. Throughout the war, there were covert connections between French officials in Hanoi and Chongqing, with the French consul in Longzhou, Siguret, acting as intermediary.[27] The French army in Indochina managed to maintain its control of the border with Guangxi and kept Japanese troops from getting to the border. The French civilian and military authorities close to the border had direct and friendly contacts with the Chinese forces on the other side, and they believed that it would be a disaster if Indochina were to be embroiled in the war.

These were strictly local connections and had little to do either with Vichy policy or with the stance of French diplomats in China. The official French closeness to Japan did not go without a Chinese response. The French betrayal of China, as the Chinese government saw it, became a pretext for Chinese support of anti-French revolutionaries from Indochina in both Yunnan and Guangxi.[28] The anti-Communist general Zhang Fakui, who was commander of the Fourth War Zone, which held Guangxi for much of the war, gave sanctuary to anti-French revolutionaries, many of them Communists, at his headquarters in Liuzhou, where they were "protected, instructed and kept under surveillance" by his men.[29] Both the Vichy and the non-Vichy French took this support, "la menace Vietminh" (the Viet Minh threat), seriously. In July 1943, de Gaulle's representative in Chongqing reported as follows: "The Chinese often use, for present and future ends, Annamites in China, either refugees or residents. Annamites from the school in Liuzhou have recently been sent to the border region; their mission is to prepare a movement of revolt for the moment when Chinese troops penetrate into Indochina."[30]

The End of the War and the Chinese Civil War

Those French in Hanoi who took a long-term view of relations with China and with Japan turned out to be right: France had no fundamental interest in dealing with the Japanese and no advantage to gain from the relationship. The Japanese had little respect for the French, whom they treated as puppets, in much the same way that they treated the regimes in China. In March 1945, the Japanese turned against the French, eliminated the French administration in Indochina, and arrested most of its officials, killing some of them. The illusion of common interests between France and Japan was shattered.

By this time, the cross-border relationship was almost irrelevant to Guangxi. The second Japanese invasion had done terrible damage to the province. The major cities were burned to the ground as part of a terrible scorched-earth policy on the part of the defenders of the province. The fighting spirit of Guangxi had drained away. The war left the province weak, dispirited, and physically and psychologically damaged.

Indochina was not much better off. The territory had to deal with the sudden influx of Yunnanese troops at the end of the war, with the departure of the Japanese, and with having to settle the bitter animosities between the "new" French and those who had worked enthusiastically for Vichy.

This was the start of yet another convoluted phase of French relations with China. The border between Guangxi and Indochina reverted to what it had long been – quiet but troubled and potentially dangerous. In 1949, the danger surfaced. A great number of Guomindang (GMD) troops fled from Guangxi into Indochina, at what seemed to be the end of the Chinese civil war. The French administrators had to find ways to deal with this situation while simultaneously making sure that they kept the lid on the potential Communist threat the Viet Minh posed to their own rule. There were two enemies in China at once – the defeated GMD (who wanted to flee into Indochina) and the Communist forces that had driven them out (and might now be helping the enemies of France inside Indochina). For the first time, the border became very important indeed; now the French had to keep their Chinese enemies out. It was no longer a question of the French wanting to invade China, as they had in the 1870s, but, rather, of China presenting a major threat to Indochina. And that was what the border – now a very clear fortified line – meant during the French attempts to hold on in Indochina as well as during the Vietnam War. China was the threat.

But the threat evaporated. Not until after the Americans had been ousted and Vietnam was "free" did the Chinese menace materialize – and when it did, it had quite a different effect than what had been imagined. In 1978, Chinese armies invaded across the border and ran straight into a much tougher, much better-equipped army in Vietnam. The vainglorious attack turned out to be the last hurrah of ultra-leftism in China. China's total and humiliating defeat produced a miserable flood of ethnic Chinese refugees out of Vietnam – and a sense that China could not go on like this. The defeat became a stimulus for the changes that led China to the reforms of the 1980s.

Zhennanguan had been renamed Youyimen – the Friendship Gate – by the Chinese Communist Party. In the 1980s and 1990s, as capitalism flourished and cross-border trade grew, for the first time the gate was worthy of its name.

Notes

1 For a vivid description of what northern Chinese thought about the Far South, see Edward Shafer, *The Vermillion Bird* (Berkeley: University of California Press, 1967).

2 Leo Shin, *State and Ethnicity in Ming China: "March toward the Tropics" Revisited* (Cambridge: Cambridge University Press, 2006).

3 Ma Yuan had become, by the fifth century, a local deity, worshipped in the border region by Han in-migrants "to counter threats from the original inhabitants, the climate and the general misgivings" of people moving into the region, a comforter of those far from home. See Keith Stevens, *Chinese Gods* (London: Collins, 1997), 147.

4 Lai Yen-yu, *Guangxi yilan* [Glimpses of Guangxi] (Nanning: Kwangsi Provincial Government Press, 1936), Frontiers, 7.

5 Henri Cordier, *Histoire des relations de la Chine avec les puissance occidentales, 1860-1902* [The history of China's relations with the Western powers] (Paris: F. Alcan, 1901-2), 1:235-36.

6 Lai Yen-yu, *Guangxi yilan,* 8-10.

7 *Longzhou xianzhi* [Longzhou gazetteer] (Nanning: Guangxi renmin chubanshe, 1993), 367.

8 I call these "hills" instead of "mountains" because, although they are very rugged, they are not very high.

9 Wen Ruopeng, Zhang Bingxun, and Sun Kegui, *Zhongnan dajiaofei* [The Great Extermination of Bandits in the Central South] (Beijing: Guofang daxue chubanshe, 1997).

10 Pierre Famin, *Au Tonkin et sur la frontiere de Kouang-si* [In Tongking and on the frontier of Guangxi] (Paris: Challamel, 1895), 353.

11 Joseph Dautremer, "Yunnan et Kouang-si: frontieres Indo-Chinoise" [Yunnan and Guangxi: Indochinese frontiers], in *Bulletin de l'association amicale Franco-Chinoise,* 1909, 282.

12 Dautremer, "Yunnan et Kouang-si," 469.

13 Jean Beauvais, *Documents geographiques, historiques et linguistiques sur la ville et la region de Long-tcheou.*[Geographical, historical and linguistic documents on the town and the region of Longzhou] (Hanoi: Imprimerie d'extreme orient, 1909).

14 *Through the Consul's Eye,* Tanguera Films 1999, promotional materials.

15 Diana Lary, *Region and Nation: The Kwangsi Clique in Republican Politics* (Cambridge: Cambridge University Press, 1975), 26.

16 The dream of canonization for Chapdelaine and for one of his close associates, Lawrence Pe-man, was finally achieved in 2000, after a process that lasted 146 years. The two were beatified in 1900 and canonized a century later. The canonization, along with that of eighty-two other Chinese Catholics and thirty-two other missionaries who had died in China between 1648 and 1930, evoked fury in Beijing, officially because of "outside interference" but probably because, once again, the Vatican had shown that, in terms of diplomatic manoeuvring, it has no rivals – even in the Beijing mandarinate.

17 *Longzhou xianzhi,* 366.

18 Joseph Cuenot, *Au pays des pavillons noirs* [In the Land of the Black Banners] (Hong Kong: Imprimerie de Nazareth, 1925).

19 There were substantial numbers of Overseas Chinese in northern parts of Indochina from a part of China that is now Guangxi but was then Guangdong. These are the counties that make up the Nanlu region, an entirely Cantonese-speaking region that belonged to Guangdong until 1961.

20 Franz Heger, *Alte metaltrmmeln aus sudost Asien* [Old metal drums from Souhteast Asia] (Leipzig: Hiersemann, 1902); and B. Hirth, "Uber hinterindischen Bronze-trommeln" [On Nether-Indian bronze drums], *Toung-pao* 1 (1890): 135-42.

21 Fabienne Mercier, *Vichy face à Chiang Kai-shek: Histoire diplomatique* [Vichy's dealings with Chiang Kai-shek: A diplomatic history] (Paris: L'Harmattan, 1995), 22.

22 Jacques Guillermaz, *Une vie pour la Chine* [A Life for China] (Paris: Robert Lafont, 1989).

23 Guillermaz, *Une vie pour la Chine,* 104-5.

24 John Israel, *Lianda: A Chinese University in War and Revolution* (Stanford: Stanford University Press, 1998).

25 Guillermaz, *Une vie pour la Chine,* 77.

26 Wesley Bagby, *The Eagle-Dragon Alliance: America's Relations with China in World War II* (Newark: University of Delaware Press, 1992), 132.

27 Mercier, *Vichy face à Chiang Kai-shek,* 16.

28 Ibid., 12.

29 Guillermaz, *Une vie pour la Chine,* 76.

30 Mercier, *Vichy face à Chiang Kai-shek,* 251.

11

Border Banishment: Rightists in the Army Farms of Beidahuang

Wang Ning

For thousands of years, China's governments have used the border regions as places of banishment. As early as the Qin dynasty (third century BCE), emperors deported convicts, disgraced officials, and people in disfavour to remote regions in the south and the north.[1] Reasons for this practice ranged from the removal of disruptive elements to the rehabilitation of offenders, from the colonization of the frontiers to the assimilation of ethnic minorities.

In the late imperial period, one of the major regions for the disposal of undesirable elements was Manchuria, as documented by Yang Bin and Joanna Waley-Cohen. Under the Ming, Liaodong (present-day Liaoning) received a large number of military exiles (*junfan*); the Qing government designated Shangyangbao (Liaoning), Ningguta, and Chuanchang (Heilongjiang) as exile destinations.[2] The peoples banished to Manchuria in the Qing were mostly "common criminals such as robbers, counterfeiters, and smugglers" as well as the secondary participants in popular rebellions that posed serious threats to the existing order.[3] Because of the cold, the remoteness, and the harsh physical conditions, banishment to the Manchuria frontier regions was considered among the harshest of penalties.

In the twentieth century, the Communist government raised Manchurian banishment to a new level. In terms of location, with the expansion of the frontier and the effective delineation of the Sino-Soviet border, it sent exiles further northeast than the Qing had done, to areas close to the border. In a demographic sense, it banished not only criminal offenders but also other groups – demobilized soldiers, secondary school graduates, the urban unemployed, and so on.[4] In a political sense, it banished not only real political opponents and critics but also those who were considered to have the potential to pose threats and even, sometimes, its loyal followers.

This chapter examines the massive wave of banishment to the Manchurian frontier that followed the political campaigns of 1957. I focus on the experience of a group of Chinese intellectuals and government employees who were sent from Beijing to the army farms of Beidahuang, the Great Northern Wilderness, in eastern Heilongjiang. I examine the process of banishment, the work and life of the exiles, and their physical and emotional suffering; I analyze the social consequences of border banishment, of practising social control through coercion and manipulation; I look at how the border regions served the purposes of the People's Republic of China (PRC) government; and, finally, I examine why and how the so-called "rehabilitation of offenders" was undermined at local levels.

Background

In the spring of 1957, the Chinese Communist Party (CCP) encouraged intellectuals and students to speak out against abuses of party and government officials, with the alleged intention of improving governance and facilitating social progress. But when criticisms were directed at a wide range of party policies and at the whole political system, the party shifted tack and cracked down overnight – in the Anti-Rightist Campaign. Those who had called for intellectual and political freedom and for putting a stop to corruption were accused of political subversion.[5] In a nationwide campaign, more than half a million intellectuals out of five million, along with open-minded party cadres and government employees, were labelled "rightists" or "counterrevolutionaries," essentially the "enemies of the people."[6]

Along with political labelling, the CCP envisaged policies for the treatment of those labelled. Although insisting that the enmity between the party and the rightists was really a "contradiction between ourselves and the enemy," the party advocated a solution based on "contradictions among the people" as a sign of its leniency and willingness to "save" those who had gone astray but wished to repent.[7] The lenient treatment was "to give a way out" to the rightists – that is, to send them to factories, rural areas, or frontier areas to engage in "reform through labour" (*laodong gaizao*) or "ideological remoulding" (*sixiang gaizao*), rather than putting them in jail.[8] It is estimated that, from late 1957 to early 1958, a majority of those labelled rightists (over 300,000) lost, or were suspended from, their jobs and were sent to rural areas or the border regions.[9]

Thousands of Beijing rightists were sent to a variety of locations to perform manual labour. Those labelled in the municipal authority and its affiliated organs were sent to local farms or construction sites, while many student rightists from Peking University were sent to coal mines west of Beijing.[10] Journalist Liu Binyan (later a well-known dissident) was banished to Shanxi; the young writer Liu Shaotang was sent to his home village in Hebei to herd cows. Some rightists were allowed to choose their place of banishment, but most were not.[11]

Rightists from central organizations were often sent to army farms in Beidahuang. The most serious offenders – the "ultra-rightists" and the "counterrevolutionaries" – were sent to labour camps. The rightists whose offences were deemed less serious were allowed to retain their jobs or were sent to farms close to Beijing.[12] This chapter focuses on the rightists sent to the army farms of Beidahuang.

Relocation to Beidahuang

The decision to send the rightists from the central organizations (hereafter Beijing rightists) away from Beijing was made in early 1958, a time that coincided with unprecedented development in northeast China, especially land reclamation in Heilongjiang, which demanded a cheap labour force. In 1954, the government used demobilized soldiers for reclamation work in eastern Heilongjiang. Tens of thousands of men were sent as pioneers to the virgin lands of Mishan, Hulin, Baoqing, and Raohe, where they established army farms.[13] In the early stages of the establishment of these farms, agricultural, construction, and forestry labour was in great demand.

In the spring of 1958, the land reclamation program was in full force, under the rubric of the Great Leap Forward. More demobilized soldiers were ordered to relocate, but the numbers were still insufficient. Wang Zhen, the minister of national land reclamation, demanded more settlers. Young peasants from Shandong and Hebei (known as frontier youth), convicts from northern and eastern China, and rightists were all incorporated into his grand recruitment plan. The State Council decided to send the rightists from the central organizations to eastern Heilongjiang.[14]

Little is known about how the CCP made the decision to send down the Beijing rightists; nor is it clear how the central ministries carried out the coordinated plan for mass relocation. The recollections of the political exiles, however, provide valuable sources on the process. Ding Ling recalled the experience of her husband Chen Ming: "A couple of days after the New Year, the Beijing Movie Studio of the Ministry of Culture informed Chen Ming of his verdict: while he was to keep his post, he was to be deprived of his rank and to be sent to 'labor under supervision' in Mishan, Heilongjiang. He was given three days before reporting to a meeting place in an eastern suburb."[15]

Other recollections (Liu Meng, Yin Yi) point to similar situations: the rightists, after being stripped of their posts, were ordered to designated meeting places (Qianmen Station, for instance) to board trains for Beidahuang; cadres from their work units supervised their departure. Some trains were "rightist expresses" (*youpai zhuanlie*) reserved by the Ministry of Land Reclamation, but most were not.[16]

The rightists banished to Beidahuang came from agencies of the State Council, from professional associations, and from institutions of higher learning; they ranged from senior revolutionaries to members of the non-party elite, from college graduates to office clerks. Many were prestigious figures who had held important posts in managerial, economic, cultural, literary, or other fields. Figures such as Ding Ling, Ai Qing, Wu Zuguang, and Ding Cong were famous in the literary and art worlds; Wang Zuoru (director of protocol at the foreign ministry) and Xie Hegeng (senior CCP intellectual, graduate of Cornell University) were revolutionary veterans.[17] Military personnel were not immune from banishment. Of seven thousand People's Liberation Army (PLA) officers, cadets, and technicians who were labelled, more than a hundred were sent to Beidahuang.[18]

Beidahuang: An Imagined World

The term Beidahuang, the Great Northern Wilderness, was first constructed by Han Chinese during the Qing dynasty (1644-1912). Considering Manchuria as their homeland, Qing rulers in the late seventeenth century implemented an exclusion policy in Manchuria. They planted two lines of willows – the Willow Palisades – in southern Manchuria to prohibit Han Chinese migration, preserve the Manchu way of life, and retain control over the valuable products of the region.[19] The Han who lived south of the Willow Palisades called the boundless northern land Beidahuang.[20] With the Qing's lifting of the ban on migration to Manchuria in the second half of the nineteenth century, and the massive influx of Han migrants, the imagined world of Beidahuang was reduced in scope. By the time of the Communist takeover, the term Beidahuang referred to the vast plains north of Harbin and Yilerhuli mountain; the Three River Plain (*Sanjiang pingyuan*) bounded by the Amur, Ussuri, and Sungaris rivers; and the Mudan River Plain (*Mudanjiang pingyuan*). The ecology there was still one of "hunting roe deer with clubs, netting fish with gourd ladles, and watching pheasants fly into the kitchen."[21]

In the massive land reclamation of the mid-1950s, four counties – Mishan, Hulin, Baoqing, and Raohe in the eastern frontier region of Heilongjiang – were the location of large numbers of army farms, the destination of the Beijing rightists.[22] Later, during the Cultural Revolution, Beidahuang, as the destination of hundreds of thousands of sent-down youths, was the generic name of the whole Heilongjiang wilderness.

Beidahuang has a bad reputation. Although arable land is abundant and the soil fertile, its climate (–30°C on average in winter), its isolation from China proper, and the difficulty of communication make people flinch at the name. A diet based on coarse grain (corn, sorghum), and the lack of vegetables in winter were also deterrents. Even after the Qing lifted their exclusion policy, Han Chinese, except for some Shandong and Hebei migrants, avoided this desolate land.[23] In the 1930s, Japanese colonizers attempted to open this area but failed.[24]

Beidahuang historically provided a perfect site for the rulers of China to banish undesirable elements; its harsh physical environment and isolation generated immense fear in offenders, including the political offenders of

1957. When told that they would be sent to Beidahuang, sadness and despair overwhelmed the Beijing rightists. Many of them did not know whether they would come back alive or whether they would see their families again. Some appealed to be sent to another location, but they were harshly refused.[25]

A considerable number of Beijing rightists, however, were not afraid of being sent to Beidahuang, and some volunteered to go even though they were offered other options. According to a directive of the central authorities (in Note Eight), only rightists assigned to the first and second levels of punishment were to be sent to difficult regions for "labour re-education" or "labour under supervision." Some rightists, such as writers Ding Ling and Nie Gannu, asked to go to Beidahuang.[26] The reasons for these requests were complex.

Some political exiles were impressed by the landscape of the northeast. With the tidal wave of land reclamation, media coverage of the landscape and the social transformation of Manchuria had dramatically increased; this contributed to people's knowledge of Manchuria and led to an idealized image of Beidahuang. Ding Ling was among many who were impressed by the Heilongjiang forests depicted in the books she collected.[27] Journalist Cong Weixi was impressed by the boundlessness, the natural beauty, and the fertility of Beidahuang. Cong believed that, for people without families to worry about, Beidahuang was an oasis far away from mundane life: "I was infatuated with the northeast, especially in winter when it was decorated by the white snow, so I went to this silvery white world twice in the winter 1956 and spring 1957."[28] To young idealists, life in the great wilderness could help with spiritual growth.

A second reason some writers chose to go to Beidahuang had to do with finding literary inspiration from ordinary people. Taking to heart Mao's injunction in the Yan'an Talks, some writers sincerely believed that it was necessary to go to the grassroots and write about the masses.[29] Ding Ling, for instance, insisted that a revolutionary writer should enthusiastically go down to the rural areas and observe and learn from the real life of the masses, even through adversity. She presumed that living close to the soil would nourish her literary creativity; her writing would present the epic transformation of heaven and earth.[30] Another example is essayist Nie Gannu. With his record as a revolutionary veteran, Nie, after being labelled a rightist, was offered the option of retiring or working at a lower rank at the People's Literature Press, but he declined the "kindness." "Life is the source of writing," he said, "As a writer I should experience all kinds of life. Now that I have become a rightist, I would like to lead the real life of this kind."[31] In a sense, what these intellectuals sought was self-banishment.

A third reason some of these people opted for Beidahuang had to do with their desire to show their commitment to redeeming themselves through ideological remoulding. Many, such as artists Ding Cong and Huang Miaozi, were told by the party apparatus that they had committed serious crimes against the party and the nation and that they needed to redeem themselves through hard labour in the most arduous areas. Beidahuang, with its physical hardship and its revolutionary changes since 1949, was the ideal place to go. They were told that, through hard labour and physical suffering, they could transcend their past faults and their deep-seated bourgeois ideologies. Driven by this propaganda, they were willing to go to Beidahuang to prove their commitment to self-reform.[32]

For most rightists, however, revolutionary hyperbole could not make Beidahuang more attractive. Nonetheless, Beidahuang could offer an escape. Having been demonized and having experienced harsh attacks and insults, the rightists were notorious among their colleagues and neighbours. A rightist would always have to lower his or her head in deep embarrassment even when coming across a friend. Even their families were persuaded to condemn them and to announce the breakdown of the family relationship.[33] The social isolation the rightists felt was unbearable. Given this situation, going to Beidahuang seemed, to some extent, to be a relief. Many rightists assumed that, in an exile community established in a remote location, everybody would be equal. They believed that the smell of the black earth meant hope.[34] When their fates were sealed and discrimination on the part of their colleagues and neighbours escalated, many wanted to seek refuge in the wilderness in order to free themselves from political pressure.

Arrival in Beidahuang

When they first arrived at their place of banishment, the chief concern of the Beijing rightists was how long they would have to stay there. Things did not seem so grim at this point. Before leaving Beijing, many rightists were given hints by heads of their work units to the effect that, as long as they did well, they might be recalled within one or two years.[35] There were other signs that "reform through manual labour" was likely a temporary period: bosses of many work units advised the rightists not to let their professional expertise get rusty. The rightists from the Central Orchestra in Beijing, for instance, were allowed to take their musical instruments with them. Journalists from the Xinhua News Agency were encouraged to take English books and English-Chinese dictionaries.[36] Many exiles, therefore, expected that their frontier banishment would not be that harsh and would not last long. As long as they sincerely engaged in "reform through labour," they assumed, the party would give them a chance to go back to normal life and continue their work in their fields of expertise. Journalist Dai Huang recalls: "when taking the journey with a box of books, I was full of confidence in pursuing a bright future in the wilderness."[37] Even though it is hard to tell whether Dai's feelings were typical, it seems that some political exiles did not feel entirely hopeless.

From early March 1958, thousands of Beijing rightists arrived at various locations in Beidahuang. Ding Ling was assigned to Tangyuan; Ai Qing, the famous poet, and his family were sent to Farm 852; and the majority of the Beijing rightists were sent to Farms 850 and 853.[38] Nie Gannu and Xie Hegeng, Ding Cong and artist Huang Miaozi, as well as journalists Dai Huang, Wu Yongliang, Yin Yi, and Liu Meng were sent to Farm 850, the first army farm set up in Beidahuang. English literature specialist Huang Wu, playwrights Wu Zuguang and Wang Zheng, and journalists Zheng Xiaofeng and Sun Zhanke were sent to Farm 853, as was Chen Ming (before being allowed to join Ding Ling in Tangyuan).[39] In these farms, the Beijing rightists worked with demobilized soldiers, convicts, and people who had completed their terms but were retained in labour camps.

For most of those in Farm 850, their experience in the first months was not bad. In contrast to their debased status in Beijing, their formal status in the farms was "agricultural worker" (*nonggong*) rather than "rightist." The farm authorities designated 120 demobilized officers to supervise their daily life and to organize their work.[40] The farm authorities did not, however, develop clear measures regarding how to ideologically remould these people. The managerial and ideological control over the rightists was relatively loose in the first months, which enabled them to enjoy considerable freedom to learn, to talk, and to relax after work. They sang Peking opera, practised

Forced labour allocation in the relevant army farms of Beijing rightists (1958)

	Forced labourers				
			Rightists		
Name of farm	Demobilized soldiers	Convicted criminals	Beijing	Local	Military
Farm 850	12,800	5,074	828	61	97
Farm 852	10,600		Ai Qing and his Family	261 (including other "bad elements")	
Farm 853	4,668		484	60	19
Tang Yuan		14,000	Ding Ling and her family		

Sources: Bawuling nongchangshi [Gazetteer of Farm 850] (Hulin: Bawuling nongchangshi bianxie bangongshi, 1986), 30; *Bawusan nongchangzhi* [Gazetteer of Farm 853] (Jiamusi: Bawusan nongchangzhi bianxie bangongshi, 1986), 2; Zheng Jiazhen, *Zhongguo dongbeijiao* [The northeast corner of China] (Harbin: Heilongjiang renmin chubanshe, 1998), 66; *Wang Zhen zhuan* [The Biography of Wang Zhen] (Beijing: Dangdai zhongguo chubanshe, 2001), 68, 81; *Heilongjiang shengzhi guoying nongchang zhi* [Gazetteer of state farms in Heilongjiang] (Harbin: Heilongjiang renmin chubanshe, 1992), 76.

painting, played bridge, conducted research, and read foreign language texts.[41] While living conditions were hard – they lived in ramshackle sheds – and the physical work heavy, the rightists led passable lives until the summer of 1959, when food shortages started to be felt. The situation was similar at Farm 853, where, as journalist Zheng Xiaofeng recalls, the political exiles did not feel much pressure. The demobilized PLA officers in Zheng's work team treated the rightists quite politely, addressing them as "sent-down cadres" (*xiafang ganbu*). Except for daily work, the lives of political exiles were not badly disturbed, and discrimination against them was kept at a minimum.[42]

Some party officials in charge of the land reclamation took a moderate attitude towards the rightists. Wang Zhen, the minister of land reclamation, seemed to be rather helpful to the rightists that he recruited from Beijing. He visited them in Farms 850 and 853 shortly after they arrived and tried to cheer them up by suggesting that they would have a "bright future" if they took a positive attitude towards labour reform. What delighted the rightists was that Wang addressed them as "comrades," which helped to remove the humiliation they suffered under the Anti-Rightist Campaign.[43] Under Wang's instructions, the farm authorities took measures to improve their living conditions (generating electricity, for instance) and reassigned some of them to work on local literature magazines, in art troupes, at movie theaters, and in schools. Many rightists in Farm 850 went so far as to refer to their experience as "civilized banishment."[44]

The rightists were normally allowed to bring family members with them. Although few of them had the heart to make their families experience such hardship, some of them did. Han Yuan, an ordinary employee in the Ministry of Culture, went with her husband, following the example of the heroic wives of Russian Decembrists, with whom she was familiar through Soviet movies.[45] When Nie Gannu worked in Farm 850, he met several women who had accompanied their husbands. For a period they had to live with other male labourers in a newly built shed that housed about ninety people. "At night, the wives slept at both ends of the wide *kang* (northern style bed), with their husbands close to them, and the rest of the men jammed together on the other side of the husbands. With women about, the men tried to show better behavior; and the dirty jokes that used to circulate among men totally disappeared."[46] Couples in such surroundings were unable to enjoy conjugal life, but the warmth and kindness of the exile community was felt and appreciated.

Most rightists left their wives or husbands behind. In cases where both members of the couple were labelled and banished, their children were left in Beijing. Even though divorce due to political disgrace was not as common as it had been in the Cultural Revolution, there were cases in which one member of a couple would attempt to avoid being implicated by drawing a political line between him/herself and the once beloved partner who had now become an "enemy of the people." While there are many stories about unwavering commitment to marriage (e.g., Wu Zuguang, Huang Miaozi, and Ding Cong), there are also cases in which spouses of rightists showed their commitment to the party by asking for a divorce (e.g., Xu Zimei and Dai Huang).[47] Some rightists, however, broke off engagements, asked their spouses to divorce them, or announced a break with their families in order to avoid bringing trouble to their loved ones.[48]

Daunting Labour

The early, relaxed stage of life in Beidahuang turned out to be transitory. It was not long before the rightists realized that things would not work out as they expected, and they came to see how harsh conditions were. During 1958-59, the nationwide economic adventure – the Great Leap Forward – featured huge and wasteful inputs of labour. In Beidahuang, the state's agenda to establish a national grain base spelled daunting manual work in agriculture and forestry, the daily job of the rightists.

Beidahuang was, in a physical sense, the toughest region of all Manchuria. When the involuntary migrants (demobilized soldiers, convicts, and rightists) gathered in the area in early 1958, it was a vast stretch of swamp and boggy grassland as far as the eye could see.[49] Since the level of mechanization was extremely low in the early stages, all the tilling, sowing, and reaping had to be done manually. Put into special "rightist teams," the political exiles had to do all kinds of work, including cultivating the land, harvesting crops, building reservoirs, cutting wood, excavating earth, making bricks, erecting barracks, building roads, and raising livestock. The work was backbreaking for intellectuals who had only done academic and managerial work. Dai Huang provided examples of the daily work of the political exiles in the Yunshan Branch:

> Right after the soybean harvest in the early winter of 1958, dozens of us went into the Wanda Mountains to cut hard oak trees ... Less than one month afterward (December 1st, 1958), we were ordered to leave the mountains, to go to the grassland for an irrigation project ... The people in our platoon had to strive to finish work quotas. We used pickaxes to break up the frozen topsoil, sometimes close to one meter thick, then dug out the unfrozen soil ... It was still dark when the reveille was sounded in the morning. We had to leave our barracks and rushed dozens of *li* to work, and have breakfast in the fields. During that winter, we usually slept for no more than four hours a day.[50]

Work hours on average ranged from twelve to sixteen hours a day in summer. People had to get up at three or four o'clock in the morning and work until dark. In some branch farms, weekends were cancelled in the summer of 1958 (during the Great Leap Forward).[51] The rightists were driven to ceaseless physical exertion.

Forestry work in winter was another ordeal for the banished intellectuals. As poet Huang Wu recalls:

> In the winters of 1958 and 1959, we rightists were twice ordered to go into the Wanda Mountains to cut wood. We went into the mountain in September and left in March the next year, which was the coldest season in this remote frontier area ... The mountain valleys were deep and the forest dense without a trace of human habitation, where we had to share the forests with wolves, bears and wild boars day and night. The tree felling was not without danger; it was easy for us to get hurt or even killed by the falling trees.[52]

Due to their unfamiliarity with the new work and to working in the dark, the rate of accidental death among those working in the forests was high. In Huang Wu's team of fifty-six, two were killed by falling trees and one badly injured during the winter of 1958-59. Dai Huang also recalls that four of his fellow exiles died in the forests that winter.[53] Like winter forestry, charcoal making was also an ordeal. In order to produce charcoal of good quality, they had to go into the kilns to bring out the charcoal while the kilns were still filled with hot smoke and ash. Strong people could manage to do this quickly, but those in poor physical shape often fainted inside. Some were rescued by their fellows, and some died with charcoal ash on their faces.[54]

The rightists, like the demobilized soldiers and convicts, were put into a quasi-military system organized along military lines: regiment, company, platoon, squadron, and so on, with demobilized officers (now cadres) as their heads above company level. Some officers showed a degree of concern for the physical fitness of the rightists and assigned the elderly and the weak to lighter work.[55] Other officers, driven by quotas from above and enmeshed in the fanatical fervour of the Great Leap Forward, treated the exiles as slaves and even required them to engage in competitions with demobilized soldiers and convicts. In the busiest seasons (such as harvest), unreasonable work quotas were set: the cadres "wanted to wring every ounce of sweat and blood out of us." When work quotas were not filled, the rightists were often denied rest and food.[56]

Despite their seemingly equal status with peasants, the rightists, during most of the period of their banishment, were treated worse than were demobilized soldiers. In Farm 850, when the rightists had to sleep outside during work rushes, the demobilized soldier workers were provided with barracks. In Farm 853, the soldiers could refuse to work due to food shortages, while the rightists had to go to work with empty stomachs.[57] The political status of the rightist was highlighted in the farms.

The harsh climate posed huge difficulties for the rightists. The first difficulty was the extreme cold. As early as mid-October, the cold wind began to slice through the mountains and wilderness. Between January and March, the land is frozen solid, and any agricultural activity is impossible. Northeasterners (*dongbeiren*) stayed indoors, doing nothing but drinking and gambling and perhaps occasionally hunting deer. After the Communist takeover, however, the winter season was used for hydraulic projects, road construction, and forest work. This was what the rightists experienced. During the day, they were exposed to temperatures of minus thirty degrees Celsius, and at night they lived in makeshift shacks made of birch logs with thatched roofs. The temperature outside could go down to minus forty degrees Celsius, while the temperature inside was not much better as wind and snow could blow in.[58] Many rightists drank alcohol to warm up before sleep and wore cotton-padded hats. Eating after work was not easy. When the food (usually corn or sorghum breads) was sent to the work sites, it was often frozen solid; people had to cut it into pieces with axes in order to eat it. The bitter cold meant that one had to work without stopping.[59]

In summertime, a major difficulty came in the form of insects, especially mosquitoes. Nourished in the marshland, gigantic in size, they tortured everyone in Beidahuang. Writer Wang Zheng recalls: "Once wakened, these extremely vicious creatures would swarm those of us who worked on the marshland, and would try to get into our noses, eyes, ears, and mouths as well as our collars. People would go mad in this situation."[60] Exposed skin led to instant bites. Short of wearing cumbersome, insect-proof suits, the exiles had to keep moving to try to hold the mosquitoes at bay. For many political exiles, mosquitoes were a nightmare during their time in Beidahuang.[61]

Ideological Remoulding

Recent Western scholarship has contrasted Mao-era efforts at the political indoctrination of labour camp inmates with Soviet-era efforts. Some academics assume that political study was a distinguishing feature of Maoist labour camps.[62] This argument is true of the general practice in Maoist labour camps and concurs with the CCP's claims about the significance of "thought reform." During the Great Leap Forward and its aftermath, however, and in Beidahuang in particular, little effort was made to implement thought reform, even though higher authorities saw manual labour as a way to remould those who had committed political errors and even though the rightists in Beidahuang did not refuse political indoctrination.[63]

Generally speaking, when they first arrived in Beidahuang, the Beijing rightists displayed a certain degree of commitment to "thought reform through labour." While many felt they had been wrongly labelled, they recognized the role physical labour played in ideological remoulding and in cleansing them of their "bourgeois ideologies." As mentioned earlier, Ding Ling and Nie Gannu looked at their labour in Beidahuang as an opportunity to be with the working class and rural world, to cast off their old selves, and to achieve spiritual regeneration. Nie Gannu, for instance, wrote in his "thought report": "I was born into a non-working class family, and thus had neither experience of physical labor nor access to working people. Therefore, I am glad to join working people, going into the countryside or mountainous area, to participate in physical labor or work at grass level in order to change my ideology ... I am now prepared for a long-term self-remolding anywhere."[64]

Nie Gannu's self-reflection should not be treated as simple affectation: it was consistent with his request to go to Beidahuang and with his willingness to engage in physical labour while there. Others, such as Huang Miaozi and Dai Huang, took a positive attitude towards labour reform. In the early period, they wrote poems and essays in praise of the party's labour reform policy and expressed their willingness to make a new start.[65] Some had brought political books with them to improve their minds through political study after work.[66]

Nevertheless, before long, the rightists found out that the army farm authorities essentially saw them as mere slave labourers and that it was unrealistic for them to expect to benefit from any "ideological remoulding." After fourteen hours of backbreaking labour, any form of study session was virtually impossible. Yin Yi recalls that, during the years of the Great Leap Forward, "the repertoire of daily life was reduced to an endless circle of working, eating and sleeping, plus the morning call of a cadre, Lu. There was nothing more than that."[67] As long as work quotas were filled, cadres did not bother with study sessions. At times, the rightists were asked to submit their "thought summaries" (*sixiang zongjie*), but these summaries, which the workers had taken pains to compose, were used by the leaders as toilet paper.[68]

An exception with regard to political indoctrination was Farm 850. Wu Yongliang recalls that the cadre, Zhu, arranged newspaper readings at breakfast to update the rightists concerning national politics, especially regarding high crop yields. Demobilized soldiers were brought in to give political talks to these well-educated yet "bourgeois" rightists.[69]

The most common political instruction given by cadres was known as "rebuking," or "dressing down" (*xunhua*). When cadres found that the rightists had failed to finish designated work quotas, or when they perceived a less than positive work attitude, this meant a *xunhua*, the denial of food, and/or the imposition of extra work hours. The language used was insulting, including phrases such as *yiqun cunzhu* (herd of pigs), *laomianyang* (old sheep), *fulu* (captives), or *tufei* (bandits).[70] Cadres also used *xunhua* to keep pressure on the rightists. Topics would include the rightists' "bourgeois taste," their ignorance of agriculture, and their lack of physical strength. They were reminded of their inferiority to "working people" and their need to engage in "long-term" reform.[71] The *xunhua* were often given before breakfast and at evening roll call, but they could be given at any time and without notice. Political indoctrination was reduced to reprimand, and "reform through labour" to forced labour.

This form of political lecture brought a negative reaction rather than a positive one, and it undermined the confidence of the political exiles engaged in "thought reform." Being deprived of dignity, and being driven as forced labourers, the rightists came to realize that Beidahuang was far from a refuge and that land reclamation or any kind of manual labour was, for them, no more than physical and psychological punishment. As Yin Yi puts it, the maltreatment meted out in his branch made his fellow exiles realize that "thought reform through labour" was merely camouflage, that punishment through labour was in fact what was happening.[72] When the food shortages started to loom large from mid-1959, the question of how to survive in Beidahuang rather than how to achieve ideological renewal or how to redeem oneself became the overwhelming concern. Having gone through years of forced labour, few people held a positive attitude towards their experience with banishment. The result of the ideological remoulding, or thought reform, turned out to be contrary to the stated expectations of the CCP leadership.

In assessing the experience of the political exiles in Beidahuang, the relationship of the rightists with their officers (the cadres) needs to receive special attention. Although the exiles were generally maltreated in Beidahuang, to a great extent their lot was in the hands of individual cadres – that is, branch leaders (*fenchangzhang*), brigade leaders (*duizhang*), and political instructors (*zhidaoyuan*), whose attitudes and managerial styles were by no means uniform, varying according to location and time. Under a considerate and sympathetic officer, the rightists would fare well even if their workload was heavy and the cold chilled them to the bone. Those in Farm 853 fared better than did those in Farm 850. Ding Ling in Tangyuan and Ai Qing in Farm 852 fared best of all.[73]

Most cadres had to obey rules set by higher authorities. Nonetheless, they could manipulate arrangements to favour the rightists with regard to food and living conditions. In Branch Four (Farm 850), when Nie Gannu felt pressured to improve his soy bean sowing quota, his two officers helped him – something that deeply impressed Nie and other exiles.[74] In Farm 853, brigade leader Li Fuchun worked with the rightists, treated them well, and tried to help with food supplies.[75] Under compassionate cadres, the exiles felt respected and were motivated to work hard. These cadres stood between the demanding regime and the disfavoured group.

Different cadres treated the same group well or badly. When Dai Huang's helpful political instructor Liu Wen was replaced, the situation of the rightists in Yunshan deteriorated; the new officers, Zhu and Yin, treated them harshly and reprimanded them frequently.[76] The death rate in Yunshan was much higher than was that in other farms.

Starvation, Death, and Suicide

The banishment of the rightists overlapped with the nationwide famine in China (1959-61). From the summer of 1959, food shortages began to be increasingly felt. In both Farms 850 and 853, grain rations for workers were set and then kept at a low level. During the worst months of 1960, a rightist in Farm 853 had only an eight *jin* grain ration monthly (1 *jin* = 1.1023 pounds).[77] Since there was no meat or cooking oil, the exiles had to subsist mainly on their skimpy grain rations, which, in the form of hard corn buns, washed down by watery vegetable soup, hardly alleviated the hunger pangs of those engaged in strenuous manual labour.

Since their food was far from sufficient, the rightists tried, whenever allowed, to search the vast fields for food – wild herbs, edible weeds, birds' eggs, and roots. They even searched rat holes for caches of grain stored underground. Wild animals also became valuable sources of food: some exiles dug in the ground for field mice or snakes. During the most difficult year, 1960, food substitutes, straw, corn stalks, sorghum stalks, corncobs, and leaves became part of the diet.[78] All of these measures, however, brought only temporary relief. As the food shortages continued, many rightists and other workers died of starvation and related diseases. In Farm 850, rightists died of edema (caused by malnourishment), while others contracted tuberculosis and fever (also caused by prolonged malnutrition). In the Yunshan Branch alone, twenty-eight rightists died of starvation from May to December 1960.[79] Dai Huang describes how six fellow exiles died of edema within a month in the fall of 1960. Some died on the road while searching for food, and some died at night after work. It was common that a man who had worked in the fields one day would be found dead in bed the next morning.[80]

The mass deaths in Beidahuang were also the consequence of the intensive use of forced labour and the lack of basic humanitarian concern on the part of a number of army cadres. On 13 October 1960, around one hundred rightists in Yunshan were herded out to harvest soy beans; seven of them died on the road home after a day of ceaseless work in the snow. When the emergency was reported, the heads of Yunshan Branch did not even bother to send for doctors to treat those in danger.[81] In Yunshan Branch, some died after being denied food or medical care. Ren Yaozhang, for instance, repeatedly pleaded for medical leave to treat his acute tuberculosis but was refused by his farm cadres. In September 1960, he finally died. The next month, Luo Xiangcheng, a thin, sick man denied food by his team leader because he could not work, died by the roadside.[82] According to the personal memoirs published by the political exiles, maltreatment by cadres was the chief reason for these tragic deaths.

Some political exiles died in despair. When the sense of isolation and depression became too difficult to overcome, when bad news arrived from their families, or when they found the work and physical hardship insurmountable, many chose suicide. The death of Tong Aicheng, Dai Huang's campmate, had its roots in his deep depression. After he was sent to Farm 850, his wife divorced him and left their two children without proper care in Beijing. Tong did not have sufficient money to support them from his Renminbi 32 allowance, nor could he return to take care of them. An unbearable workload crushed him. Tong hanged himself from a tree.[83]

Another rightist who committed suicide in Farm 850 was an overseas Chinese who returned to serve the "New China." Desperate with hunger in Beidahuang, he wrote to his father in Britain for milk powder, for which he was repeatedly condemned by cadres for "having disgraced the socialist motherland." Feeling this humiliation to be unbearable, he drowned himself.[84] Having witnessed so many friends lose their lives one after another, those who survived the Beidahuang banishment were deeply traumatized. Many, such as Wu Yongliang, Huang Wu, and Dai Huang, continued to experience intense emotional strain whenever they thought of their dead fellow inmates and their own painful experiences in Beidahuang.[85]

Fortunate Exiles: Ding Ling, Ai Qing, and Others

Not everyone was as miserable as the discussion above suggests. Compared to those who laboured in Farms 850 and 853, Ding Ling fared well thanks to the patronage of Wang Zhen, her friend from the pre-1949 period. Jonathan Spence describes the experience of Ding Ling in post-1957 Beidahuang:

> During this period Ding Ling was assigned to duty in the chicken coops of Tang Yuan. She has recorded that she grew absorbed in the task of raising the fowl and expert at looking after the ailing chickens, some of which she nursed back to health on the heated *kang* in her own hut ... She began to take a genuine interest in the problems of developing the best methods for raising a healthy flock, and during her spare time even built models of an ideal chicken complex, using the cardboard from old toothpaste containers or any other materials she could find.[86]

Spence provides a close-up of Ding's life and her seeming ability to adapt to her surroundings. Other sources, including her memoir of 1986, piece together a more comprehensive picture of her life. When assigned to Tangyuan, Ding lived in a chicken shed with her husband. Because of her illness (osteomyelitis), she was assigned light work – selecting eggs for hatching and feeding the chickens around her dormitory. At times, when her husband was sent to build roads during the winter, she was asked to engage in literacy projects for the benefit of the local community. She enthusiastically participated in local affairs such as mediating neighbourhood feuds and fixing roads. Due to the patronage of Wang Zhen, she did not lack supplies of paper, special food, and medicine in the famine years. The good relationships she enjoyed in the village actually made her hesitate to return to her job in Beijing when the opportunity arose.[87] It seems that living in Beidahuang did not bother her at all: she was satisfied with being a chicken run manager and doing light physical labour. "Why should not a writer raise chickens when common people can do it?" she said.[88] Ding did not consider her decade in Beidahuang to be a form of political banishment.[89]

Like Ding Ling, poet Ai Qing was also fortunate. Thanks to his personal connection to Wang Zhen, Ai Qing received favourable treatment in Farm 852. For him, physical labour was only symbolic, as his major work came in the form of writing poetry in praise of labour heroes and the great cause of land reclamation. He was appointed deputy director of a forestry centre and was offered his own house.[90] The experience of Ding and Ai show the importance of personal networks, even for those who were in disgrace.

As for artists, playwrights, and engineers who did not have personal connections with important figures, their professional expertise made their life easier. After working for several months on reservoir construction, Ding Cong, thanks to his ability to draw cartoons, was transferred to a part-time job editing a magazine entitled *Beidahuang wenyi* (Literature and Art in Beidahuang). Wu Zuguang had a similar experience. He served in an army art troupe writing plays in praise of land pioneers. Although they still needed to do some physical labour, their new posts provided them with benefits that other political exiles could hardly dream of – better living conditions, freedom to go to county towns, the chance to display their expertise, and, most important, better food.[91] In the difficult years, less manual labour and better food meant a greater chance of survival.

The End of Beidahuang Banishment

The political exiles granted favourable treatment were few in number. Of the thousands of Beijing rightists in Beidahuang, no more than twenty were transferred to less strenuous work before October 1959.[92] For the vast majority, the only chance to leave lives mired in hunger and hardship rested with periodic "removal of caps" (*zaimào*), which started in the fall of 1959. On the eve of the tenth anniversary of the People's Republic, CCP chairman Mao Zedong proposed to remove "rightist" labels from a proportion of people who were deemed to have behaved well during labour reform.[93] On Mao's suggestion, the CCP central authorities cautiously implemented plans to restore a small number of rightists. When the first phase of the plan was completed at the end of 1959, 37,506 people had their "caps" removed – 8.5 percent of all rightists.[94]

For rightists in the border regions, the process of cap removal started in early October 1959. Central observation teams were sent to army farms in Beidahuang, checking the files of the banished, consulting with leaders, and determining the number of those who should be rehabilitated.[95] Trying to leave Beidahuang, many Beijing rightists strove to perform well in their daily work. To their dismay, only a small portion of them was designated as rehabilitated. Of 925 rightists from central organizations and the military system in Farm 850, for instance, only forty-six had their labels removed. They were allowed to leave for new jobs in Beijing, Gansu, Shanxi, or better locations in Heilongjiang.[96] Those left behind were advised to continue their efforts. Disillusioned with this episode, many exiles realized that the end of their banishment and the return to normal life was not determined by their efforts but by other factors, such as designated quotas set from above. Disappointment set in.[97]

Ultimately, it was mass starvation and death that helped put an end to the internal exile. By the fall of 1960, incessant reports of deaths of Beidahuang rightists reached Beijing. This caused apprehension in the central government and prompted the acceleration of the processes of cap removal and the evacuation of rightists from the "death land."[98] In November 1960, central observation teams were again sent to Beidahuang to implement the second round of cap removal, which was much larger in scale than was that of the year before. In Farm 850, 127 had their caps removed and were relocated to interior provinces.[99] While the observation teams were discussing the performance of individual rightists, however, the deaths continued. Within less than one month, according to Dai Huang, four rightists on his team died of starvation and related illnesses.[100] Alerted to the flood of deaths, the central authorities made a quick decision. In January 1961, the observation teams announced that all the rightists from central government organs were to be allowed to leave the army farms.[101] From the end of 1960 to early 1961, Beijing rightists left the army farms of Beidahuang, where many of their fellow exiles lay forever. Some were assigned jobs in the interior and some were reallocated to less demanding locations in Heilongjiang.

Conclusion

During the post-1949 period, China's northern frontier regions have been used by the Communist government to facilitate its agendas of state consolidation and economic development. In the case of the northeastern frontier of Beidahuang, by banishing thousands of political offenders to that region, the government aimed to crush real or imagined forces of opposition, to remove undesirable elements from China's core, to facilitate land reclamation, and to facilitate the ideological renewal of offenders. Due to the severity of its physical environment, the importance of the exiles it received, and the way the government implemented this internal exile, Beidahuang can be seen as a window through which to view broader issues of frontier banishment in the PRC (though its isolation and remoteness made it a particularly fearsome place).

The social consequences of border banishment were devastating. The banishment caused tremendous suffering (physical and psychological) to the exiles and negatively affected the lives of their family members. The waste of human talent in China's educated elite is obvious as well. By punishing those who criticized but actually supported the regime, the CCP damaged its social foundation.

The government boasted of its achievements with regard to "reform through labour." The case of Beidahuang shows the opposite, however. Although the influx of thousands of political exiles into Beidahuang provided labour for land reclamation, lumbering, and the building of infrastructure, these contributions to economic growth were outweighed by the huge waste of intelligence. The influx of political exiles also added to the negative impact of land reclamation on the ecology of Beidahuang.

The party's alleged attempt at the ideological renewal of various offenders was undermined at local levels. The party leadership may have wished to focus on controlled rehabilitation rather than on meting out suffering; however, on the ground, under various cadres, political indoctrination was reduced to reprimand and "thought reform through labour" was reduced to slave labour. Political exiles who went to the border region with a degree of enthusiasm and with the intention of ideologically remoulding themselves came back with severe grievances against the government. In this sense, persecution and border banishment were not only destructive of China's educated elite but also detrimental to the party itself.

Notes

1 Joanna Waley-Cohen, *Exile in Mid-Qing China: Banishment to Xinjiang, 1758-1820* (New Haven: Yale University Press, 1991), 36-37.

2 Ibid., 48-49, 57; and Yang Bin, *Liubian jilue* [Notes from the Willow Palisades] (Taibei: Guangwen shuju, 1968), 18.

3 Waley-Cohen, *Exile in Mid-Qing China*, 57. According to Waley-Cohen, such crimes ranked among the most serious under the Qing law, and many of these exiles "had originally been sentenced to death but had had their sentence commuted."

4 According to aggregate statistics released by the Chinese government, for instance, around 12 million urban youths were sent down to rural areas from 1968 to 1975. See Thomas Bernstein, *Up to the Mountains and Down to the Villages: The Transfer of Youth from Urban to Rural China* (New Haven: Yale University Press, 1977), 2-3.

5 Frederick Teiwes, *Politics and Purges in China, Rectification and the Decline of Party Norms, 1950-1965* (Armonk, NY: M.E. Sharpe, 1993), 216-20; and Merle Goldman, "The Anti-Rightist Campaign," in *The Cambridge History of China*, vol. 14 (Cambridge: Cambridge University Press), 250-57.

6 Bo Yibo, *Ruogan zhongda juece yu shijian de huigu* [Reflections on several important decisions and events] (Beijing: Zhonggong zhongyang dangxiao chubanshe, 1993), 2:620; and

see Teiwes, *Politics and Purges*, 228-29. Some rightists tried to appeal their cases only to get their political status escalated to "counterrevolutionaries," due to their refusal to admit their "crimes" or "wrongdoings," and were sent to prison camps. See, for instance, the case of Hongda Harry Wu in his book *Bitter Winds*: a *Memoir of My Years in China's Gulag* (New York: John Wiley and Sons, 1994), 45-46.

7 With the triumph over the literati deviants at hand, Mao began to focus on leniency. At CCP internal conferences in December 1957 and January 1958, he stated that "we need to take disciplinary action against those rightists, but not too harsh"; that "we need to criticize them seriously but treat them leniently"; and that "the discipline is necessary, but a way out needs to be left for them." See Mao's speeches on 8 December 1957 and on 28 January 1958 in *Mao Zedong sixiang wansui* [Long live Mao Zedong's thought] (Beijing, 1967), 180, 190-91.

8 The stipulations on treatment were elaborate. According to a directive the central government issued in January 1958, the punishment meted out to rightists was to be broken down into six levels. Those with the first-level punishment were to be removed from their jobs and sent to "labour re-education camps"; those with the second were to be removed from their jobs and sent to "labour under supervision" in various locations; the other punishments included removal from posts, retaining jobs on a probationary basis, accepting reduced salaries, and so on. See Central Committee of the CCP and State Council, "The Stipulations on Disposal of the Rightists among State Employees and University Students" (29 January 1958), in *Zhou Enlai nianpu* [Chronicle of Zhou Enlai], edited by Zhongyang wenxian yanjiushi, 122-23 (Beijing: Zhongyang wenxian chubanshe, 1997). These modes of punishment constituted a formal institutional basis for banishment.

9 The severity of the penalty did not necessarily match the severity of the political denunciations the rightists received. Many famous rightists who suffered harsh condemnation by the CCP high leaders were not sent to labour reform but remained in Beijing, living a relatively easy life. Consider, for instance, the case of Zhang Bojun as presented in Zhang Yihe, *Wangshi bingbu ruyan* [Do not let bygones be bygones] (Beijing: Renmin wenxue chubanshe, 2004), 87.

10 For instance, those from the Beijing municipal government and the *Beijing Daily* were sent to a road construction site in a western suburb of Beijing. See Cong Weixi, *Zouxiang hundun* [Going to chaos] (Beijing: Zhongguo shehui kexue chubanshe, 1998), 48-49.

11 See Niu Han and Deng Jiuping, eds., *Jingji lu: Jiyi zhong de fan youpai yundong* [The thorny road: The anti-rightist campaign in memory] (Beijing: Jingji ribao chubanshe, 1998), 338. Although sending the rightists down to manual labour was a government decision and they were strongly pressured to leave, there was a degree of flexibility regarding their destinations. Liu Meng, a junior cadre in the Ministry of Communications, was originally to be relocated to Qinghai in the northwest, but when he asked to go to a land reclamation region in Heilongjiang, his request was approved. See Liu Meng, *Chuntian de yu qiutian qing* [Rain in spring, clear skies in autumn] (Beijing: Zhongguo gongren chubanshe, 2004), 63, 67.

12 Some "counterrevolutionaries" singled out from central organizations were sent to Xingkaihu labor reform camp, which is very close to the army farms of Beidahuang. Liu Naiyan of New China News Agency was one case. See his *Mirror: A Loss of Innocence in Mao's China* (Philadelphia: Xlibris Corp, 2001).

13 *Heilongjiang shengzhi guoying nongchang zhi* [Gazetteer of state farms in Heilongjiang] (Harbin: Heilongjiang renmin chubanshe, 1992), 6; *Wang Zhen zhuan*, [The biography of Wang Zhen] (Beijing: Dangdai zhongguo chubanshe, 2001), 68-70. In addition to the army farms, there were eight collective farms established in the nearby counties by "frontier youths" recruited from interior provinces. See *Heilongjiang shengzhi guoying nongchang zhi*, 85.

14 *Wang Zhen zhuan*, 70, 74-78; *Heilongjiang shengzhi guoying nongchang zhi*, 92-4. Li Hui, *Renzai xuanwo* [People in the eddy] (Jinan: Shandong huabao chubanshe, 1998), 297.

15 Ding Ling, *Fengxue renjian* [Blizzard world] (Xiamen: Xiamen daxue chubanshe, 1986), 3.

16 Yin Yi, for instance, recalls that he took a "rightist express" to Beidahuang, see his *Huishou canyang yihan shan* [The setting of the sun over the mountain] (Beijing: Shiyue wenyi chubanshe, 2003), 26; however, Dai Huang indicates that he and his five fellows went to

Beidahuang in small groups without any supervision. See Dai Huang, *Jiusi yisheng* [Narrow escape from death] (Beijing: Zhongyang bianyi chubanshe, 1998), 95.

17 Wu Yongliang, *Yuxue feifei* [Floating rain and snow] (Beijing: Zhongguo xiju chubanshe, 2002), 30-31, 43.

18 Hu Ping, *Chan Ji: Kunan de jitan* [Allegorical words: Bitter sacrificial altar] (Guangzhou: Guangdong luyou chubanshe, 1998), 454.

19 Yang Bin, *Liubian jilue* (Taibei: Guangwen shuju, 1968), 4, 12; Thomas Gottschang and Diana Lary, *Swallows and Settlers: The Great Migration from North China to Manchuria* (Ann Arbor: University of Michigan Press, 2000), 46.

20 See Mei Jimin, *Beidahuang* (Taibei: Shuifurong chubanshe, 1975), 5-6. Mei believes that, because the vast territory in eastern Siberia was legally under Qing jurisdiction due to the Treaty of Nerchinsk (signed by China and Russia in 1689), the term Beidahuang bore a broader implication.

21 Ibid., 6.

22 Zhang Linchi, *Dangdai Zhongguo de nongken shiye* [Land reclamation in contemporary China] (Beijing: Zhongguo shehui kexue chubanshe, 1986), 24-26.

23 For a general account of Shandong migration to Manchuria, see Gottschang and Lary, *Swallows and Settlers*.

24 Jiang Dongping, "Weiman riben kaituotuan de zuie lishi" [The evil history of Japanese pioneer groups in Manchuria], in *Zongheng* 4 (1999): 47-49; *Heilongjiang shengzhi guoying nongchang zhi*, 4.

25 Wu Yongliang, *Yuxue feifei*, 8. According to Wu, a journalist, You Zai of the *Dagong Daily*, appealed to remain in Beijing on the grounds of his health problem, only to be declined immediately by his work unit and scolded by anti-rightist activists.

26 Ding Ling, *Fengxue renjian*, 16-8; Zhou Jianqiang, *Nie Gannu Zhuan* [Biography of Nie Gannu] (Chengdu: Sichuan renmin chubanshe, 1987), 219-20.

27 Ding Ling, *Fengxue renjian*, 16-7. One of Ding's pastimes was to go through copies of *People's Pictorial* looking at scenes of the Xing'an Mountains in Manchuria.

28 Cong Weixi, *Zouxiang hundun*, 7, 121.

29 In May 1942, Mao made his famous "Talks at the Yan'an Forum of Literature and Art," in which he required writers and artists to adhere to the party line – to go down to the grassroots and write about them so that they might serve the masses well and thus qualify as progressive writers. The Yan'an Talks served as a guideline for the production of literature and art in Maoist China. See Mao Zedong, *Mao Zedong xuanji* [Selected Works of Mao Zedong] (Beijing: Remin chubanshe, 1967), 807-8.

30 Ding Ling, *Fengxue renjian*, 17.

31 Zhou Jianqiang, *Nie Gannu Zhuan*, 220.

32 Xin Suwei, *Ding Cong zhuan* [Biography of Ding Cong] (Beijing: Zhongguo gongren chubanshe, 1993), 182-84.

33 Zheng Xiaofeng, *Ding Ling zai Beidahuang* [Ding Ling in Beidahuang] (Wuhan: Hubei renmin chubanshe, 1989), 78. Many other rightists indicated that they went through similar experiences after the campaign. Wu Yongliang recalls that, given the instructions from above to isolate rightists, "there was no nodding, no hello, no smile from friends, who began to treat us as strangers and shunned us as "a contagious disease." See Wu Yongliang, *Yuxue feifei*, 14. Ding Ling and leading rightists Zhang Bojun and Chu Anping were renounced by their children and/or cut off from familial relationships. See Ding Ling, *Fengxue renjian*, 64; Hu Ping, *Chan Ji*, 508-10. Opera actress Xin Fengxia's boss tried to persuade her to divorce her husband Wu Zuguang, but she refused. See Niu Han and Deng Jiuping, *Jingji lu*, 87.

34 Ding Ling, *Fengxue renjian*, 17-8; Xu Chengbei, "Nie Gannu zai Beidahuang (Nie Gannu in Beidahuang)," in *Yuan shang cao: jiyi zong de fanyoupai yundong* [Grass on the land: The anti-rightist campaign in memory], edited by Niu Han and Deng Jiuping (Beijing: Jingji ribao chubanshe, 1998), 308.

35 When Ding Cong was about to leave for Beidahuang, the director of his work unit encouraged him to show his best performance in labour reform and promised to get him back in one year. See Xin Suwei, *Ding Cong zhuan*, 186.

36 Dai Huang, *Jiusi yisheng*, 97.

37 Ibid.

38 According to the farm gazetteers, 925 rightists were sent from Beijing to different branches of Farm 850, and 486 rightists were to Farm 853, totalling 1,411. See *Bawuling nongchangshi* [Gazetteer of Farm 850] (Hulin: Bawuling nongchangshi bianxie bangongshi, 1986), 30; and *Bawusan nongchangzhi* [Gazetteer of Farm 853] (Jiamusi: Bawusan nongchangzhi bianxie bangongshi 1986), 2. The figures of Beijing rightists provided by the two gazetteers are not consistent with those given by other sources, however. For instance, *Wang Zhen zhuan* (2:78) indicates 1,039, and Zheng Jiazhen, *Zhongguo dongbeijiao* [The northeast corner of China] (Harbin: Heilongjiang renmin chubanshe, 1998), 66, indicates 1,327. A possible reason for this discrepancy is that these gazetteers include the rightists sent from various military units of Beijing, while others did not. Another possible reason is that the spouses of the Beijing rightists who came along might have been incorporated into the rightist list in some sources but not in others. See Dai Huang, *Jiusi yisheng*, 103.

39 Significant information about these political exiles may be drawn from their memoirs and biographies. Zheng Jiazhen, in his lengthy report *Zhongguo dongbeijiao*, also describes the lives of Ding Ling, Ai Qing, Nie Gannu, and Wu Zuguang in Beidahuang.

40 *Bawuling nongchangshi*, 30.

41 Dai Huang, *Jiusi yisheng*, 117-18.

42 Zheng Xiaofeng, interview (Beijing, 5 July 2004). Huang Wu also recalls that Farm 853 "was a new world, where we felt liberated psychologically, and there was no discrimination from outside anymore." See Huang Wu, *Mahuatang waiji* [Mahua Hall ephemera] (Guangzhou: Guangdong wenhua chubanshe, 1989), 189.

43 *Bawuling nongchangshi*, 31; Dai Huang, *Jiusi yisheng*, 113-15; Liu Meng, *Chuntian de yu qiutian qing*, 94-96; *Wang Zhen zhuan*, 78-79; and Ding Ling, *Fengxue renjian*, 14-5. All acknowledge Wang Zhen's visit and his paternal care for the rightists. Wang Zhen's warm gesture was seen as a sign of the party's concern for the banished intellectuals.

44 *Bawuling nongchangshi*, 31; Dai Huang, *Jiusi yisheng*, 115. Regarding rightist comments on "civilized banishment," see Dai Huang, *Jiusi yisheng*, 119-20.

45 Dai Huang, *Jiusi yisheng*, 103.

46 Xu Chengbei, "Nie Gannu zai Beidahuang," in *Yuan shang cao*, 309.

47 Dai Huang, *Jiusi yisheng*, 108, Liu Meng, *Chuntian de yu qiutian qing*, 108-10; Wu Yongliang, *Yuxue feifei*, 87-9; Yin Yi, *Huishou canyang yihan shan*, 41 (see also various documented family crises, most of which ended in divorce).

48 Huang Wu, *Mahuatang waiji*, 5, 16, 26.

49 Zhang Linchi, *Dangdai Zhongguo de nongken shiye*, 18-19.

50 Dai Huang, *Jiusi yisheng*, 125-26.

51 Ibid., 120; Wu Yongliang, *Yuxue feifei*, 7, 64. Johanna Waley-Cohen shows that Qing exiles were allowed to do business or to work in post stations and on river patrol (see Waley-Cohen, *Exile in Mid-Qing China*, 58, 224). However, the recollections of the rightists all indicate that their regular work involved heavy manual labour. Dai Huang recalls that he and his fellow exiles were once forced to work for fifty-six hours with very little sleep when constructing an irrigation canal. See Dai Huang, *Jiusi yisheng*, 127.

52 Huang Wu, *Mahuatang waiji*, 189.

53 Ibid., 37, 59; Dai Huang, *Jiusi yisheng*, 141-43.

54 Hu Ping, *Chan Ji*, 601; Dai Huang, *Jiusi yisheng*, 175. Dai Huang was himself a survivor of charcoal making; he once fainted and fell into a charcoal kiln, whereupon he was rescued by his friends and given artificial respiration.

55 See Niu Han and Deng Jiuping, *Jingji lu*, 309-10.

56 Dai Huang, *Jiusi yisheng*, 158-9.

57 Yin Yi, *Huishou canyang yihan shan*, 49. Zheng Xiaofeng interviews.

58 Wu Yongliang, *Yuxue feifei*, 79-80. Wu recalls that, when his team was working in the mountains, it was so cold inside their huts that "neither pen nor ball-pen could be used since ink would simply freeze."

59 Dai Huang, *Jiusi yisheng*, 127-8; Yin Yi, *Huishou canyang yihan shan*, 64; Hu Ping, *Chan Ji*, 618-19.

60 Wang Zheng, "Menghui huangyuan" [Dreaming back to the wilderness], in *Lishi zai shenpan* [Retrial of History], edited by Liu Meng (Chengdu: Sichuan renmin chubanshe, 1996), 338.

61 Many survivors of Beidahuang banishment said that having to deal with mosquitoes was one of their worst experiences there. See Yin Yi, *Huishou canyang yihan shan*, 33; Wu Yongliang, *Yuxue feifei*, 60; Zheng Jiazhen, *Zhongguo dongbeijiao*, 67.

62 Philip Williams and Yenna Wu note that Russia's gulag almost never compelled its inmates to listen to propaganda or write self-criticisms and confessions. In contrast, in Maoist China indoctrination sessions were persuasive and were usually taken extremely seriously in labour camps. See Philip Williams and Yenna Wu, *The Great Wall of Confinement: The Chinese Prison Camp through Contemporary Fiction and Reportage* (Berkeley: University of California Press, 2004), 112-13.

63 Given the nature of forced labour, the restriction of individual freedom, and the practice of physical and psychological abuse, the army farms in Beidahuang could certainly be considered to constitute a special form of labour camp – the camp "without walls."

64 Nie Gannu, *Nie Gannu zixu* [Autobiography of Nie Gannu] (Beijing: Tuanjie chubanshe, 1998), 450, 452.

65 A much sung song, "Let's Build Our Beautiful Beidahuang," was composed by an enthusiastic rightist after exhausting work. See Dai Huang, *Jiusi yisheng*, 119.

66 Huang Miaozi recalls that, in the early months of his stay in Beidahuang, he read *Red Flag* (a leading party journal) and the works of Marx and Engels (Li Hui, *Renzai xuanwo*, 307). Nie Gannu also brought many of Mao's works with him. See, Niu Han and Deng Jiuping, "Yuan shang cao," *Jingji lu*, 309.

67 Yin Yi, *Huishou canyang yihan shan*, 63.

68 Wu Yongliang, *Yuxue feifei*, 97-98.

69 Ibid., 70.

70 In the Yunshan Branch, directors Lu and Zhu frequently used coarse language to scold rightist workers during their xunhua for their failure to fulfill work quotas. See Dai Huang, *Jiusi yisheng*, 131; Yin Yi, *Huishou canyang yihan shan*, 51.

71 Li Hui, *Renzai xuanwo*, 305; Wu Yongliang, *Yuxue feifei*, 66-67.

72 Yin Yi, *Huishou canyang yihan shan*, 63.

73 Analysis of memoirs of the political exiles (Liu Meng, Nie Gannu, Huang Wu, Dai Huang, Wang Zheng, Yin Yi, and Wu Yongliang) shows that, of all the rightists who were banished to Beidahuang, those in Yunshan Branch suffered the most. They worked longer hours, had poorer accommodation, less food, and higher death rates during the famine year.

74 Niu Han and Deng Jiuping, *Jingji lu*, 311-2. Even in Yunshan Branch there were helpful cadres who, like political instructor Liu Wen, were cherished by Dai Huang, Yin Yi, and Wu Yongliang. Liu cared about the well-being of the rightists and showed great respect for them. See Yin Yi, *Huishou canyang yihan shan*, 34-6; Dai Huang, *Jiusi yisheng*, 128-29; Wu Yongliang, *Yuxue feifei*, 37-8.

75 Wang Zheng "Meng hui huangyuan," in Liu Meng, *Chuntian de yu qiutian qing*, 347-48.

76 Dai Huang, *Jiusi yisheng*, 131-33.

77 *Bawusan nongchangzhi*, 132.

78 Yin Yi, *Huishou canyang yihan shan*, 66; Dai Huang, *Jiusi yisheng*, 213; Liu Meng, *Chuntian de yu qiutian qing*, 9. Wu Yongliang also recalls that, at times, he and his fellows were sent to dig up rat holes for soy beans that had been stored by field rats. Six days of doing this brought back more than ten bags of soy beans, which was an important supplement to their food supply. Wu Yongliang, *Yuxue feifei*, 112-13. Many survivors of Beidahuang banishment, such as Dai Huang, Liu Meng, and Huang Wu, ate field rats and/or snakes. For consumption of "food substitutes," see Zheng Jiazhen, *Zhongguo dongbeijiao*, 159.

79 Yang Congdao, "Bawuling Yunshan xumuchang liuren feizhengchang siwang mingdan" [List of abnormal deaths in the Yunshan Branch of Farm 850], Unpublished Note.

80 Dai Huang, *Jiusi yisheng*, 244-47.

81 Ibid., 225-32. This mass death is also documented by Yin Yi (Yin Yi, *Huishou canyang yihan shan*, 87-89); and Wu Yongliang (Wu Yongliang, *Yuxue feifei*, 133-34). Dai Huang believes

that more than one year of prolonged hunger made rightists in this branch extremely weak and pale, which, compounded by intensive labour in vile weather, resulted in many deaths.

82 Yang Congdao, "Bawuling Yunshan xumuchang liuren feizhengchang siwang mingdan"; and Dai Huang, *Jiusi yisheng*, 241.

83 Dai Huang, *Jiusi yisheng*, 193.

84 Ibid., 247.

85 For instance, the dead fellow campmates frequently entered the dreams of Huang Wu, which saddened and disturbed him. Huang Wu, *Mahuatang waiji*, 48-49, 56-59. Wu Yongliang also says that his experience in Beidahuang gave rise to endless nightmares that obsessed him for dozens of years after he was released. See Wu Yongliang, *Yuxue feifei*, 2.

86 Jonathan Spence, *The Gate of Heavenly Peace: The Chinese and Their Revolution, 1895-1980* (New York: Penguin Books, 1982), 339.

87 Ding Ling, *Fengxue renjian*, 48-56; Tani Barlow and Gary Bjorge, eds., *I Myself Am a Woman: Selected Writings of Ding Ling* (Boston: Beacon Press, 1989), 44; Zheng Xiaofeng, *Ding Ling zai Beidahuang*, 19-23.

88 Zheng Xiaofeng, *Ding Ling zai Beidahuang*, 73.

89 After being released and getting her case reversed in the late 1970s, Ding Ling expressed an even more positive attitude towards the party. She seldom talked about her personal afflictions in Beidahuang but considered her suffering during the Maoist period to be a special trial the party afforded to her as well as a good opportunity to steel her revolutionary spirit. See Zheng Xiaofeng, *Ding Ling zai Beidahuang*, 84.

90 Zhou Hongxing, *Ai Qing zhuan*. [Biography of Ai Qing] (Beijing: Zuojia chubanshe, 1993), 441-44; Zheng Jiazhen, *Zhongguo dongbeijiao*, 76-77.

91 Xin Suwei, *Ding Cong zhuan*, 188-89, 192; Zhang Jie, *Wu Zuguang beihuan qu* [Wu Zuguang: Vicissitudes of life] (Chengdu: Sichuan wenyi chubanshe, 1986), 343-44.

92 Ding Cong, interview, 16 August 2003; Yang Congdao, interview 28 July 2004.

93 *Zhongyang wenxian yanjiushi*, *Jianguo yilai zhongyao wenxian xuanbian* [Selected collection of important documents since the establishment of the PRC] (Beijing: Zhongyang wenxian chubanshe, 1996) 12:528-29.

94 Hu Ping, *Chan Ji*, 660.

95 Yin Yi, *Huishou canyang yihan shan*, 70-71; Wu Yongliang, *Yuxue feifei*, 108-9; Dai Huang, *Jiusi yisheng*, 168.

96 Yu Shanpu, "Beidahuang liuren mingdan" [Name list of the Beidahuang exiles], unpublished note. In Team Six of Farm 853, as far as Zheng Xiaofeng can remember, only five or six Beijing rightists (out of more than one hundred) got their rightist caps removed in the fall of 1959. Zheng Xiaofeng, interview, 5 July 2004, Beijing.

97 Yin Yi, *Huishou canyang yihan shan*, 70-71; Dai Huang, *Jiusi yisheng*, 168-69.

98 No official source has disclosed how the central government made the decision to evacuate the Beidahuang rightists. According to journalists Zheng Xiaofeng and Dai Huang, however, when Zhou Enlai, in the fall of 1960, discovered the discrepancy between the numbers of Beijing rightists who had been sent to Beidahuang and those still alive, he demanded an explanation from Wang Jingkun, director of Mudanjiang Land Reclamation Bureau. When Zhou found out, from the ambivalent report Wang provided, that the majority of deaths were the result of edema, malnutrition, and disease, he realized the jeopardy these people were in and immediately demanded the withdrawal of the Beijing rightists. Zheng Xiaofeng, interview; Dai Huang, *Jiusi yisheng*, 267-68.

99 The names of those whose labels were removed are recorded by Yu Shanpu.

100 Dai Huang, *Jiusi yisheng*, 253-55.

101 Yu Shanpu, "Beidahuang liuren mingdan."

12
L'état, c'est nous, or We Have Met the Oppressor and He Is Us: The Predicament of Minority Cadres in the PRC

Stevan Harrell

A Sad Story of a Young Man Torn

In the last chapter of *The Age of Wild Ghosts,* his magnificent ethnography of the experience of a Lolopo (Yi) township in Yunnan through fifty years of the People's Republic of China, Erik Mueggler tells the story of one Qi Haiyun. Qi Haiyun was a twenty-five-year old, middle-school educated man who was made brigade party secretary in the early 1990s, a time when the county government had decided to carry out a sterilization program in order to consolidate the local implementation of the national planned-birth campaign. Qi had attended a two-day conference of local cadres in the county seat, where he was given instructions to arrange the sterilization, by tubal ligation, of every woman under forty-two years of age who had already borne the allowed maximum of two children.[1] Qi announced his decision at an outdoor film showing, saying that lists of women to be sterilized would be posted at regular intervals and that those whose names appeared on the lists were to walk to the township clinic to have the procedure performed. Those who did not go voluntarily would be captured, handcuffed, and led to the clinic, where the sterilization would be performed without anaesthesia. In addition to this, their families would have all their livestock confiscated.

A few women were intimidated by the threats and had the procedure performed, but before long resistance developed. This resistance was based on a local belief that tubal ligation would stop the flow of sexual fluids from the ovaries into the uterus and, thus, not only render women incapable of enjoying sex but also sap their physical energy to the point where even ordinary household labour would be difficult. Whether due to this belief or to the crude way in which the sterilizations were performed or both, many women did, in fact, become ill and/or very weak after the procedure, and soon those who had not been sterilized began refusing to go. In addition, women began to get together and hound the party secretary. They would gather outside Qi's house and heckle him, follow him around the village, taunt him, throw things, and make his life increasingly miserable. Eventually he was compelled, with the assent of higher-level officials, to call off the compulsory sterilizations. But the pressure did not stop; his own wife lay in bed, recovering slowly, if at all, from the procedure, and he had to scramble to do both the women's and the men's work in his household. Finally, desperate, Qi hanged himself. Unfortunately, the rope broke, so he was forced to continue living. People then backed off a little, figuring that, as his life was now ruined, they didn't need to harass him any further.[2]

The Position of Minority Cadres in the People's Republic of China

The story of Qi Haiyun should be familiar to those who know the local-level workings of China's birth-control campaign; similar stories can be found in Huang Shu-min's *The Spiral Road*, in which a local party secretary negotiates, more successfully than Qi but not without cost, enough abortions for his village to make its birth quota for the year[3] as well as in other ethnographic accounts. In every part of China, ever since the beginning of the People's Republic of China, the so-called basic-level cadres (*jiceng ganbu*) have been called upon to play a dual role that involves representing the state to the community and representing the community to the state. Basic-level cadres are those at the village and township levels, or, during the collective period, at the team, brigade, and commune levels. Team and brigade level cadres are almost always drawn from the population of the unit they lead. This dual role has placed them in the kind of double-bind situation common to people who find themselves in the position of being state-community intermediaries, be they the *kapitans China* of overseas Chinese communities in the Dutch Empire or government-appointed chiefs in various colonial situations from British-ruled Africa to US Indian reservations. Throughout PRC history, the ability of basic-level cadres to negotiate state-community relations has been seen as crucial to the success of policy implementation.[4]

But Qi Haiyun's situation is somewhat different from that of the majority of basic-level cadres because he is a Lolopo, a member of the Yi nationality, an officially designated minority nationality with about 7.5 million members living mostly in Yunnan, Guizhou, and Sichuan.[5] As a Lolopo cadre, Qi was a broker not only between the state and local community but also between a local culture and a modernizing state dominated by a hegemonic national culture associated primarily with the majority Han nationality. As so many authors have pointed out,[6] in PRC state discourse, modernity, progress, wealth, and, in the Maoist period, revolution, have been associated with the "advanced" Han people. Han people comprise not only the majority of China's population (about 91 percent at present) and almost all the leaders of the central party and government but also the great majority of the highly educated, urban, and wealthy segments of the Chinese populace. This means that the Communist Party has implemented what I elsewhere refer to as a "civilizing project," an attempt to "raise" the economic, educational, cultural, and moral level of the non-Han peoples up to that of the Han majority.[7] From the viewpoint of state policy makers, there is thus an additional component to the backwardness of people like the Lolopo. They are not only poor, illiterate, and ignorant like ordinary Han peasants,[8] but they also have the further handicap of being part of a culture seen to be full of superstition, ignorance, and remnants of the slave and early feudal stages of human development.[9]

From the standpoint of people like the Lolopo, the situation looks both different and similar. They and other minority peoples view the Chinese state as a Han state, as a creation of people not only ethnically, linguistically, and culturally different from themselves but also often their oppressors. Sometimes they also display a kind of self-stigmatization,[10] being resigned to the idea of the Han as their moral and cultural superiors. It is clear to just about everyone in China that the state is a Han creation: its language, its ideas, its policies, its national leaders all come from the Han cultural tradition (as mediated, of course, by Western ideas such as Marxism, revolution, and development) and from the Han ethnic group. The Chinese state celebrates itself in its constitution and its propaganda as a "unified state of diverse nationalities" (*tongyi de duo minzu guojia*), but its direction and its directors come from the Han. Local minority communities thus are potentially more separated, more alienated, from state policy and its policy makers than are ordinary Han local communities; ethnic, linguistic, and cultural differences are piled on top of the differences of wealth, power, literacy, and education that separate high-level leaders from members of Han village communities.

If state-minority relations, or state-community relations in minority areas, were Han-minority relations, there would be very little to write about. We would have a situation of clear and direct colonial rule, a case for international human rights and self-determination activists, and an academic topic that could do little more than catalogue injustices, outrages, and oppression. But the Chinese state, Han in its policy-making leadership and in its intellectual and policy directions, is not entirely Han in its personnel. An important part of minority policy and state administration in minority areas is to bring minority people into the state as cadres at various levels: not only the basic-level brigade or village cadres like the unfortunate Qi Haiyun but also salaried government cadres at the commune or township, county, prefectural, and provincial levels of administration. This policy has several manifestations. First, the constitution of the PRC states that, in any of the minority autonomous districts at the provincial ("region"), prefectural, or county level, the titular head of government (who is always outranked by the party secretary but nevertheless is usually a powerful person in any administrative unit), must be a member of the minority nationality to whom the so-called autonomous administrative status is granted. Second, there has been, since the early 1950s, and before that in some areas such as Western Inner Mongolia,[11] a consistent program to train members of minorities as state cadres. In the southwest in the 1950s, for example, every autonomous prefecture had its Minority Cadre School (*minzu ganbu xuexiao*), where promising young minority boys were taught everything from basic literacy to Marxist-Leninist theory and administrative and technical skills, preparing them to take up administrative, cultural, or (less often) technical positions in the local bureaucracy. At the same time, nationalities institutes (*minzu xueyuan*), some of which have recently been "promoted" to the status of universities (*minzu daxue*), were established in Beijing and several regions and provinces for the primary purpose of training both teachers and cadres to staff educational and bureaucratic institutions in their home areas.

As a consequence of these policies, minorities predominate both in higher level administrative positions and in certain bureaus of most minority prefectures and counties (they are numerically dominant primarily in the general administrative, educational, cultural, and police fields, less so in the economic, financial, technical, and scientific fields, where they are often considered to lack the proper training).[12] They are perhaps less predominant in the provincial-level autonomous region bureaucracies, partly because three of the five regions, despite their "autonomous" status, have Han majority populations (Ningxia, Inner Mongolia, and Guangxi) and perhaps partly because the other two autonomous regions (Xinjiang and Tibet) harbour serious separatist movements and, in some ways, are treated by the central government as occupied territories. But even in the autonomous regions, minorities form a substantial portion of cadres at all administrative levels. In addition, in several provinces that do not have formal "autonomous" status but have had large minority populations (Yunnan and Guizhou, Gansu, Qinghai, and Sichuan), at least since the early 1980s, one governor, lieutenant-governor, or vice-secretary has been a minority person. There are also national-level bodies, the State Nationalities Commission and the Nationalities Commission of the National People's Congress, that are customarily led and staffed primarily by members of minority groups.

Finally, there has been an effort to have minorities represented in various deliberative bodies at the provincial and national levels. The National People's Congress and the Chinese People's Political Consultative Conference (*zhengxie*) have high proportions of minority representation, and, in fact, people in Beijing around the time of these decorative assemblies' yearly meetings often comment on the visual spectacle of minority deputies, dressed not in the everyday Chinese work clothes that they would wear to the office but, rather, in the "national costumes" of their respective "nationalities."

In addition, in recent years the State Council has always included at least one minority councillor or vice-premier.

It is thus clear that minorities play a large part in the administration of many regions of China. They do so, however, primarily by virtue of their status as members of minority nationalities. It is rarer for a minority person to be appointed as a provincial- or ministerial-level official in a post that has nothing to do with the constitutional position of minorities in the "multinational" state. This does happen, of course, since some minorities manage to move out of the minority educational and bureaucratic tracks into the "mainstream" tracks, but my impression (I have not been able to find any figures) is that this is relatively rare.[13]

Where minorities have hardly ever been represented, however, is in the actual policy-making apparatus of the party-state. Only one non-Han person has held even alternate membership in the Political Bureau of the Central Committee or has risen to a state post as high as that of government or party vice-chairman. This was Ulanhu, a non-Mongolian speaking Mongol Communist anti-Japanese activist of the 1940s who, at various times, was party secretary, governor, military commander, and PLA political commissar of Inner Mongolia as well as an alternate politburo member and vice-premier. Paradoxically, the ethnic conflict embodied in Ulanhu's position was actually not very different from that of an ordinary village cadre like Qi Haiyun, and his case will be discussed in more detail below. But it is important to remember that he is the only one who ever made it close enough to the centre of power to have any influence at all on national policy.

It would be tempting to see minorities who rise to leadership positions at whatever level simply as co-opted by the Han party-state and its projects, or as assimilated into the mainstream Han culture, or even, in some cases, as shameless collaborators with an occupying power. After all, state policy recognizes minority cultures as backward and minority people as targets of ultimate assimilation, and participating in state administrative or educational bureaucracies is, in one sense, to display complicity with the state's overall program of first revolution and then modernization – both of which point ultimately to the elimination of "backwardness" and cultural difference. Many minority cadres, especially those from the second or third generation of cadre families (but see Ulanhu, above) do not speak their "native" languages, spend little time in the villages where the majority of non-Muslim minorities live,[14] often marry Han, and act in much of their everyday lives, from their eating habits to their personal interactions with fellow-bureaucrats, just like their Han counterparts. In other words, their lives are those of ordinary Chinese citizens. But my personal experience with minority cadres at levels from the production group to the prefecture, as well as my reading of ethnographic sources from other regions of the

People's Republic, leads me to question the assumption that minority cadres are nothing but stooges for the majority. Instead, I see the position of minority cadres, not only at the basic levels but at all levels up to the prefecture and higher, as characterized by the same tug between community and state interests as was evident in the sad case of Qi Haiyun, who was trying to be part of a Lolopo family and a Lolopo community at the same time that he was trying to implement the state birth-control policy. Simply put, minority cadres at all levels are trapped between the state and the local community. The state not only employs them but convinces most of them of the rightness of its basic directions, if not necessarily of all its detailed policies. The local community, variously defined as village, ethnic group, or state-defined *minzu* or "nationality," commands both their practical and their emotional loyalty. In the remainder of this article, I want to describe this internal tug-of-war and the way it works for individual minority cadres, some of them personal acquaintances of mine, and some of them people like Qi Haiyun or Ulanhu, whom I have read about in books but never met. In doing so, I hope to illustrate some of the paradoxes of the Chinese state at the (internal) borders as well as some of the questions for the future development of the People's Republic of China as a professed multinational state.

Some Minority Cadres

Leader Hxielie Nzyhxa[15]

When I first met him in 1994, Nzyhxa was sixty years old, a recently retired high administrative official of Liangshan Yi Autonomous Prefecture in southwestern Sichuan, a poor and difficult to reach administrative unit with a population of about 4.5 million people. Half of these people are members of the Nuosu ethnic group, classified by the state, like the Lolopo, as members of the Yi minzu (see note 2). I was told by others that he had been nominated for an even higher post but that complaints had been raised by bureaucratic rivals and so he was passed over for the position and had instead gone to the prefectural People's Consultative Conference, a typical sinecure for someone whose climb up the administrative ladder has been halted in late middle-age. After dinner one evening, I and another Nuosu friend were invited to the family home, a pleasant series of rooms around a tree-shaded courtyard with a night-time view of the city lights of Xichang. The interior was, I quickly noticed, decorated entirely with Nuosu-themed artwork, from the oil painting on the wall, showing a young woman in a pleated skirt and embroidered top, to the gold- and silver-coloured bas-relief depictions of Nuosu legends wrapped around the pillars in the second-floor sitting room, to the red-yellow-black-lacquered cups into which Nzyhxa poured strong liquor to welcome me to Liangshan and wish me success in my work with local Nuosu scholars. What was immediately striking to me was the ethnicity of it all. Here was a man who was a Communist Party member, a former city-level party secretary who had a desk full of typical Chinese government bureaucratic memos and reports that he had either written or needed to review for his work, who had in his younger years played a part in suppressing the ethnic rebellion against the Democratic Reforms of 1955-57, which abolished the slave-holding system in Nuosu areas and weakened the political power of local clans and clan leaders. But he wanted to talk to me about the glories of Yi culture, to thank me for coming from such a far and wealthy country to pay attention to the Yi, and to encourage me to continue cooperating with local scholars and with Yi scholars generally to make Yi culture better known to the world at large. Unlike just about all Han cadres and scholars whom I had met, he said nothing to me about China, about Chinese culture, about my coming from a rich country to a poor country to help out. I was welcome (and he would have his chauffeur take me to a village to conduct field research the next day) because I was interested in the Yi. That's what he was interested in – he who had been a high official in the Chinese government.

Nzyhxa was born in 1934 in a village in a county north of Xichang whose population is about half Nuosu and half Han. As he and members of his family emphasized to me many times, his clan was one of the most prominent in that area and, already in the 1930s, boasted a few boys with enough education to read, write, and speak basic Chinese, though their everyday language was Nuosu. Nzyhxa himself, at the age of one year, moved from his native village to his mother's native village, in the flatlands north of Xichang, and was raised until age eight by his mother's relatives, members of a community that was strongly bilingual and bicultural (unlike the Nuosu of his native area). This undoubtedly gave him a head start in understanding Han language and culture and, perhaps, contributed to his later success as a Chinese bureaucrat. Immediately after the CCP takeover of Liangshan in 1950, and before the Democratic Reforms, Nzyhxa was selected to attend the Ethnic Cadres School and was several times selected as a "leading person in promoting ethnic harmony." From there he was accepted to a university in Beijing, where he finished a regular bachelor's degree and, significantly, met his wife, a woman of mixed Han and minority ancestry from Inner Mongolia, who was working as a professional host and guide in the Nationalities Palace in the capital.

After returning to Liangshan, Nzyhxa took up various posts in the then prefectural capital of Zhaojue; he rose rapidly through the bureaucratic hierarchy and, although he was briefly forced from office during the Cultural Revolution, quickly resumed his climb up the administrative ladder beginning in the mid-1970s, taking high-level posts in the government and party of the city of Xichang after the prefectural capital was moved there in 1979.

During his tenure in these posts, Nzyhxa was by all reports a creative, able, and popular official precisely because of the things he was perceived to have done for the Yi. Most important of these was his legendary role in getting money from the State Education Commission in Beijing to build the prefectural Minority Middle School on the outskirts of town. Xichang, despite its status as capital of a Yi autonomous prefecture, has a population that is about 90 percent Han, and to have a prestigious middle school that was dedicated primarily to educating the Yi and other minorities from all over the prefecture not only provided an avenue of social mobility for talented Nuosu children but also was a matter of cultural pride. But, at first, Nzyhxa did not succeed in obtaining the requisite financing from provincial authorities. Frustrated after many attempts, the story goes, he got on the train to Beijing, packing his *vala*, or Nuosu fringed cape, in his suitcase. For several days, he practically camped out in the State Education Commission Office, from opening to closing, dressed in his vala, until the relevant officials approved his request for the money to build the school. This sounded apocryphal to me when I first heard it, but later I asked Nzyhxa if he had indeed worn his vala, and he smiled and said that he had. Nzyhxa also advocated establishing the prefectural Nationalities Research Institute, presided over the rebuilding of the Museum of Slave Society, and established the International Torch Festival first held in August of 1992 and several times since.

Since his retirement, Nzyhxa has busied himself, like any influential local person in China, with attracting foreign and domestic investment to his prefecture; he has also, however, busied himself with promoting Yi cultural activities, and he was instrumental in securing many of the important artifacts that were displayed in an exhibit that I and two Nuosu scholars curated in Seattle in 2000. Still, despite our repeated urgings, he would not use the funds I had secured to travel to Seattle to speak at the exhibit opening. He said he was delighted to have been of service to a project that introduced Yi culture to the world but that someone else should use the money.

Leader Luovu Lapu

I have only met Lapu once, though I am well acquainted with his classificatory brother[16] and one of his daughters, who has an American PhD. I met him at the Central Nationalities Institute in 1994; he had heard of my efforts on behalf of the Yi and had told his daughter that he wanted to meet me. At this time he was head of the Nationalities Commission of the National People's Congress, and I of course assumed that I would go to see him and be received with great formality and not much substance. Nervously, I dialled the number his daughter had given me, and to my surprise Chairman Lapu answered the phone himself (it must have been his private line) and insisted that, since he had a car and a chauffeur, it would be very easy for him to come to see me in the rather embarrassingly ramshackle reception room at the foreigners' dormitory at the institute, which he did. I was impressed with his height (we stood back-to-back and he turned out to be a centimetre or so taller than I, or a tad over six-feet-one), the total lack of a southwestern accent in his Chinese, and his courtly, charismatic manner. We chatted about this and that, but he wanted to find out whether I could really speak his native language; and, when I could, he got sad. He said, "Here you are, a foreigner, and you can converse with me in Nuohxo, and even two of my three daughters don't speak it very well, and many of my nieces and nephews not at all. We're losing our culture. How do we regain it?"

Lapu has had a much more illustrious career in the Chinese bureaucracy than has Hxielie Nzyhxa. He was born into an aristocratic family[17] in the 1930s in Mianning county, just to the north of Xichang. His cousin, a prominent Nuosu scholar of about the same age, told me that the two of them left their village to walk to a nearby town to go to school to learn Chinese, beginning with opposites: *anuo* (black) and *aqu* (white) were *hei* and *bai; asho* (long) and *isho* (short) were *chang* and *duan*, and so forth. By the time of the Communist takeover, Lapu had taken the same educational route as had Nzyhxa but was even more successful, rising through a series of prefectural and then provincial positions, and was noticed at some point by Hu Yaobang, whom Deng Xiaoping made general secretary of the Communist party in 1980. Hu appointed Lapu to a succession of posts, culminating in vice-chairman of the Nationalities Commission. Then, in 1985, as part of Hu's policy to try to win some measure of loyalty back from the Tibetans after the disasters of the Cultural Revolution, Hu appointed Lapu as party secretary of the Tibet Autonomous Region, the only member of a minority ever to hold that post. No Tibetan has ever held it.[18]

By reports,[19] Lapu's appointment was at first resisted by prominent Tibetans. After all, the Yi were a slave society before Liberation, and the Tibetans were a feudal society, so it was something of an insult to appoint a Yi as party secretary of Tibet (or perhaps it was just because the Tibetans rightly felt that one of their own deserved the post). But he quickly became popular; a polyglot from his youth, he quickly learned to speak some simple Tibetan, and on holidays he would dress up in Tibetan clothes and address the crowds (haltingly, perhaps) in their own language, again something no previous (Han) party secretary had ever done. It is realistic to think that, had Hu Yaobang not fallen from grace in 1987, his protégé Luovu Lapu might well have continued to rise in the national hierarchy and become a vice-premier or even a politburo member. But Hu fell, and not long afterwards militant monks set off anti-government rioting in Tibet, whereupon Lapu was first sidelined and then removed outright from power in early 1988, to be replaced by one Hu Jintao, whose rise was not similarly interrupted.[20]

Lapu returned to Beijing (to my knowledge he has never lived permanently in Liangshan since at least the 1970s) and took up a succession of sidelined posts, including chair of the Nationalities Commission of the National People's Congress (NPC) and member of the NPC standing committee, not quite sinecures but off the track for those who would enter the policy-making level of government.

Both Lapu and Nzyhxa are completely bicultural people who operate just as well in a Chinese bureaucratic environment as they do in a Nuosu village environment, and, despite their immersion in bureaucratic life, they are both almost universally known to the ordinary Nuosu villagers of Liangshan. If one of them shows up, for whatever reason, in a town or village in the Nuosu hinterland, villagers will probably feel obliged to kill an ox for a celebratory feast; and if one of their eldest daughters (both anthropologists, one with a Chinese and one with an American PhD) shows up to conduct field research in a village, she will immediately be known as her father's daughter, which will open research doors for her. But at the same time, their reputations are somewhat different. Lapu is a local boy made really, really good, but his recent bureaucratic career has taken him away from Liangshan, so he is not remembered for his actual administrative actions. Nzyhxa, on the other hand, never rose so high or went so far away as did Lapu and, thus, is better known. In addition, Nzyhxa married a non-Nuosu, which, to conservative locals, is reprehensible, but Lapu's marital history is even more questionable. Unlike Nzyhxa, he comes from an aristocratic clan, and his first wife was an aristocrat. Due to complex politics having to do with the Anti-Rightist Campaign and then the Cultural Revolution, they divorced, and his second wife came from a commoner clan, something that is anathema to conservative aristocrats and that is generally considered to be more reprehensible than marrying outside the Nuosu ethnic group altogether.

Leader Shama Vuho

I had taken Vuho's picture in 1993 at a Nuosu wedding in a village near Baiwu in Yanyuan county, attended by local and minor county officials, but it was only when I returned home and had my slides developed that I realized that Vuho, also known locally as Ma Yanjingr (Glasses Ma), was the guy in my picture sitting on the mat munching on a chunk of mutton. After the wedding, I saw him several times that winter and learned that he was a bureau head in the county government, and a few weeks later I was invited to his house for boiled sheep. Still later, when I and Vuho's uncle were finishing our field research in Yanyuan and returning to Xichang, Vuho commandeered a sedan and driver from his bureau, stuck a live sheep in the trunk for later slaughter, and we headed down the mountain together. We stopped at a riverside restaurant and had fish, the first fresh anything except meat I had eaten in several weeks. In all our conversations since – and we have become quite good friends and talk about a lot of things – I don't think I have ever heard him say anything about the Yi or what I was doing for them.

Vuho is two years younger than I, and perhaps for that reason, or perhaps because he has only been a county bureau head, I have always thought of him as a friend and equal rather than as a superior who could do me favours. He was born near the aforementioned village in 1949 and started school in the township seat when he was about eleven or twelve years old. He never went beyond elementary school, but early on he developed a love of books and reading, and this brought him the glasses that became his nickname. He and his uncle, six years his junior, used to lie beneath trees in the spring and fall, when it's not raining but not too cold, and read together; his uncle later became a professor. During the Cultural Revolution decade, Vuho joined the army (he's a tall, strong fellow and a good basketball player), and there learned to speak a passable version of Mandarin, though he much prefers either the local Chinese dialect or his native Nuosu, and even when he tries really hard he still has a Liangshan accent. With the rough-and-ready education that the army provided, he got a low-level post in the county government, and through his high intelligence and ability to get things done he rose to be vice-head of one county bureau and then head of another bureau. At one point, he took some sort of adult course that was supposed to give him a high-school equivalent level of education, but he told me he didn't learn a thing; all it got him was a twenty-*kuai*-a-month raise. For a few years in the late 1990s, he held some sort of sinecure in the prefectural government that allowed him to stay in his native Yanyuan county and not do much of a bureaucratic nature, but he was not idle. When some foreign and domestic friends of his uncle's decided to build an experimental elementary school in their native village, Vuho was the one who really got things done. He kept the accounts, arranged for tax breaks, got permits issued, secured the lumber in an era when there was a general logging ban, worked with the contractors, and organized the villagers (many of them his clan mates or affines) to contribute free labour. He was made a member of the school board, and he also helped university students when they went to the area to do ecological field research. Recently, he has been made vice-chair of the county People's Congress, so he has work to do again; he has also, like so many local cadres, gone into business, buying a restaurant and a mid-size bus (*zhongba*) that plies the dirt road between Baiwu and the county seat.

Whereas Lapu spends his life in a primarily mainstream Chinese context, and Nzyhxa spends his going back and forth between mainstream culture and the promotion of Yi culture, Vuho's life is still firmly grounded in Nuosu culture. He speaks Nuosu regularly with his colleagues in the county government and with his friends, though his urban-raised children don't speak it very well. But, for Vuho, being Yi is a fact of life, not something to be promoted, and when foreigners seek him out, he doesn't immediately enter the discourse of minority backwardness and gratitude for outside help, nor does he go on about the glories of Nuosu history and culture. He is very comfortable being a Nuosu and being a Chinese official and educator. He is passionately interested in local history, in the affairs of his clan, and in the ecological research that I and my colleagues have begun to conduct in his hometown. His identification is with his village, his township, and his Shama clan rather than with any abstraction like the Nuosu or the Yi. And, more than anything, he is concerned with getting results, something that puts him in great demand among his relatives and colleagues.

Leader Ulanhu[21]

Ulanhu, as mentioned above, is the only minority person ever to hold even alternate membership in the policy-making Political Bureau of the Communist Party; he was also vice-chairman of the People's Republic and vice-chair of the National People's Congress. He was born in 1906 in a suburb of Hohhot and was a member of a group of Mongols called the Tumed, who had sedentarized and adopted the Chinese language early in the Qing dynasty. In his twenties, he developed an enthusiasm for communism and joined the Chinese Communist Party (CCP), forming the first party organization among Mongols. During the Anti-Japanese War, he allied with the Chinese Communists in their struggle against Japan and managed to unite several eastern and western Mongol factions behind the Inner Mongolia Autonomous Government, formed under CCP sponsorship in 1947. He became the first party secretary and governor of the Inner Mongolian Autonomous Region when it was founded later that year. All through the 1950s and early 1960s, he held these posts along with those of commander and political commissar of the Inner Mongolia Military Region. He became a vice-premier of the State Council in 1954 and alternate member of the Politburo in 1956, making him one of the twenty most powerful men in China.

Despite his lofty positions and his direct access to Mao Zedong and other central leaders, however, Ulanhu's position between the central state and his ethnic community (which, in his case, included all the Mongols in China) was little different from that of the other leaders I have described. In the 1950s, he managed to prevent both the redistribution of property in herding areas and the extensive reclamation of grasslands for agriculture, arguing successfully that these centrally mandated policies were unsuitable for the local conditions of Inner Mongolia or the pastoral livelihood of the traditional Mongols. He even promoted language rights: he gave a public speech in Mongolian (he did not actually speak the language, so he read phonetically from a Cyrillic text) on the tenth anniversary of the founding of the autonomous region. He thus managed successfully to represent his constituency within the Chinese state while never having his credentials questioned as a loyal Chinese patriot or a faithful party member; after all, he had delivered the Mongols to the CCP and always praised Chairman Mao's leadership and the Communist Party.

This changed in the Cultural Revolution, when the party-state's nationalities policy changed to one of immediate acculturation and attempts at ethnic assimilation; Ulanhu was attacked as a local chauvinist, a rightist in disguise, "the Chinggis Khan of our time" – an epithet that, at that moment, was not an accolade. He was removed from all his posts.

After the Cultural Revolution, however, as the central leaders wished to emphasize the very real turn towards pluralism that their policies had taken, Ulanhu once again was praised and was elevated to the high-level honorific positions of state vice-chairman and NPC vice-chairman – a post he held at the time of his death in 1988.

After he died, Ulanhu became the object of a cult of veneration among Mongols. An immense mausoleum (slightly larger than the one for Chinggis Khan in the Ordos) was built in Hohhot, fronted by a huge statue of the leader wearing a military overcoat. This was similar to the many statues of his patron Mao Zedong, whom he uncannily resembled. Nowadays Mongol intellectuals venerate Ulanhu because, despite his participation in the highest structures of the Chinese party and state, he always conducted his political business with a "Mongol heart," embodying the ideal of Mongols, and incidentally other nationalities, as proud and equal citizens of a multinational China.

The Han State?

All the minority cadres I have portrayed here, in ascending order of rank – Qi Haiyun, Shama Vuho, Hxielie Nzyhxa, Luovu Lapu, and Ulanhu – have, through their participation in the Chinese political situation, been placed into a kind of "Pushmipullyu" position. On the one hand, they are sincerely motivated by their membership in a local community. This might be a village or a clan in the case of Qi or Vuho, an ethnic group of varying size in the case of the higher-ranking leaders. But all of them feel loyalty and emotional attachment to those whom they lead or represent. On the other hand, all of them are agents (and, with the exception of Qi, salaried employees) of the Chinese party-state. In addition, again with the exception of Qi, for whom I have no information, they are all sincere and dedicated patriots, and all are members of the Communist Party. They sincerely believe, or did at one time, in some version of something called socialism, and they have all worked to support party policies that they thought would bring health, wealth, literacy, and modernity in general to their own people just as they would to Han citizens throughout China. There are certainly people, particularly Uighurs and Tibetans, but also Mongols and Yi, who see these two kinds of loyalties, two kinds of goals, as mutually contradictory. Only through getting rid of the Chinese yoke, according to these separatists, can the Uighurs or Mongols or Tibetans or Yi truly liberate themselves to pursue real health, wealth, and modernity as well as real autonomy. But there are others, and the leaders profiled here are among them, who feel that, despite the Han origins of the structures and policies of the PRC state, the idea of a multinational China is a feasible and desirable one. Partly, of course, this is a matter of necessity. Tibet or Xinjiang or even a united Inner and Outer Mongolia (with the southern urban and agricultural strip cut off, perhaps, to eliminate large numbers of Han residents) might be a viable nation-state, but Liangshan, surrounded on three sides by Han and on the other by Tibet, poor and mountainous with no outlet to anywhere, certainly would not be. A greater Yi-land, composed of a series of Bantustans widely separated by Han and other ethnic areas, would be even less feasible. Yi leaders from Sichuan, Yunnan, and Guizhou have long dreamed of a province-level Yi autonomous region, on a par with Xinjiang, Tibet, Guangxi, Ningxia, and Inner Mongolia, but I have never heard them speak of it as a potentially independent country.

In this context, some may perhaps see minority cadres as sell-outs, collaborators, people co-opted by a Han policy implemented by a Han state, unwitting or even cynically careerist stooges. This has, in fact, been a danger in East Asia for a long time. When the Ming and Qing states implemented the *tusi*, or local ruler system, appointing heads of local polities or clans to positions as agents of the imperial state, they did so at least partly as a conscious step towards acculturation and assimilation. The local rulers, more often than not, adopted written Chinese as an administrative language (whether they had their own local written languages or not), sometimes participated in the imperial examination system, and often espoused Confucian moral principles. In some cases, such as in many of the Yi areas of Yunnan, this eventually led to the formation of hybrid cultures or even to the full assimilation of people who no longer considered themselves to be different from the Han Chinese. In other areas, this led to resistance. As early as the Ming, several tusi were established in Liangshan, chosen from a super-elite stratum of Nuosu society known as the *nzymo*. Many of these households indeed sinified culturally, to the point where at least one scion of such a household in the early twentieth century, Leng Guangdian of Ganluo county, attended the Huangpu Military Academy and served as an officer in the Guomindang army, returning later to his native county to establish the first modern elementary school. But in other areas, the sinicized tusi stirred nothing but resentment as agents of the Ming and the Qing states, and a series of revolts on the part of *nuoho* aristocrats drove many of the tusi from the core of Nuosu territory out to the marginal areas, where Nuosu were mixed with Han. There must have been plenty of times during the history of the PRC when local members of minority groups saw their local minority cadres as the equivalent of these sinified tusi and considered driving them out; the revolt of 1957-64 in Liangshan was the one instance in which some of them actually tried. In the case of the Lolopo, about whom Mueggler has written, driving representatives of the state out of the community has been out of the question. But people have paid a terrible emotional price, incessantly mentally tormented by the restless ghosts that originated when the state would not allow proper funeral rituals for victims of the Great Leap Forward famine or the political struggles of the Cultural Revolution.

At the same time, the equation of "the state" with "the Han" is a terribly problematical one. I remember discussing the Nuosu revolt of the late 1950s with a group of Nuosu cadres and intellectuals, and asking about why local aristocrats took up arms in guerrilla warfare against the Communist Party. One professor immediately piped up and said, "They were not opposed to the Communist Party; they were opposed to the Han." In another case, a Nuosu scholar tells the story of his father's being strung up by the wrists and beaten by Nuosu red guards during the Cultural Revolution. After they finally cut the man down, he managed to crawl to the door of his room where a rooster was cowering, wring the bird's neck, and call forth a curse on the Red Guards, all their descendants, and the idiotic policies of the Han.[22] The old man had, and has to this day, several blood-brother pacts with Han neighbours (his son calls them *shushu* or "uncle"), and the red guards who strung him up were all Nuosu. It appears, therefore, that for many minority people, "Han" does not necessarily mean "people of the Han minzu"; Rather it means the state that sometimes oppresses them, the modern consumer culture to which many of them aspire, and often the vices of mendacity and slippery manipulation that they identify as ethnic character traits when they see them (often enough, but far from always) in Han people whom they know.

We thus have a paradox. Minority people, when the state opposes their interests in certain ways, almost reflexively direct their anger at the Han, even in cases like that of the 1950s revolt in Liangshan, where almost all the state agents carrying out the Democratic Reform policies were ethnically Nuosu (as were both the targets and the beneficiaries of the reforms). At the same time, minority people actively participate as cadres in the various local projects of the state. From their own standpoint, they are not doing it particularly to serve China (though that may be one motivation) but, rather, to better the life, the position, the respect given to members of their own ethnic group. I have never heard a minority cadre of any rank say that he or she was trying to "Hanify" people of his own nationality, even when carrying out policies such as education in the Chinese language or promotion of entrepreneurship, a stereotypically Han sort of behaviour. In fact, of course, all national and almost all local state policies originate with Han leaders, so it is appropriate to blame the Han when the state becomes oppressive. But, at the same time, minority people in many areas, particularly the southwest, consider themselves to be unambiguously Chinese, and when they participate in state projects, they are doing so for their relatives and coethnics, whom they view as equal and respectable (though not always respected) citizens of China. In Xinjiang and Tibet, identification with China is much less unanimous, and there are many people who see the Chinese state as illegitimate in their areas. But there are others who, like minorities in the southwest, assert their rights as Chinese citizens, in much the same way as First Nations assert their rights as Canadian citizens.

Ordinary people, when they view the actions of minority cadres in their communities and regions, thus often see anything oppressive as a manifestation of the "Han-ness" of the state, regardless of the ethnicity of the state representatives who carry out the policy. But when they support what the minority cadres do, they see their actions as contributing to the welfare of their community or ethnic group in its capacity as a section of the China whose welfare is intertwined with theirs. Perhaps the view of minority cadres can be best summarized as alternating between *"L'état, c'est nous,"* and "We have met the oppressor and he is us."

Back to the Cadres

Minority cadres at different levels experience the paradox of their broker position somewhat differently. Lapu, like his even more prestigious predecessor Ulanhu, comfortable physically and culturally in the halls of power in Beijing, is protected from any possible local opposition in his home territories and, in some ways, can act exactly like a Han official with regard to that aspect of his life. But this does not lift Lapu out of the context of the Yi community altogether. He is still part of, and responsible to, the community of minority officials and intellectuals that resides in the capital. He will always attend, for example, Beijing celebrations of the Yi New Year every fall. And he reportedly has a lot to say about which Yi are appointed to middle-level posts in government agencies in Beijing or in his native province of Sichuan. But he is one step removed from any geographic Yi or Nuosu community.

Nzyhxa, by contrast, despite his competence in Han culture, spends most of his time in Xichang and travelling around Liangshan, involved as a senior adviser and mentor to prefectural and county officials and working to attract outside investment to Liangshan. He is not the least bit insulated from local opinion; in fact, he seeks it out in Xichang and when he travels to Liangshan communities. It would be difficult for him to rationalize working for a "Han state" if he did not sincerely feel that what he was doing was for the good of the Nuosu or at least the Yi minzu.

Vuho's situation is again different. Working for the local state, he has a lot of contact with Han people and is competent and comfortable in Chinese bureaucratic culture, but he really does not have to face any tug on his own identity. Unlike Lapu or Nzyhxa, he sees members of his own clan and natives of his own village all the time; in a sense, he has not been lifted out of the ordinary context of kin relations that is Nuosu society. Lapu and Nzyhxa have obligations of kinship outside their immediate families, but they are not a big part of either one's everyday life. Vuho builds a school for his clan and village, attends weddings and funerals among his kin, and remains connected with his social and cultural background in a daily way. Perhaps this is why he says so little about the Yi or their history or culture. He does not need to reinforce, on an ideational level, what he experiences daily as part of his own life. Lapu is sad when his young relatives don't speak Nuohxo and Nzyhxa spends much of his time promoting Yi culture, partly because these things are semi-objectified for them. Vuho, and I suspect also Qi Haiyun (assuming he has recovered from his depression and suicide attempt), experience the paradox of being in the middle in a much more mundane and realistic way.

We thus have two modes of experiencing being in the middle, and the officials portrayed here reside at different points on the continuum between them. There is a mode exemplified by higher-level minority cadres, who, despite their physical and institutional removal from their ethnic communities, still feel a strong emotional and ideological attachment. Because of this attachment, perhaps, they reify or objectify the fact of their ethnicity. The farther they move out of the daily sphere of local life, the more this objectification takes over. For them, the opposition is between a policy reality and a cultural or emotional ideal. Officials at lower levels still experience a paradox, but it takes place much more at the level of policy itself. They have no need to reify or objectify or ideologize their ethnic identity as they live it daily. But they still, like all state agents who are members of ethnic minority communities, face daily conflicting loyalties and wrestle with hard decisions about how they can serve the community and the state at the same time.

Acknowledgments

I am grateful to Diana Lary for inviting me to the conference in honour of Alexander Woodside in Vancouver in January 2004, where I presented a preliminary version of this chapter. I owe particular thanks to Bamo Ayi for comments on an earlier draft.

Notes

1 The planned-birth policy of the PRC (*jihua shengyu zhengce*) varies greatly among different ethnic minority regions. In some places, minority couples are allowed two children, or two if the first is a girl, or three, or three if the first two are girls. In a few areas, mostly in the remote pastoral regions of northern Tibet, there are no limitations.

2 Erik Mueggler, *The Age of Wild Ghosts: Memory, Violence, and Place in Southwest China* (Berkeley: University of California Press, 2001), 302-16.

3 Shu-min Huang, *The Spiral Road: Change in a Chinese Village through the Eyes of a Communist Party Leader* (Boulder: Westview Press, 1989), 175-85.

4 Susan H. Whiting, *Power and Wealth in Rural China: The Political Economy of Institutional Change* (Cambridge: Cambridge University Press, 2001).

5 The category Yi was first used in the 1950s to encompass a large number of closely related Tibeto-Burman-speaking groups in the southwest, and it includes speakers of six major dialect groups and many local dialects and vernaculars. The Lolopo, about whom Mueggler writes, as well as the Nuosu (to which several of the cadres portrayed below belong) are now classified as subgroups or branches (*zhixi*) of the Yi.

6 See Dru C. Gladney, *Muslim Chinese: Ethnic Nationalism in the People's Republic* (Cambridge, MA: Harvard University Press, 1991); Louisa Schein, *Minority Rules: The Miao and the Feminine in China's Cultural Politics* (Durham: Duke University Press, 1999); and Ralph Litzinger, *Other Chinas: The Yao and the Politics of National Belonging* (Durham: Duke University Press, 2000).

7 Stevan Harrell, "Introduction: Civilizing Projects and the Reactions to Them," in *Cultural Encounters on China's Ethnic Frontiers*, edited by S. Harrell, 3-36 (Seattle and London: University of Washington Press, 1995).

8 Myron L. Cohen, "Cultural and Political Inventions in Modern China: The Case of the 'Peasant,'" *Daedalus* 122, 2 (1993): 151-70.

9 According to the orthodox Marxist-Leninist ethnohistory formulated in the Soviet Union and adopted just about wholesale in China in the 1950s, all societies go through a progression of social formations, or modes of production, from primitive, to slave, to feudal, to capitalist, to socialist, and, perhaps someday, to communist. In China, the Nuosu (or Yi of Liangshan) were the only group determined to be at the slave stage at the time of the Democratic Reforms of the 1950s. Other groups were classified as belonging to the early, or manorial, substage of feudalism, to distinguish them from the rural Han Chinese, who were at the later, or landlord economy, substage of feudalism.

10 Hsieh Shih-chung, "*Rentong de wuming: Taiwan yuanzhumin de zuqun bianqian*" [Stigmatized identity: Ethnic change among Taiwan's aborigines] (Taipei: Ziyou Wanbal She, 1987).

11 Uradyn Erden Bulag, *The Mongols at China's Edge: History and the Politics of National Unity* (Lanham, MD: Rowman and Littlefield, 2002).

12 In Xide county in Liangshan prefecture, Sichuan, which has a population of 85 percent Yi and 15 percent Han, about two-thirds of the party secretaries in the general administrative, military, and government offices were Nuosu; about two-thirds of the party secretaries in the functional departments such as finance, construction, and so on were Han. This one small example shows that, when Han predominate in party positions, at least in this one minority area, they predominate in positions requiring more technical or specialized knowledge.

13 One current vice-premier, Hui Langyu, a member of the Hui *minzu,* was formerly governor of Jiangsu, a province with a very small minority population. In a certain sense, he may be the exception that proves the rule since the Hui Muslims are linguistically and culturally closer to the Han majority than are any other minority group, and the Hui have long played important roles in the Chinese state at various levels.

14 The only minority peoples in China whose population, at least until very recently, had a large urban component were the Hui, who lived in almost every city in China, and the Uighurs and Tatars of Xinjiang. All were traditionally Muslim peoples.

15 I have chosen to use pseudonyms for all the cadres I portray here except Ulanhu, who was a well-known historical figure.

16 Nuosu are very loose, whether speaking Nuohxo or Chinese, with the distinction between brothers and agnatic cousins. The two men are in fact third or fourth cousins, but in the Nuosu view of things this makes them more closely related than are a lot of "brothers."

17 Nuosu society is divided into several ranks, or strata, distinguished by "hardness of bone," or what Chinese and Europeans would call purity of blood. The aristocrats, or *nuoho*, were the traditional rulers and constiuted between 5 percent and 10 percent of the population; the commoners, or *quho*, constituted about 50 percent, and various serf and slave strata (*mgajie*, *gaxy*, etc.) constituted the rest.

18 Tsering Shakya, *The Dragon in the Land of Snows: A History of Modern Tibet since 1947* (New York: Columbia University Press, 1999), 400-2.

19 Ibid., 402-3.

20 Ibid., 429.

21 This account of the life and works of Ulanhu (sometimes spelled Ulanfu or Wulanfu, after the *pinyin* rendition of the Chinese characters used to write his name) is taken from Bulag, *The Mongols at China's Edge*.

22 Mgebbu Lunzy (Ma Erzi), "Nuosu and Their Neighbors through the Eyes and Ears of the Mgebbu Clan," *Asian Ethnicity* 4, 1 (2003): 129-45.

13
Theoretical and Conceptual Perspectives on the Periphery in Contemporary China

Pitman B. Potter

China exists geographically and conceptually at the centre of an ever-widening series of concentric borderlands. The traditional nomenclature of the "Central Kingdom" was applied not only to distinguish China from external principalities but also to differentiate non-Han groupings within the boundaries of the Chinese empire. Whether we consider the ancient Qin dynasty with its capital of Chang'an (now Xian) at the bend of the Yellow River or the People's Republic of China (PRC) whose heart is Beijing, the North China Plain has served for millennia as both the physical and spiritual centre of China. True, important dynasties such as the Southern Song and early Ming, as well as the Republic of China, were centred or began in the south. But for most of the imperial and modern periods, China's cultural centre rested along the course of the Yellow River.

Looking outward, China's cultural perspective was soon confronted by societies whose structure, belief systems, and behaviour conflicted fundamentally with those of the Han. Moving westward, the Chinese came into conflict with Central Asian cultures of the Tarim Basin, whose nomadism and religiosity contrasted with the secular urbanism of the Han.[1] Moving north, the Chinese confronted the pastoral societies of the Gobi, with similarly conflicted results.[2] While some of these contacts (especially in the Tarim Basin) were violent, even when relatively peaceful, relentless intrusion from China resulted in the displacement and marginalization of local people. In its relations with the borderlands, the Chinese state (whether Imperial, Republican, or Socialist) tended to view local denizens with a mixture of contempt and fear. As the archetypal "other," the peoples of these outer regions were considered both inferior and challenging, unequal to the cultural superiority of the Han but also militarily powerful and threatening. Chinese dynasties sought to suppress those barbarians (*yi*, meaning "not yet sinicized") who ventured too close to the Han homeland, to dominate peaceful border areas through settlement and military garrison, and to convert societies to the benefits of Han culture.[3] Thus, through much of Chinese history, management of the periphery has loomed large as an imperative of governance.

Today, China's relations with its borderlands continue to reflect a combination of cultural superiority and deep-seated unease, standing against the context of the policy imperatives of national integration. The areas of the "inner periphery," particularly Inner Mongolia, Tibet, and Xinjiang, are administrative components of the PRC state. Governance of these minority nationality "autonomous regions" has long been a central feature of PRC policy and is presented as an improvement on the policies of domination associated with Imperial China and, to some extent, the Nationalist period.[4] Despite their formal designations, however, these regions often enjoy less actual autonomy than is conferred by the centre on the Chinese provinces. National integration of minority nationality areas has run the gamut from relatively benign accommodation to military control but is unavoidably coloured by the spectre of Han chauvinism – either as an unfortunate feudal remnant to be gradually educated away or as a lethal complement to socialist transformation that worked to displace local sociocultural arrangements. Thus, China's national integration priorities in Inner Mongolia, Tibet, and Xinjiang have included policies of Han migration, economic development, and political control.[5]

From Beijing's perspective, the "outer periphery," comprising Hong Kong, Macao, and Taiwan, reflects historical influences of imperialism and internationalization that have drawn these mainly Chinese societies into greater integration with the world political economy. In the outer periphery, national integration policies are reflected in the "One Country-Two Systems" (*yiguo liangzhi*, or 1C2S) model applied to Hong Kong and Macao after their return to China in 1997.[6] This typology continues to inform China's proposals for unification with Taiwan,[7] although with limited success in the face of continued resistance from successive Taiwan governments. While the Anti-Session Law, 2005, eschews direct reference to 1C2S, the law's promise of a "high degree of autonomy" parallels this foundational principle.

In both the inner and the outer periphery, relations with China proper and the central government are conflicted by differences of expectation about autonomy; by differences in perspectives of place that construct the peripheries alternatively as homelands or as border zones of key strategic importance to China; and by differences in ethnicity, language, and culture that affect dynamics of development and organization. Comparison both within and between the inner and outer peripheries can yield important insights not only into China's relations with these areas – an issue important in its own right – but also into China's sense of itself. Such comparisons can reveal the ways in which pursuit of national integration in China remains contingent upon central and local conditions, interests, and expectations.

China's Peripheries: Local Conditions and Perspectives

China's policies on governance in the periphery purport to acknowledge the central government's understanding and appreciation of the local conditions.[8] This is a daunting task, however. Each of the areas within the inner and outer peripheries has distinctive local conditions. While their shared status as contested peripheral areas invites generalization, each of the areas under study here has a unique history and culture that defies unified approaches to governance.

The Inner Periphery: Governance of Minority Nationalities

China's inner periphery comprises areas traditionally inhabited by ethnic minorities. This is recognized explicitly in Inner Mongolia, Xinjiang, and Tibet but is evident as well in provinces such as Gansu and Sichuan, which have large minority populations. Ningxia is accorded autonomous region status linked to the Hui nationality: even though these people are ethnically Han, their Muslim culture is deemed sufficiently distinct to warrant a social classification separate from that of other Han social groups.[9] Due to the role of ethnicity in the identity of the peripheral status of Inner Mongolia, Xinjiang, and Tibet, this article focuses particularly on these three sectors of the inner periphery.

Inner Mongolia

The Great Wall of China is mute but powerful testimony to China's historical insecurities about its northern frontier in the face of more or less constant threat of incursion by nomadic tribes from the north.[10] Whether the Xiongnu of the Han period, the Mongols who defeated the Song and founded the Yuan dynasty, or the Manchus who collaborated with Mongols and defecting Chinese generals to defeat Ming China, peoples from the north frequently challenged the integrity and security of traditional China.[11] The establishment of the Inner Mongolian Autonomous Region in 1947 bears the imprint of a historical legacy that includes the Qing division of Inner from Outer Mongolia, Nationalist efforts to integrate Inner Mongolia, and the alliance of the Communist Tumed Mongols under Ulanhu with the Chinese Communist revolutionary base at Yan'an.[12] China's policies towards Inner Mongolia have reflected broad tensions between Chinese imperatives of national integration and security and local concerns with identity and place. The Mongols themselves are distinguished by tribe and locale, such as the so-called "Western" Mongols (mostly Tumed Communists associated with Ulanhu) and their Ordos Mongol affiliates, and the "Eastern" Mongols (mostly returned from Japanese colonialism in Manchuria). China's efforts at co-aptation and control have been carried out through Mongol cadres such as Ulanhu, who professed loyalty to Beijing. Security dimensions have also played an important role – particularly during periods of tension in Sino-Russian relations. Conflicts between the nomadic culture of the steppe and the settled culture of the Han Chinese also play an important role in social and economic development policy. More recently, questions of desertification and degradation of the grasslands, competition for control of the lucrative cashmere industry, and urbanization have all come to dominate China's relations with Inner Mongolia. Against these broad themes of identity, environment, economy, and security, tensions remain over the meaning and extent of autonomy in local governance.

Xinjiang

China's relationship with Xinjiang reflects historical factors of conflict between successive Chinese dynasties and the vigorous cultures of the Silk Road.[13] The commercial importance of the Silk Road invited social discourse but also raised the possibility of conflicts over control. The emergence of ocean trade routes from Arabia, expansion of the Tibetan empire into the Tarim basin in the seventh and eighth centuries, and the gradual displacement of local Buddhist cultures by militant Islam all contributed to the decline of the Silk Road. The rise of the Mongols linked the Yuan dynasty with the Tarim region, although the succeeding Ming focused dynastic interests inward to China proper. The Manchus reasserted China's control over the Tarim and Dzungerian Basins, defeating Mongol competitors and retaining suzerainty through the reigns of Kangxi and Qianlong. The story of the "Fragrant Concubine" whose tomb still graces the outskirts of Kashgar epitomizes the exoticism that Imperial China associated with the western frontier of Xinjiang.[14] Qing decline in the nineteenth century, coupled with the "Great Game" of resurgent British and Russian imperialism, saw Xinjiang dominated by local satraps such as Yakub Beg.[15] Although he died facing nearly certain defeat at the hands of Qing general Zuo Zongtang, Beg's kingdom of Eastern Turkestan casts a powerful image in the minds of Chinese and Uighurs alike. Under the Nationalists, China continued to assert its interests in Xinjiang, although the stability promised by Chinese dominion was often undermined by a combination of venal administration, the resiliency of local warlord armies, and a series of localized Islamic and Turkic rebellions. By the time of the Anti-Japanese War, Nationalist government control was tenuous at best and came to depend on an alliance with the Uighur and Kazakh-dominated Eastern Turkistan Republic (ETR). Ultimately, the ETR was undermined by Soviet dissembling and Chinese communist duplicity, and PRC control over the region was finally secured with the arrival of the People's Liberation Army in 1949.

China's policies in Xinjiang reflect the importance of the region to Beijing's conception of national interest.[16] Xinjiang has multiple natural resources, including oil and natural gas, which are seen as essential to China's economic development. Xinjiang's strategic location in central Asia has leant particular importance to China's policies,[17] most recently the Chinese government's attempt to use the US-led anti-terrorism campaign as justification for suppression of Islamic separatists.[18] Yet Xinjiang remains a highly contested community whose multiple ethnic groups and largely Islamic culture are wholly distinct from those of Han China.[19] While Chinese immigration has changed the face of the provincial capital Urumqi, local nationalities – particularly Uighurs and Kazakhs – remain dominant in the south of the autonomous region (*Jiang nan*). The area around Kashgar remains a centre of Uighur nationalism – the Idhkah Mosque near the centre of the city standing as the symbolic centre of anti-Han sentiment. Signs throughout the interior of the mosque extolling in Chinese, Uighur, and English the virtues of ethnic unity and prohibiting "splittist" (*fenlie*) activities seem curiously maladroit as the only readers are Chinese and foreign tourists. This mixing of religion and national identity is also evident in privately funded mosques established in such places as Artush despite the denial of state funding. China's policy makers seem acutely aware of the power of these local religious and nationalist sentiments,[20] although often China's policies of social control in the service of national integration seem unresponsive.

Tibet

Tibet's relationship with China also reflects historical legacies, ranging from periods of subordination to the Mongols (who later founded the Yuan dynasty in the thirteenth century) and to the Qing (during periods of the eighteenth century), interspersed with long periods in which Tibet enjoyed functional independence in the face of Chinese imperial weakness.[21] Caught between the territorial ambitions of China and imperialist Britain in the late eighteenth and early nineteenth centuries, Tibet sought to preserve its legal autonomy even as China attempted to establish its sovereignty. While Nationalist China's de facto control over Tibet had been minimal prior to 1949, upon taking power, the PRC began to assert ever more strident claims to authority over Tibet. In the face of Chinese military conquest of eastern Tibet in 1950, the fourteenth Dalai Lama concluded a "17 Point Agreement" recognizing Chinese sovereignty in return for commitments with regard to local autonomy. Ongoing tensions with China, complicated by US overtures encouraging resistance and by China's socialist transformation policies (most notably the collectivization of land), led ultimately to a full-fledged Chinese military occupation in 1959. Thereafter, China instituted policies aimed at dismantling traditional Tibetan society and culture and replacing these with Maoist institutions and practices of socialist revolution.

During the post-Mao period, the government of Deng Xiaoping adopted more moderate policies aimed at correcting the self-defeating excesses of the Maoist era, in part by promoting economic development and providing broader economic and political opportunities for local Tibetan elites. Despite Hu Yaobang's six-point reform proposal announced in 1980, a secret meeting between Hu and the Dalai Lama's brother Gyalo Thondup in 1981, and negotiations in Beijing in 1982 over the possible return of the Dalai Lama to China, a successful reconciliation was elusive.[22] Internal political battles in China leading to the dismissal of Hu in 1987, the 1986 launch of an international campaign for Tibet on the part of the government in exile in Dharamsala (which contributed to the Dalai Lama's receiving the Nobel Peace Prize in 1989), and, ultimately, the riots in Lhasa in 1987 and 1988 led to a hardening of Beijing's negotiating position. While the 1990s saw little progress in Sino-Tibetan relations, more recently discussions have been restarted, with visits led by the Dalai Lama's envoy Lodi Gyari in 2002-4. However, these were held under the auspices of the Communist Party of China's United Front Work Committee, signalling their "non-governmental" character and potentially limiting their political impact.

China's military occupation of Tibet has left a legacy of tension and resistance.[23] China's national integration program for Tibet is pursued through local development programs combined with ongoing criticism of the Dalai Lama's "government in exile."[24] During the past several years, public airing of policy perspectives and the convening of direct discussions between China and the Tibet government in exile suggest possibilities for change in the relationship. However, China has also moved aggressively to curb local dissent, to control religious activities that challenge Beijing's dominance, and to promote urbanization and infrastructure development under its "Western Development Strategy."[25] Yet restiveness remains, as China's migration policies have brought large numbers of Han Chinese into the Tibet Autonomous Region, and tensions between the goals of assimilation and those of accommodation continue to challenge Beijing's policies.

The Outer Periphery: Challenges of Internationalization

China's relations with the outer periphery are coloured less by factors of ethnicity than by internationalization and local identities. The colonial legacy of Britain and Portugal determined much of China's approach to the recovery of Hong Kong and Macao. (China's relations with Hong Kong set the tone for its relationship with Macao, even to the point of parallel provisions in the Basic Laws for these two "Special Administrative Regions." Accordingly, I focus on Hong Kong as an example of China's postcolonial policies in the outer periphery.) For Taiwan, colonial practices by Japan played an important role in relations with the Mainland, while more recently the influence of the United States and globalization more broadly have much to do with China's perception of its interests in Taiwan. In Hong Kong and Taiwan, local identities also play a significant role, along with historical isolation from China proper, language differences, and changing economic conditions.

Hong Kong

Hong Kong occupies a special place in China's self-awareness and its perception about relations with the world at large. The legacies of European colonialism and imperialism are particularly poignant in Hong Kong and often overshadow the reality of historical tensions in social, economic, and political relations between northern and southern China generally and between Beijing and Guangdong in particular.[26] Yet these internal tensions are powerful. Mongol and later Manchu domination of north China contributed to southern Chinese identities of cultural purity and contempt for the rustics of the North China Plain. Northerners, on the other hand, hold to their identities as descendants of the Yellow Emperor and often view their southern compatriots with ambivalence. The multiple southern dialects of Chinese, particularly those of Guangdong, are considered unintelligible by many northerners, who prize their own dialects as "standard." North-south relations in China are complicated by ethnic disparities as well. Purported to be of northern, possibly Xiongnu, origins, the Hakka were driven south at the time of the Mongol invasion in the thirteenth century and have been seen by the local Han as displaced "guests" (*kejia*) and have been marginalized since at least the Yuan dynasty.[27] Thus, the Chinese cultural relationships around Hong Kong are conflicted by internal factors unrelated to the colonial legacy.

Yet, China's view of Hong Kong is inextricably linked with the colonial experience. The story of Britain's wresting of Hong Kong and Kowloon from Qing control is well known.[28] What is often overlooked, however, is the comic-tragedy of relations between two great empires being driven by cultural representatives drawn not from national elites but, rather, from local frontier society. Neither the British nor the Qing merchants whose actions led ultimately to British rule in Hong Kong could be considered the sociocultural elite of either country: both the Jardines and Mathesons and the clans of Mowqua and Howqua were rather tawdry standard bearers for their respective cultures.[29] Nor did the government officials in either country command significant political authority as each state was dismissive of the other's claims to status and prestige. Chinese nationalist sentiment over Hong Kong has itself been historically conflicted. While anti-Manchu nationalism called for "overthrowing the Qing and restoring the Ming" (*fan Qing fu Ming*), the prospect of a foreign bourgeois empire defeating the militant literati culture of the Central Kingdom even under Manchu rule was particularly galling to China's sense of itself. The combination of a nationalist commitment to retaking control of Hong Kong from imperialist Europeans and a general sense of northern chauvinist disdain for the south works to ensure that Beijing retains a strong hand over Hong Kong, even while striving to ensure that Hong Kong has little influence in China proper. More recently, the power of Shanghai political interests in the regime of Jiang Zemin worked to further marginalize Hong Kong's status and influence.

The result is a contested society. On the one hand, Hong Kong retains its international character. Despite challenges from resurgent Shanghai (and also Singapore and Tokyo), Hong Kong remains an important financial centre. With its manufacturing enterprises moving into the Pearl River Delta, Hong Kong has attempted to expand its financial and professional service sectors and to present itself as an essential gateway to China.[30] The continued (albeit somewhat diluted) commitment to the rule of law has persuaded many international private and public actors to base their China activities in the Hong Kong Special Administrative Region (SAR), while the generally high level of human resource development remains an important impetus for local postindustrial development.

On the other hand, China exerts considerable influence in Hong Kong. China's control over Hong Kong's political system has ensured that PRC interests are protected and promoted. Much of the political history of the post-handover period has centred on conflicts between Beijing's policy preferences and those of local interests. Yet, political questions over such issues as the right of abode for children of Hong Kong residents, protection for political dissent, the structure and process for Legislative Council elections, public security policy and practice, and the appointment of the chief executive have generally been resolved in favour of Beijing. As with areas of the inner periphery, Hong Kong has seen significant levels of inward migration from China. For Chinese whose personal or professional prospects in the Mainland are limited, Hong Kong offers considerable opportunities. As well, China has actively promoted commercial and institutional linkages that would ensure a pro-PRC voice among the population. Elite circulation has played an important role in this regard as the colonial elite whose status depended on ties with and loyalty to Britain has largely been replaced by a new elite with close ties and loyalty to China.

Taiwan

Over the past two decades, Taiwan has undergone far-reaching social, economic, and political changes that affect its relationship with Mainland China.[31] Economic relations between Taiwan and the Mainland are close, driven by relative parallels in the timing and focus of economic reform policies in the two regions, and drawing on advantages of shared language and culture. However, while there are aspects of shared history and culture upon which reconciliation might be based,[32] important socioeconomic and political changes in Taiwan have stimulated systemic divergence with China and encouraged local claims to autonomy and possibly independence.[33] Ever-widening differences in legal and political culture reflect contrasts in institutional performance driven by different degrees of commitment to reform. Taiwan's legal system has become more institutionalized and internationalized than has China's.[34] Political reforms in Taiwan have seen the voluntary ceding of power by the ruling Kuomintang (KMT) following its electoral defeat in 2000, which contrasts directly with the continued refusal by Beijing to permit non-Communist policies and politicians any meaningful role in governance. Thus, Taiwan's experience with a transformative democratizing economy in which political and economic reforms coexist presents a direct contrast to the policies of the PRC government and to the legitimacy of the Chinese party-state.

The election of President Chen Shui-bian in 2000 and his re-election in 2004 were watershed events in Taiwan's relations with the Mainland.[35] During his first term, Chen succeeded in steadily pushing China to accept new dimensions of acceptable discourse on Taiwanese autonomy. On the one hand, Chen sought to expand links with China, without making further concessions to China's claims to sovereignty over Taiwan. Acknowledging the principle of "one China," Chen declined to accept China's interpretation of its meaning and implications, adopting instead a principle of "agreeing to disagree" (*bu gongshi de gongshi*).[36] Chen's "three acknowledgements, four recommendations" (*sange renzhi sige jianyi*), posed in 2000, while implying the possibilities of further coordination with the Mainland, nonetheless underscored the separateness of Taiwan's constitutional and legal systems and its claim to distinct international status.[37] Chen's discourse of "political integration" (*zhengzhi tonghe*) implied a degree of separation significantly greater than that contemplated under Beijing's preferred "reunification" (*tongyi*) language.[38]

However, through much of 2002-3, economic problems borne of global recession and uncertainties about the China relationship had diluted Chen's popular support. Despite, or perhaps because of, his increasingly vigorous challenge to Beijing's claims of sovereignty over Taiwan, Chen seemed unable to build significant popular support for a second term. The "Pan-Blue" team, comprising an alliance between the KMT and the People First Party (PFP), seemed to be capitalizing effectively on popular dissatisfaction with corruption and mismanagement associated with Chen's Democratic Progressive Party (DPP) government. The alliance of the KMT's Lien Chan with the PFP's James Soong offered a potentially powerful alliance of traditionalist, mainlander-based political organizations. The apparent popularity of local KMT candidates like Taipei mayor Ma Ying-jeou, suggested potential depth in the opposition to Chen's presidency. While Taipei and northern

Taiwan remained a centre of KMT support, Chen Shui-bian's support in southern Taiwan (including Kaohsiung and Tainan) seemed to be growing northward along class lines. Spontaneous non-structured interviews with cab drivers, students, and market hawkers in Taipei during 2003-4 revealed to me a deep-seated resentment of KMT privilege and entitlement and raised open questions about the KMT's willingness to help Taiwan's workers, who had been buffeted by economic decline and increased unemployment. However, Chen's razor-thin victory in the presidential election and his loss in the local elections of December 2004 and resulting resignation as chair of the DPP signalled the extent to which his China policies, and particularly his localization policies in Taiwan, remain controversial. The visit to China by KMT chief Lien Chan in April 2005 underscored the importance of Mainland relations in Taiwan's domestic politics.

Thus, conditions in China's inner and outer peripheries serve as an essential context for understanding China's policies of governance and control. While differences of local culture, ethnicity, and economic and political conditions caution against over-generalization, the shared reverence for local identity, claims to autonomy from Mainland China, and local conflicts over how to manage relations with Beijing are common factors. These affect not only local perceptions but also China's approach to governance and control.

China's Policies of Governance and Control

China's management of its relations with the regions of the inner and outer peripheries is based formally on their classification as political and legal entities under the PRC Constitution. In the inner periphery, constitutional arrangements for local governance in the "autonomous regions" of Inner Mongolia, Tibet, and Xinjiang pose exceptions to the unitary state model applied elsewhere. Yet tensions borne of ethnic difference continue to challenge Beijing's authority. In the outer periphery, Hong Kong and Taiwan are objects of Beijing's effort to establish the "Special Administrative Region" as yet another constitutional model for governance.[39] Yet China's practices of governance in Hong Kong and its proposals for unification with Taiwan reflect continued tensions between Beijing's perspectives on national integration and local concerns with autonomy.

Perspectives on Federalism, Multiculturalism, and Development

Discussion of political dimensions of China's relations with its periphery can draw usefully on policy discourses of federalism, which offer insights into the dilemmas of central-local relations that inform national integration programs.[40] In China generally, central-local relations have been an important dynamic in economic, legal, and political reform processes.[41] While the PRC Constitution provides that China is a unitary rather than a federal state, in practice, the interplay of power and politics between the central and subnational governments echoes practices of federalism,[42] and the policy and scholarly discourse in China have come increasingly to accept the need for federalist principles.[43] Often, however, this has been limited to writings by political dissidents.[44]

Analysis of China's political relations with the inner periphery (Inner Mongolia, Xinjiang, and Tibet) has tended to focus on human rights issues,[45] while historical analyses[46] have provided a general context for understanding relations with China. Regional surveys[47] have provided useful local information about these important regions. Existing work on China's minority policies raises important questions as to whether these empower or marginalize non-Han cultural groups.[48] Legal research has generated useful compilations of treaties and domestic legislation.[49]

With regard to the outer periphery, federalist issues of centre-local relations are central to the discourse of local autonomy.[50] Issues of democratization,[51] sovereignty,[52] strategic and security relations,[53] economic interdependence,[54] and international legal relations[55] have stimulated greater interest in building federalist-type relationships between China and its outer periphery.

The complexities of China's effort to build political structures for management and governance in its borderlands are compounded by the intricacies of social and economic relations between peripheral areas and China proper. Social changes across China in the wake of the economic growth policies of the past twenty years have been well documented.[56] The quest for economic growth and the simultaneous reduction of the role of the state in social and economic life has brought on what might be termed a condition of "post-Socialism," where the party-state continues to wield significant political and administrative control but chooses to remain uninvolved in the social and economic welfare of the people. Yet the social conditions in the periphery, particularly on issues such as religion and culture, offer a vastly different picture than do the conditions of post-Socialist China. Ethnic variation in the inner periphery of Inner Mongolia, Tibet, and Xinjiang exists in close relationship with localized patterns of social organization that differ widely from those in China proper. While the areas of Hong Kong and Taiwan embody many elements of Han society in China proper, the greater internationalization of these areas has created social conditions that are quite distinct. These variations present significant challenges for China's programs of management and control.

Social relations involving China's periphery may be examined by reference to scholarly discourses of multiculturalism in areas such as policy process,[57] legal institutions,[58] minority relations,[59] and jurisdictional issues.[60] While the PRC Constitution and various laws and regulations affirm the rights of China's national minorities, Han privilege has often led to the suppression of local cultures.[61] This multiculturalism approach can also assist in understanding PRC law and policy on national integration with Hong Kong and Taiwan as differences between China and its outer periphery invite appreciation of cultural diversity, even within the broader ambit of Han societies. As debate continues over the potential for cultural affinity,[62] the resurgence of local traditional customs and perspectives, particularly around religion, suggests potentially significant differences between Hong Kong and Taiwan and China that warrant analysis through discourses of multiculturalism. Language too plays a role as the local languages of Hong Kong (Guangdong dialect) and Taiwan (Min-nan dialect) present opportunities to express and validate local identity.

Economic relations within the inner and outer peripheries and between the peripheries and China proper offer another useful vector for comparative analysis. On the one hand, areas such as Inner Mongolia, Tibet, and Xinjiang have lagged significantly behind the dramatic economic growth rates that China has posted over the past twenty years. Hong Kong and Taiwan, by contrast, have boasted economic successes of their own, supported by greater integration with the world political economy. Yet in each of these areas, local economic conditions are affected significantly by China's programs of governance. The Western Development Strategy, for example, has had a significant effect on the character and consequences of economic change in Inner Mongolia, Xinjiang, and Tibet. China's effort to induce investment from Hong Kong and Taiwan to the Mainland have created opportunities for integration, while still raising questions about the politicization of economic relations.

The dynamics of social, economic, and political relations thus pose particular challenges for China's relations with its peripheral areas. Of particular interest is the increasingly central role that law plays in governance in China and also the extent to which law remains an instrument of policy. As a case study, the examination of law and policy on China's relations with its peripheral areas shows how policies are articulated and implemented through law and political-legal institutions. Legal reform in China since 1978 has focused primarily on supporting economic reform.[63] More recently, however, China's legal reform efforts are linked more closely with issues of national integration.[64] In the inner periphery, the Chinese government has attempted to lend greater authority to its rule through references to the rule of law, which serves as an expression of state policy and an instrument for its enforcement.[65] In the outer periphery, by contrast, legalization discourses serve as contested domain wherein China's commitment to rule of law is challenged. The government of Taiwan has on several occasions suggested that reunification will depend on China's completing its efforts to build a rule of law system.[66] Hong Kong's relations with China have repeatedly involved disputes over constitutional questions about jurisdiction, political authority, and the rule of law.[67] Thus, China's law and policy on national integration with its peripheral areas reveals much about official legal culture regarding such questions as institutional jurisdiction and process, the role of law in policy enforcement, and legal restraints on state action.

The Inner Periphery: Policy, Law, and Challenges of Institutional Capacity

The legal framework for governance in China's borderlands derives primarily from the PRC Constitution and its extension to the inner periphery through the Nationality Region Autonomy Law (NRAL) and to the outer periphery through the Hong Kong Basic Law and the Anti-Secession Law. These measures are augmented through particular regulations and through a broader context of policy discourse.

Constitution of the PRC

The Constitution of the PRC provides the overall legal principles from which all other legislation is to proceed. The Chinese Constitution, Section VI, addresses governance autonomy in nationality areas. Viewed in light of CPC policy dictates and broader official discourses on governance autonomy in nationality areas, these provisions reveal features of particular interest in the context of institutional capacity.

Article 113 of the Constitution provides for appropriate representation at the local people's congresses (PC) for nationalities inhabiting a minority autonomous area region, prefecture, or county but not being members of the nationality(ies) in whose name the area is designated. While aimed ostensibly to ensure that local minorities are included in local PC representation, this provision also has the effect of ensuring representation of Han Chinese residents in minority nationality areas. Articles 113 and 114 require that the chair and at least one vice-chair of the autonomous area People's Congress Standing Committee be held by a member of the local nationality and that the administrative head of the area be from a local nationality. However, no parallel provisions govern appointment to party organs. The pervasive influence of the Chinese Communist Party is such that local minority administrative leaders are often perceived as impotent followers of the Han-dominated CPC.[68]

Article 115 affirms the functions and powers of local governance organs but qualifies these by the limitations of the Constitution, the NRAL, and other laws. These limitations, particularly in light of China's unitary state ideal, effectively prohibit local governments from directly opposing policy directions from higher levels, although local governance departments are permitted to adapt state laws and policies to local conditions. Article 116 permits local People's Congresses to enact regulations in light of local characteristics, although these must be submitted to the NPC Standing Committee for approval. Apparently, draft legislation on local governance in the Nationality Autonomous Regions has been prepared by several autonomous region governments, but as yet none has been approved by Beijing.

Articles 117-19 extend significant authority to local autonomous area governments in areas of financial management, local economic development, education, science, culture, public health, and physical culture. Yet these remain subject to policy interpretation in light of central party and government priorities. Local development plans must also operate under the guidance of state plans, while state initiatives like the Western Development Strategy (*Xibu Da Kaifa*) remain outside the purview of local control. Constitutional grants of local autonomy over administration of education, science, and culture are qualified by the requirement of protecting and putting in order (*zhengli*) cultural heritage and promoting cultural development. These normative standards are then interpreted to mean conformity with Han educational, scientific, and cultural criteria, even as these are portrayed in non-ethnic terms such as socialism, modernization, development, and opening up.[69]

The potential for state intrusion on security matters is underscored in Article 120, which allows local governments to organize local public security forces to respond to concrete local needs in accordance with the state military system and subject to State Council approval. This allows for state direction of local security activities – particularly in peripheral areas where border security and perceived threats of separatism and terrorism have been used to justify expanded national security initiatives.[70] However, central concerns over security often conflict with local priorities over standard policing.

Article 121 addresses issues of local language usage in governance activities. While some autonomous regions, such as Tibet, have enacted regulations promoting local language use, the revised Nationality Region Autonomy Law (2001) lowered the age at which Chinese must be taught in minority areas, thus underscoring the potential for displacement of local languages. And indeed, Chinese language usage continues to dominate social and political life in minority areas.[71] While the enactment in 2000 of a law on simultaneous language usage was heralded as an example of the government's commitment to protecting local minority languages, its very enactment and challenges to its full implementation suggest that minority language usage remains marginalized.[72]

Article 122 commits the central government to providing financial, material, and technical assistance to autonomous areas and assisting with training local minority cadres. Unfortunately, this tends to entrench patterns of Han domination of minority areas as the assistance and training are unresponsive to local concerns and priorities[73] or are expressly intended to strengthen central control and to ensure policy compliance with central level policy priorities, many of which are not supported locally.[74]

Nationality Region Autonomy Law

The law of the PRC on autonomy in nationality regions (Nationality Region Autonomy Law [NRAL]) summarizes China's national policies and historical experience in managing relations with its indigenous minorities. Enacted initially in 1984, the law was amended in 2001 to account primarily for inclusion of issues related to economic development. The 2001 amendments also reflected the content of the State Council's 1999 *White Paper on National Minority Policies*.[75] While the autonomy of nationality areas (*minzu quyu*) is presented as essential to national development, the tasks associated with local autonomy are confined to implementation of national laws and regulations, cadre recruitment and training under national guidelines, contribution to national development, and subordination to national programs for local development.

The Nationality Region Autonomy Law affirms the overarching authority of the Chinese Communist Party and the central government. The NRAL derives from the PRC Constitution[76] and requires compliance with it.[77] This necessarily involves obedience to the Four Basic Principles – which are listed specifically along with other *tifa* (authoritative slogans), including socialist democracy and the legal system as bases for managing local autonomy in nationality areas.[78] This, in turn, involves party policy as the basis for legal norms and behaviour. The NRAL confers on local governments the authority to administer economic development programs, subject to national planning.[79] Yet "higher level organs" are accorded considerable authority and responsibility to assist and direct local development.[80] While local governments are given responsibility for education, the Minority Autonomy Law charges higher level organs with responsibility for assisting with cadre recruitment and training.[81] This follows constitutional provisions[82] requiring central government assistance for autonomous region governments, and it allows the party to retain control over the content and process for minority cadres' training.[83]

The Nationality Region Autonomy Law entrenches principles of unification and centralism through requiring that local autonomy remain subject to central state and party leadership.[84] Policy subordination to party leadership requires adherence to the principles of safeguarding national unity, preserving national interests, ensuring the equality and unity of all national groups, and conditioning central government assistance on policy compliance.[85] The NRAL repudiates notions of "ethnic autonomy" (*minzu zizhi*), "local autonomy" (*difang zizhi*), and federalism, instead limiting grants of autonomy to narrowly delegated administrative subject areas such as culture and education. Moreover, the law focuses on autonomy for regions rather than peoples, thus undermining the potential for shared minority identities among, for example, Tibetans living in the Tibet Autonomous Region, Gansu, and Qinghai.

At root, the NRAL is aimed at delegating to autonomous region governments limited autonomy within which to handle civic affairs that are deemed by the party to be a legitimate focus of minority nationality control. Under the label "masters of their own house," minority nationalities are granted authority to manage matters such as cultural expression, heritage and tradition, family relations, and so on, as long as this does not intrude on the policy priorities of the central party-state. And it is the party-state's apprehension that issues of minority identity, religion, language, and culture will serve as alternate sources of legitimacy and loyalty that motivate the central government to restrict expressions of autonomy on such issues. Thus, the NRAL exemplifies the basic quandary faced by the Han-dominated regime – how to gain legitimacy by appearing to grant autonomy, while at the same time restricting that autonomy so that it does not pose a threat to the power of the party-state. The contradictions of the NRAL reflect this more fundamental contradiction of China's policies towards governance in the inner periphery.

The Challenge of Institutional Capacity

China's legal system development can generally be understood in terms of institutional capacity.[86] Institutional capacity can be particularly useful in examining China's approach to governance in the inner periphery. Factors of institutional purpose, location, orientation, and cohesion come into sharp relief in the context of China's governance in the inner periphery, particularly with reference to law and policy issues pertaining to regional autonomy, minority affairs, and regulation of religion. Institutional purposes centred on implementation of party policy on autonomy, minority nationalities, and religion; institutional location questions involving disparities of viewpoint and language between Beijing and minority nationality areas; issues of institutional orientation revealing tensions over approaches to local development; and factors of institutional cohesion affecting cadre selection and administration all have a significant impact on the performance of the legal and regulatory system that governs China's inner periphery.

The PRC Constitution and the NRAL reveal issues of *institutional purpose* around broader policy themes of accommodation and control of local minority nationalities and religion. Party policy on minority affairs has evolved considerably over the course of the PRC.[87] While the party leadership has avowed an increased sensitivity to the issues of minority nationalities,[88] the specifics of party policy remain heavily weighted in favour of state-centric governance. National unity remains the fundamental priority of the party and government to which minority nationalities owe fealty.[89] Constitutional and NRAL provisions subjecting local autonomy to the leadership of the state are supplemented by requirements of central party leadership.[90] Safeguarding the unity of the Chinese state remains an overriding priority: "only when China's sovereignty and territorial integrity are maintained will all ethnic groups truly come to enjoy freedom, equality, development and progress. People of all ethnic groups must further enhance their unity to safeguard the country's sovereignty and territorial integrity."[91]

In Xinjiang, state interests are presented as paramount, subordinating local social and economic relations to national unity goals.[92] For Tibet, unity of the Chinese state is presented as the primary policy goal, to which issues of development are subordinated.[93] Yet these principles conflict significantly with China's minorities' aspirations for self-government. This conflict of institutional purpose poses a significant challenge to China's governance regime.

Factors of *institutional location* are also evident. Aside from the obvious elements of location present in the interpretation of a national statute concerned with local governance, particular institutional location questions arise over issues about local knowledge. China's governance of the inner periphery has traditionally exhibited features of colonialism, with significant Han-dominated oppression of local culture.[94] Case studies from Xinjiang, for example, reveal the extent to which central policies on minority affairs are disconnected from local realities.[95] While Beijing focuses on propaganda efforts to protect social stability, local people seem more interested in substantive improvements in their social and economic conditions.[96] Factors of institutional location are also evident in comparisons between central and local views on development, where central priorities focused on economic accumulation and output contrast with local concerns in regard to cultural and religious identity and social well-being in Xinjiang and Tibet.[97] While minority autonomy in fields of language, religion, and "folkways and customs" are to be respected, central control remains the dominant operational principle for policy development and implementation: "Regional autonomy for ethnic minorities in China means that, under the unified leadership of the state, regional autonomy is practiced in areas where people of ethnic minorities live in compact communities."[98]

The Constitution and the NRAL reveal the dynamics of *institutional orientation* in the way they address purposes and indicators of local development in minority areas. The Western Development Strategy exemplifies the tensions between local autonomy and state oversight on issues of development. On the one hand, the program has seen significant state investment in local infrastructure in the periphery.[99] Economic development in the periphery is seen as a possible solution to issues of ethnic unrest.[100] Yet local concerns with social well-being are often overlooked as development is constructed primarily in terms that conflict with traditional social arrangements.[101] Explicitly rejecting "postmodern" viewpoints that extol the virtues of local identity and tradition, authoritative treatments of the Western Development Program call for development to be achieved through reform in local practices.[102] Local cultural values are then relegated to performance arts, social customs, and literature but not to forms for economic change.[103]

Factors of institutional cohesion are also present as the capacity for implementation of local autonomy under the Constitution and the NRAL will depend significantly on recruiting and training of officials drawn from local nationalities. The NRAL requires that local governments achieve an appropriate balance in their operational units between local minority cadres and cadres of other nationalities.[104] Yet Chinese analysts claim that local governments in Western China are characterized by the "low quality" of their personnel.[105] The content and purpose of minority cadre training remains focused on displacing traditional cultural norms with socialism and cultural civilization associated with Han China.[106] Institutional cohesion is also challenged by minority cadre training approaches focused on establishing basic level cadre corps (*jiceng ganbu duiwu*),[107] which work to insulate minority cadres from participating in government administration at higher levels. This tends to underscore a perception that local minority cadres are essentially translators and implementers of governance programs rather than interpreters and designers of policy.[108]

Thus, China's "legalization" of its governance policies for the minority areas of the inner periphery are contingent on factors of institutional capacity. The institutional purposes of the Nationality Region Autonomy Law reflect party policy imperatives that often conflict with the perspectives and interests of local people. Institutional location questions are omnipresent but come into stark relief around issues of language use and Han-minority relations. Institutional orientation issues emerge around development programs that emphasize central rather than local priorities and approaches. Institutional cohesion problems are evident in the conflicted approach to minority cadre training and uncertainties about its effectiveness in co-opting local elites. Each of these elements of institutional capacity raises questions about the effective implementation of China's NRAL regime with regard to governance in the inner periphery.

The Outer Periphery: Unification and Challenges of Legal Culture

China's relations with its outer periphery are centred on efforts to recapture territory lost to historical circumstance. Issues of state sovereignty were at the heart of China's negotiated repatriation of the former British colony of Hong Kong. Contests over sovereignty also remain critical to China's relations with Taiwan. However, while sovereignty informs China's ambitions, actual relations with the outer periphery are also affected by differences of legal and political culture.

Hong Kong: The Basic Law and the Challenge of Autonomy

The legal framework for Chinese governance in Hong Kong reflects the use of legislation aimed at formalizing policy goals. Similarly, with the Nationality Autonomous Regions, the Hong Kong Special Administrative Region is created pursuant to the PRC Constitution and is subject to principles of national unity. Allowance for Special Administrative Regions with particular grants of autonomy was provided for in Article 31 of the 1982 Constitution in order to permit the accommodation of Taiwan. The "One Country-Two Systems" model envisioned in the Constitution was then applied first to Hong Kong and Macao through Basic Laws legislated by the PRC National People's Congress on the advice of specially constituted drafting committees. The drafting process for the Hong Kong Basic Law, particularly the process for selecting the members of the Drafting Committee and the weighting of the committee to ensure dominance by China,[109] confirmed Beijing's intention to use the Basic Law to entrench its policy preferences for Hong Kong. As a model of constitutional delegation of administrative authority by the central government, the Basic Law exhibits parallels with the constitutional grants of administrative authority through NRAL provisions for the Nationality Autonomous Regions.[110] While the NRAL affords considerably less autonomy than is afforded under the Hong Kong Special Administrative Region, Chinese analysts depict Hong Kong's legal status as structurally comparable with that of provinces, autonomous regions, and centrally administered cities of China, particularly in the sense that all local governance authority results from a delegation by the central government.[111] Thus, the relationship between central and local authority, as set forth in the Hong Kong Basic Law, remains a creature of Chinese constitutional law and, thus, is subject to whatever opportunities and restrictions this may entail.

Read in light of the PRC Constitution upon which it is based, the Basic Law of Hong Kong reflects the perspectives of the Chinese government on how the balance between central control and local autonomy should be achieved.[112] Article 2 of the Basic Law confers on Hong Kong a "high degree of autonomy." However, the term autonomy (*zizhi*) as interpreted in light of its usage elsewhere in the Chinese legal system confers a sense of local responsibility for self-administration. The term does not connote in Chinese the sense of insulation from outside authority that it connotes in

English. In tacit recognition that meaningful autonomy requires local activism, Hong Kong civil leaders have urged broader public participation in the processes of politics and governance.[113] While increased civil consciousness and political activism in Hong Kong may lay the ground for claims against intrusion on the part of Beijing, this is far from certain. Thus, as the Basic Law remains a creature of Chinese constitutional law, the autonomy it promises operates only through a grant of authority from the central government. The actual meaning of such "autonomy" will depend upon what interpretations that government places upon it.

The Basic Law (Article 2) affirms the importance of independent judicial power "including that of final adjudication." However, the potential remains for executive intrusion in judicial appointments, which may cloud judicial independence.[114] Moreover, as the "right of abode" cases demonstrated,[115] China views final adjudication as limited to application of law rather than final interpretation, which, under the Article 67 of the PRC Constitution, remains the province of the National People's Congress Standing Committee.

Article 4 of the Basic Law promises that the rights and freedoms of Hong Kong residents will be safeguarded. While the Basic Law contains apparent safeguards for human rights, the sustainability of these protections is uncertain as they remain subject to such interpretations and limitations as may emerge from the National People's Congress Standing Committee.[116] As the controversy over implementation of the security ordinance (Basic Law Article 23) demonstrated, these basic rights may still be diluted through amendment by the Hong Kong government or by the National People's Congress Standing Committee exercising its overall interpretive authority.[117]

Article 6 of the Basic Law provides for protection of private ownership of property. Coupled with Article 5's commitment that the "socialist system" will not be implemented in Hong Kong, this offers the promise of respect for a wide range of private rights. However, while protection is in "accordance with law" generally and thus is not limited to provisions of the Basic Law, the question arises, which law? As the debate over the appointment of the chief executive revealed,[118] China has taken the view that Chinese law should be a source for interpretations of general rights and processes to be decided "according to law."

Article 8 of the Basic Law provides that laws previously in force in Hong Kong – including the common law, rules of equity, and enacted statutes and regulations, along with customary law – will remain in effect unless in conflict with the Basic Law and that they will be subject to amendment by the Hong Kong legislature. While retention of existing law has given great comfort to those who feared the imposition of Chinese law in matters of economic and social relations, the allowance for amendments and the reference to customary law raises the possibility that existing laws and regulations may gradually be diluted by China-based rules. In light of the historical role for customary law in Hong Kong[119] and the uncertainties of interpreting customary law,[120] the potential for gradual merging of Hong Kong and Chinese law and custom remains strong.

Article 12 of the Basic Law reiterates the promise of a "high degree of autonomy" and indicates that the Hong Kong Special Administrative Region shall come directly under the Central People's Government. While this allows Hong Kong to avoid parochial governance from Guangdong province, for example, it underscores that the Chinese government retains overall political dominance. Whether through appointment of the chief executive, control over election rules and processes, or final interpretation of the Basic Law (upon which all other Hong Kong law depends), the central government retains significant power over the legal direction of Hong Kong. When viewed in light of Beijing's exercise of authority in areas of China that are directly under the central government, particularly the autonomous regions but also the directly administered cities, the protections of the Basic Law may be less effective than many hope it will be in insulating Hong Kong's social, economic, and political life from Chinese control.

Taiwan: The Challenge of the Anti-Secession Law

Consistent with the intent underlying Article 31 of the PRC Constitution, Chinese government proposals aim to add Taiwan to the special constitutional category of special administrative region. Policy proposals from China have suggested that, upon reunification with China, Taiwan will enjoy levels of autonomy that have been extended to the Hong Kong Special Administrative Region. Nonetheless, as presently conceived by Beijing, the autonomy granted Taiwan will still proceed from a grant by the central government pursuant to the PRC Constitution. The recently enacted Anti-Secession Law underscores this point: "After the country is reunited peacefully, Taiwan may (*keyi*) practice a system different from that on the Mainland, and enjoy a high degree of autonomy."

The Anti-Secession Law (ASL) reiterates that the China-Taiwan relationship will be based in the PRC Constitution,[121] thus extolling principles of national unity and territorial integrity. The ASL suggests that reunification with Taiwan may proceed on the basis of political equality between authorities on both sides of the Taiwan Strait.[122] The political status of the Taiwan government may be a subject for reunification discussions.[123] While this suggests a higher level of autonomy than is currently granted to Hong Kong, once negotiations begin, the specifics of Taiwan's political status may be diminished, as happened in the Sino-British negotiations over Hong Kong. Moreover, by requiring agreement to reunification negotiations first, China retains the negotiating advantage to determine the "political status of the

Taiwan authorities." The ASL also allows for discussion of Taiwan's "room for international operations," thus holding out the promise of some sort of international status. In the wake of China's campaign to oppose Taiwan's participation in UN organizations such as the World Health Organization, a grant of authority to participate independently in the international community may be a significant improvement for Taiwan. However, as these are simply issues for discussion, the outcome remains uncertain.

China's expectations regarding negotiations with Taiwan may be appreciated in light of the White Paper entitled *The One-China Principle and the Taiwan Issue*.[124] The White Paper added a new condition under which China might use force against Taiwan. In addition to existing conditions concerning a threat to the territorial integrity of Taiwan and/or a declaration of Taiwanese independence, the White Paper suggested force might be used in the event of Taiwan's refusal to negotiate a reunification agreement with China promptly and in good faith.[125] The Anti-Secession Law may be viewed as a consequence of this provision.

The White Paper relied heavily on an international legal argument that relied upon theories of state succession to justify claims that China-Taiwan issues are wholly domestic and therefore beyond the reach of the general prohibitions of International Law against the use of force between states. The White Paper rejected the "two German states" model associated with German reunification, which might support separate sovereignty for Taiwan and the Mainland; instead, it reiterated the commitment to "One Country-Two Systems" as a basis of reunification, allowing for a different application than that used in Hong Kong.

As with the situation in Hong Kong, the meaning of "autonomy" depends not only on its Chinese language connotations but also on the institutional arrangements for its implementation. The record in Hong Kong suggests that issues such as legislative interpretation, selection of the executive, and the sources upon which interpretation of legal rights will be based remain essential to the realization of meaningful autonomy. The language of the ASL on Taiwan's future relationship with China echoes the One Country-Two Systems model used in Hong Kong. As the "autonomy" to be enjoyed by Taiwan as envisioned by the ASL will be conferred through the dispensation of the Chinese government, it will remain contingent in ways similar to those found in the central grant of autonomy to Hong Kong under the Basic Law.

Challenges of Legal and Political Culture

The conflicted relationships between the PRC government and the regions of China's outer periphery are the product of complex historical circumstances. Local and international socioeconomic and political factors are also important. Tensions over law and policy in China's relations with the outer periphery may also be appreciated in light of differences of legal culture. Legal culture analysis permits us to appreciate the tensions between the globalized systems of liberal legal norms that inform much of legal culture in Hong Kong and Taiwan, on the one hand, and China's deeply embedded system of legal and political norms and values, on the other. Contrasting paradigms of patrimonial sovereignty and responsible agency have been applied to understanding the ways that China selectively adapts principles of liberalism associated with globalization.[126] These can also be applied to understanding the changing relationships between Beijing and Hong Kong and Taiwan.

The legal systems of Hong Kong and Taiwan are grounded in principles of liberalism.[127] Liberalism proceeds from tenets concerning human equality and natural law; the liberal tradition of political ideology asserts that government should be an agency of popular will.[128] Such agency requires accountability from political leaders through democratic elections and from administrative agencies through ensuring that they act within the limits of lawfully delegated authority. The notion of *responsible agency* suggests that regulators and their political superiors are accountable to the subjects of regulation and, thus, are subject to expectations that regulatory authority will be exercised broadly in accordance with norms of transparency and the rule of law.[129] Norms of responsible agency constitute a belief system driven by changing historical conditions of socioeconomic and political relations in Europe and North America. The general pattern of dissemination of these norms from developed to developing economies reflects imbalances in political and economic power that characterize the current dynamic of globalization. The influence of liberal norms on the legal and political cultures of Hong Kong and Taiwan remains powerful, especially as these areas of the outer periphery engage ever more closely with the dynamics of globalization.

In China, however, local norms informing China's governance culture may be described in terms of the notion of *patrimonial sovereignty*.[130] Drawing on traditional norms of Confucianism combined with ideals of revolutionary transformation drawn from Marxism-Leninism and Maoism, regulatory culture in China tends to emphasize governance by a political authority that remains largely immune to challenge.[131] During the first thirty years of the PRC, law and regulation served primarily as instruments for enforcing policies of the party-state. Norms and processes for accountability were dismissed as bourgeois artifacts deemed inappropriate to China's revolutionary conditions. By the turn of the twenty-first century, even after twenty years of legal reform, the supremacy of the party-state remains a salient feature in the regulatory process.[132] Whether the policy aim is military restrengthening, economic growth, or social welfare, accountability is determined nearly exclusively by party and governmental leaders rather than by popular participation. The patrimonialism of Confucianized Marxism-Leninism and the thoughts of Mao Zedong combine with the sovereignty of party-state supremacy to establish a powerful modality of governance in the PRC. Patrimonial sovereignty thus functions as a frame within which regulators are accountable only to their bureaucratic and political superiors. As a result, they have few obligations to heed those they rule when problems arise regarding either the process or substance of regulation.

In this regard, it is useful to recall that liberal notions about restraining state power conflict strongly with the views of many in the post-Mao period (and earlier) that a strong state is essential to China's development.[133] Chinese legal scholars and officials today remain apprehensive about the applicability of liberal legal norms to China.[134] Official statements about the proper role of law in contemporary China suggest that Chinese legal culture draws on a reservoir of Chinese tradition derived from Confucianism and its assumptions about authority and hierarchy in social organization.[135] While Confucianism and the collectivist norms it has engendered have been severely criticized by many contemporary Chinese thinkers as overly authoritarian and repressive,[136] they remain powerful restraints on the penetration of foreign legal norms associated with liberalism.

This tension between responsible agency and patrimonial sovereignty suggests that conflicts over governance models in the outer periphery will remain strong. While gradual convergence is possible, China's insistence on applying its constitutional norms (which are associated with a unitary state) suggests resistance to liberal influences that permit significant local autonomy. While China's law and policy approach to relations with the outer periphery will continue to be influenced by the international context, the underlying tension between liberal and socialist approaches to law and governance suggest that mutual accommodation will be a complex and difficult process.

Conclusion

China's relations with its peripheral areas reflect a mix of historical and contemporary factors. Governance in the inner periphery is influenced as well by the dynamics of institutional capacity. The effectiveness of Beijing's legal and policy regime faces significant challenges borne of conflicted policy goals, limited local knowledge, centrist perspectives on development, and ongoing difficulties with recruitment, training, and the promotion of minority nationality cadres. Thus, factors of institutional purpose, location, orientation, and cohesion continue to confront China's efforts to bring its legal governance regimes for the inner periphery to fruition. In the outer periphery, China's relations with Hong Kong and Taiwan are challenged by divergent legal and political cultures. China's socialist system faces significant challenges in the effort to build common purpose with local cultures of liberalism. China's ability to establish sustainable governance institutions in the outer periphery will depend on how tensions between patrimonial sovereignty and responsible agency are resolved. With its effort to bring legal reform principles to bear in managing relations with its borderlands, China will continue to face challenges borne of institutional capacity and legal culture in a changing historical context.

Acknowledgements
I would like to thank Eleanor Gill, Michelle Merry, and Harry Chao Wang, students at the UBC Faculty of Law and UBC's Institute of Asian Research, for their invaluable research and editorial assistance on this chapter. The research on which this chapter is based was supported by funding from the Social Sciences and Humanities Research Council of Canada, for which I am deeply grateful.

Notes

1 James A. Millward and Peter Perdue, "Political and Cultural History of the Xinjiang Region through the late 19th Century," in *Xinjiang: China's Muslim Borderland*, edited by S. Frederick Starr, 27-62 (Armonk, NY and London: M.E. Sharpe, 2004).

2 Uradyn E. Bulag, "Inner Mongolia: The Dialectics of Colonization and Ethnicity Building," in *Governing China's Multiethnic Frontiers*, edited by Morris Rossabi, 84-116 (Seattle: University of Washington Press, 2004); and James Reardon-Anderson, *Reluctant Pioneers: China's Expansion Northward 1644-1937* (Stanford: Stanford University Press, 2005).

3 John King Fairbank, *Trade and Diplomacy on the China Coast: The Opening of the Treaty Ports 1842-1854* (Stanford: Stanford University Press, 1953), 7-10.

4 State Council Information Office, "White Paper on National Minorities Policy and Its Practice in China" (Beijing: State Council, 1999); and State Council Information Office, "White Paper: Regional Autonomy for Ethnic Minorities in China" (Beijing: State Council, 2005).

5 Colin Mackerras, *China's Minorities: Integration and Modernization in the Twentieth Century* (Hong Kong: Oxford University Press, 1994); and Morris Rossabi, *Governing China's Multiethnic Frontiers* (Seattle: University of Washington Press, 2004).

6 Wang Zhenmin, *Zhongyang yu tebie xingzhengqu guanxi* [Relations between the centre and special administrative regions] (Beijing: Qinghua University Press, 2002).

7 Chiu Hongdah, "Koo-Wang Talks and the Prospect of Building Constructive and Stable Relations across the Taiwan Straits," *Issues and Studies* 29, 8 (1993): 1-36.

8 State Council Information Office, "White Paper on National Minorities Policy and Its Practice in China"; and State Council Information Office, "White Paper: Regional Autonomy for Ethnic Minorities in China".

9 Jonathan N. Lipman, "White Hats, Oil Cakes, and Common Blood: The Hui in the Contemporary Chinese State," in Rossabi, *Governing China's Multiethnic Frontiers*.

10 Yuan Zhiming, "River Elegy" (TV series 1988).

11 Mark Elvin, *The Pattern of the Chinese Past* (Stanford: Stanford University Press, 1973).

12 Bulag, "Inner Mongolia"; Uradyn E. Bulag, *The Mongols at China's Edge: History and the Politics of National Unity* (Lanham, MD: Rowman and Littlefield, 2002); and Reardon-Anderson, *Reluctant Pioneers*.

13 Millward and Perdue, "Political and Cultural History of the Xinjiang Region"; and Susan Whitfield, *Life along the Silk Road* (London: John Murray Publishers, 1999).

14 Christian Tyler, *Wild West China: The Taming of Xinjiang* (New Brunswick, NJ: Rutgers University Press, 2004), 57-87.

15 James A. Millward and Nabijan Tursun, "Political History and Strategies of Control, 1884-1978," in *Xinjiang: China's Muslim Borderland*, edited by S.F. Starr, 63-98 (Armonk, NY and London: M.E. Sharpe, 2004).

16 Dru Gladney, "Chinese Program of Development and Control, 1978-2002," in Starr, *Xinjiang: China's Muslim Borderland*, 101-19; and Ma Dazheng, *Guojia liyi gaoyu yiqie* [The national interest is paramount] (Urumqi: Xinjiang People's Press, 2003).
17 Nicolas Becquelin, "Xinjiang in the Nineties," *The China Journal* 44 (2000): 65-90; and Yitzhak Schichor, "The Great Wall of Steel: Military and Strategy in Xinjiang," in Starr, *Xinjiang: China's Muslim Borderland*, 120-60.
18 Vivien Pik-Kwan Chan, "War on Terrorism: Local Foes in Mainland's Sights," *South China Morning Post*, 19 September 2001.
19 Dru Gladney, *Muslim Chinese: Ethnic Nationalism in the People's Republic* (Cambridge, MA: Harvard Council on East Asian Studies, 1991); and Felix K. Chang, "China's Central Asian Power and Problems," *Orbis* 47, 3 (1997): 401-26.
20 Ma Dazheng, *Guojia liyi gaoyu yiqie*.
21 Melvin Goldstein, *The Snow Lion and the Dragon: China, Tibet and the Dalai Lama* (Berkeley: University of California Press, 1997); Harvard Project on Cold War Studies, "The Cold War and Its Legacy in Tibet: Great Power Politics and Regional Security" (conference papers, 2001); Dawa Norbu, *China's Tibet Policy* (Richmond, UK: Curzon, 2001); and Tsering Shakya, *The Dragon in the Land of Snows: A History of Modern Tibet Since 1947* (London: Pimlico, 1999).
22 Goldstein, *The Snow Lion and the Dragon*; and Xu Mingxu, *Yinmou yu qiancheng: Xizang sangluan de lai long qu mai* [Intrigue and devotion: The origins and effects of the Tibet riots] (Missasauga, ON: Mirror Books, 1999).
23 Wang Lixiong, *Sky Burial: The Fate of Tibet* (Hong Kong: Mirror Books, 1998); and Xu, *Yinmou yu qiancheng*.
24 State Council Information Office, *White Paper: New Progress in Human Rights in the Tibet Autonomous Region* (Beijing: State Council, 1998).
25 Andrew Fischer, *Poverty by Design: The Economics of Discrimination in Tibet* (Montreal: Canada Tibet Committee, 2002).
26 David S.G. Goodman and Feng Chongyi, "Guangdong: Greater Hong Kong and the New Regionalist Future," in *China Deconstructs: Politics, Trade, and Regionalism*, edited by D. Goodman and Gerald Segal, 177-201 (London and New York: Routledge, 1994).
27 Paul Hathaway, *Operation China: Introducing All the Peoples of China* (Carlisle, UK: Piquant, 2000).
28 Fairbank, *Trade and Diplomacy on the China Coast*.
29 Maurice Collis, *Foreign Mud: The Opium Imbroglio at Canton in the 1930s and the Anglo-Chinese War* (New York: W.W. Norton, 1946).
30 Tung Chee-hwa, *Chief Executive's Policy Address 2005* (Hong Kong: Government Information centre, 2005).
31 Thomas B. Gold, *State and Society in the Taiwan Miracle* (Armonk, NY: M.E. Sharpe, 1986); Richard Louis Edmonds and Steven M. Goldstein, eds., *Taiwan in the Twentieth Century: A Retrospective View* (Cambridge: Cambridge University Press, 2001); and Denis Fred Simon and Michael Y.M. Kau, eds., *Taiwan: Beyond the Economic Miracle* (Armonk, NY: M.E. Sharpe, 1992).
32 Alistair I. Johnston, "Independence through Unification: On the Correct Handling of Contradictions across the Taiwan Strait," *Fairbank Centre for East Asian Research, Contemporary Issues* 2 (1993): 4.
33 Thomas J. Bellows, *Taiwan and Mainland China: Democratization, Political Participation and Economic Development in the 1990s* (Jamaica, NY: Center of Asian Studies, St. Johns University, 2000); and Shelley Rigger, "Social Science and National Identity: A Critique," *Pacific Affairs* (Taiwan Strait, special issue) 72, 4 (1999-2000): 537-52
34 Wang Tay-sheng, "The Legal Development of Taiwan in the 20th Century: Toward a Liberal and Democratic Country," *Pacific Rim Law and Policy Journal* 11, 3 (2002): 531-59.
35 Trevor Corson, "Strait Jacket," *Atlantic Monthly* 294, 5 (2004): 54-58; Goh Sui Noi, "China Gives a Firm 'No,'" *Straits Times*, 14 October 2004; Scott Simon, Wang Fu-chang, Joseph Wong, Andre Laliberte, Robert D'A. Henderson, "Domestic and International Considerations in Taiwan's 2004 Presidential Election: An Interdisciplinary Roundtable," *Pacific Affairs* 77, 4 (2004-5): 683-712; and Tan Qingshan Forest, "Controversial Taiwan Election," *EAI Bulletin*, May 2004, 1-8.

36 Zhang Wuyue, ed., *Liangan guanxi yanjiu* [Perspectives of the relationship across the strait] (Taipei: New Wun Ching Development Publishing, 2003).
37 Xingzheng yuen dalu weiyuanhui [Mainland affairs council of the executive yuan], ed., *Zhengfu dalu zhengce zhongyao wenjian* [Important documents on the government's Mainland policy] (Taipei: Executive Yuan, 2003).
38 Zhang Wuyue, *Liangan guanxi yanjiu*, 90.
39 Wang Zhenmin, *Zhongyang yu tebie xingzhengqu guanxi.*
40 Glen Drover and and K.K. Leung, "Nationalism and Trade Liberalization in Quebec and Taiwan," *Pacific Affairs* 74, 2 (2000): 205-24.
41 Lynn T. White, *Unstately Power,* 2 vols. (Armonk, NY: M.E. Sharpe, 1998).
42 Michael Davis, "The Case for Chinese Federalism," *Journal of Democracy* 10, 2 (1999): 124-37; Sean M. Dougherty and Robert H. McGuckin, "Federalism and the Impetus for Reform in China," *China Law and Practice* 15, 4 (2002): 30-34; and Sean M. Dougherty, Robert H. McGuckin, and J. Radzin, "How Federalism – Not Just Privatization – Is Driving China's Economy," *Zhongguo jingji pinglun* [China economic forum] 1, 2 (2002): 115-19.
43 Huang Yafeng, "Political Institutions and Fiscal Reforms in China," *Problems of Post-Communism* 48, 1 (2001): 16-26; and X. Song, "Thinking Federal: The Relevance of Federalism to China," *Regional and Federal Studies* 10 (2000): 107-28.
44 Yan Jiaqi, "Federalism and the Future of Tibet," in *Tibet through Dissident Chinese Eyes*, edited by Cao Changching and James D. Seymour, 107-20 (Armonk and London: M.E. Sharpe, 1998); and Yan Jiaqi, "China's National Minorities and Federalism," *Dissent* (Summer 1996): 139-44.
45 Amnesty International, *Repression in Tibet, 1987-1992* (New York: Amnesty International, 1992); Amnesty International, *Secret Violence: Human Rights Violations in Xinjiang* (New York: Amnesty International, 1992); and Human Rights Watch, *Cutting Off the Serpent's Head: Tightening Control in Tibet, 1994-1995* (New York: Human Rights Watch, 1996).
46 Goldstein, *The Snow Lion and the Dragon*; Melvin Goldstein, William Siebenschuh, and Tashi Tsering, *The Struggle for Modern Tibet: The Autobiography of Tashi Tsering* (Armonk, NY: M.E. Sharpe, 1999); and Shakya, *The Dragon in the Land of Snows.*
47 Doak Barnett, *China's Far West: Four Decades of Change* (Boulder, CO: Westview Press, 1993).
48 Barry Sautman, "Preferential Policies for Ethnic Minorities in China: The Case of Xinjiang," *Nationalism and Ethnic Politics* 4, 1-2 (1998): 88-118; Solomon M. Karmel, "Ethnic Tension and the Struggle for Order: China's Policies in Tibet," *Pacific Affairs* 68, 4 (1995-96): 485-508; Colin Mackerras, "The Minorities: Achievements and Problems in the Economy, National Integration and Foreign Relations," in *China Review 1998*, edited by Joseph Y.S. Cheng, 281-311 (Hong Kong: Chinese University of Hong Kong Press, 1999); and Wang, *Sky Burial: The Fate of Tibet.*
49 Theodore C. Sorensen and David L. Phillips, *Legal Standards and Autonomy Options for Minorities in China: The Tibetan Case* (Cambridge, MA: Belfer Center for Science and International Affairs, Harvard University, 2004); International Committee of Lawyers for Tibet, *Legal Materials on Tibet*, 2nd ed. (Berkeley, CA: International Committee of Lawyers for Tibet, 1997).
50 Chu Yun-han, "The Challenge of the 1997 Hong Kong Handover for Taiwan," *Pacific Affairs* (Taiwan Strait, special issue) 72, 4 (1999-2000): 553-69.
51 Steve Tsang and Hung-Mao Tien, *Democratization in Taiwan: Implications for China* (New York: St. Martin's Press, 1999); Robert Weller, *Alternate Civilities: Democracy and Culture in China and Taiwan* (Boulder, CO: Westview Press, 1999); and Yash Ghai, *Hong Kong's New Constitutional Order: The Resumption of Chinese Sovereignty and the Basic Law* (Hong Kong: Hong Kong University Press, 1999).
52 Lee Che-fu, "China's Perception of the Taiwan Issue," *New England Law Review* 32 (1998): 695-706.
53 Zhao Suisheng, "Military Coercion and Peaceful Offence: Beijing's Strategy of National Reunification with Taiwan," *Pacific Affairs* (Taiwan Strait, special issue) 72, 4 (1999-2000): 495-512; and Brian Job, Andre Laliberte, and Michael Wallace, "Assessing the Risks of Conflict in the PRC-ROC Enduring Rivalry," *Pacific Affairs* (Taiwan Strait, special issue) 72, 4 (1999-2000): 513-35.

54 Hsing Youtien, "Blood, Thicker Than Water: Interpersonal Relations and Taiwanese Investment in Southern China," *Environment and Planning* 28 (1996): 2241-61.
55 Jonathan Charney and J.R.V. Prescott, "Resolving Cross-Strait Relations between China and Taiwan," *American Journal of International Law* 94 (2000): 453-77.
56 Elizabeth J. Perry and Mark Selden, eds. *Chinese Society: Change, Conflict, and Resistance* (London and New York: Routledge, 2000); and Arif Dirlik and Maurice Meisner, eds., *Marxism and the Chinese Experience* (Armonk, NY: M.E. Sharpe, 1989).
57 Michael E. Brown, "The Impact of Government Policies on Ethnic Relations," in *Government Policies and Ethnic Relations in Asia and the Pacific*, edited by M. Brown and S. Ganguly, 511-75 (Cambridge and London: MIT Press, 1997).
58 Constance Backhouse, *Color-Coded: A Legal History of Racism in Canada, 1900-1950* (Toronto: University of Toronto Press, 1999).
59 Ann Gomer Sunahara, *The Politics of Racism* (Toronto: James Lorimer, 1981).
60 Richard H. Bartlett, *Indian Reserves and Aboriginal Lands in Canada: A Homeland* (Saskatoon: University of Saskatchewan Native Law Centre, 1990); and Paul Tennant, *Aboriginal Peoples and Politics: The Indian Land Question in British Columbia, 1849-1989* (Vancouver: UBC Press, 1990).
61 June Teufel Dreyer, "Ethnicity and Economic Development in Xinjiang," *Inner Asia* 2, 2 (2000): 137-54; Mackerras, *China's Minorities*; and Colin Mackerras, "The Minorities: Achievements and Problems in the Economy, National Integration and Foreign Relations," in Cheng, *China Review 1998*, 281-311.
62 Johnston, "Independence through Unification: On the Correct Handling of Contradictions across the Taiwan Strait," 4; and Shelley Rigger, "Social Science and National Identity: A Critique," 537-52.
63 Pitman B. Potter, *The Chinese Legal System: Globalization and Local Legal Culture* (London: Routledge, 2001).
64 Duncan Hewitt, "Clash as Hong Kong Court Bars Immigrants," BBC News, 3 December 1999.
65 State Council Information Office and Xinhua (New China News Agency), "China's Top Lawmaker Stresses Regional Autonomy in Xinjiang," news release, 14 March 2002.
66 Chiu, "Koo-Wang Talks and the Prospect of Building Constructive and Stable Relations across the Taiwan Straits," 1-36.
67 Ghai, *Hong Kong's New Constitutional Order: The Resumption of Chinese Sovereignty and the Basic Law*); and Albert Chen, "The Provisional Legislative Council of the SAR," *Hong Kong Law Journal* 27 (1997): 1.
68 Justin Rudelson and William Jankowiak, "Acculturation and Resistance: Xinjiang Identities in Flux," in Starr, *Xinjiang: China's Muslim Borderland*, 309.
69 Wu Shimin, *Zhongguo minzu zhengce duben* [Reader on China's nationalities policy] (Beijing: Central Nationalities University Press, 1998), 165-67.
70 Ma, *Guojia liyi gaoyu yiqie* [The national interest is paramount]; and Chan, "War on Terrorism: Local Foes in Mainland's Sights."
71 Gardner Bovington, "Heteronomy and Its Discontents: 'Minzu Regional Autonomy' in Xinjiang," in *Governing China's Multiethnic Frontiers*, edited by Morris Rossabi, 133-37 (Seattle: University of Washington Press, 2004).
72 "Xuexiao shi guanche shishi 'Guojia tongyong yuyan wenzi fa' de jiben zhendi" (Schools are the basic front for fully implementing the Law on Simultaneous Language Usage by the state), in *Zhonghua renmin gonghe guo guojia tongyong yuyan wenzi fa xuexi duben* [Study reader on the Simultaneous Language Law of the PRC], edited by NPC Committee on Education, Science, Culture and Health and Ministry of Education, 34-36 (Beijing: Language Press, 2001).
73 Xu, *Yinmou yu qiancheng: Xizang sangluan de lai long qu mai* [Intrigue and devotion: The Origins and effects of the Tibet riots], 265-73.
74 Wu, *Zhongguo minzu zhengce duben* [Reader on China's nationalities policy], 47-49, 181-82.
75 State Council Information Office, *White Paper on National Minorities Policy and Its Practice in China*.
76 Nationality Region Autonomy Law (NRAL), Article 1.

77 Ibid., Article 5.
78 NRAL, preface.
79 NRAL, Articles 15-16.
80 NRAL, Chapter 6.
81 NRAL, Articles 71-72.
82 Constitution, Article 122.
83 Hu Jintao, "Gaodu zhongshi, qieshi zuohao shaoshu minzu ganbu de peiyang xuanba gongzuo" [Raise the emphasis and completely excel in minority cadre training and selection work], in *Minzu gongzuo wenzhai xuanbian 1990-2002* [Collection of documents on nationalities work – 1990-2002], edited by State Nationalities Affairs Commission and CPC Central Archives, 66-81 (Beijing: Beijing Central Archives Press, 2003).
84 State Council Information Office, *White Paper on National Minorities Policy and Its Practice in China*; and Xinjiang CPC Propaganda Department.
85 Xinjiang CPC Propaganda Department; and Song Caifa, ed., *Minzu quyu zizhifa tonglun* [General survey on the law on autonomy in minority areas] (Beijing: Nationalities Press, 2003), 51-57.
86 Pitman B. Potter, "Legal Reform in China: Institutions, Culture, and Selective Adaptation," *Law and Social Inquiry* 28, 4 (2004): 465-95.
87 Mackerras, *China's Ethnic Minorities and Globalisation*; and Barry Sautman, "Ethnic Law and Minority Rights in China: Progress and Constraints," *Law and Policy*, 21, 3 (1999): 283-314.
88 "Hu Jintao Addresses CPC Politburo Study Session, Calls for Common Prosperity," *Xinhua* Domestic Service, 22 October 2004, in *FBIS Daily Report: China,* FBIS-CHI 2004-1022, 22 October 2004; "New Historic Chapter of China National Solidarity," *People's Daily Online,* 11 March 2005; and "President Hu Calls for Good Implementation of Policies on Ethnic Minorities, Religions," *People's Daily Online*, 10 March 10, 2005. See http://english.people.com.cn/200503/09/eng20050309_176097.html.
89 State Nationalities Affairs Commission, *Zhongguo gongchandang guanyu minzu wenti de jiben guandian he zhengce* [Basic approaches and policies of the Chinese Communist Party on nationalities issues] (Beijing: Nationalities Press, 2002), 46.
90 Constitution, Article 115; NRAL Preface and Article 5; and Wu, *Zhongguo minzu zhengce duben* [Reader on China's nationalities policy], 43.
91 State Council Information Office, *White Paper: Regional Autonomy for Ethnic Minorities in China*.
92 Miao Pusheng, "Xinjiang zai Zhongguo tongyi de duominzu guojia xingcheng, fazhan, he gonggu guocheng zhong de lishi diwei" [Xinjiang's historic role in the process of the formation, development, and consolidation of unified China as a multi-ethnic state], in *Xinjiang yanjiu wenlun xuan, di yi ji* [Collection of essays on the study of Xinjiang, vol. 1], edited by Tie Muer and Mao Gangning, 52-64 (Beijing: Nationalities Press, 2003).
93 State Nationalities Affairs Commission, *Zhongguo gongchandang guanyu minzu wenti de jiben guandian he zhengce* [Basic approaches and policies of the Chinese Communist Party on nationalities issues] (Beijing: Nationalities Press, 2002), 53.
94 Bulag, "Inner Mongolia: The Dialectics of Colonization and Ethnicity Building," 84-116; Susan K. McCarthy "The State, Minorities, and Dilemmas of Development in Contemporary China," *Fletcher Forum on World Affairs* 26, 2 (2002): 107-18; and June Teufel Dreyer, *China's Forty Millions: Minority Nationalities and National Integration in the People's Republic of China* (Cambridge, MA: Harvard University Press, 1976).
95 Tie Muer and Mao Gongning, ed., *Xinjiang yanjiu wenlun xuan, di yi ji* [Collection of essays on the study of Xinjiang, vol. 1] (Urumqi: Xinjiang People's Press, 2003); and Ma Dazheng, *Guojia liyi gaoyu yiqie* [The national interest is paramount].
96 Ling Jun, "Xitong yanjiu he zhengque xuanquan Xinjiang de lishi, wei Xinjiang de wending he fazhen fuwu" [Systematic research and precise propaganda on Xinjiang's history serve stability and development in Xinjiang], in *Xinjiang yanjiu wenlun xuan, di yi ji* [Collection of essays on the study of Xinjiang, vol. 1], edited by Tie Muer and Mao Gongning, 43-51 (Urumqi: Xinjiang People's Press, 2003).
97 Compare "Xizang de xiandaihua fazhan" [Development of modernization in Tibet] (2001), in State Nationalities Affairs Commission and CPC Central Archives, *Minzu gongzuo wenzhai*

xuanbian, 1990-2002 [Collection of documents on nationalities work, 1990-2002], 447-74 (Beijing Central Archives Press, 2003) with Wang Lixiong, *Sky Burial: The Fate of Tibet*, 372-374; Compare Wang Luolin and Wei Houkai, *Zhongguo xibu dakaifa zhengce* [China's western development policy] (Beijing: Economic Management Publishing, 2003), 7-18, with Tyler, *Wild West China: The Taming of Xinjiang*, 214-21.

98 State Council Information Office, *White Paper: Regional Autonomy for Ethnic Minorities in China*.

99 Sautman, "Preferential Policies for Ethnic Minorities in China."

100 Qing Jue, Zhang Zhuyin, Xu Jinhua, and Zhou Zhuanhui, "Xinjiang jingji shehui fazhen due minzu guanxi de yingxiang" [Effects of economic and social development on nationalities relations in Xinjiang], in *Xinjiang yanjiu wenlun xuan, di yi ji* [Collection of essays on the study of Xinjiang, vol. 1], edited by Tie Muer and Mao Gongning, 196-224 (Urumqi: Xinjiang People's Press, 2003); and Ma, *Guojia liyi gaoyu yiqie* [The national interest is paramount], 138-42.

101 Wang Luolin and Wei Houkai, *Zhongguo xibu dakaifa zhengce* [China's western development policy], chap. 13.

102 Ni Guoliang, *Zhongguo xibei diqu xiandaihua zhong de jingji yu wenhua guanxi* [Relations between economy and culture in the course of modernization in China's northwest] (Lanzhou: Gansu People's Press, 1998), intro.

103 Ma Zifu, ed., *Xibu kaifa yu duominzu wenhua* [Western China development and multi-ethnic cultures] (Beijing: Huaxia Press, 2003).

104 NRAL, Article 18.

105 Lai Bangfan, ed., *Xibu kaifa zhengfu guanli yanjiu* [Study of government administration in China's western development] (Beijing: National Administration Institute, 2002), 30 et seq.

106 State Nationalities Affairs Commission, *Zhongguo gongchandang guanyu minzu wenti de jiben guandian he zhengce* [Basic approaches and policies of the Chinese Communist Party on nationalities issues] (Beijing: Nationalities Press, 2002), 169-71.

107 "Zhonggong zhongyang zuzhi bu, Zhonggong zhongyang tongzhanbu, Guojia minwei guanyu jinyibu zuohao peiyang xuanba shaoshu minzu ganbu gongzuo de yijian" [Opinion of the CPC Organization Department, CPC United Front Work Deptartment, and State Nationalities Ministry on continuing to do a good job of training and selecting minority cadres], in Central Party School Nationalities and Religious Theory Office 1998, *Xin shiqi minzu zongjiao gongzuo xuanchuan shouce* [Propaganda handbook on minority religions work in the new era) (Beijing: Religion and Culture Press, 2002), 136-41.

108 "Hu Jintao Addresses CPC Politburo Study Session, Calls for Common Prosperity," *Xinhua* Domestic Service, 22 October 2004, in *FBIS Daily Report: China*, FBIS-CHI 2004-1022 (22 October 2004).

109 Mark Roberti, *The Fall of Hong Kong: China's Triumph and Britain's Betrayal*, rev. ed. (New York: John Wiley, 1996).

110 Wang, *Zhongyang yu tebie xingzhengqu guanxi* [Relations between the centre and special administrative regions], 50-54.

111 Dai Xiaoming, *Minzu fazhi wenti tansuo* [Inquiry on nationalities issues] (Beijing: Nationalities Press, 2002), 44-46.

112 Peter Wesley-Smith, ed., *Hong Kong's Basic Law: Problems and Prospects* (Hong Kong: Hong Kong University Faculty of Law, 1990); and Yash Ghai, *Hong Kong's New Constitutional Order: The Resumption of Chinese Sovereignty and the Basic Law* (Hong Kong: Hong Kong University Press, 1999).

113 Lu Gonghui and Civic Exchange, eds., *Rang minyi shenyin xiangqilai* [Let ring the sound of the will of the people] (Hong Kong: Hong Kong University Press, 2002).

114 Berry Hsu, "Judicial Independence under the Basic Law," *Hong Kong Law Journal*, vol. 34, pt. 2 (2004), 279-302.

115 *Ng Ka Ling v. Director of Immigration* [1999] (HKLRD 315); Johannes Chan, Fu Hualing, and Yash Ghai, *Hong Kong's Constitutional Debate: Conflict over Interpretation* (Hong Kong: Hong Kong University Press, 2000); and Benny Tai, "Why Second-Generation Mainland Children Have No Right of Abode in Hong Kong," *Hong Kong Law Journal* 29, 2 (1999): 208-15.

116 Michael (Dai Dawei) Davis, "Jiben fa, renquan he minzhu: Lilun yu shijian" [The basic law, human rights, and democracy: Theory and practice], in *Chuangjian minzhu* [Establishing

democracy], edited by Lu Gonghui and Civil Exchange, 9-19 (Hong Kong: Hong Kong University Press, 2003).

117 Fu Hualing, Carole J. Peterson, and Simon N.M. Young, eds., *National Security and Fundamental Freedoms: Hong Kong's Article 23 under Scrutiny* (Hong Kong: Hong Kong University Press, 2005).

118 Janus Lam, "Beijing Misstep over New Hong Kong Head," *Asia Times On-Line*, 2 April 2005); Chris Hogg, "China to Settle New HK Chief Row," BBC, 6 April 2005; and "Hong Kong Lawmaker to Legally Challenge China," *Taipei Times*, 25 March 2005.

119 Austin Coates, *Myself a Magistrate: Memoirs of a Special Magistrate* (Hong Kong: Oxford University Press, 1968).

120 Su Yigong, "The Application of Chinese Law and Custom in Hong Kong," *Hong Kong Law Journal* 29, 2 (1999): 267-93.

121 Anti-Secession Law, Article 1.

122 Ibid., Article 7.

123 Ibid., Article 7.4.

124 Taiwan Affairs Office and Information Office of the State Council, "The One-China Principle and the Taiwan Issue" (Beijing: State Council, 2000).

125 *Pacific Affairs* (Taiwan Strait, special issue) 72, 4 (1999-2000).

126 Potter, "Legal Reform in China," 465-495.

127 Herbert H.P. Ma, *Law and Contemporary Society: Essays in Honor of the Seventieth Birthday of Professor Herbert Han-pao Ma* (Taipei: Si shang shu wu, 1996); and Berry Hsu, *The Common Law System in Chinese Context: Hong Kong in Transition* (Armonk, NY: M.E. Sharpe, 1992).

128 Will Kymlicka, *Liberalism, Community and Culture* (Oxford: Clarendon Press, 1991).

129 Potter, "Legal Reform in China."

130 Ibid.

131 Kenneth Lieberthal, *Governing China* (New York: W.W. Norton, 1995); and State Council Information Office, *White Paper: Progress in China's Human Rights Cause* (Beijing: State Council, 2001).

132 Potter, *The Chinese Legal System.*

133 Lieberthal, *Governing China.*

134 Gong Piyang, "Zhongguo fa zhi xiandaihua mianju de si da maodun" [Four major contradictions in the modernization of Chinese law], *Tansuo yu zhengming* [Inquiry and Debate] 3 (1995): 3-6.

135 Anne Kent, *Between Freedom and Subsistence: Human Rights in China* (Hong Kong: Oxford University Press, 1993).

136 Wang Ruoshui, *Wei rendao zhuyi bianhu* [In defense of humanism] (Beijing: United Press, 1986).

Bibliography

Alekseev, A.I. *Amurskaya Ekspeditsiya 1849-1855 gg.* [Amur expedition, 1849-1855]. Moscow: Mysl', 1974.

–. *Russian Geographic Explorations in the Far East and in the Northern America, XIX-beginning of the XX centuries*. Nauka: 1976.

Amnesty International. *Repression in Tibet, 1987-1992*. New York: Amnesty International, 1992.

–. *Secret Violence: Human Rights Violations in Xinjiang*. New York: Amnesty International, 1992.

Andrade, Tonio. "Commerce, Culture and Conflict: Taiwan under European Rule, 1623-1662." PhD diss., Yale University, 2001.

Anuchin, V.A. *Geograficheskie ocherki Manchzhurii* [Essays on geography of Manchuria]. Moscow: Gosudstvennoe Izdatelstvo Geograficheskoi Literatury, 1948.

Anzaldina, Gloria. *Borderlands/La Frontera: The New Mestiza*. San Francisco: Aunt Lute Books, 1999.

Armitage, David. *The Ideological Origins of the British Empire*. Cambridge: Cambridge University Press, 2000.

Arseniev, V.K. "Kraikii fiziko-geograficheskii ocherk basseina reki Amura" [Protokol of public meeting of the Russian Geographic Society] (6 June 1916).

Atwood, Christopher P. *Encyclopedia of Mongolia and the Mongol Empire*. New York: Facts on File, 2004.

Backhouse, Constance. *Color-Coded: A Legal History of Racism in Canada, 1900-1950*. Toronto: University of Toronto Press, 1999.

Bagby, Wesley. *The Eagle-Dragon Alliance: America's Relations with China in World War II*. Newark: University of Delaware Press, 1992.

Baker, Alan. *Fraternity among the French Peasantry: Sociability and Voluntary Associations in the Loire Valley, 1815-1914*. Cambridge: Cambridge University Press, 1999.

Barfield, Thomas. *The Perilous Frontier: Nomadic Empires and China*. Cambridge, MA: B. Blackwell, 1989.

Bargow, Leo. "A Few Remarks on Maps of the Amur, the Tartar Strait and Sakhalin." *Imago Mundi* 12 (1955): 129-30.

Barlow, Tani, and Gary Bjorge, eds. *I Myself Am a Woman: Selected Writings of Ding Ling*. Boston: Beacon Press, 1989.

Barnett, Doak. *China's Far West: Four Decades of Change*. Boulder, CO: Westview Press, 1993.

Bartlett, Richard H. *Indian Reserves and Aboriginal Lands in Canada: A Homeland*. Saskatoon: University of Saskatchewan Native Law Centre, 1990.

Bawuling nongchangshi [Gazetteer of farm 850]. Hulin: Bawuling nongchangshi bianxie bangongshi, 1986.

Bawusan nongchangzhi [Gazetteer of farm 853]. Jiamusi: Bawusan nongchangzhi bianxie bangongshi, 1986.

Beauvais, Jean. *Documents geographiques, historiques et linguistiques sur la ville et la region de Long-tcheou* [Geographical, historical and linguistic documents on the town and the region of Longzhou]. Hanoi: Imprimerie d'extreme orient, 1909.

Becquelin, Nicolas. "Xinjiang in the Nineties." *China Journal* 44 (2000): 65-90.

Bellows, Thomas J. *Taiwan and Mainland China: Democratization, Political Participation and Economic Development in the 1990s*. Jamaica, NY: Center of Asian Studies St. Johns University, 2000.

Bergholz, Fred W. *The Partition of the Steppe: The Struggle of the Russians, Manchus and the Zunghar Mongols for Empire in Central Asia, 1619-1758 – A Study in Power Politics*. New York: Peter Lang, 1993.

Bernstein, Thomas. *Up to the Mountains and Down to the Villages: The Transfer of Youth from Urban to Rural China*. New Haven, CT: Yale University Press, 1977.

Blum, Susan, and Lionel Jensen, eds. *China Off Center: Mapping the Margins of the Middle Kingdom*. Honolulu: University of Hawaii Press, 2003.

Bo Yibo. *Ruogan zhongda juece yu shijian de huigu* [Reflections on several important decisions and events], 2 vols. Beijing: Zhonggong zhongyang dangxiao chubanshe, 1991-93.

Bolotov, A.A. *Amur I ego Bassein* [Amur and its basin]. Khabrin, 1925.

Bourdieu, Pierre. *Practical Reason: On the Theory of Action*. Stanford, CA: Stanford University Press, 1998.

Bovington, Gardner. "Heteronomy and Its Discontents: 'Minzu Regional Autonomy' in Xinjiang." In *Governing China's Multiethnic Frontiers*, edited by Morris Rossabi, 133-37. Seattle: University of Washington Press, 2004.

Bowers Museum. *Symbols of Power: Masterpieces from the Nanjing Museum*. Anaheim, CA: Bowers Museum, 2002.

Brown, Michael E. "The Impact of Government Policies on Ethnic Relations." In *Government Policies and Ethnic Relations in Asia and the Pacific*, edited by Michael E. Brown and S. Ganguly, 511-75. Cambridge, MA; London: MIT Press, 1997.

Bui Xuan Dinh. *Le Lang Phep Nuoc* [Village customs and state law]. Hanoi: Phap Ly, 1985.

Bulag, Uradyn E. "Inner Mongolia: The Dialectics of Colonization and Ethnicity Building." In *Governing China's Multiethnic Frontiers*, edited by Morris Rossabi, 84-116. Seattle: University of Washington Press, 2004.

–. *The Mongols at China's Edge: History and the Politics of National Unity*. Lanham, MD: Rowman and Littlefield, 2002.

Cammann, Schuyler. "The Evolution of Magic Squares in China." *Journal of the American Oriental Society* 80 (1960): 116-24.

Chan, Johannes, Fu Hualing, and Yash Ghai. *Hong Kong's Constitutional Debate: Conflict over Interpretation*. Hong Kong: Hong Kong University Press, 2000.

Chan, Vivien Pik-Kwan. "War on Terrorism: Local Foes in Mainland's Sights." *South China Morning Post*, 19 September 2001.

Chang, Felix K. "China's Central Asian Power and Problems." *Orbis* 47, 3 (1997): 401-26.

Chang Yü-chüan. *Wang Shou-jen as a Statesman*. Peking: Chinese Social and Political Science Association, 1940.

Charney, Jonathan, and J.R.V. Prescott. "Resolving Cross-Strait Relations between China and Taiwan." *American Journal of International Law* 94 (2000): 453-77.

Chen, Albert. "The Provisional Legislative Council of the SAR." *Hong Kong Law Journal* 27 (1997): 1.

Chen Cheng. *Chen Zhushan xian sheng wen ji* [Collected writings of Chen Cheng]. Reprint. Jinan: Qi Lu shu she chuban she, 1997.

Ch'en, Kenneth. "Matteo Ricci's Contribution to, and Influence on, Geographical Knowledge in China." *Journal of the American Oriental Society* 59, 3 (1939): 325-59.

Chen Minsun. "Ferdinand Verbiest and the Geographical Works by Jesuits in Chinese 1584-1674." In *Ferdinand Verbiest, S.J. (1623-1688): Jesuit Missionary, Scientist, Engineer, and Diplomat*, edited by John Witek, 123-64. Nettetal: Steyler Verlag, 1994.

Chen Zilong, ed. *Huang Ming jingshi wenbian* [A collection of statecraft essays of the imperial Ming court]. Taipei: Guofeng chubanshe, 1964 ed.

–. *Ming jingshi wenbian* [Compendium of statecraft documents of the Ming], 6 vols. Reprint. Beijing: Zhonghua shuju, 1987.

Cheng Chongde. "Qingdai xianqi bianjiang tonglun, xia" [A general discussion of the earlier period Qing borderlands, part 2]. *Qingshi yanjiu* [Studies in Qing history], 1998, 1:14-27.

Cheng K'o-ch'eng. "Cheng Ch'eng-kung's Maritime Expansion and Early Ch'ing Coastal Prohibition." In *Development and Decline of Fukien Province in the 17th and 18th Centuries*, edited by E.B. Vermeer, 228-44. Leiden and New York: E.J. Brill, 1990.

Chiu Hongdah. "Koo-Wang Talks and the Prospect of Building Constructive and Stable Relations across the Taiwan Straits." *Issues and Studies* 29, 8 (1993): 1-36.

Cho Kwang. "Chosŏn hugi ŭi py'ŏngy'ŏng ŭisik" [Border consciousness in late Chosŏn]. *Paeksan hakpo* 16 (1974): 164.

Chu Yun-han. "The Challenge of the 1997 Hong Kong Handover for Taiwan." *Pacific Affairs* (Taiwan Strait, special issue) 72, 4 (1999-2000): 553-69.

Chung, Chai-sik. *A Korean Confucian Encounter with the Modern World: Yi Hang-no and the West*. Berkeley, CA: Institute of East Asian Studies, 1995.

Cimeddorji, Jaqa. *Die Briefe des Kang-Hsi-Kaisers aus den Jahren 1696-97 an den Kronprinzen Yin-Cheng aus mandschurischen Geheimdokumenten: ein Beitrag zum ersten Dsungarenkrieg der Ching 1690-1697* [The letters of the Kangxi emperor from the years 1696-1697 to the crown prince Yinzheng, from secret Manchu documents: a contribution to the study of the first Qing Zunghar war]. Wiesbaden: Otto Harrassowitz, 1991.

Coates, Austin. *Myself a Magistrate: Memoirs of a Special Magistrate*. Hong Kong: Oxford University Press, 1968.

Cohen, Myron L. "Cultural and Political Inventions in Modern China: The Case of the 'Peasant.'" *Daedalus* 122, 2 (1993): 151-70.

Cohen, Paul A. *Discovering History in China: American Historical Writings on the Recent Chinese Past*. New York: Columbia University Press, 1984.

–. *History in Three Keys: The Boxers as Event, Experience, and Myth*. New York: Columbia University Press, 1997.

Collis, Maurice. *Foreign Mud: The Opium Imbroglio at Canton in the 1930s and the Anglo-Chinese War*. New York: W.W. Norton, 1946.

Cong Peiyuan, and Zhao Mingqi, eds. *Cao Tingjie ji* [Collected works by Cao Tingjie], vol. 2. Beijing: Zhonghua shuju, 1985.

Cong Weixi. *Zouxiang hundun* [Going to chaos]. Beijing: Zhongguo shehui kexue chubanshe, 1998.

Constitution of the People's Republic of China.

Cordier, Henri. *Histoire des relations de la Chine avec les puissances occidentales, 1860-1902* [The history of China's relations with the western powers], 3 vols. Paris: F. Alcan, 1901-2.

Corson, Trevor. "Strait Jacket." *Atlantic Monthly* 294, 5 (2004): 54-58.

Crossley, P.K. *A Translucent Mirror: History and Identity in Qing Imperial Ideology*. Berkeley: University of California Press, 1999.

Cuenot, Joseph. *Au pays des pavillons noirs* [In the land of the black banners]. Hong Kong: Imprimerie de Nazareth, 1925.

Da Qing Lichao Shilu [Veritable records of the Qing], 93 vols. Reprint. Taibei: Huawen Shuju, 1963-4.

Dai Huang. *Jiusi yisheng* [Narrow escape from death]. Beijing: Zhongyang bianyi chubanshe, 1998.

Dai Xiaoming. *Minzu fazhi wenti tansuo* [Inquiry on nationalities issues]. Beijing: Nationalities Press, 2002.

Dai Yi. *Jianming Qingshi*, 2 vols. Beijing: Renmin chubanshe, 1984.

Dai Yingcong. "A Disguised Defeat: The Myanmar Campaign of the Qing Dynasty." *Modern Asian Studies* 38, 1 (2004): 145-88.

Dalizhabu, Bao. *Mingdai mo nan Menggu lishi yanjiu* [Studies in the history of the southern deserts of Mongolia in the Ming period]. Hailaer: Nei Menggu wenhua chuban she, 1997.

Dautremer, Joseph. "Yunnan et Kouang-si: frontieres Indo-Chinoise" [Yunnan and Guangxi: Indochinese frontiers]. In *Bulletin de l'association amicale Franco-Chinoise*, 1909.

Davis, Michael. "The Case for Chinese Federalism." *Journal of Democracy* 10, 2 (1999): 124-37.

Davis, Michael (Dai Dawei). "Jiben fa, renquan he minzhu: Lilun yu shijian" [The basic law, human rights, and democracy: theory and practice]. In *Chuangjian minzhu* [Establishing democracy], edited by Lu Gonghui and Civil Exchange, 9-19. Hong Kong: Hong Kong University Press, 2003.

Day, John. "The Search for the Origins of the Chinese Manuscript Copies of Matteo Ricci's Maps." *Imago Mundi* 47 (1995): 94-117.

D'Elia, Pasquale M. "Recent Discoveries and New Studies (1938-60) on the World Map in Chinese of Father Matteo Ricci S.J." *Monumenta Serica* 20 (1961): 82-164.

De Heer, Philip. *The Care-Taker Emperor: Aspects of the Imperial Institution in Fifteenth-Century China as Reflected in the Political History of the Reign of Chu Ch'i-yü*. Leiden: E.J. Brill, 1986.

Di Cosmo, Nicola. "Military Aspects of the Manchu Wars against the Čaqars." In *Warfare in Inner Asian History (500-1800)*, edited by Nicola Di Cosmo, 337-67. Leiden: E.J. Brill, 2002.

Di Cosmo, Nicola, and Dalizhabu Bao. *Manchu-Mongol Relations on the Eve of the Qing Conquest*. Leiden: E.J. Brill, 2003.

Ding Ling. *Fengxue renjian* [Blizzard world]. Xiamen: Xiamen daxue chubanshe, 1986.

Ding Peihua. "Luelun 'Shanghai wuguo' fazhan de jichu" [A brief discussion of the basis of development of the "Shanghai Five" countries]. *Shehui kexue* [Social sciences] 7 (2001): 45-49.

Ding Shouhe, comp. *Zhongguo lidai zhiguo ce xuancui* [Selected highlights of Chinese state administration policies through the centuries]. Beijing: Gaodeng jiaoyu chubanshe, 1994.

Dirlik, Arif, and Maurice Meisner, eds. *Marxism and the Chinese Experience*. Armonk, NY: M.E. Sharpe, 1989.

Dougherty S., and R. McGuckin. "Federalism and the Impetus for Reform in China." *China Law and Practice* 15, 4 (2002): 30-34.

Dougherty S., R. McGuckin, and J. Radzin. "How Federalism – Not Just Privatization – Is Driving China's Economy." *Zhongguo jingji pinglun* [China economic forum] 1, 2 (2002): 115-19.

Dreyer, June Teufel. *China's Forty Millions: Minority Nationalities and National Integration in the People's Republic of China*. Cambridge, MA: Harvard University Press, 1976.

–. "Ethnicity and Economic Development in Xinjiang." *Inner Asia* 2, 2 (2000): 137-54.

Drover, Glen, and K.K. Leung. "Nationalism and Trade Liberalization in Quebec and Taiwan." *Pacific Affairs* 74, 2 (2000): 205-24.

Du Weiyun. *Qing Qianjia shidai zhi shixue yu shijia* [Historians and historical studies in the Qianlong and Jiaqing eras]. Taibei: Wenshi zongkan, 1962.

Duyvendak, Jan Julius Lodewijk. *Ma Huan Re-examined*. Amsterdam: Noord-Hollandsche uitgeversmaatschappij, 1933.

Edmonds, Richard L. "The Willow Palisade." *Annals of the Association of American Geographers* 69, 4 (1979): 611-21.

Edmonds, Richard Louis, and Steven M. Goldstein, eds. *Taiwan in the Twentieth Century: A Retrospective View*. Cambridge: Cambridge University Press, 2001.

Eggert, Marion. "A Borderline Case: Korean Traveler's Views of the Chinese Border (Eighteenth to Nineteenth Century)." In *China and Her Neighbours: Borders, Visions of the Other, Foreign Policy, 10th to 19th Century*, edited by Sabine Sabringhaus and Roderich Ptak. Wiesbaden: Harrossowitx Verlag, 1997.

Eisenstadt, S.M. *Revolution and the Transformation of Societies: A Comparative Study of Civilizations*. New York: The Free Press, 1878.

Elliott, J.H. *The Old World and the New, 1492-1650*. Cambridge: Cambridge University Press, 1970.

Elliot, Mark. "The Limits of Tartary: Manchuria in Imperial and National Geographies." *Journal of Asian Studies* 59, 3 (2000): 603-46.

–. *The Manchu Way: The Eight Banners and Ethnic Identity in Late Imperial China*. Stanford, CA: Stanford University Press, 2001.

Elman, Benjamin. *A Cultural History of Civil Examinations in Late Imperial China*. Berkeley: University of California Press, 2000.

–. *From Philosophy to Philology: Social and Intellectual Aspects of Change in Late Imperial China*. 2nd ed. Los Angeles: UCLA Asia Institute Monograph Series, 2001.

–. *On Their Own Terms: Science in China, 1550-1900*. Cambridge, MA: Harvard University Press, 2005.

Elverskog, Johan. *The Jewel Translucent Sūtra: Altan Khan and the Mongols in the Sixteenth Century*. Leiden: E.J. Brill, 2003.

Elvin, Mark. *The Pattern of the Chinese Past*. Stanford, CA: Stanford University Press, 1973.

Fairbank, John King. *China: A New History*. Cambridge, MA: Harvard University Press, 1992.

–. *Trade and Diplomacy on the China Coast: The Opening of the Treaty Ports, 1842-1854*. Cambridge, MA: Harvard University Press, 1953.

Fairbank, J.K., and S.Y. Teng. "On the Ch'ing Tributary System." *Harvard Journal of Asiatic Studies* 6 (1941): 161.

Fairbank, J.K., E.O. Reischauer, and A.M. Craig. *East Asia: Tradition and Transformation*. Boston: Houghton Mifflin Press, 1973.

Famin, Pierre. *Au Tonkin et sur la frontiere de Kouang-si* [In Tongking and on the frontier of Guangxi]. Paris: Challamel, 1895.

Fang Junyi. "Shili shiyi shuo" [Hereditary clerks and hereditary office servants]. In *Huangchao jingshi wen xubian* [A continuation of the statecraft essays of the present court], compiled by Sheng Kang. Taipei: Wenhai, 1972.

Farquhar, David M. "The Origins of the Manchus' Mongolian Policy." In *The Chinese World Order*, edited by John K. Fairbank, 198-205. Cambridge, MA: Harvard University Press, 1968.

Farquhar, Judith B., and James L. Hevia. "Culture and Postwar American Historiography of China." *Positions* 1, 2 (1993): 486-525.

Fei Xin. *Hsing-ch'a-sheng-lan: The Overall Survey of the Star Raft by Fei Hsin*, translated by J.V.G. Mills and revised, annotated, and edited by Roderich Ptak. Amsterdam: Noord-Hollandsche uitgeversmaatschappij, 1933.

Feng Shiyang et al., eds. *Annan lai wei tu ce* [Album concerning the submission of Annam]. Reprint. Beijing: Shumu wenxian chuban she, 1988.

Fischer, Andrew. "Poverty by Design: The Economics of Discrimination in Tibet." Montreal: Canada Tibet Committee, 2002.

Fisher, Carney. *The Chosen One: Succession and Adoption in the Court of Ming Shizong*. Sydney: Allen and Unwin, 1990.

Fletcher, Joseph. "Turco-Mongolian Monarchic Tradition in the Ottoman Empire." *Harvard Ukrainian Studies* 3/4 (1979-80): part 1, 236-51.

Foret, Phillipe. *Mapping Chengde: The Qing Landscape Enterprise*. Honolulu: University of Hawai'i Press, 2000.

Foss, Theodore. "A Western Interpretation of China Jesuit Cartography." In *East Meets West: The Jesuits in China, 1582-1773*, edited by Charles Ronan and Bonnie Oh. Chicago: Loyola University Press, 1988.

Fu Hualing, Carole J. Peterson, and Simon N.M. Young, eds. *National Security and Fundamental Freedoms: Hong Kong's Article 23 under Scrutiny*. Hong Kong: Hong Kong University Press, 2005.

Fuchs, Walter. "Materialen zur Kartographie der Mandju-Zeit, part 1" [Materials on cartography of the Manchu period, part 1]. *Monumenta Serica* 1 (1935-36): 395-96; "Materialen zur Kartographie der Mandju-Zeit, part 2" [Materials on cartography of the Manchu period, part 2]. *Monumenta Serica* 3 (1938): 189-231.

–. "Der Jesuiten-Atlas der Kanghsi-Zeit" [The Jesuit atlas of the Kangxi period]. *Monumenta Serica*, Monograph Series 4 (1943): 60-75.

Fujiwara Riichirō. "Reichō zenki no Min to no kankei (1428-1527)" [Early relations between the Le dynasty and the Ming]. In *Betonamu Chūgoku kankeishi*, edited by Yamamoto Tatsurō. Tokyo: Yamakawa Shuppansha, 1975.

Geiss, James. "The Chia-ching Reign, 1522-1566." In *The Cambridge History of China*. Vol. 7: *The Ming Dynasty, 1368-1644, Part 1*, edited by Frederick Mote and Denis Twitchett. Cambridge: Cambridge University Press, 1988.

Ghai, Yash. *Hong Kong's New Constitutional Order: The Resumption of Chinese Sovereignty and the Basic Law*. Hong Kong: Hong Kong University Press, 1999.

Giersch, C. Patterson. *Chinese Borderlands: Indigenes, Migrants, and Empires on Qing China's Yunnan Frontier*. Cambridge, MA: Harvard University Press, 2005.

Giles, Lionel. "Translations from the World Map of Father Ricci." *Geographical Journal* 52, 6 (1918): 367-85; and *Geographical Journal* 53, 1 (1919): 19-30.

Gladney, Dru C. *Muslim Chinese: Ethnic Nationalism in the People's Republic*. Cambridge, MA: Harvard University Press, 1991.

–. "Chinese Program of Development and Control, 1978-2002." In *Xinjiang: China's Muslim Borderland*, edited by S.F. Starr. Armonk, NY: M.E. Sharpe, 2004.

Goh Sui Noi. "China Gives a Firm 'No.'" *Straits Times*, 14 October 2004.

Gold, Thomas B. *State and Society in the Taiwan Miracle*. Armonk, NY: M.E. Sharpe, 1986.

Goldman, Merle. "The Anti-Rightist Campaign." In *The Cambridge History of China*. Vol. 14: *The People's Republic, Part 1: The Emergence of Revolutionary China, 1949-1965*, edited by Roderick MacFarquhar and John K. Fairbank. Cambridge: Cambridge University Press, 1987.

Goldstein, Melvin. *The Snow Lion and the Dragon: China, Tibet and the Dalai Lama*. Berkeley: University of California Press, 1997.

Goldstein, Melvin, William Siebenschuh, and Tashi Tsering. *The Struggle for Modern Tibet: The Autobiography of Tashi Tsering*. Armonk, NY: M.E. Sharpe, 1999.

Gong Piyang. "Zhongguo fa zhi xiandaihua mianju de si da maodun" [Four major contradictions in the modernization of Chinese law]. In *Tansuo yu zhengming* [Inquiry and debate] 3 (1995): 3-6.

Gong Zizhen. *Gong Ding'an Quanji Leibian* [Complete works of Gong Zizhen]. Shanghai: Shijie shuju, 1937.

–. *Gong Zizhen quanji* [The complete works of Gong Zizhen]. Shanghai: Renmin Chubanshe, 1975.

Goodman, David S.G., and Feng Chongyi. "Guangdong: Greater Hong Kong and the New Regionalist Future." In *China Deconstructs: Politics, Trade, and Regionalism*, edited by Goodman and Gerald Segal. London and New York: Routledge, 1994.

Goodrich, L.C., et al., eds. *Dictionary of Ming Biography*, 2 vols. New York: Columbia University Press, 1976.

Gossman, Lionel. *The Empire Unpossess'd: An Essay on Gibbon's "Decline and Fall."* Cambridge: Cambridge University Press, 1981.

Gottschang, Thomas, and Diana Lary. *Swallows and Settlers: The Great Migration from North China to Manchuria*. Ann Arbor, MI: University of Michigan Press, 2000.

Grossheim, Martin. "Village Laws (*huong uoc*) as Source for Vietnamese Studies." In *Vietnam: Sources and Approaches*, Proceedings of the 2nd EuroViet Conference, edited by Philippe le Failler and Jean Marie Mancini. Aix-en-Provence: Publications de l'Université de Provence, 1996.

Guillermaz, Jacques. *Une vie pour la Chine* [A life for China]. Paris: Robert Lafont, 1989.

Guy, R. Kent. *The Emperor's Four Treasuries: Scholars and the State in the Late Ch'ien-lung Era*. Cambridge, MA: Harvard University Press, 1987.

Haboush, Jahyun Kim. "Constructing the Center: The Ritual Controversy and the Search for a New identity in Seventeenth-Century Korea." In *Culture and State in Late Chosŏn Korea*, edited by J. Haboush and M. Deuchler. Cambridge, MA: Harvard University Press, 1999.

Hahn, Roger. *The Anatomy of a Scientific Institution: The Paris Academy of Sciences, 1666-1803*. Berkeley: University of California Press, 1971.

Hao Zhenhua. "Ferdinand Verbiest and Sino-Russian Relations." In *Ferdinand Verbiest, S.J. (1623-1688): Jesuit Missionary, Scientist, Engineer, and Diplomat*, edited by John Witek. Nettetal: Steyler Verlag, 1994.

Harrell, Stevan. "Introduction: Civilizing Projects and the Reactions to Them." In *Cultural Encounters on China's Ethnic Frontiers*, edited by S. Harrell. Seattle and London: University of Washington Press, 1995.

Hartwell, Robert M. "Historical Analogism, Public Policy, and Social Science in 11-12th-Century China." *American Historical Review* 76 (1971): 690-728.

Harvard Project on Cold War Studies. "The Cold War and Its Legacy in Tibet: Great Power Politics and Regional Security." Conference papers, 2001.

Hathaway, Paul. *Operation China: Introducing All the Peoples of China*. Carlisle, UK: Piquant, 2000.

Hauf, Kandice. "The Community Covenant in Sixteenth Century Ji'an Prefecture, Jiangxi." *Late Imperial China* 17, 2 (1996): 1.

He Changling. *Huangchao Jingshi Wenbian* [Collected essays on statecraft]. Shanghai: Zhongxi shuju, 1899.

Heger, Franz. *Alte Metaltrmmeln aus sudost Asien* [Old metal drums from Souhteast Asia]. Leipzig: Hiersemann, 1902.

Heilongjiang shengzhi guoying nongchang zhi [Gazetteer of state farms in Heilongjiang]. Harbin: Heilongjiang renmin chubanshe, 1992.

Heissig, Walther. *Die Zeit des letzten mongolischen Großkhans Ligdan (1604-1634)* [The time of the last Mongolian great khan Ligdan]. Opladen: Westdeutscher Verlag, 1979.

Henderson, John. *The Development and Decline of Chinese Cosmology*. New York: Columbia University Press, 1984.

Heuschert, Dorothea. "Legal Pluralism in the Qing Empire: Manchu Legislation for the Mongols." *International History Review* 20, 2 (1998): 310-24.

Hevia, James. *Cherishing Men from Afar: Qing Guest Ritual and the Macartney Mission of 1793*. Durham, NC: Duke University Press, 1995.

Hewitt, Duncan. "Clash as Hong Kong Court Bars Immigrants." BBC News, 3 December 1999.

Hirth, B. "Uber hinterindischen Bronze-trommeln" [On Nether-Indian bronze drums]. *Toung-pao* 1 (1890): 135-42.

Hobsbawm, Eric J. "The New Threat to History (Address to the Central European University, Budapest)." *New York Review of Books*, 16 December 1993.

Hogg, Chris. "China to Settle New HK Chief Row." BBC, 6 April 2005.

Hong Set'ae. "Paektusan'gi." In *Kando yŏngyu'gwŏn kwan'gye charyojip* [Materials relating to the rights of possession of Kando], edited by No Yakhyon. Seoul: Paeksan charyowŏn, 1993, 2:35.

Hosie, Alexander. *Manchuria: Its People, Resources and Recent History*. Boston: J.B. Millet Co., 1910.

Hostetler, Laura. *Qing Colonial Enterprise: Ethnography and Cartography in Early Modern China*. Chicago: University of Chicago Press, 2001.

–. "Qing Connections to the Early Modern World: Ethnography and Cartography in Eighteenth-Century China." *Modern Asian Studies* 34, 3 (2000): 623-62.

Hsieh Shih-chung. *Rentong de wuming: Taiwan yuanzhumin de zuqun bianqian* [Stigmatized identity: ethnic change among Taiwan's aborigines]. Taipei: Ziyou Wanbao She, 1987.

Hsing Youtien. "Blood, Thicker than Water: Interpersonal Relations and Taiwanese Investment in Southern China." *Environment and Planning* 28 (1996): 2241-61.

Hsu, Berry. *The Common Law System in Chinese Context: Hong Kong in Transition*. Armonk, NY: M.E. Sharpe, 1992.

–. "Judicial Independence under the Basic Law." *Hong Kong Law Journal* 34, 2 (2004): 279-302.

Hu Jintao. "Gaodu zhongshi, qieshi zuohao shaoshu minzu ganbu de peiyang xuanba gongzuo" [Raise the emphasis and completely excel in minority cadre training and selection work]. In State Nationalities Affairs Commission and CPC Central Archives, *Minzu gongzuo wenzhai xuanbian, 1990-2002* [Collection of documents on nationalities work, 1990-2002], 66-81. Beijing Central Archives Press, 2003.

"Hu Jintao Addresses CPC Politburo Study Session, Calls for Common Prosperity." *Xinhua* Domestic Service, 22 October 2004, in *FBIS Daily Report: China,* FBIS-CHI 2004-1022 (22 October 2004).

Hu Minghui. "Measuring the Cosmos: The Rise of Precision Narratives in Qing China." Paper presented at the Colloquium sponsored by the Center for the Cultural Studies of Science, Medicine, and Technology, UCLA History Department, 6 May 2002.

Hu Ping. *Chan Ji: Kunan de jitan* [Allegorical words: bitter sacrificial altar]. Guangzhou: Guangdong luyou chubanshe, 1998.

Huai Xiaofeng, ed. *Da Ming lü* [The Ming code]. Beijing: Falü chubanshe, 1999.
Huang, Ray. "The Liaotung Campaign of 1619." *Oriens Extremus* 28 (1981): 29-54.
Huang Shu-min. *The Spiral Road: Change in a Chinese Village through the Eyes of a Communist Party Leader*. Boulder, CO: Westview Press, 1989.
Huang Wu. *Mahuatang waiji* [Mahua Hall ephemera]. Guangzhou: Guangdong wenhua chubanshe, 1989.
Huang Yafeng. "Political Institutions and Fiscal Reforms in China." *Problems of Post-Communism* 48, 1 (2001): 16-26.
Huangchao jingshi wen xubian [A continuation of the statecraft essays of the present court], compiled by Sheng Kang. Taipei: Wenhai, 1972.
Huangchao wenxian tongkao [Comprehensive analysis of civil and military institutions during the Qing dynasty]. In *Shitong* [The ten comprehensive encyclopedias of civil and military governance]. Shanghai: Commercial Press, 1935-37.
Human Rights Watch. *Cutting Off the Serpent's Head: Tightening Control in Tibet, 1994-1995*. New York: Human Rights Watch, 1996.
Hummel, Arthur et al. *Eminent Chinese of the Ch'ing Period*. Washington, DC: US Printing Office, 1943.
Huong Uoc cua lang La Doi, Tong La Doi, Phu Nam Sach, Tinh Hai Duong (The community convention of La Doi Village, in La Doi Hamlet, Nam Sach Prefecture, Hai Duong Province). Hanoi: Thong Tin Khoa Hoc Xa Hoi (HU 1443), 1936.
Hwang Hyŏn. *Maech'ŏn yarok*. Seoul: Kuksa p'yŏnch'anwiwŏnhoe, 1961.
International Committee of Lawyers for Tibet. *Legal Materials on Tibet*, 2nd ed. (Berkeley CA: International Committee of Lawyers for Tibet, 1997).
Israel, John. *Lianda: A Chinese University in War and Revolution*. Stanford, CA: Stanford University Press, 1998.
Jagchid, Sechin. "Mongolian-Manchu Intermarriange in the Ch'ing Period." In *Zentralasiatische Studien* 19 (1986): 68-87.
Jiang Dongping. "Weiman riben kaituotuan de zuie lishi" [The evil history of Japanese pioneer group in Manchuria], *Zongheng* 4 (1999): 47-49.
Job, Brian, Andre Laliberte, and Michael Wallace. "Assessing the Risks of Conflict in the PRC-ROC Enduring Rivalry." *Pacific Affairs* (Taiwan Strait, special issue) 72, 4 (1999-2000): 513-35.
Johnston, Alastair I. *Cultural Realism: Strategic Culture and Grand Strategy in Chinese History*. Princeton, NJ: Princeton University Press, 1995.
–. "Independence through Unification: On the Correct Handling of Contradictions across the Taiwan Strait." *Fairbank Centre for East Asian Research, Contemporary Issues* 2 (1993): 4.
Kanda, Nobuo et al., trans. and annot. *Manbun Rōtō. Tongki fuka sindaha hergen i dangse*, 7 vols. Tokyo: Tōyō Bunko, 1955-63.
Kara, G. *Chants d'un Barde Mongol* [Songs of a Mongol bard]. Budapest: Akadémiai Kiadó, 1970.
Karmel, Solomon M. "Ethnic Tension and the Struggle for Order: China's Policies in Tibet." *Pacific Affairs* 68, 4 (1995-96): 485-508.
Kaup, Katherine. *Creating the Zhuang: Ethnic Politics in China*. Boulder: Lynne Reiner, 2000.
Kent, Anne. *Between Freedom and Subsistence: Human Rights in China*. Hong Kong: Oxford University Press, 1993.
Kermode, Frank. *The Classic*. Cambridge, MA: Harvard University Press, 1983.
Khâm định Đại Nam hội điển sự lệ [Official compendium of institution and usages of imperial Vietnam], 15 vols. Hue: Thuan Hoa, 1993.
Kirillov, A., ed. *Geografichesko-statisticheskii slovar' Amurskoi I Primorskoi oblastei s vkluchеniem nekotorykh punktov sopredel'nykh s nimi stran* [Geographic-statistical dictionary of the Amur and Maritime regions including selected parts of the neighboring countries]. Blagoveshchensk: D.O. Mokin I Ko, 1894.
Kristof, Ladis K. D. "The Nature of Frontiers and Boundaries." *Annals of the Association of American Geographers* 49, 3 (1959): part 1.
Kropotkin, Petr. *Memoirs of a Revolutionist*. New York and Montreal: Black Rose Books, 1898.

Kuhn, Philip A. "Ideas behind China's Modern State." *Harvard Journal of Asiatic Studies* 55 (1995): 301.

Kymlicka, Will. *Liberalism, Community and Culture.* Oxford: Clarendon Press, 1991.

Lai Bangfan, ed. *Xibu kaifa zhengfu guanli yanjiu* [Study of government administration in China's western development]. Beijing: National Administration Institute, 2002.

Lai Yen-yu. *Guangxi yilan* [Glimpses of Guangxi]. Nanning: Kwangsi Provincial Government Press, 1936.

Lam, Janus. "Beijing Misstep over New Hong Kong Head." *Asia Times On-Line,* 2 April, 2005.

Lam, Truong Buu. "Intervention versus Tribute in Sino-Vietnamese Relations, 1788-1790." In *The Chinese World Order: Traditional China's Foreign Relations,* edited by John King Fairbank. Cambridge, MA: Harvard University Press, 1968.

Lary, Diana. *Region and Nation: The Kwangsi Clique in Republican Politics.* Cambridge: Cambridge University Press, 1975.

Lattimore, Owen. *Inner Asian Frontiers of China.* Reprint. Boston: Beacon Press, 1962; original. New York: American Geographical Society, 1940.

–. "Origins of the Great Wall of China: A Frontier Concept in Theory and Practice." In *Studies in Frontier History: Collected Papers, 1928-1958.* London: Oxford University Press, 1962.

Ledyard, Gari. "Cartography in Korea." In *The History of Cartography,* vol. 2, no. 2, edited by J.B. Hartley and David Woodward. Chicago: University of Chicago Press, 1994.

–. "Confucianism and War: The Korean Security Crisis of 1598." *Journal of Korean Studies* 6 (1988-89): 81-119.

Lee Che-fu. "China's Perception of the Taiwan Issue." *New England Law Review* 32 (1998): 695-706.

Lee, Peter ed. *Sourcebook of Korean Civilization,* vol. 2. New York: Columbia University Press, 1996.

Lee, Robert H.G. *The Manchurian Frontier in Ch'ing History.* Cambridge, MA: Harvard University Press, 1970.

Leonard, Jane Kate. "Qing History, Wei Yuan and Contemporary Political Dialogue." In *New Directions in the Social Sciences and Humanities in China,* edited by Michael B. Yahuda. London: Macmillan, 1987.

–. *Wei Yuan and China's Rediscovery of the Maritime World.* Cambridge, MA: Harvard University Press, 1984.

Li Chi. *The Travel Diaries of Hsu Hsia-k'o.* Hong Kong: Chinese University Press, 1974.

Li, Gertraude Roth. "State Building before 1644." In *The Cambridge History of China.* vol. 9.1: *The Ch'ing Dynasty to 1800,* edited by Willard J. Peterson. Cambridge: Cambridge University Press, 2002.

Li Guangtao. *Ji Qianlong Nian Pingding Annan Zhi Yi* [Record of the pacification campaigns against Annam during the Qianlong years]. Taipei: Zhongyang yanjiu yuan lishi yuyan yanjiu suo, 1976.

Li Hui. *Renzai xuanwo* [People in the eddy]. Ji'nan: Shandong huabao chubanshe, 1998.

Li Jingyu. *Zhongguo yu Dongbei Ya quyu jingji hezuo zhanlue duice* [China and its strategic measures for Northeast Asian economic cooperation]. Beijing: Renmin chubanshe, 1999.

Li, Lilian. "Introduction: Food, Famine, and the Chinese State." *Journal of Asian Studies* 41, 4 (1982): 696.

Li Xian et al. eds. *Da Ming yi tong zhi* [Union gazetteer of the Great Ming]. Reprint, Taipei: Wenhai chuban she, 1965.

Li Yushu, comp. *Xinjiang tuzhi* [Illustrated gazetteer of Xinjiang]. Taipei: Wenhai, 1965 ed.

Lieberthal, Kenneth. *Governing China.* New York: W.W. Norton, 1995.

Lieven, Dominic. *Empire.* London: Pimlico, 2003.

Lin Tongji. "Bianjiang wenti yu lishi jiaoyu" [The border areas question and history education]. *Duli pinglun* [The independent critic], 18 November 1934, 8-12.

Lin Tongyang. "Ferdinand Verbiest's Contribution to Chinese Geography and Cartography." In *Ferdinand Verbiest, S.J. (1623-1688): Jesuit Missionary, Scientist, Engineer, and Diplomat,* edited by John Witek. Nettetal: Steyler verlag, 1994.

Ling Jun. "Xitong yanjiu he zhengque xuanquan Xinjiang de lishi, wei Xinjiang de wending he fazhen fuwu" [Systematic research and precise propaganda on Xinjiang's history serve stability and development in Xinjiang]. In *Xinjiang yanjiu wenlun xuan, di yi ji* [Collection of essays on the study of Xinjiang, vol. 1], edited by Tie Muer and Mao Gangning. Beijing: Nationalities Press, 2003.

Lionnet, Françoise. "'Logiques métissage': Cultural Appropriation and Postcolonial Representations." In *Order and Partialities: Theory, Pedagogy and the "Postcolonial,"* edited by Kostas Myrsiades and Jerry McGuire. New York: State University of New York Press, 1995.

Lipman, Jonathan N. "White Hats, Oil Cakes, and Common Blood: The Hui in the Contemporary Chinese State." In *Governing China's Multiethnic Frontiers*, edited by Morris Rossabi. Seattle: University of Washington Press, 2004.

Litzinger, Ralph. *Other Chinas: The Yao and the Politics of National Belonging*. Durham, NC: Duke University Press, 2000.

Liu Junmei, and Wu Huajia. "Guanyu jianli huan Ribenhai siguo keji lianmeng de kexingxing yanjiu" [On studying the feasibility of building a science and technology alliance of the four countries around the Japan Sea]. *DongBei Ya luntan* [Northeast Asia forum] 1 (2002): 65-68.

Liu, Lydia. "Legislating the Universal: The Circulation of International Law in the Nineteenth Century." In *Tokens of Exchange: The Problem of Translation in Global Circulations*, edited by Lydia Liu. Durham, NC: Duke University Press.

Liu Meng. *Cuntian de yu qiutian qing* [The rain in spring, clear skies in autumn]. Beijing: Zhongguo gongren chubanshe, 2004.

Liu Naiyan. *Mirror: A Loss of Innocence in Mao's China*. Philadelphia: Xlibris Corp., 2001.

Liu Yuantu, ed. *Zaoqi Zhong-E dongduan bianjie yanjiu* [Research on the eastern section of the Sino-Russian border in the early period]. Beijing: Zhongguo shehui kexue chubanshe, 1993.

Lo Jung-pang. "The Decline of the Early Ming Navy." *Oriens Extremus* 5, 2 (1958): 147-68.

–. "Policy Formulation and Decision-Making on Issues Respecting Peace and War." In *Chinese Government in Ming Times: Seven Studies*, edited by Charles O. Hucker. New York: Columbia University Press, 1969.

Longzhou xianzhi [Longzhou gazetteer]. Nanning: Guangxi renmin chubanshe, 1993.

Lu Gonghui, and Civic Exchange, eds. *Rang minyi shenyin xiangqilai* [Let ring the sound of the will of the people]. Hong Kong: Hong Kong University Press, 2002.

Luk, Bernard Hung-kay. "A Study of Giulio Aleni's *Chih-fang wai-chi*." *Bulletin of Oriental and African Studies* 40 (1977): 58-84.

Luong Nhat Tuan. "Quoc dan ta voi quan-niem kinh-te" [Our people and views of the economy]. *Bao Dong Phap* [Indochina-France news], 30 January 1932.

Lyon, John A. "Recalculating French Army Growth during the Grand Siecle, 1650-1715." *French Historical Studies* 18, 4 (1994): 881-906.

Ma Dazheng. *Guojia liyi gaoyu yiqie* [The national interest is paramount]. Urumqi: Xinjiang People's Press, 2003.

Ma, Herbert H.P. *Law and Contemporary Society: Essays in Honor of the Seventieth Birthday of Professor Herbert Han-pao Ma*. Taipei: Si shang shu wu, 1996.

Ma Zifu, ed. *Xibu kaifa yu duominzu wenhua* [Western China development and multi-ethnic cultures]. Beijing: Huaxia Press, 2003.

Mackerras, Colin. *China's Ethnic Minorities and Globalisation*. London: Routledge, 2003.

–. *China's Minorities: Integration and Modernization in the Twentieth Century*. Hong Kong: Oxford University Press, 1994.

–. "The Minorities: Achievements and Problems in the Economy, National Integration and Foreign Relations." In *China Review 1998*, edited by Joseph Y.S. Cheng. Hong Kong: Chinese University of Hong Kong Press, 1999.

Major, John. "A Note on the Translation of Two Technical Terms in Chinese Science: *Wuhsing* and *Hsiu*." *Early China* 2 (1976): 1-3.

Mancall, Mark. *Russia and China: Their Diplomatic Relations to 1728*. Cambridge, MA: Harvard University Press, 1971.

Mao Zedong sixiang wansui [Long live Mao Zedong thought]. Beijing, 1967.

Mao Zedong. *Mao Zedong xuanji* [Selected works of Mao Zedong]. Beijing: Remin chubanshe, 1967.

Marks, Robert. "The State of the China Field, or the China Field and State." *Modern China* 11, 4 (1985): 461-509.

Matsumura, Jun. "The Queens and Royal Concubines of the Emperor Ch'ing T'ai-tsung." *Bulletin of the Institute of China Border Area Studies* 3 (1972): 55-76.

Maxwell, Neville. "A Note on the Amur/Ussuri Sector of the Sino-Soviet Boundaries." *Modern China* 1, 1 (1975): 116-26.

McCarthy, Susan K. "The State, Minorities, and Dilemmas of Development in Contemporary China." *Fletcher Forum on World Affairs* 26, 2 (2002): 107-18.

Mei Jimin. *Beidahuang*. Taipei: Shuifurong chubanshe, 1975.

Menard, Orville. "Leon Bourgeois, Antoine de Saint-Exupery and Solidarité." *International Social Sciences Review* 68, 1 (1993): 4.

Menegon, Eugenio. *Un solo Cielo: Giulio Aleni S.J. (1582-1649)*. Rome: Grafo, 1994.

Meng Sen. "Qing Taizu gaotian qi da hen zhi zhenben yanjiu." In *Qingshi luncong*. Hong Kong: Dadong tushu gongsi, 1977.

Menzies, Gavin. *1421: The Year China Discovered America*. New York: HarperCollins, 2002.

Mercier, Fabienne. *Vichy face à Chiang Kai-shek: Histoire diplomatique* [Vichy's dealings with Chiang Kai-shek: a diplomatic history]. Paris: L'Harmattan, 1995.

Mgebbu Lunzy (Ma Erzi). "Nuosu and Their Neighbors through the Eyes and Ears of the Mgebbu Clan." *Asian Ethnicity* 4, 1 (2003): 129-45.

Miao Pusheng. "Xinjiang zai Zhongguo tongyi de duominzu guojia xingcheng, fazhan, he gonggu guocheng zhong de lishi diwei" [Xinjiang's historic role in the process of the formation, development, and consolidation of unified China as a multi-ethnic state]. In *Xinjiang yanjiu wenlun xuan, di yi ji* [Collection of essays on the study of Xinjiang, vol. 1], edited by Tie Muer and Mao Gangning. Beijing: Nationalities Press, 2003.

Miasnikov, Vladimir. "Ferdinand Verbiest and His Role in the Formation of Sino-Russian Diplomatic Relations." In *Ferdinand Verbiest, S.J. (1623-1688): Jesuit Missionary, Scientist, Engineer, and Diplomat*, edited by John Witek. Nettetal: Steyler verlag, 1994.

Millward, James A. *Beyond the Pass: Economy, Ethnicity, and Empire in Qing Central Asia, 1759-1864*. Stanford, CA: Stanford University Press, 1998.

–. "Coming onto the Map: 'Western Regions' Geography and Cartographic Nomenclature in the Making of the Chinese Empire in Xinjiang." *Late Imperial China* 20, 2 (1999): 61-98.

Millward, James A., and Peter Perdue. "Political and Cultural History of the Xinjiang Region through the late 19th Century." In *Xinjiang: China's Muslim Borderland*, edited by S. Frederick Starr. Armonk, NY: M.E. Sharpe, 2004.

Millward, James A., and Nabijan Tursun. "Political History and Strategies of Control, 1884-1978." In *Xinjiang: China's Muslim Borderland*, edited by S.F. Starr. Armonk, NY: M.E. Sharpe, 2004.

Ming shilu [Veritable records of the Ming], 500 vols. Nanjing: Liang Hongzhi, 1940.

Miura Kunio, "Orthodoxy and Heterodoxy in Seventeenth Century Korea: Song Siyŏl and Yun Hyu." In *The Rise of Neo-Confucianism in Korea*, edited by Wm. Theodore de Bary and Jahyun Kim Haboush. New York: Columbia University Press, 1985.

Mo-Trung, Mlle. "Tinh hinh sinh hoat cua chi em nuoc ta ngay nay" [The living situation of our sisters today]. *Bao Dong Phap*, 6 January 1932.

Mote, Frederick W. *Imperial China: 900-1800*. Cambridge, MA: Harvard University Press, 1999.

–. "The T'u-mu Incident of 1449." In *Chinese Ways in Warfare*, edited by Frank Kierman, Jr. and John Fairbank, 243-72. Cambridge, MA: Harvard University Press, 1974.

Mueggler, Erik. *The Age of Wild Ghosts: Memory, Violence, and Place in Southwest China*. Berkeley and Los Angeles: University of California Press, 2001.

Munck, Ronaldo. "Mutual Benefit Societies in Argentina: Workers, Nationality, Social Security, and Trade Unionism." *Journal of Latin American Studies* 30 (1998): 573-90.

Muthu, Sankar. *Enlightenment against Empire*. Princeton, NJ: Princeton University Press, 2003.

Myasnikov, V.S. *Russko-Kitaiskie Dogovorno-Pravovye Akty (1689-1916)* [Sino-Russian treaties and legal acts, 1689-1916]. Moscow: Pamyatniki Istoricheskoi Mysli, 2004.

Myasnikov, V.S., and Ye. D. Stepanov, ed. *Granitsy Kitaya: Istoriya Formirovaniya* [China's borders: history of their development]. Moscow: Pamyatniki Istoricheskoi Mysli, 2001.
Naitô Konan. "'Qinbian Jilue' no 'Gardan zhuan.'" In *Naitô Konan Zenshû* [The complete works of Naitô Konan], 14 vols. Tokyo: Chikuma Shobo, 1969-76, 7:380-425.
Needham, Joseph. *Science and Civilisation in China*, multiple volumes. Cambridge: Cambridge University Press, 1954-.
Ng V. Thuoc. "Nguyen nhan cai nan tri-thuc that nghiep" [The cause for unemployment problem among intellectuals]. *Bao Dong Phap*, 28 May 1932.
Ngo Si Lien et al., eds. *Dai Viet su ky toan shu* [Complete history of the Great Viet]. Tokyo: Tokyo Daigaku Tōyō Bunka Kenkyūjo Fuzoku Tōyōgaku Bunken Sentaa, 1984-86.
Nguyen Dong Chi. "Vai net ve bien phap cuu te tuong tro trong lang xa Viet Nam" [Some aspects of mutual-aid relief in Vietnamese villages before the revolution]. In *Nong thon Viet Nam trong lich su* [Vietnamese countryside in history], vol. 2, edited by Vien Lich Su [Institute of history]. Hanoi: Khoa Hoc Xa Hoi, 1978.
Nguyen The Anh. *Kinh te va xa hoi Viet Nam duoi cac vua trieu Nguyen* [Economy and society in Vietnam during the Nguyen dynasty]. Saigon: Lua-Thieng, 1970.
Nguyen-Marshall, Van. "Issues of Poverty and Poor Relief in Colonial Northern Vietnam." PhD diss., University of British Columbia, 2002.
Ni Guoliang. *Zhongguo xibei diqu xiandaihua zhong de jingji yu wenhua guanxi* [Relations between economy and culture in the course of modernization in China's northwest]. Lanzhou: Gansu People's Press, 1998.
Nie Gannu. *Nie Gannu zixu* [Autobiography of Nie Gannu]. Beijing: Tuanjie chubanshe, 1998.
Niu Han and Deng Jiuping eds. *Jingji lu: jiyi zhong de fan youpai yundong* [The thorny road: the anti-rightist campaign in memory]. Beijing: Jingji ribao chubanshe, 1998.
Nivison, David. *The Life and Thought of Chang Hsueh-ch'eng*. Stanford, CA: Stanford University Press, 1966.
Norbu, Dawa. *China's Tibet Policy*. Richmond, UK: Curzon, 2001.
Oyunbilig, Borjigidai. *Zur überlieferungsgeschichte des Berichts über den persönlichen Feldzug des Kangxi Kaisers gegen Galdan* [The compilation of the personal campaign history of the Kangxi Emperor against Galdan] *(1696-1697)*. Wiesbaden: Harrassowitz, 1999.
Palais, James. *Politics and Policy in Traditional Korea*. Cambridge, MA: Harvard University Press, 1975.
Pan Guangdan. *Minzu yanjiu wenji* [A collection of writings on nationalities research]. Beijing: Minzu chubanshe, 1955.
Pavlov, S.I., ed. *Bol'shaya Sovetskaya Entsiklopedia* [Great Soviet Encyclopaedia], vol. 2. Moscow: State Scientific Society "Bol'shaya Sovetskaya Entsiklopedia," 1950.
Percival, Sir David, trans. *Chinese Connoisseurship, the Ko Ku Yao Lun: The Essential Criteria of Antiquity*. London: Faber, 1971.
Perdue, Peter C. "Boundaries, Maps, and Movement: Chinese, Russian, and Mongolian Empires in Early Modern Central Eurasia." *International History Review* 20, 2 (1998): 263-86.
–. *China Marches West: The Qing Conquest of Central Eurasia*. Cambridge, MA: Harvard University Press, 2005.
–. "Military Mobilization in Seventeenth and Eighteenth Century China, Russia and Mongolia." *Modern Asian Studies* 30, 4 (1996): 757-93.
–. "The Qing Empire in Eurasian Time and Space." In *The Qing Formation* in *World-Historical Time*, edited by Lynne A. Struve. Cambridge, MA: Harvard University Press, 2004.
Perry, Elizabeth J., and Mark Selden, eds. *Chinese Society: Change, Conflict, and Resistance*. London and New York: Routledge, 2000.
Phan Ke Binh. *Viet Nam phong tuc* [Vietnamese customs]. Reprint. Ho Chi Minh City: Tong Hop Dong Thap, 1990.
Phu Nu Thoi Dam [Women's Herald]. Hanoi, 1930-32.
Potter, Pitman B. *The Chinese Legal System: Globalization and Local Legal Culture*. London: Routledge, 2001.
–. "Legal Reform in China: Institutions, Culture, and Selective Adaptation." *Law and Social Inquiry* 28, 4 (2004): 465-95.

Priest, Quinton G. "Portraying Central Government Institutions: Historiography and Intellectual Accommodation in the High Ching." *Late Imperial China* 7 (1986): 39.

Qing Jue, et al. "Xinjiang jingji shehui fazhen due minzu guanxi de yingxiang" [Effects of economic and social development on nationalities relations in Xinjiang]. In *Xinjiang yanjiu wenlun xuan, di yi ji* [Collection of essays on the study of Xinjiang, vol. 1], edited by Tie Muer and Mao Gangning. Beijing: Nationalities Press, 2003.

Qu Dajun. *Guangdong xinyu* [New discourses of Guangdong]. Hong Kong: Zhonghua shuju, 1974.

Qu Jiusi. *Wanli wu gong lu* [Record of military accomplishments during the Wanli reign]. Reprint. Taipei: Yiwen yinshu guan, 1980.

Rawski, Evelyn S. *The Last Emperors: A Social History of Qing Imperial Institutions.* Berkeley: University of California Press, 1998.

Reardon-Anderson, James. *Reluctant Pioneers: China's Expansion Northward 1644-1937.* Stanford, CA: Stanford University Press, 2005.

Renmin ribao [People's Daily], 20 July 1995.

–. 28 September 1999.

Rigger, Shelley. "Social Science and National Identity: A Critique." *Pacific Affairs* (Taiwan Strait, special issue) 72, 4 (1999-2000): 537-52.

Roberti, Mark. *The Fall of Hong Kong: China's Triumph and Britain's Betrayal* (rev. ed.). New York: John Wiley, 1996.

Rong Zhaozu. "Yan Ruoju de kaozhengxue" [The *kaozheng* studies of Yan Ruoju]. *Lingnan xuebao* 1, 4 (1930): 90-91.

Rossabi, Morris. *China and Inner Asia: From 1368 to the Present Day.* London: Thames and Hudson, 1975.

–. "The Ming and Inner Asia." In *The Cambridge History of China.* Vol. 8: *The Ming Dynasty, 1368-1644,* Part 2, edited by Dennis Twitchett and Frederick W. Mote. Cambridge: Cambridge University Press, 1998.

–, ed. *Governing China's Multiethnic Frontiers.* Seattle: University of Washington Press, 2004.

Roth, Gertraude. "The Manchu-Chinese Relationship, 1618-1636." In *From Ming to Ch'ing: Conquest, Region, and Continuity in Seventeenth-Century China,* edited by Jonathan D. Spence and John E. Wills, Jr. New Haven, CT: Yale University Press, 1979.

Rudelson, Justin, and William Jankowiak. "Acculturation and Resistance: Xinjiang Identities in Flux." In *Xinjiang: China's Muslim Borderland,* edited by S.F. Starr. Armonk, NY: M.E. Sharpe, 2004.

Sahlins, Peter. *Boundaries: The Making of France and Spain in the Pyrenees.* Berkeley: University of California Press, 1989.

Saso, Michael. "What Is the *Ho-t'u?*" *History of Religions* 17, 3 and 4 (1978): 399-416.

Sautman, Barry. "Ethnic Law and Minority Rights in China: Progress and Constraints." *Law and Policy* 21 (1999): 88-118.

–. "Preferential Policies for Ethnic Minorities in China: The Case of Xinjiang." *Nationalism and Ethnic Politics* 4, 1-2 (1998): 88-118.

Schafer, Edward H. *Pacing the Void: T'ang Approaches to the Stars.* Berkeley: University of California Press, 1977.

–. *The Vermilion Bird: T'ang Images of the South.* Berkeley: University of California Press, 1967.

Schein, Louisa. *Minority Rules: The Miao and the Feminine in China's Cultural Politics.* Durham, NC: Duke University Press, 1999.

Schichor, Yitzhak. "The Great Wall of Steel: Military and Strategy in Xinjiang." In *Xinjiang: China's Muslim Borderland,* edited by S.F. Starr. Armonk, NY: M.E. Sharpe, 2004.

Schmid, Andre. *Korea between Empires, 1895-1919.* New York: Columbia University Press, 2002.

Semenov, P., ed. *Geografichesko-statisticheskii slovar' Rossiiskoi Imperii* [Geographic-statistical dictionary of the Russian empire]. St. Petersburg: Tip. Bezobrazova, 1863.

Serruys, Henry. "Oaths in the Qalqa Jirum." *Oriens Extremus* 19 (1972): 131-41.

–. "Sino-Mongol Relations during the Ming." In *Melanges Chinois et Bouddhiques.* Vol. 1: *The Mongols in China during the Hung-wu Period, 1368-1398,* and Vol. 2: *The Tribute System and the Diplomatic Missions* (1967). Brussels: Institut Belge des Hautes etudes Chinoises, 1959.

Shakya, Tsering. *The Dragon in the Land of Snows: A History of Modern Tibet since 1947*. New York: Columbia University Press, 1999.

Shen Minhua. "Zhongguo dui Gelunbu yanjiu de pingxi" [A critical analysis of the Chinese approach to Columbus studies]. *Shehui kexue* [Social sciences] 11 (1992): 67-70.

Shi Fang, and Gao Ling. *Chuantong yu biange* [Tradition and change]. Haerbin: Heilongjiang renmin chubanshe, 1995.

Shin, Leo K. "The Last Campaigns of Wang Yangming." Unpublished paper.

–. *The Making of the Chinese State: Ethnicity and Expansion on the Ming Borderlands*. Cambridge: Cambridge University Press, 2006.

Shulman, N.K., ed. *Amurskaya oblast': Opyt entsiklopedicheskogo slovaria* [Amur region: encyclopaedic dictionary]. Blagoveshchensk: Khabarovskoye knizhnoye izdatel'stvo, 1989.

Siku quanshu zongmu [General catalog for the complete collection of the four treasuries]. Reprint. Taipei: Commercial Press, 1983-86.

Simon, Denis Fred, and Michael Y.M. Kau, eds. *Taiwan: Beyond the Economic Miracle*. Armonk, NY: M.E. Sharpe, 1992.

Simon, Scott, Wang Fu-chang, Joseph Wong, Andre Laliberte, Robert D'A. Henderson. "Domestic and International Considerations in Taiwan's 2004 Presidential Election: An Interdisciplinary Roundtable." *Pacific Affairs* 77, 4 (2004-5): 683-712.

Sivin, Nathan. "Wang Hsi-shan." In *Dictionary of Scientific Biography*, edited by Charles Gillispie. New York: Scribner's Sons.

Smith, Richard J. *Chinese Maps: Images of All under Heaven*. Oxford: Oxford University Press, 1996.

–. *Fortune-Tellers and Philosophers: Divination in Traditional Chinese Society*. Boulder, CO: Westview Press, 1991.

–. "Mapping China's World: Cultural Cartography in Late Imperial Times." In *Landscape, Culture and Power in Chinese Society*, edited by Yeh Wen-hsin. Berkeley: University of California, Berkeley, Center for East Asian Studies, 1998.

Song, X. "Thinking Federal: The Relevance of Federalism to China." *Regional and Federal Studies* 10 (2000): 107-28.

Sorensen, Theodore C., and David L. Phillips. *Legal Standards and Autonomy Options for Minorities in China: The Tibetan Case*. Cambridge, MA: Harvard University, Belfer Center for Science and International Affairs, John F. Kennedy School of Government, 2004.

Sotheby's. *The Library of Philip Robinson*, Part 2. London: Sotheby's Auction Catalogue (1988): 77-95.

Spence, Jonathan D. *The Gate of Heavenly Peace: The Chinese and Their Revolution, 1895-1980*. New York: Penguin Books, 1982.

–. *The Search for Modern China*. New York: W.W. Norton, 1999.

Stakheev, Dmitrii. *Za Baikalom I na Amure: putevye kartiny* [Beyond the Baikal Lake and along the Amur River: images of travel]. St. Petersburg: Tip. K. Vul'fa, 1869.

Starkov, G.F., and A.A. Stepanov. "Important Monument to Far Eastern Cartography." In *Voprosy Geografii Dal'nego Vostoka*, vol. 6. Khabarovsk: Geograficheskoe obshchestvo SSSR, Priamurskii filial, 1963.

Stary, Giovanni. "La politica mancese delle 'sette accuse.' Una costante per giustioficare la conquista della Cina e della Corea." In *Studi Eurasiatici in Onore di Mario Grignaschi* [Eurasian studies in honour of M. Grignaschi], edited by G. Bellinger and G. Vercellin, 43-55. Venezia: Libreria univeristaria, 1988.

State Council Information Office. *White Paper on National Minorities Policy and Its Practice in China*. Beijing, 1999.

–. *White Paper: New Progress in Human Rights in the Tibet Autonomous Region*. Beijing, 1998.

–. *White Paper: Progress in China's Human Rights Cause*. Beijing, 2001.

–. *White Paper: Regional Autonomy for Ethnic Minorities in China*. Beijing, 2005.

State Council Information Office and Xinhua [New China News Agency]. "China's Top Lawmaker Stresses Regional Autonomy in Xinjiang," 14 March 2002.

State Nationalities Affairs Commission. *Zhongguo gongchandang guanyu minzu wenti de jiben guandian he zhengce* [Basic approaches and policies of the Chinese Communist Party on nationalities issues]. Beijing: Nationalities Press, 2002.

Stevens, Keith. *Chinese Gods*. London: Collins, 1997.

Su Yigong. "The Application of Chinese Law and Custom in Hong Kong." *Hong Kong Law Journal* 29, 2 (1999): 267-93.

Sunahara, Ann Gomer. *The Politics of Racism*. Toronto: James Lorimer, 1981.

Sutton, Donald S. "A Case of Literati Piety: The Ma Yuan Cult from High-Tang to High-Qing." *Chinese Literature: Essays, Articles, Reviews (CLEAR)* 11 (1989): 79-114.

Suzuki Chûsei. "Kenryû Annan ensei kô" [A study of the Qianlong expedition to Annam]. *Tôyô gakuhô* 50, 2 (1967): 1-23; 50, 3 (1967): 79-106.

–. "Reichô Kôki No Shin to No Kankei." In *Betonamu-Chûgoku Kankeishi*, edited by Yamamoto Tatsurô, 405-92. Tokyo: Yamakawa Shuppansha, 1975.

Swetz, Frank, trans. *The Sea Island Mathematical Manual: Surveying and Mathematics in Ancient China*. University Park: Pennsylvania State University Press, 1992.

Swope, Kenneth. "Crouching Tigers, Secret Weapons: Military Technology Employed during the Sino-Japanese-Korean War, 1592-1598." *Journal of Military History* 69, 1 (2005): 11-41.

Sun Jiji. *Kang-Yong-Qian shiqi yutu cehui yu jiangyu xingcheng yanjiu* [Study of maps and surveys during the Kangxi, Yongzheng, and Qianlong periods and the formation of territorial boundaries]. Beijing: Zhongguo renmin daxue chuban she, 2003.

Szczesniak, Boleslaw. "The Seventeenth Century Maps of China: An Inquiry into the Compilations of European Cartographers." *Imago Mundi* 13 (1956): 116-36.

Tai, Benny. "Why Second-Generation Mainland Children Have No Right of Abode in Hong Kong." *Hong Kong Law Journal* 29, 2 (1999): 208-15.

Tai, Hue-Tam Ho. *Radicalism and the Origins of the Vietnamese Revolution*. Cambridge, MA: Harvard University Press, 1992.

Taiwan Affairs Office and Information Office of the State Council. "The One-China Principle and the Taiwan Issue." Beijing, 2000.

Tan Qingshan, Forest. "Controversial Taiwan Election." *EAI Bulletin* (2004): 1-8.

Taylor, Keith W. "The Early Kingdoms." In *The Cambridge History of Southeast Asia*. Vol. 1, Part 1: *From Early Times to c. 1500*, edited by Nicholas Tarling. Cambridge: Cambridge University Press, 1999.

Teiwes, Frederick. *Politics and Purges in China: Rectification and the Decline of Party Norms, 1950-1965*. Armonk, NY: M.E. Sharpe, 1993.

Tennant, Paul. *Aboriginal Peoples and Politics: The Indian Land Question in British Columbia, 1849-1989*. Vancouver: UBC Press, 1990.

Through the Consul's Eye, Tanguera Films 1999, Promotional materials.

Tie Muer and Mao Gangning, ed. *Xinjiang yanjiu wenlun xuan, di yi ji* [Collection of essays on the study of Xinjiang, vol. 1]. Beijing: Nationalities Press, 2003.

Ting Wen-chiang. "On Hsu Hsia-k'o (1586-1641): Explorer and Geographer." *New China Review* 3, 5 (1921): 325-37.

Tombs, Robert. *France, 1814-1914*. New York: Longman, 1996.

Trương Hữu Quýnh, Bùi Quý Lộ, and Đào Tố Uyên. *Lịch Sử Việt Nam (Từ Thế Kỉ X – 1858: Giáo Trình Dào Tạo Giáo Viên Trung Học Cơ Sở Hệ Cao Dẳng Sư Phạm*. [History of Vietnam from the tenth century to 1858: a basic curriculum for middle school students]. Hà Noi: Nhà xuât bản Giáo dục, 1998.

Tsang, Steve, and Hung-Mao Tien. *Democratization in Taiwan: Implications for China*. New York: St. Martin's Press, 1999.

Tu, Wei-ming. *Neo-Confucian Thought in Action: Wang Yang-ming's Youth (1472-1509)*. Berkeley: University of California Press, 1976.

Tung Chee-hwa. "Chief Executive's Policy Address 2005." Hong Kong: Government Information Centre, 2005.

Tung Phong. "Tinh hinh kinh-te nam 1931" [The economic situation in 1931], *Bao Dong Phap*, 3 January 1932.

Turnbull, David. "Cartography and Science in Early Modern Europe: Mapping and the Construction of Knowledge Spaces." *Imago Mundi* 48 (1996): 5-24.

Tyler, Christian. *Wild West China: The Taming of Xinjiang*. New Brunswick, NJ: Rutgers University Press, 2004.

Ubelhor, Monika. "The Community Compact (Hsiang-yueh) of the Sung and Its Educational Significance." In *Neo-Confucian Education: The Formative Stage*, edited by William Theodore de Bary and John Chaffee. Berkeley: University of California Press, 1989.

Veit, Veronika. "Die mongolischen Völkerschaften vom 15. Jahrhundert bis 1691" [The Mongolian tribes from the fifteenth century to 1691]. In *Die Mongolen: Beiträge zu ihrer Geschichte und Kultur* [The Mongols: contributions on their history and culture], edited by Michael Weiers. Darmstadt: Wissenschaftliche Buchgesellschaft, 1986.

–. "Die Mongolen: von der Clanföderation zur Volksrepublik" [The Mongols: from tribal confederation to people's republic]. In *Die Mongolen: Beiträge zu ihrer Geschichte und Kultur* [The Mongols: contributions on their history and culture], edited by Michael Weiers. Darmstadt: Wissenschaftliche Buchgesellschaft, 1986.

Vu Duy Men. "Nguon goc va dieu kien xuat hien huong uoc trong lang xa o vung Dong Bang-Trung Du Bac Bo" [The origin and condition for the appearance of huong uoc in villages of the Northern Delta and Midland regions]. *Nghien cuu lich su* 1, 1 and 2 (1999): 49-50.

–. "Vai net ve qua trinh dieu chinh va bo sung huong uoc Quynh Doi" [Modifications and popularization of Quynh Doi's huong uoc]. *Nghien cuu lich su* 6, 1 and 12 (1985): 49.

Vu Duy Men, and Bui Xuan Dinh. "Huong uoc: khoan uoc trong lang xa" [Huong uoc: Khoan uoc in the villages]. *Nghien cuu lich su* 4 (1982): 45.

Wada Sei. "Some Problems Concerning the Rise of T'ai-tsu the Founder of Manchu Dynasty." Memoirs of the Research Department of the Toyo Bunko 16 (1957): 51-63.

Wade, Geoff, trans. *Southeast Asia in the Ming Shi-lu: An Open Access Resource*. Singapore: Asia Research Institute and the Singapore E-Press, National University of Singapore, 2005, available from http://epress.nus.edu.sg/msl.

Wakeman, Frederic, Jr. *The Great Enterprise: The Manchu Reconstruction of Imperial Order in Seventeenth-Century China*, 2 vols. Berkeley: University of California Press, 1985.

Waldron, Arthur. *The Great Wall of China: From History to Myth*. Cambridge: Cambridge University Press, 1990.

Waley-Cohen, Joanna. "Commemorating War in Eighteenth-Century China." *Modern Asian Studies* 30, 4 (1996): 869-99.

–. *Exile in Mid-Qing China: Banishment to Xinjiang, 1758-1820*. New Haven, CT: Yale University Press, 1991.

–. "The New Qing History." *Radical History Review* 88 (2004): 193-206.

Wallis, Helen. "The Influence of Father Ricci on Far Eastern Cartography." *Imago Mundi* 19 (1965): 35-45.

Wang Gungwu. *Community and Nation: China, Southeast Asia and Australia*. St. Leonards, Australia: Allen and Unwin, 1992.

Wang Jiguang. "Hongwu san shi nian Zhong Yue ling tu jiao she de yuan shi wen jian" [Primary documents concerning the border disputes between China and Vietnam during the thirtieth year of the Hongwu reign (1397)]. *Zhongguo bian jian shi di yan jiu* [Studies in the history of China's border regions] 14, 4 (2004): 119-23.

Wang Lixiong. *Sky Burial: The Fate of Tibet*. Hong Kong: Mirror Books, 1998.

Wang Luolin et al. *Zhongguo xibu dakaifa zhengce* [China's western development policy]. Beijing: Economic Management Publishing, 2003.

Wang Ruoshui. *Wei rendao zhuyi bianhu* [In defence of humanism]. Beijing: United Press, 1986.

Wang Sen ed. *Yuexi wen zhai* [Anthology of belle-lettres of Guangxi]. Ying yin Wenuan ge Siku quan shu, ed. Reprint. Taipei: Taiwan Shang wu yinshu guan, 1986.

Wang Shaoguang and Hu Angang. *Zhongguo guojia nengli baogao* [A report on the Chinese state's capabilities]. Hong Kong: Oxford University Press, 1994.

Wang Shouren. *Wang Yangming quanji* [The complete works of Wang Yangming]. Shanghai: Shanghai guji chubanshe, 1992.

Wang Tay-sheng. "The Legal Development of Taiwan in the 20th Century: Toward a Liberal and Democratic Country." *Pacific Rim Law and Policy Journal* 11, 3 (2002): 531-59.

Wang Zhen zhuan [The biography of Wang Zhen]. Beijing: Dangdai zhongguo chubanshe, 2001.

Wang Zheng. "Menghui huangyuan" [Dreaming back to the wilderness]. In *Lishi zai shenpan* [Retrial of history], edited by Liu Meng. Chengdu: Sichuan renmin chubanshe, 1996.

Wang Zhenmin. *Zhongyang yu tebie xingzhengqu guanxi* [Relations between the centre and special administrative regions]. Beijing: Qinghua University Press, 2002.

Wang Zhonghan. "Empress Xiao Duan Wen of the Borjigit Clan." In *Biographical Dictionary of Chinese Women: The Qing Period, 1644-1911*, edited by Lily Xiao Hong Lee, A.D. Stefanowska, and Clara Wing-Chung Ho. Armonk, NY: M.E. Sharpe, 1998.

Ward, Julian. *Xu Xiake (1587-1641): The Art of Travel Writing*. Richmond, UK: Curzon, 2001.

Wei Jun. *Qiao nan suo ji* [Miscellaneous notes on Guangxi]. Bai bu congshu ji cheng ed. Reprint. Taipei: Yiwen yinshu guan, 1966.

Wei Yuan. *Shengwuji* [Record of sacred military victories]. Beijing: Zhonghua Shuju, 1984.

Weiers, Michael. "Der Manschu-Khortsin Bund von 1626." In *Documenta Barbarorum: Festschrift für Walther Heissig zum 70*, edited by Karl Sagaster and Michael Weiers. Wiesbaden: O. Harrassowitz, 1983.

–. "Die Kuang-Ning Affäre, Beginn des Zerwürfnisses zwischen den Mongolischen Tsakhar und den Mandschuren" [The Kuang-ning affair: The beginning of the hostility between Chakhar Mongols and Manchus]. *Zentralasiatische Studien* 13 (1979): 73-91.

- "Zum Mandschu-Kharatsin Bund des Jahres 1628" [On the Manchu-Qaračin alliance of the Year 1628]. *Zentralasiatische Studien* 26 (1996): 84-119.

Weintrob, Lori. "From 'Petite Patrie' to National 'Solidarité': Regionalism and Inter-Class Alliances in Mutual Aid Societies." *Proceedings of the Western Society for French History* (1999). Greeley: University Press of Colorado, 2001.

Weller, Robert. *Alternate Civilities: Democracy and Culture in China and Taiwan*. Boulder, CO: Westview Press, 1999.

Wen Ruopeng et al. *Zhongnan dajiaofei* [The great extermination of bandits in the central south]. Beijing: Guofang daxue chubanshe, 1997.

Wesley-Smith, Peter, ed. *Hong Kong's Basic Law: Problems and Prospects*. Hong Kong: Hong Kong University Faculty of Law, 1990.

Whitbeck, Judith. "Kung Tzu-chen and the Redirection of Literati Commitment in Early Nineteenth-Century China." *Ch'ing-shih Wen't'i* 4 (1983): 1-32.

White, Lynn T. *Unstately Power*, 2 vols. Armonk, NY: M.E. Sharpe, 1998.

Whitfield, Susan. *Life along the Silk Road*. London: John Murray Publishers, 1999.

Whiting, Susan H. *Power and Wealth in Rural China: The Political Economy of Institutional Change*. Cambridge: Cambridge University Press, 2001.

Whitmore, John K. *Vietnam, Ho Quy Ly, and the Ming (1371-1421)*. New Haven, CT: Yale Center for International and Area Studies, 1985.

Widmer, Eric. *The Russian Ecclesiastical Mission in Peking during the Eighteenth Century*. Cambridge, MA: Harvard University East Asian Research Center, 1976.

Will, Pierre-Etienne. *Bureaucracy and Famine in Eighteenth-Century China*. Stanford, CA: Stanford University Press, 1990.

Williams, Philip, and Yenna Wu. *The Great Wall of Confinement: The Chinese Prison Camp through Contemporary Fiction and Reportage*. Berkeley: University of California Press, 2004.

Wills, John Jr. "Maritime China from Wang Chih to Shih Lang." In *From Ming to Ch'ing: Conquest, Region, and Continuity in Seventeenth-Century China*, edited by Jonathan Spence and John Wills. New Haven, CT: Yale University Press, 1979.

Wong, R. Bin. "Food Riots in the Qing Dynasty." *Journal of Asian Studies* 12, 4 (1983): 768-69.

Wong, Shirleen S. *Kung Tzu-chen*. Boston: Twayne Publishers, 1975.

Woodside, Alexander B. "The Ch'ien-lung Reign." In *The Cambridge History of China*. Vol. 9, Part 1, *The Ch'ing Dynasty to 1800*, edited by Willard J. Peterson, 230-309. Cambridge: Cambridge University Press, 2002.

–. "The Development of Social Organizations in Vietnamese Cities in the Late Colonial Period." *Pacific Affairs* 44 (1971): 39-64.

–. "Early Ming Expansionism (1406-1427): China's Abortive Conquest of Vietnam." *Papers on China* 17 (1963): 1-37.
–. *Vietnam and the Chinese Model: A Comparative Study of Nguyễn and Ch'ing Civil Government in the First Half of the Nineteenth Century*. Cambridge, MA: Harvard University Press, 1971.
Wu Hongda, Harry. *Bitter Winds*: A *Memoir of My Years in China's Gulag*. New York: John Wiley and Sons Inc., 1994.
Wu Shimin. *Zhongguo minzu zhengce duben* [Reader on China's nationalities policy]. Beijing: Central Nationalities University Press, 1998.
Wu Yongliang. *Yuxue feifei* [Floating rain and snow]. Beijing: Zhongguo xiju chubanshe, 2002.
Wylie, Alexander. *Notes on Chinese Literature*. Reprint. Taibei: Book Shop Limited, 1970; Original. Shanghai: American Presbyterian Press, 1867.
Xiao Dehao and Huang Zheng, comp. *Zhong Yue bianjie lishi ziliao* [Anthology of documents about the history of the Chinese-Vietnamese frontier]. Beijing: Shehui kexue wenxian, 1992.
Xiao Yishan. *Qingdai Tongshi* [Comprehensive history of the Qing dynasty]. Beijing: Zhonghua shuju, 1986.
Xin Suwei. *Ding Cong zhuan* [Biography of Ding Cong]. Beijing: Zhongguo gongren chubanshe, 1993.
Xingzheng yuen dalu weiyuanhui [Mainland Affairs Council of the Executive Yuan], ed. *Zhengfu dalu zhengce zhongyao wenjian* [Important documents on the government's Mainland policy]. Taipei: Executive Yuan, 2003.
Xinhua yuebao [New China Monthly Report], 9 (1995): 110-15.
–. 12 (1999): 138-47.
Xinjiang CPC Propaganda Department and Song Caifa, ed. *Minzu quyu zizhifa tonglun* [General survey on the law on autonomy in minority areas]. Beijing: Nationalities Press, 2003.
"Xizang de xiandaihua fazhan" [Development of modernization in Tibet] (2001). In State Nationalities Affairs Commission and CPC Central Archives, *Minzu gongzuo wenzhai xuanbian 1990-2002* [Collection of documents on nationalities work, 1990-2002], 447-74. Beijing: Beijing Central Archives Press, 2003.
Xu Chengbei. "Nie Gannu zai Beidahuang" [Nie Gannu in Beidahuang]. In *Yuan shang cao: Jiyi zong de fanyoupai yundong* [Grass on the land: the anti-rightist campaign in memory], edited by Niu Han and Deng Jiuping. Beijing: Jingji ribao chubanshe, 1998.
Xu Hongzu. *Xu Xiake you ji* [The travel records of Xu Xiake]. Shanghai: Shanghai guji chuban she, 1995 [1987].
Xu Mingxu. *Yinmou yu qiancheng: Xizang sangluan de lai long qu mai* [Intrigue and devotion: the origins and effects of the Tibet riots]. Missasauga, ON: Mirror Books, 1999.
Xu Songling. "Zhongguo: Dongbei Ya guojia zhi jian de huanjing hezuo" [Environmental cooperation between China and the countries of Northeast Asia]. *Donbgbei Ya luntan* [Northeast Asia Forum] 1 (2002): 49-54.
"Xuexiao shi guanche shishi 'Guojia tongyong yuyan wenzi fa' de jiben zhendi" [Schools are the basic front for fully implementing the Law on Simultaneous Language Usage by the State]. In *Zhonghua renmin gonghe guo guojia tongyong yuyan wenzi fa xuexi duben* [Study reader on the Simultaneous Language Law of the PRC], edited by the National People's Congress Committee on Education, Science, Culture and Health and Ministry of Education. Beijing: Language Press, 2001.
Yamamoto Tatsurō, ed. *Betonamu Chūgoku kankeishi* [History of international relations between Vietnam and China]. Tokyo: Yamakawa Shuppansha, 1975.
Yan Chongnian. *Nu'erhachi zhuan* [Biography of Nurhaci]. Beijing: Beijing chuban she, 1983.
Yan Jiaqi. "China's National Minorities and Federalism." *Dissent* (Summer 1996): 139-44.
–. "Federalism and the Future of Tibet." In *Tibet through Dissident Chinese Eyes*, edited by Cao Changching and James D. Seymour. Armonk, NY: M.E. Sharpe, 1998.
Yan Ruoju. *Qianqiu zhaji* [Yan Ruoju's Reading Notes]. Taipei: Commercial Press, 1973.
Yang Bin. *Liubian jilue* [Notes from the Willow Palisades]. Taipei: Guangwen shuju, 1968.

Yang Congdao. "Bawuling Yunshan xumuchang liuren feizhengchang siwang mingdan" [List of abnormal deaths in the Yunshan Branch of Farm 850]. Unpublished Note.

Yang Zhaoquan and Sun Yumei. *Zhong Chao bianjie shi* [A history of the Sino-Korean border]. Changchun: Jilin wenshi chubanshe, 1993.

Yee, Cordell. "A Cartography of Introspection: Chinese Maps as Other Than European." *Asian Art* 5 (1992): 29-45.

–. "Traditional Chinese Cartography and the Myth of Westernization." In *The History of Cartography*. Vol. 2: Book 2: *Cartography in the Traditional East and Southeast Asian Societies*, edited by J.B. Harley and David Woodward. Chicago: University of Chicago Press, 1994.

Yin Yi. *Huishou canyang yihan shan* [The setting of the sun over the mountain]. Beijing: Shiyue wenyi chubanshe, 2003.

Ying Jia, Ling Yunyi, and Liu Yaohui, eds. *Cangwu zong du jun men zhi* [Record of the Office of the Supreme Commander at Cangwu]. Beijing: Quan guo tushu guan wenxian shu wei fu zhi zhongxin, 1991 [1581].

You Ji. *The Armed Forces of China*. London: I.B. Tauris, 1999.

Yu Guangyuan. *Yu Guangyuan duanlun ji* [A collection of the brief writings of Yu Guangyuan]. Shanghai: Huadong shifan daxue, 2001.

Yu Shanpu. "Beidahuang liuren mingdan" [Name list of the Beidahuang exiles]. Unpublished note.

Yuan Zhiming. *He shang* [River Elegy]. CCTV television series, 1988.

Zhang Cunwu. *Qing Han zongfan maoyi, 1637-1894* [Qing-Korean Tributary Trade, 1637-1894]. Taipei: Zhongyang yanjiuyuan jindaishi yanjiusuo, 1978.

–. *Qingdai ZhongHan guanxi wenji* [Essays on Sino-Korean relations during the Qing dynasty]. Taipei: Shangwu yinshuguan, 1986.

Zhang Hao et al. *Zhongguo jindai kaifa Xibei wenlun xuan* [Selected officials discussions of China's modern development of the northwest]. Lanzhou: Lanzhou daxue chubanshe, 1997.

Zhang Huang. *Tushu bian* [Compendium of maps and materials]. Reprint. Taibei: Chengwen chuban she, 1971.

Zhang Jie. *Wu Zuguang beihuan qu* [Wu Zuguang: Vicissitudes of life]. Chengdu: Sichuan wenyi chubanshe, 1986.

Zhang Linchi. *Dangdai Zhongguo de nongken shiye* [Land Reclamation in Contemporary China]. Beijing: Zhongguo shehui kexue chubanshe, 1986.

Zhang Tingyu, ed. *Ming shi* [Dynastic history of the Ming], 28 vols. Beijing: Zhonghua shuju, 1974.

Zhang Wuyue, ed. *Liangan guanxi yanjiu* [Perspectives of the relationship across the strait]. Taipei: New Wun Ching Development Publishing, 2003.

Zhang Wuyue. "President Chen's Cross-century Remarks." *Liangan guanxi yanjiu* [Perspectives of the relationship across the strait]. Taipei: New Wun Ching Development Publishing, 2003.

Zhang Yihe. *Wangshi bingbu ruyan* [Do not let the bygones be bygones]. Beijing: Renmin wenxue chubanshe, 2004.

Zhao Shufang. "Elousi waijiao wenhua de tedian yu yingxiang" [The characteristics and influence of the Russian foreign policy culture]. *Dongbei Ya luntan* [Northeast Asia Forum], (Changchun) 204, 4:50-54.

Zhao Suisheng. "Military Coercion and Peaceful Offence: Beijing's Strategy of National Reunification with Taiwan." *Pacific Affairs* (Taiwan Strait, special issue) 72, 4 (1999-2000): 495-512.

Zhao Yi. *Huangchao Wugong Jisheng* [Record of the splendours of the military feats of the August dynasty]. Original 1799. Wenhai reprint, n.d.

–. "Ming biansheng gongjiao bingshu zui duo." In *Huangchao Jingshi Wenbian*, edited by He Changling, *juan* 71, 21-22.

Zheng Jiazhen. *Zhongguo dongbeijiao* [The northeast corner of China]. Harbin: Heilongjiang renmin chubanshe, 1998.

Zheng Xiaofeng. *Ding Ling zai Beidahuang* [Ding Ling in Beidahuang]. Wuhan: Hubei renmin chubanshe, 1989.

"Zhonggong zhongyang zuzhi bu, Zhonggong zhongyang tongzhanbu, Guojia minwei guanyu jinyibu zuohao peiyang xuanba shaoshu minzu ganbu gongzuo de yijian" [Opinion of the CPC Organization Department, CPC United Front Work Department, and State Nationalities Ministry on continuing to do a good job of training and selecting minority cadres]. In Central Party School Nationalities and Religious Theory Office 1998, 138-39.

Zhongyang wenxian yanjiushi, ed. *Jianguo yilai zhongyao wenxian xuanbian* [Selected collection of important documents since the establishment of the PRC]. Beijing: Zhongyang wenxian chubanshe, 1996.

–. *Zhou Enlai nianpu* [The chronicle of Zhou Enlai]. Beijing: Zhongyang wenxian chubanshe, 1997.

Zhou Hongxing. *Ai Qing zhuan* [Biography of Ai Qing]. Beijing: Zuojia chubanshe, 1993.

Zhou Jianqiang. *Nie Gannu Zhuan* [Biography of Nie Gannu]. Chengdu: Sichuan renmin chubanshe, 1987.

Zhu Guozhen comp. *Huang Ming da xun ji* [Imperial instructions of the Great Ming], collected in *Huang Ming shi gai* [General history of the Great Ming] (1632). Reprint. Yangzhou: Jiangsu guangling guji ke yin she, 1992.

Zhuang Jifa. *Qing Gaozong Shiquan Wugong Yanjiu*. Taipei: Guoli gugong bowuyuan, 1982.

Contributors

Timothy Brook is professor of history and principal of St. John's College, University of British Columbia.

Nicola Di Cosmo is professor of East Asian studies at the School of Historical Studies, Institute for Advanced Study.

Benjamin A. Elman is professor of East Asian studies and history, Princeton University.

Stevan Harrell is professor of anthropology at the University of Washington.

Diana Lary is professor of history and senior scholar, Centre of Chinese Research, at the University of British Columbia.

Van Nguyen-Marshall is assistant professor of history at Trent University.

Peter C. Perdue is T.W. and Wei Fong Chao Professor of Asian Civilizations and professor of history at the Massachusetts Institute of Technology.

Pitman B. Potter is professor of law and director of the Institute of Asian Research, University of British Columbia.

Andre Schmid is professor of East Asian studies at the University of Toronto.

Leo K. Shin is assistant professor of history and Asian studies at the University of British Columbia.

Wang Ning has completed his PhD in history at the University of British Columbia.

Alexander Woodside is emeritus professor of history and senior scholar, centre of Southeast Asian Research, at the University of British Columbia.

Victor Zatsepine received his PhD in history from the University of British Columbia. He is currently a postodoctoral fellow in the history department at Peking University.

Index

Printed and bound in Canada by Friesens
Set in Stone by Artegraphica Design Co. Ltd.
Copy editor: Joanne Richardson
Proofreader: Dianne Tiefensee
Indexer: Annette Lorek
Cartographer: Eric Leinberger